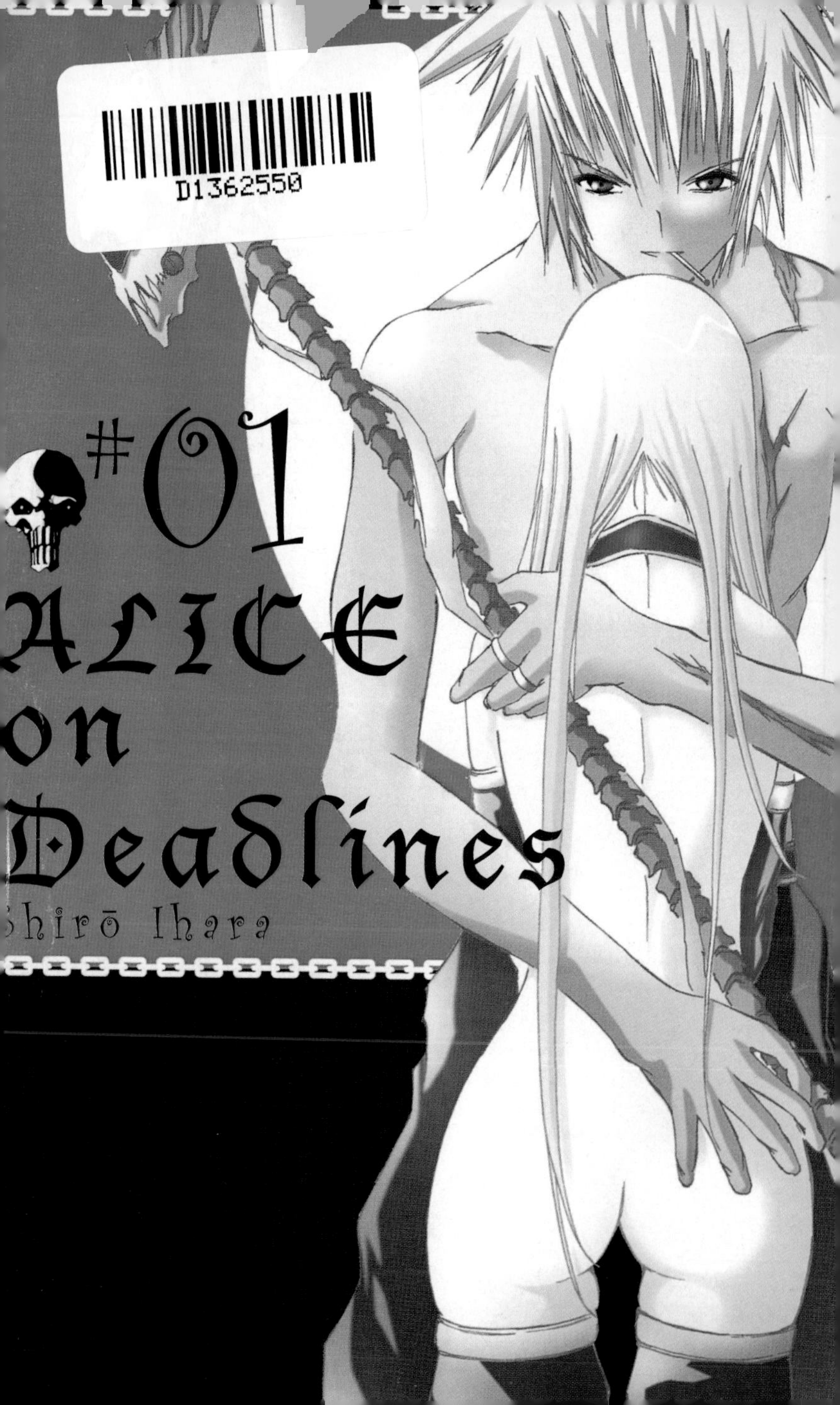
#01
ALICE
on
Deadlines
Shirō Ihara

D線上のアリス

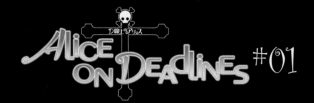

ALICE ON DEADLINES #01

CONTENTS

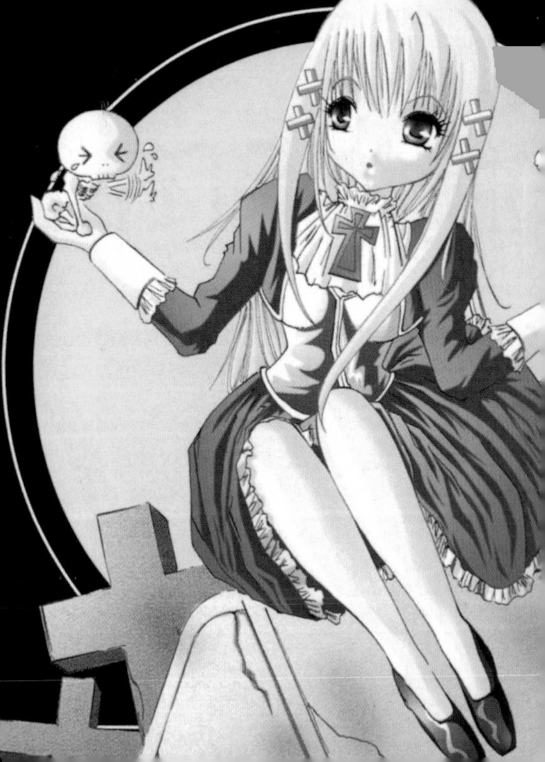

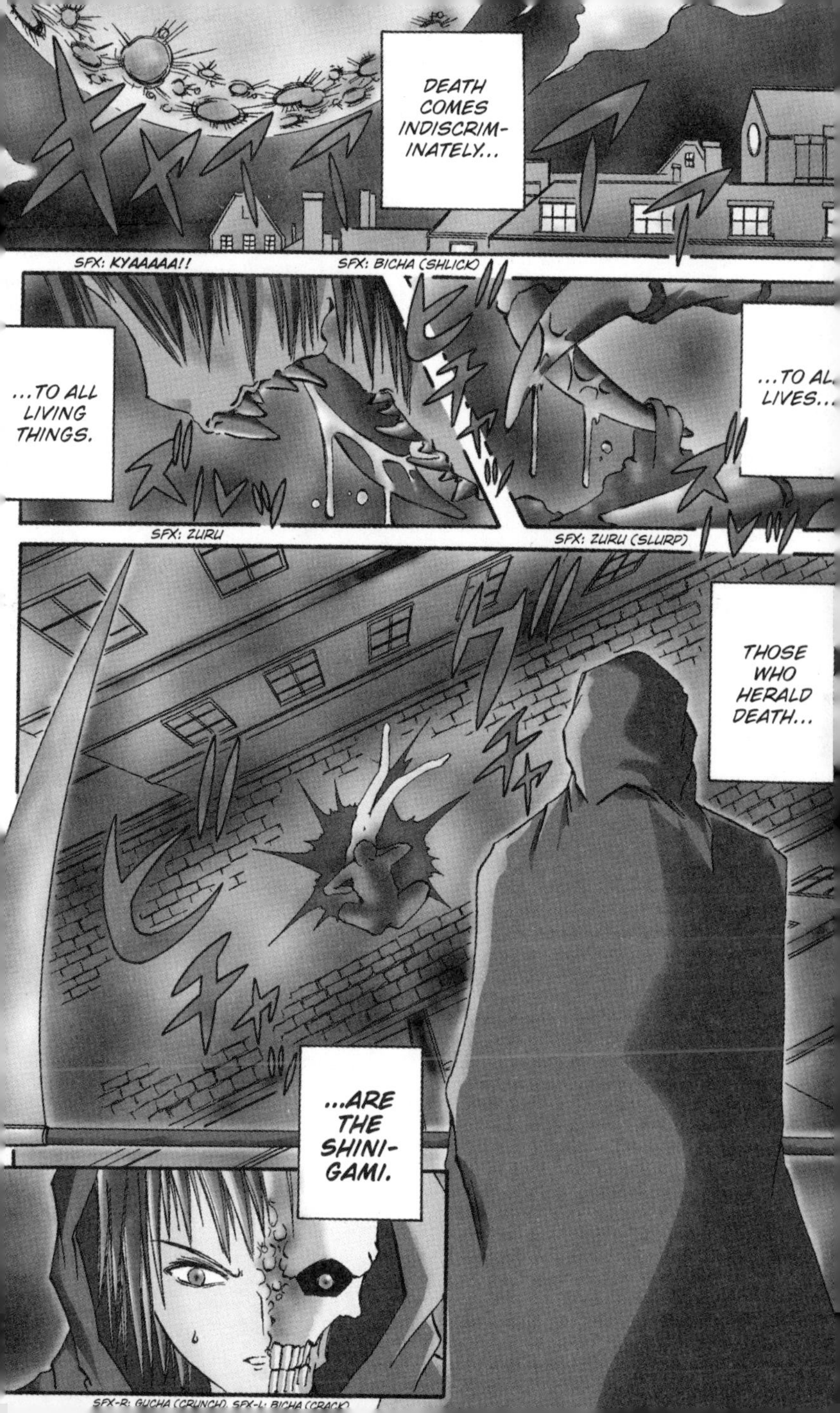
DEATH COMES INDISCRIM-INATELY...
SFX: BICHA (SHLICK)
SFX: KYAAAAA!!
...TO AL LIVES...
SFX: ZURU (SLURP)
...TO ALL LIVING THINGS.
SFX: ZURU
THOSE WHO HERALD DEATH...
...ARE THE SHINI-GAMI.
SFX-R: GUCHA (CRUNCH), SFX-L: BICHA (CRACK)

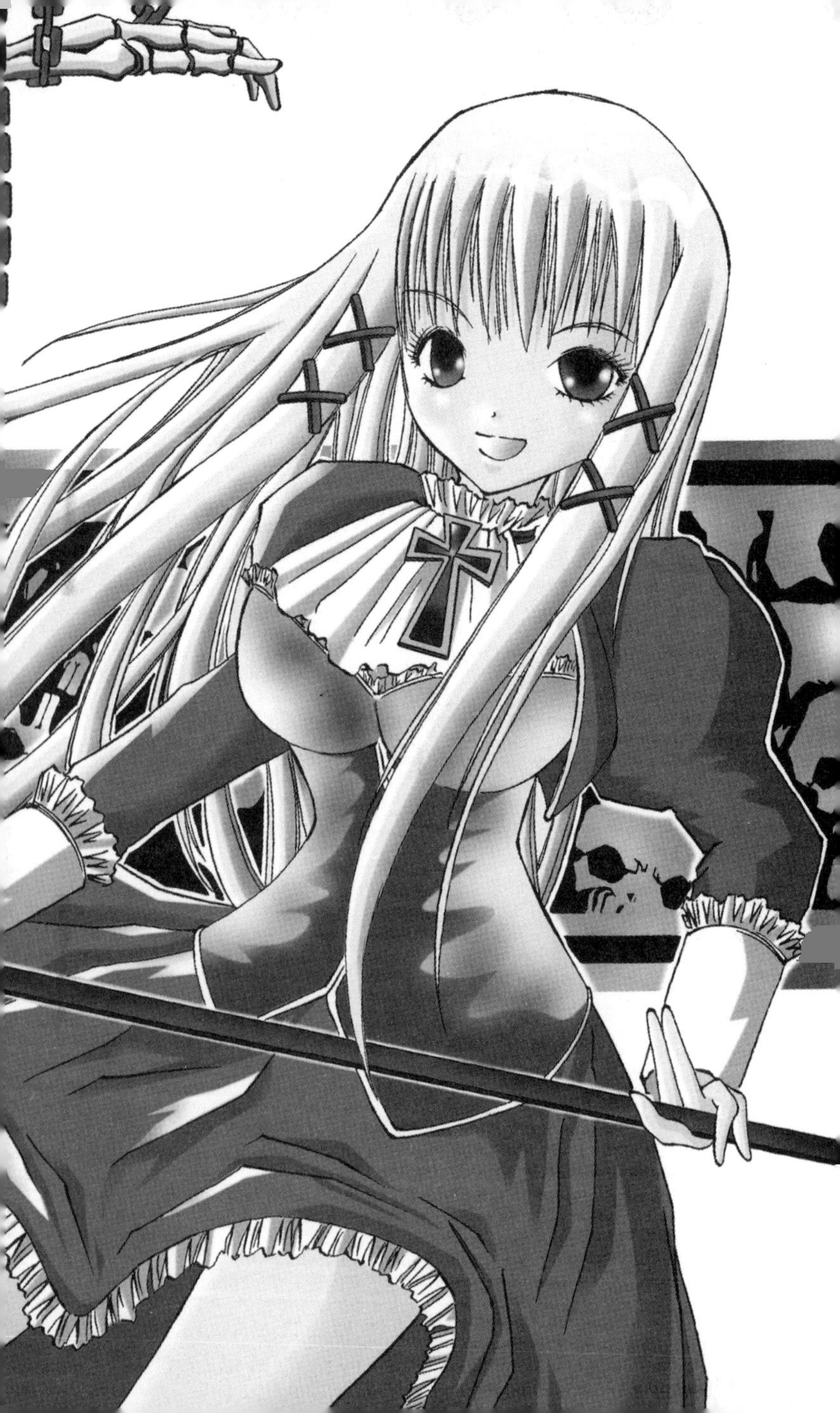

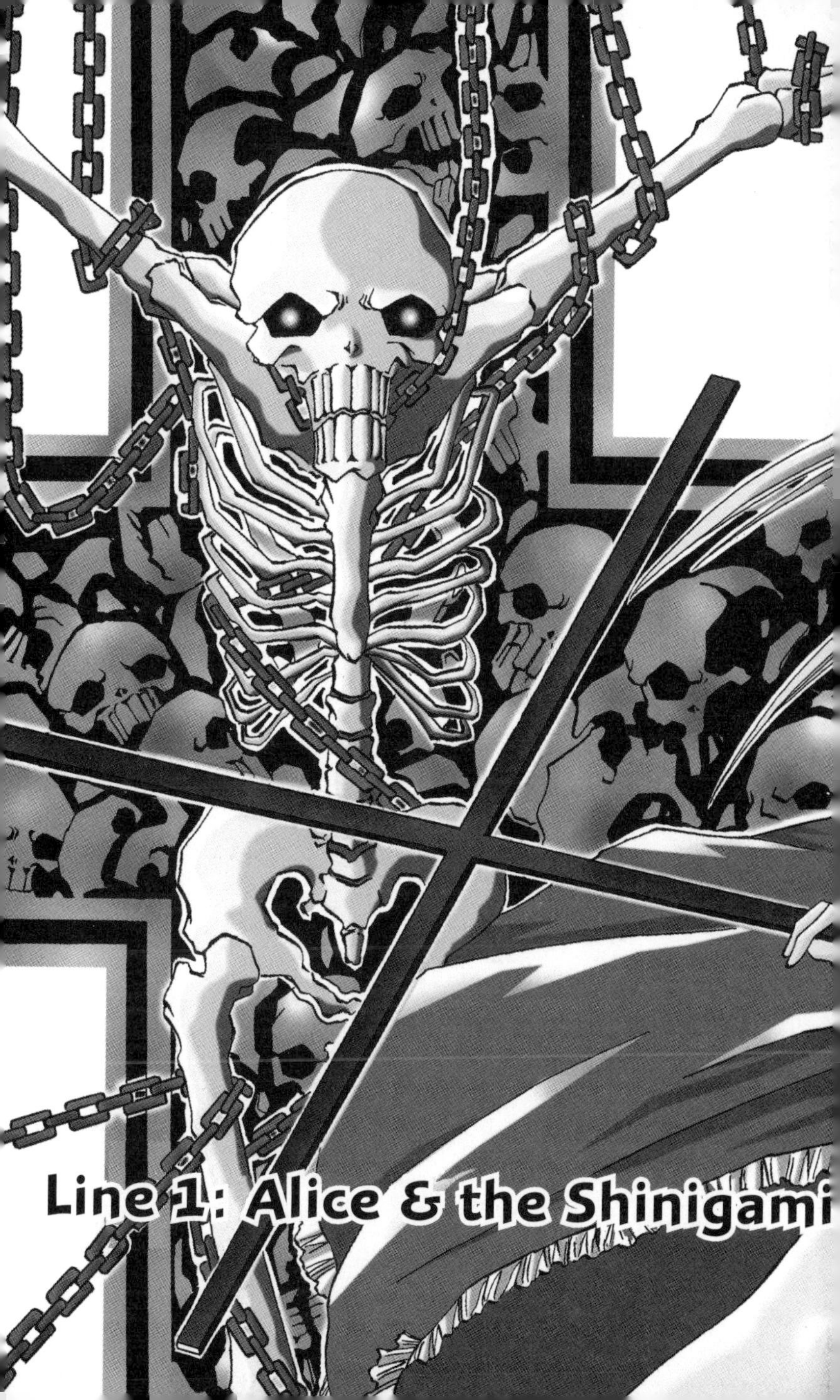
Line 1: Alice & the Shinigami

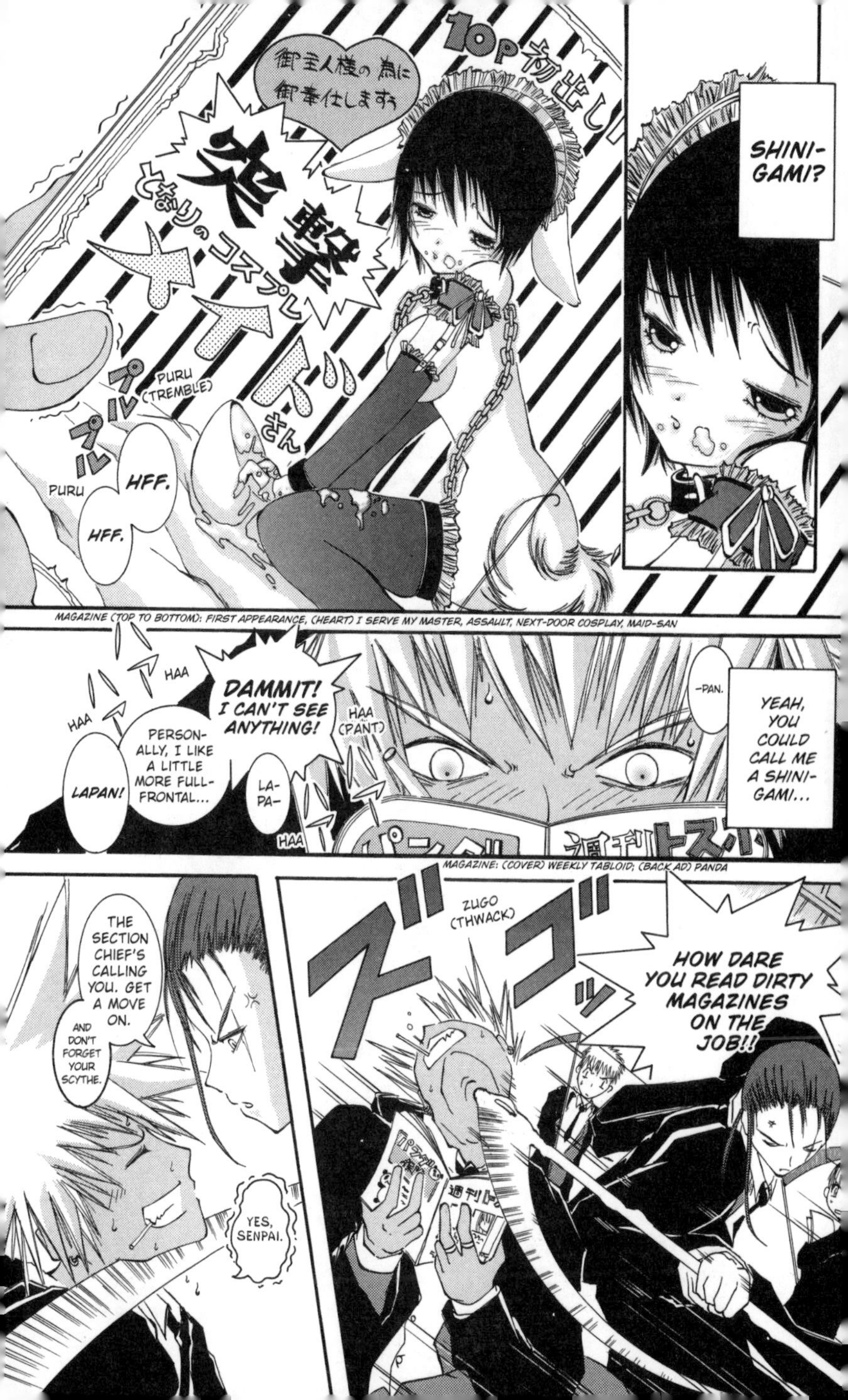
SHINI-GAMI?
10P初出し!!
御主人様の為に御奉仕しますぅ
突撃
となりのコスプレ
メイドさん
プルプル
PURU (TREMBLE)
PURU
HFF.
HFF.
MAGAZINE (TOP TO BOTTOM): FIRST APPEARANCE, (HEART) I SERVE MY MASTER, ASSAULT, NEXT-DOOR COSPLAY, MAID-SAN
YEAH, YOU COULD CALL ME A SHINI-GAMI...
-PAN.
HAA (PANT)
LA-PA-
DAMMIT! I CAN'T SEE ANYTHING!
HAA
PERSON-ALLY, I LIKE A LITTLE MORE FULL-FRONTAL...
HAA
LAPAN!
HAA
MAGAZINE: (COVER) WEEKLY TABLOID; (BACK AD) PANDA
ズゴッ
ZUGO (THWACK)
HOW DARE YOU READ DIRTY MAGAZINES ON THE JOB!!
THE SECTION CHIEF'S CALLING YOU. GET A MOVE ON.
AND DON'T FORGET YOUR SCYTHE.
YES, SENPAI.

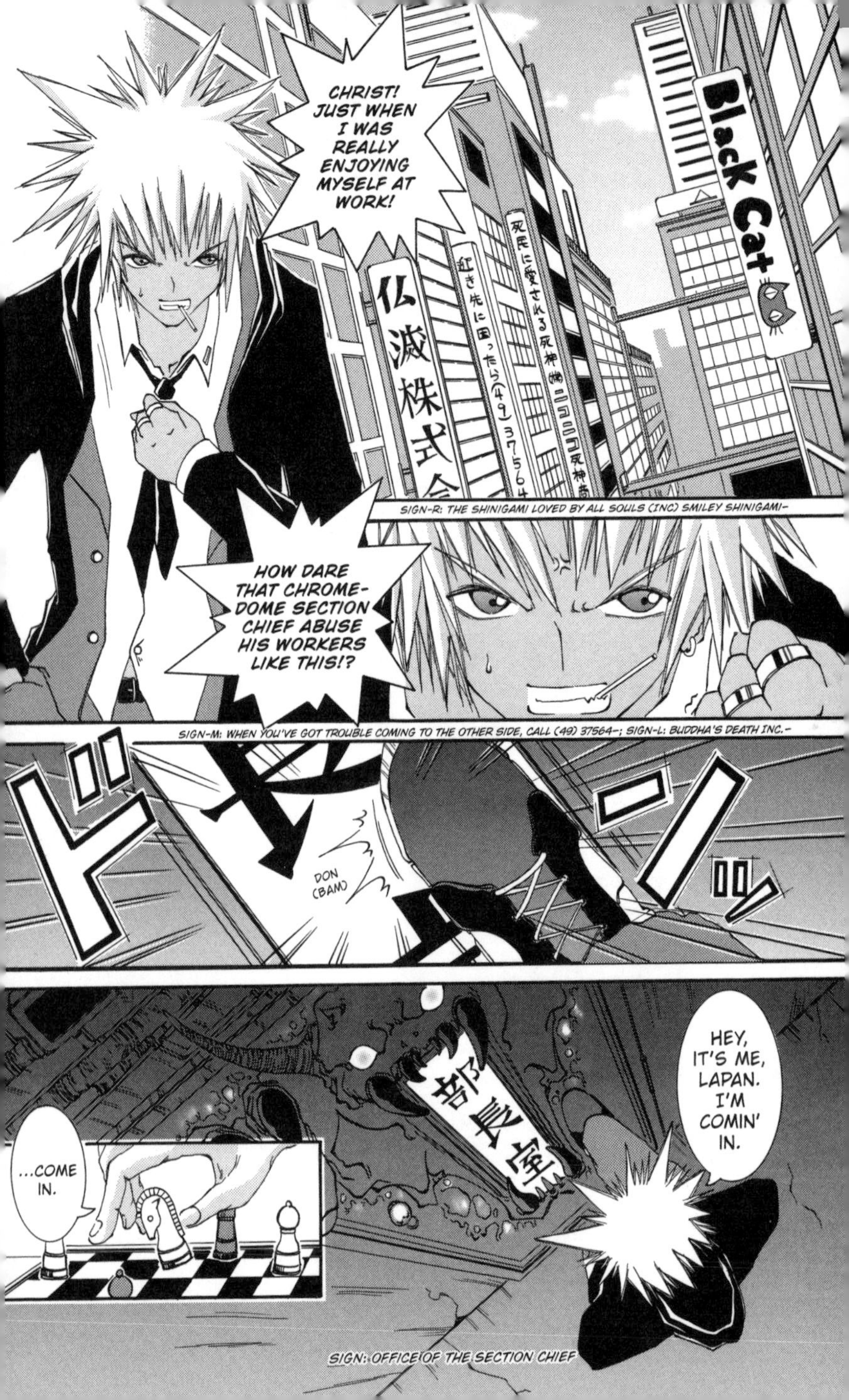
CHRIST! JUST WHEN I WAS REALLY ENJOYING MYSELF AT WORK!
Black Cat
死民に愛される死神(株)ニコニコ死神商
近き先に困ったら(49)37564
仏滅株式会
SIGN-R: THE SHINIGAMI LOVED BY ALL SOULS (INC) SMILEY SHINIGAMI-
HOW DARE THAT CHROME-DOME SECTION CHIEF ABUSE HIS WORKERS LIKE THIS!?
SIGN-M: WHEN YOU'VE GOT TROUBLE COMING TO THE OTHER SIDE, CALL (49) 37564-; SIGN-L: BUDDHA'S DEATH INC.-
ドーン
DON (BAM)
HEY, IT'S ME, LAPAN. I'M COMIN' IN.
部長室
...COME IN.
SIGN: OFFICE OF THE SECTION CHIEF

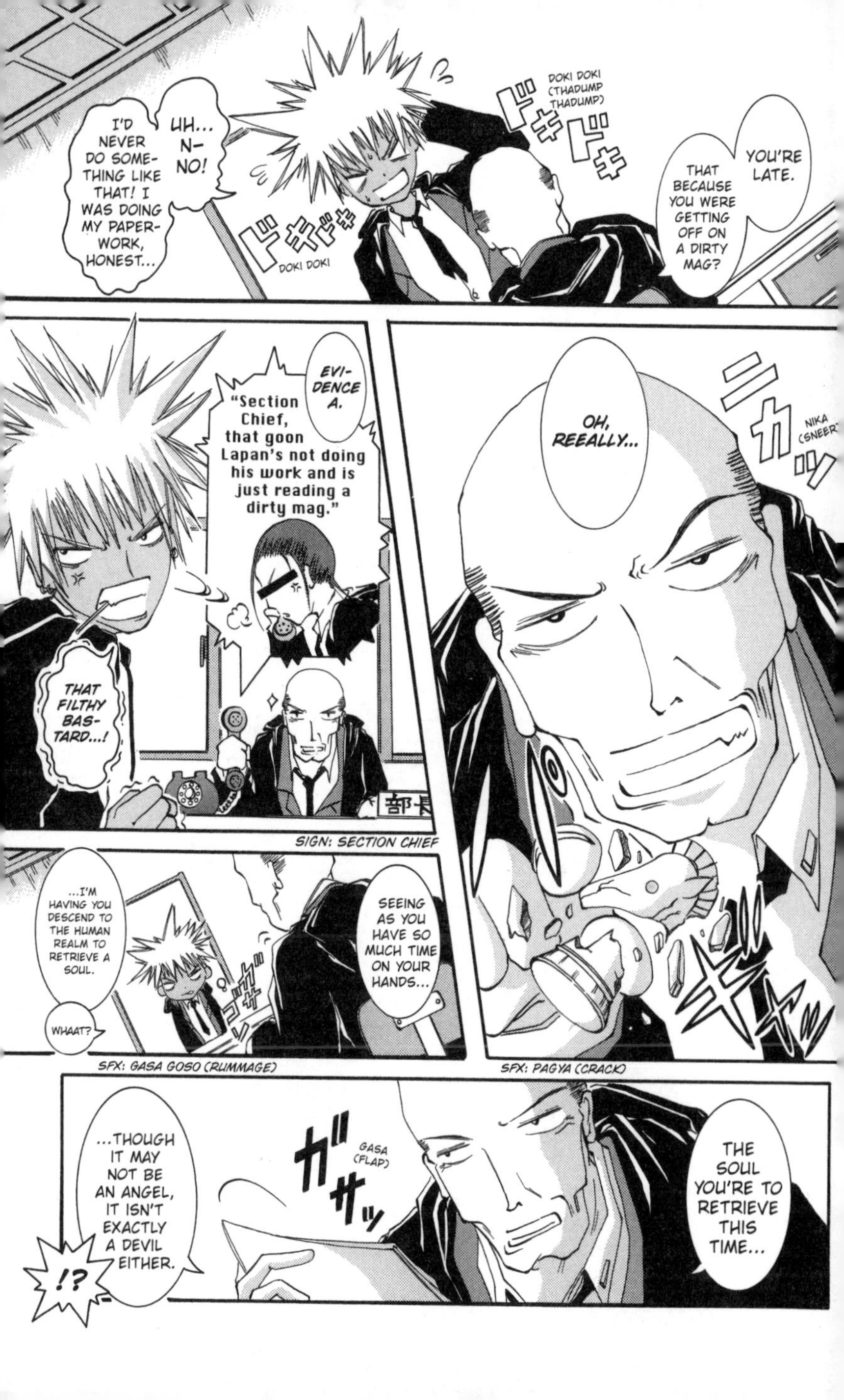
YOU'RE LATE.
THAT BECAUSE YOU WERE GETTING OFF ON A DIRTY MAG?
DOKI DOKI (THADUMP THADUMP)
UH... N-NO!
I'D NEVER DO SOME-THING LIKE THAT! I WAS DOING MY PAPER-WORK, HONEST...
DOKI DOKI
OH, REEALLY...
NIKA (SNEER)
SFX: PAGYA (CRACK)
EVI-DENCE A.
"Section Chief, that goon Lapan's not doing his work and is just reading a dirty mag."
THAT FILTHY BAS-TARD...!
SIGN: SECTION CHIEF
SEEING AS YOU HAVE SO MUCH TIME ON YOUR HANDS...
...I'M HAVING YOU DESCEND TO THE HUMAN REALM TO RETRIEVE A SOUL.
WHAAT?
SFX: GASA GOSO (RUMMAGE)
THE SOUL YOU'RE TO RETRIEVE THIS TIME...
GASA (FLAP)
...THOUGH IT MAY NOT BE AN ANGEL, IT ISN'T EXACTLY A DEVIL EITHER.
!?

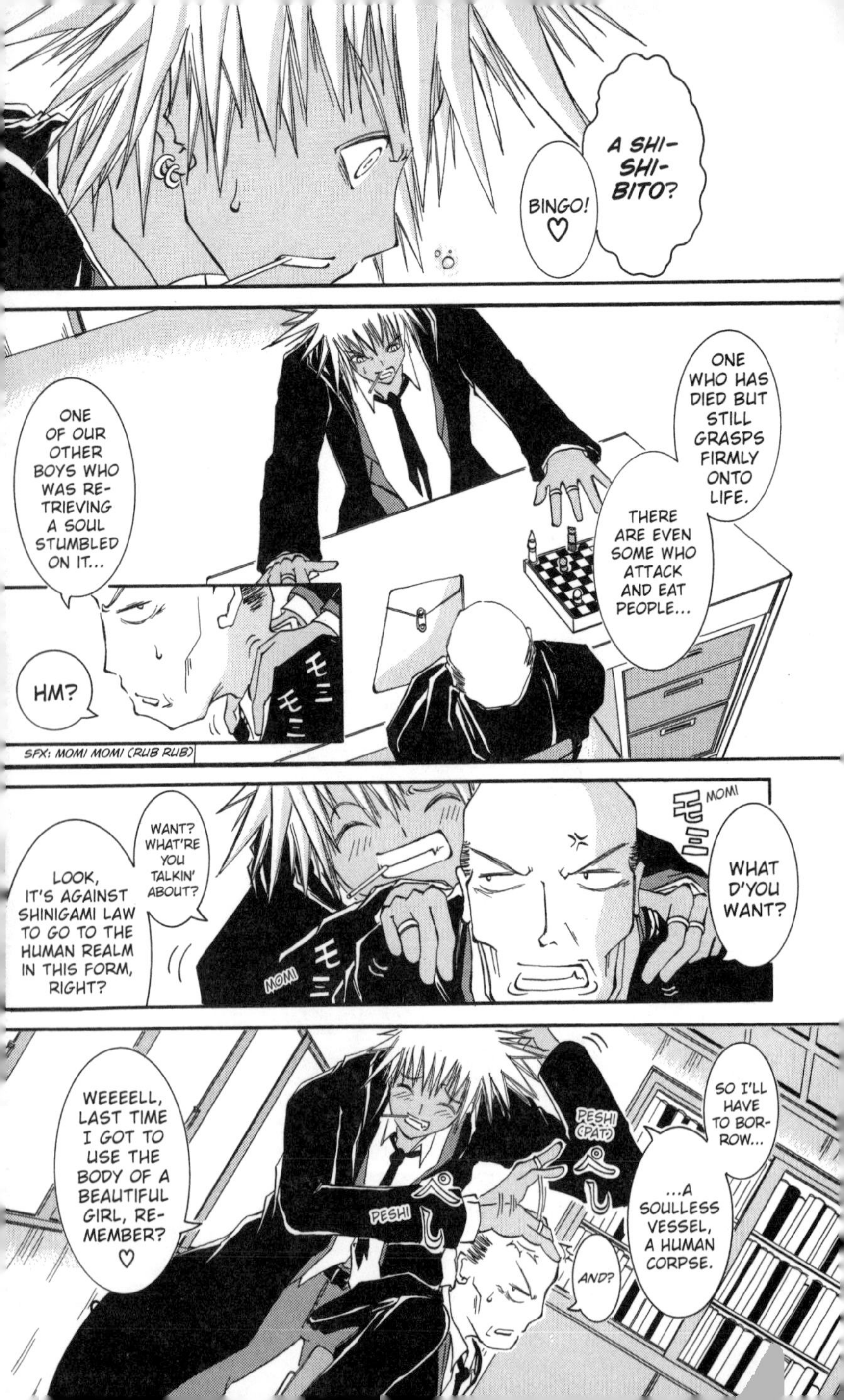
A SHI-SHI-BITO?
BINGO! ♡
ONE WHO HAS DIED BUT STILL GRASPS FIRMLY ONTO LIFE.
THERE ARE EVEN SOME WHO ATTACK AND EAT PEOPLE...
ONE OF OUR OTHER BOYS WHO WAS RE-TRIEVING A SOUL STUMBLED ON IT...
HM?
SFX: MOMI MOMI (RUB RUB)
MOMI
WHAT D'YOU WANT?
WANT? WHAT'RE YOU TALKIN' ABOUT?
LOOK, IT'S AGAINST SHINIGAMI LAW TO GO TO THE HUMAN REALM IN THIS FORM, RIGHT?
MOMI
SO I'LL HAVE TO BOR-ROW...
...A SOULLESS VESSEL, A HUMAN CORPSE.
AND?
PESHI (PAT)
PESHI
WEEEELL, LAST TIME I GOT TO USE THE BODY OF A BEAUTIFUL GIRL, RE-MEMBER? ♡

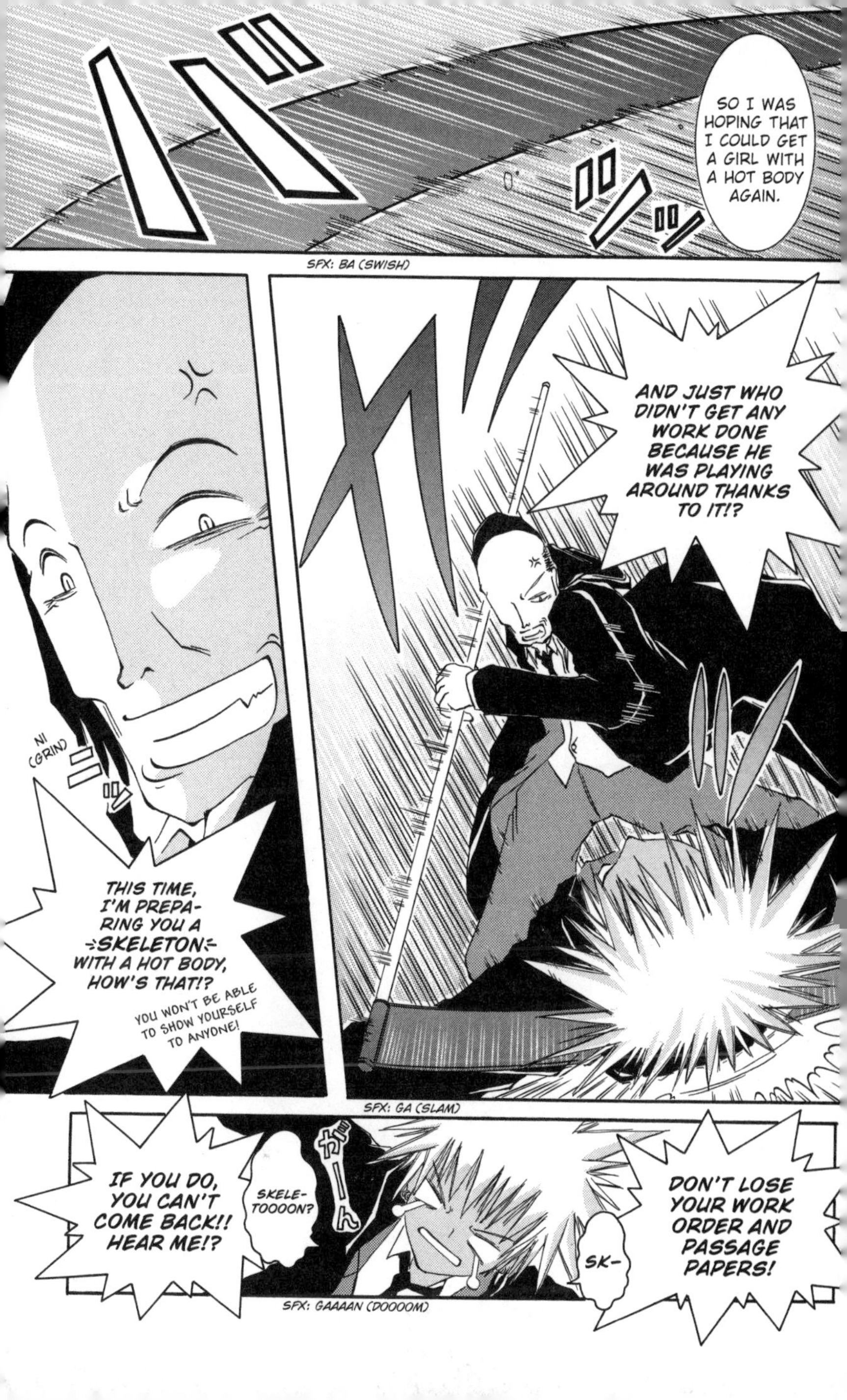
SO I WAS HOPING THAT I COULD GET A GIRL WITH A HOT BODY AGAIN.
SFX: BA (SWISH)
AND JUST WHO DIDN'T GET ANY WORK DONE BECAUSE HE WAS PLAYING AROUND THANKS TO IT!?
SFX: GA (SLAM)
NI (GRIN)
THIS TIME, I'M PREPARING YOU A ≈SKELETON≈ WITH A HOT BODY, HOW'S THAT!?
YOU WON'T BE ABLE TO SHOW YOURSELF TO ANYONE!
DON'T LOSE YOUR WORK ORDER AND PASSAGE PAPERS!
SK-
SKELE-TOOOON?
IF YOU DO, YOU CAN'T COME BACK!! HEAR ME!?
SFX: GAAAAN (DOOOOM)

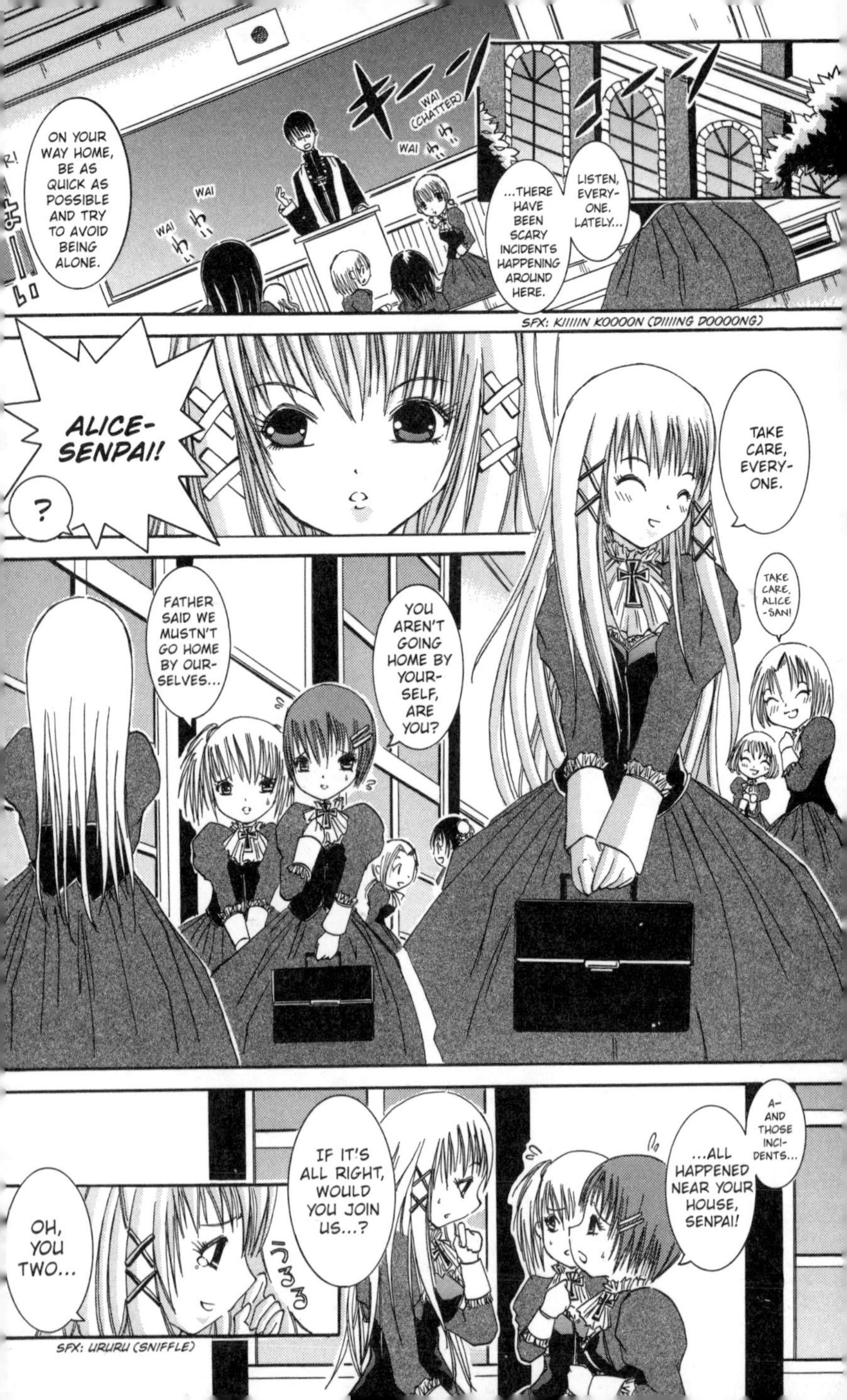
キーンコーン
LISTEN, EVERY-ONE. LATELY...
...THERE HAVE BEEN SCARY INCIDENTS HAPPENING AROUND HERE.
WAI (CHATTER)
WAI
WAI
WAI
ON YOUR WAY HOME, BE AS QUICK AS POSSIBLE AND TRY TO AVOID BEING ALONE.
SFX: KIIIIN KOOOON (DIIIING DOOOONG)
TAKE CARE, EVERY-ONE.
TAKE CARE, ALICE-SAN!
ALICE-SENPAI!
?
YOU AREN'T GOING HOME BY YOUR-SELF, ARE YOU?
FATHER SAID WE MUSTN'T GO HOME BY OUR-SELVES...
A-AND THOSE INCI-DENTS...
...ALL HAPPENED NEAR YOUR HOUSE, SENPAI!
IF IT'S ALL RIGHT, WOULD YOU JOIN US...?
OH, YOU TWO...
SFX: URURU (SNIFFLE)

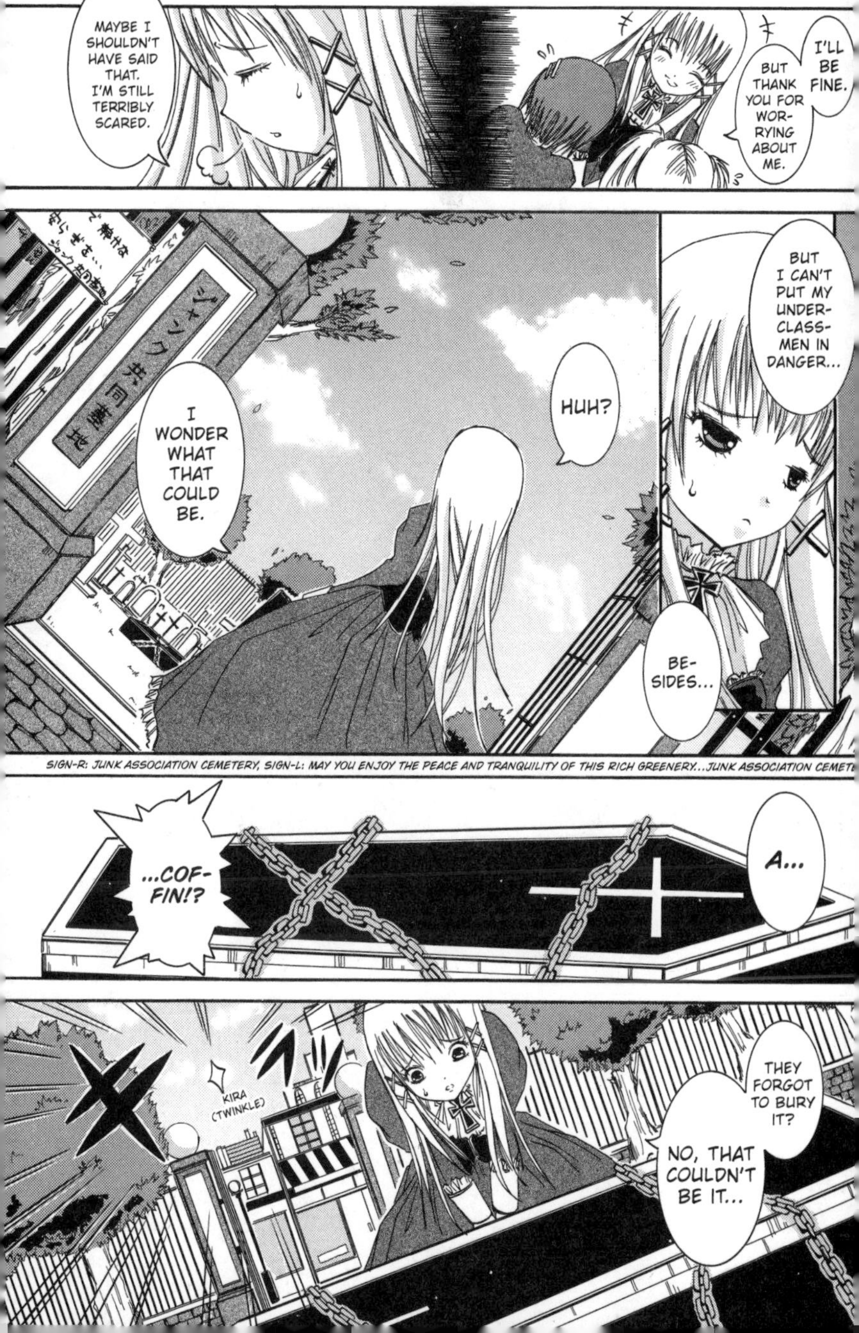
I'LL BE FINE.
BUT THANK YOU FOR WORRYING ABOUT ME.
MAYBE I SHOULDN'T HAVE SAID THAT. I'M STILL TERRIBLY SCARED.
BUT I CAN'T PUT MY UNDERCLASSMEN IN DANGER...
BESIDES...
HUH?
I WONDER WHAT THAT COULD BE.
ジャンク共同墓地
SIGN-R: JUNK ASSOCIATION CEMETERY, SIGN-L: MAY YOU ENJOY THE PEACE AND TRANQUILITY OF THIS RICH GREENERY...JUNK ASSOCIATION CEMET
A...
...COFFIN!?
THEY FORGOT TO BURY IT?
NO, THAT COULDN'T BE IT...
KIRA (TWINKLE)

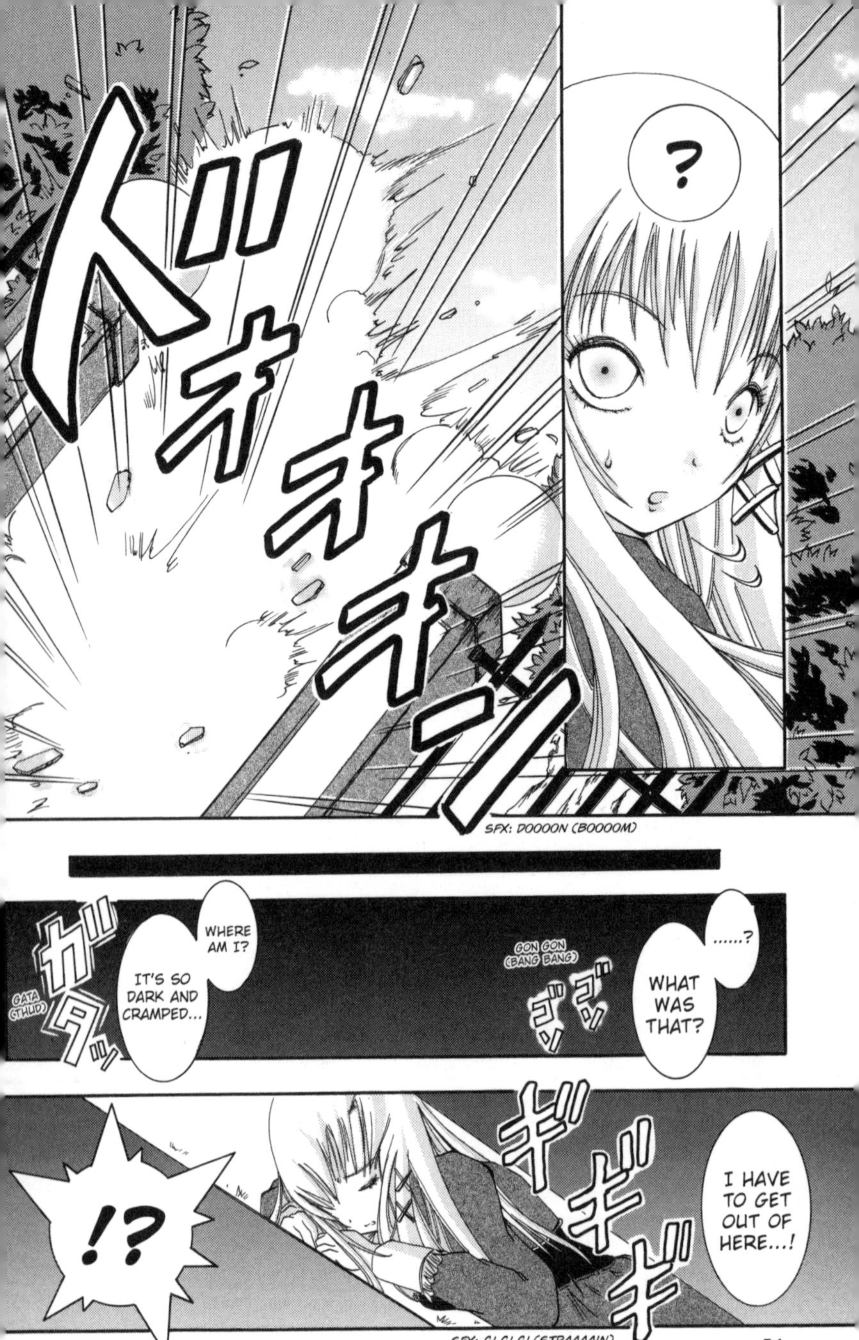
?
SFX: DOOOON (BOOOM)
......?
WHAT WAS THAT?
GON GON (BANG BANG)
WHERE AM I?
IT'S SO DARK AND CRAMPED...
GATA (THUD)
I HAVE TO GET OUT OF HERE...!
!?
SFX: GI GI GI (STRAAAAIN)

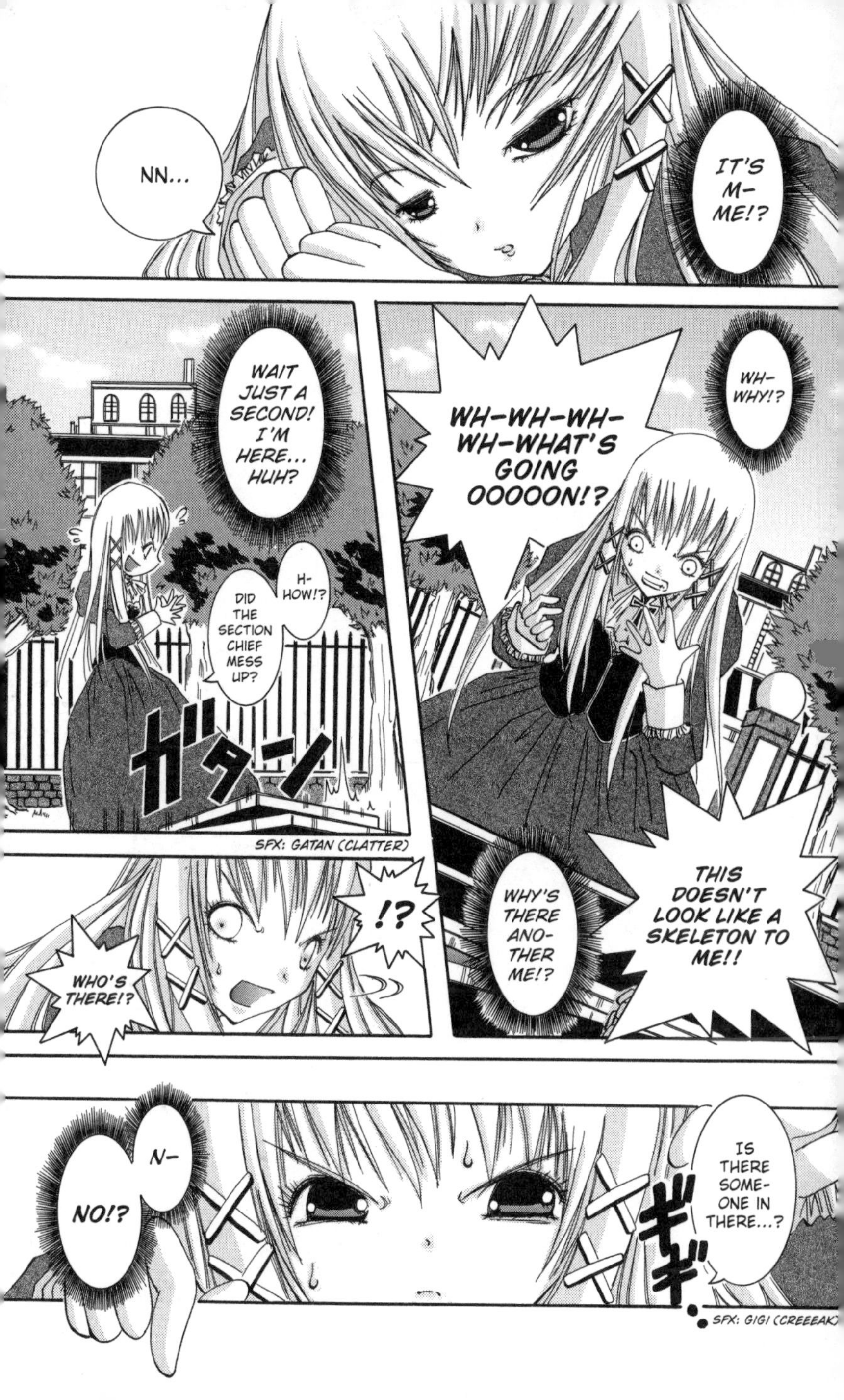
IT'S M-ME!?
NN...
WH-WHY!?
WH-WH-WH-WH-WHAT'S GOING OOOOON!?
THIS DOESN'T LOOK LIKE A SKELETON TO ME!!
WHY'S THERE ANO-THER ME!?
WAIT JUST A SECOND! I'M HERE... HUH?
H-HOW!?
DID THE SECTION CHIEF MESS UP?
ガターン
SFX: GATAN (CLATTER)
!?
WHO'S THERE!?
IS THERE SOME-ONE IN THERE...?
ギギ
SFX: GIGI (CREEEAK)
N-
NO!?

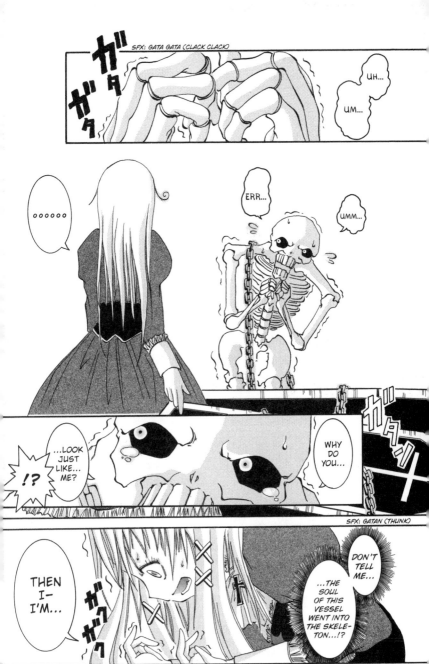

SFX: GATA GATA (CLACK CLACK)

UH...

UM...

ooooooo

ERR...

UMM...

...LOOK JUST LIKE... ME?

!?

WHY DO YOU...

SFX: GATAN (THUNK)

THEN I— I'M...

DON'T TELL ME...

...THE SOUL OF THIS VESSEL WENT INTO THE SKELETON...!?

SFX: GAKU GAKU (TREMBLE TREMBLE)

16

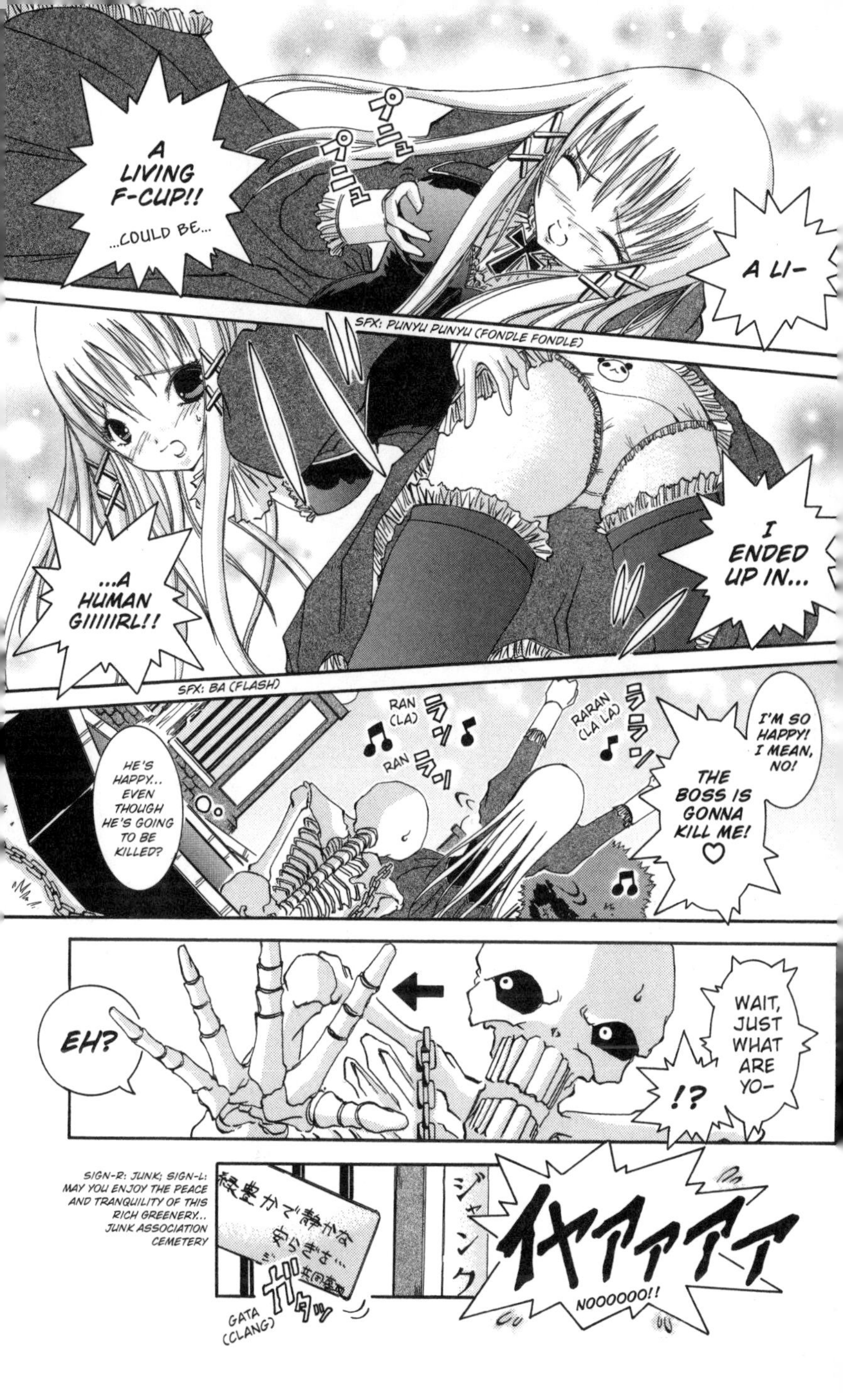

A LI-
A LIVING F-CUP!!
...COULD BE...
SFX: PUNYU PUNYU (FONDLE FONDLE)
I ENDED UP IN...
...A HUMAN GIIIIIRL!!
SFX: BA (FLASH)
I'M SO HAPPY! I MEAN, NO!
THE BOSS IS GONNA KILL ME! ♡
RARAN (LA LA)
RAN (LA)
RAN
HE'S HAPPY... EVEN THOUGH HE'S GOING TO BE KILLED?
WAIT, JUST WHAT ARE YO-
!?
EH?
イヤアアアア
NOOOOOO!!
ジャンク
ガタッ
GATA (CLANG)
SIGN-R: JUNK; SIGN-L: MAY YOU ENJOY THE PEACE AND TRANQUILITY OF THIS RICH GREENERY... JUNK ASSOCIATION CEMETERY

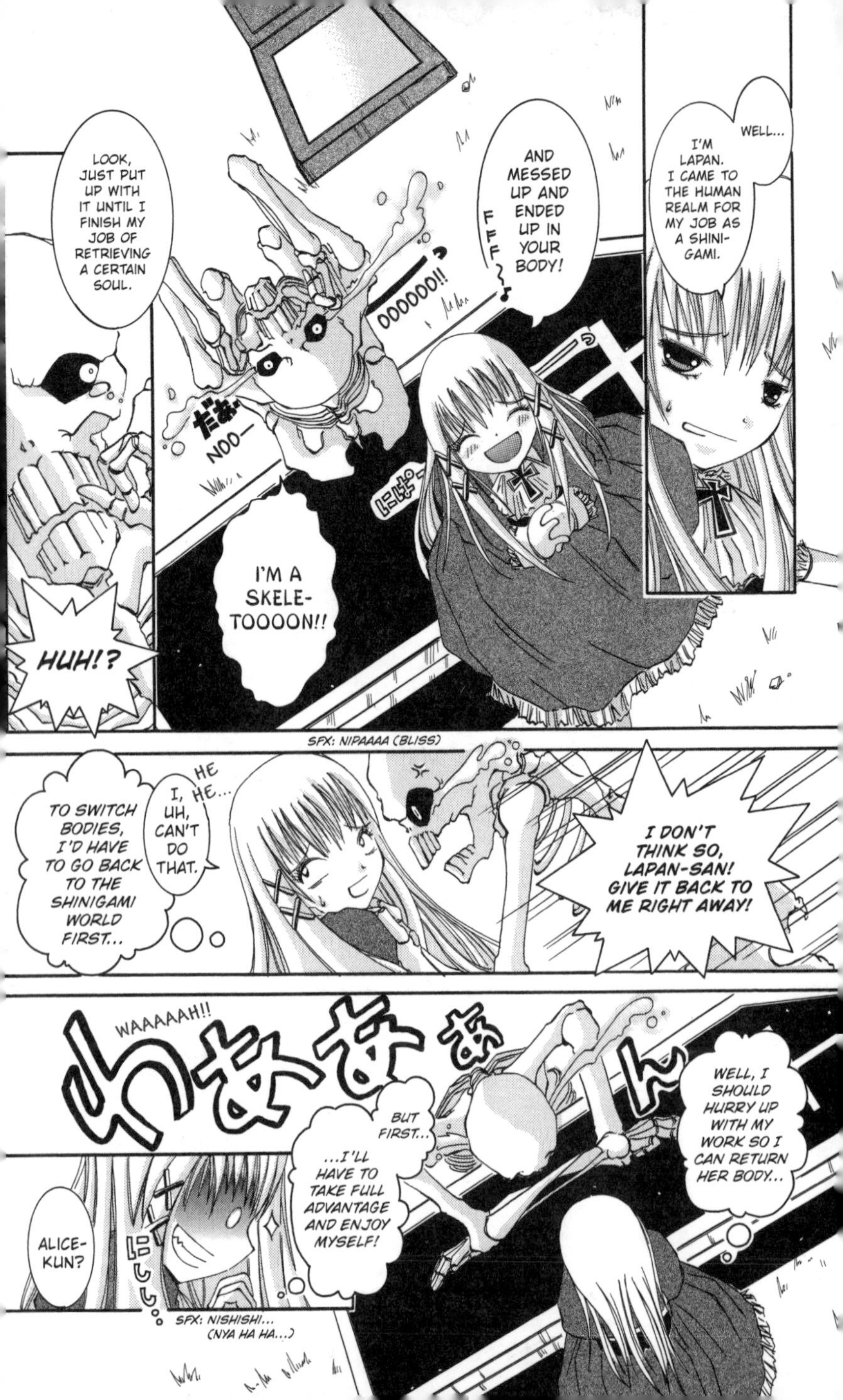
WELL...
I'M LAPAN. I CAME TO THE HUMAN REALM FOR MY JOB AS A SHINIGAMI.
AND MESSED UP AND ENDED UP IN YOUR BODY!
FFF~♪
—OOOOOO!!
NOO—
I'M A SKELE-TOOOON!!
SFX: NIPAAAA (BLISS)
LOOK, JUST PUT UP WITH IT UNTIL I FINISH MY JOB OF RETRIEVING A CERTAIN SOUL.
HUH!?
I DON'T THINK SO, LAPAN-SAN! GIVE IT BACK TO ME RIGHT AWAY!
HE HE...
I, UH, CAN'T DO THAT.
TO SWITCH BODIES, I'D HAVE TO GO BACK TO THE SHINIGAMI WORLD FIRST...
WAAAAAH!!
WELL, I SHOULD HURRY UP WITH MY WORK SO I CAN RETURN HER BODY...
BUT FIRST...
...I'LL HAVE TO TAKE FULL ADVANTAGE AND ENJOY MYSELF!
ALICE-KUN?
SFX: NISHISHI... (NYA HA HA...)

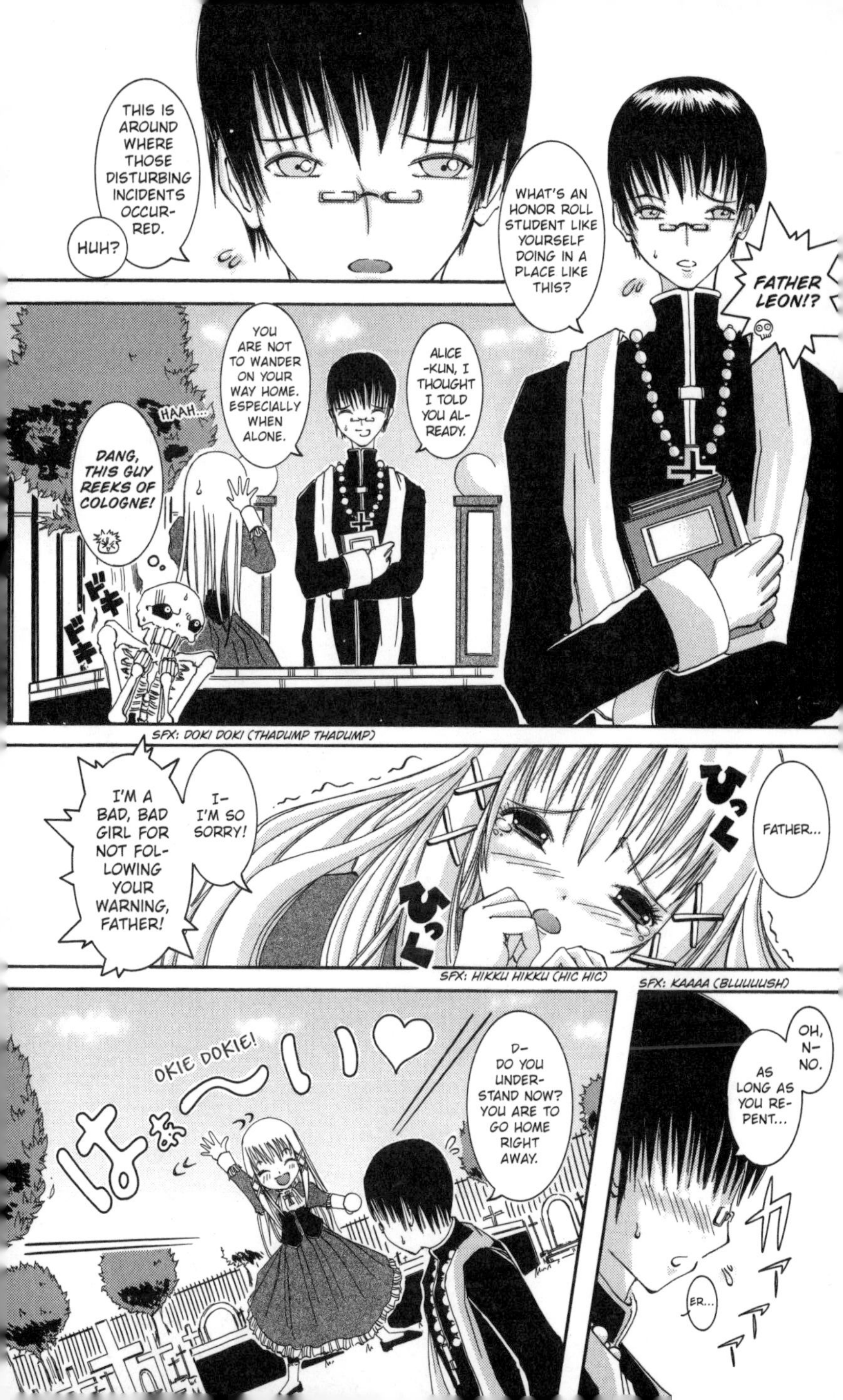
FATHER LEON!?
WHAT'S AN HONOR ROLL STUDENT LIKE YOURSELF DOING IN A PLACE LIKE THIS?
THIS IS AROUND WHERE THOSE DISTURBING INCIDENTS OCCUR-RED.
HUH?
ALICE-KUN, I THOUGHT I TOLD YOU AL-READY.
YOU ARE NOT TO WANDER ON YOUR WAY HOME. ESPECIALLY WHEN ALONE.
HAAH...
DANG, THIS GUY REEKS OF COLOGNE!
SFX: DOKI DOKI (THADUMP THADUMP)
FATHER...
I- I'M SO SORRY!
I'M A BAD, BAD GIRL FOR NOT FOL-LOWING YOUR WARNING, FATHER!
SFX: HIKKU HIKKU (HIC HIC)
SFX: KAAAA (BLUUUUSH)
OH, N- NO.
AS LONG AS YOU RE-PENT...
ER...
D- DO YOU UNDER-STAND NOW? YOU ARE TO GO HOME RIGHT AWAY.
OKIE DOKIE!

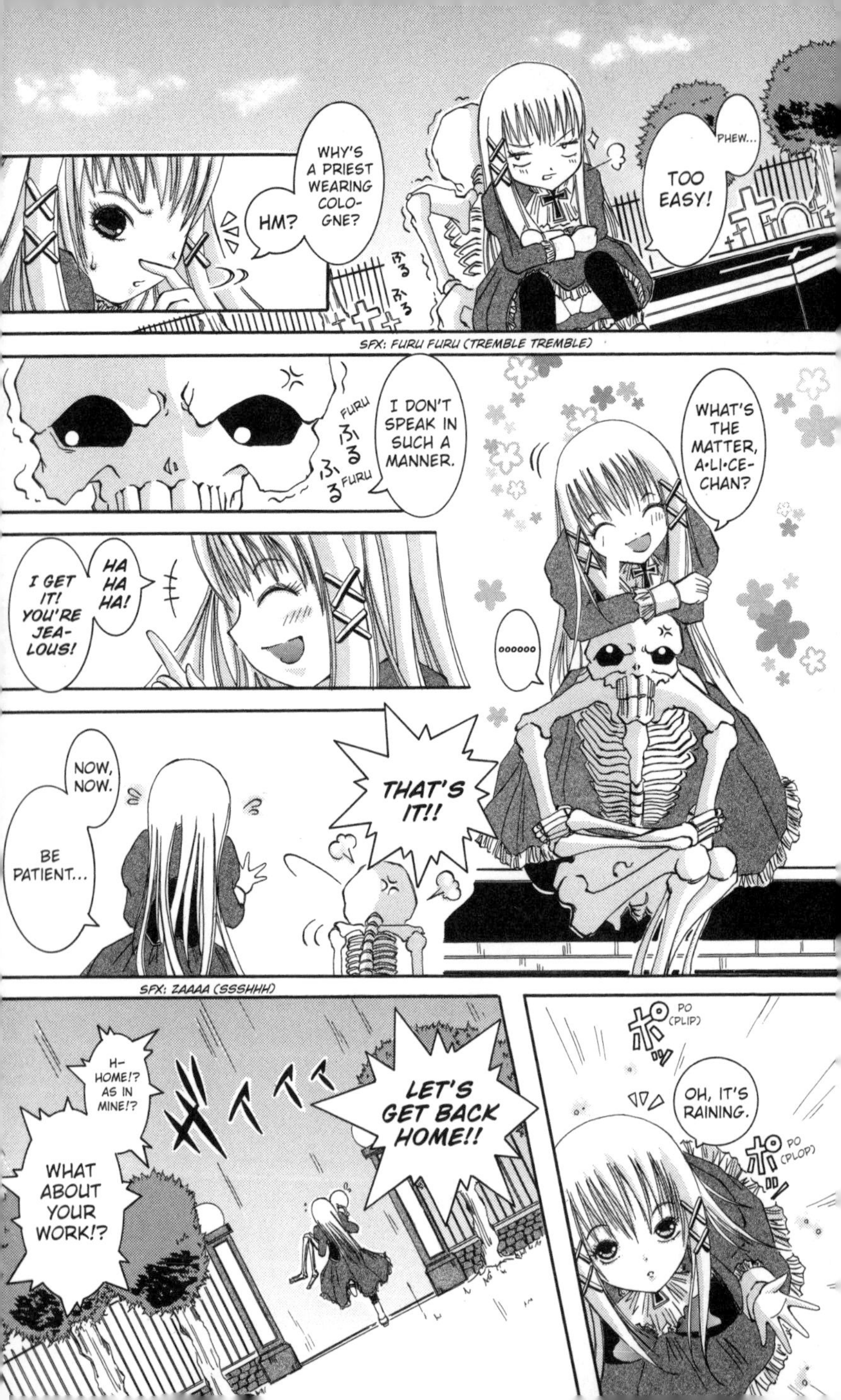
PHEW...
TOO EASY!
HM?
WHY'S A PRIEST WEARING COLO-GNE?
ふる ふる
SFX: FURU FURU (TREMBLE TREMBLE)
WHAT'S THE MATTER, A•LI•CE-CHAN?
oooooo
I DON'T SPEAK IN SUCH A MANNER.
FURU ふる ふる FURU
HA HA HA!
I GET IT! YOU'RE JEA-LOUS!
THAT'S IT!!
NOW, NOW.
BE PATIENT...
SFX: ZAAAA (SSSHHH)
ポッ PO (PLIP)
OH, IT'S RAINING.
ポッ PO (PLOP)
LET'S GET BACK HOME!!
H-HOME!? AS IN MINE!?
WHAT ABOUT YOUR WORK!?

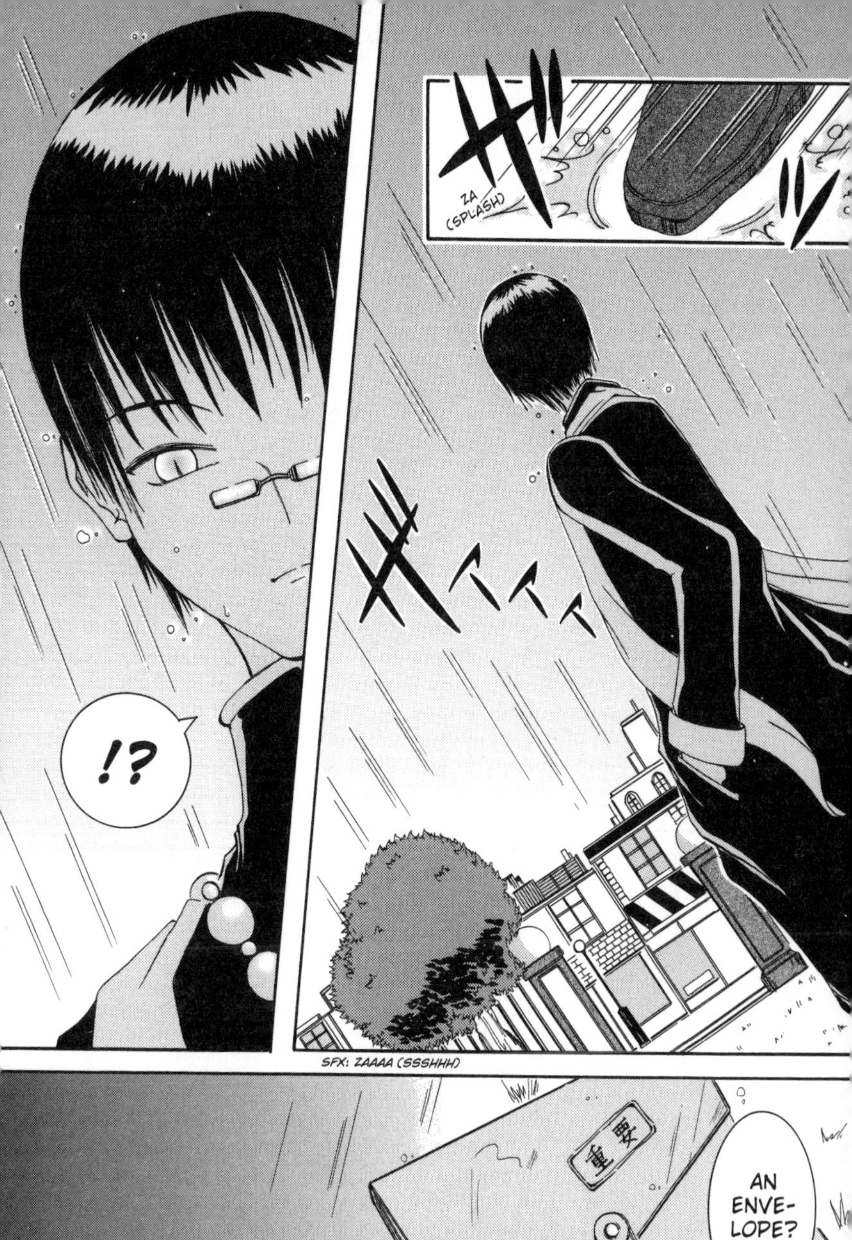
ZA (SPLASH)
!?

SFX: ZAAAA (SSSHHH)

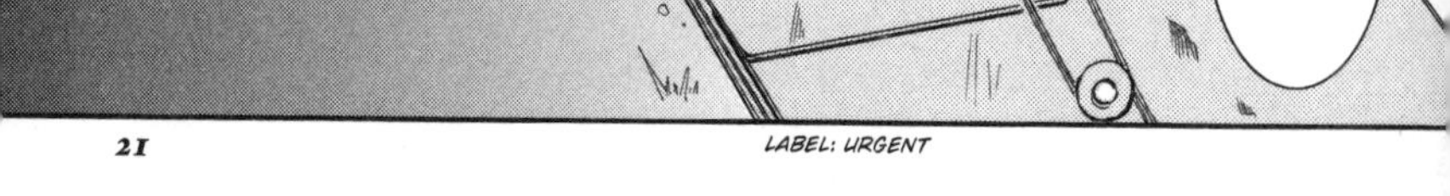
AN ENVE-LOPE?

LABEL: URGENT

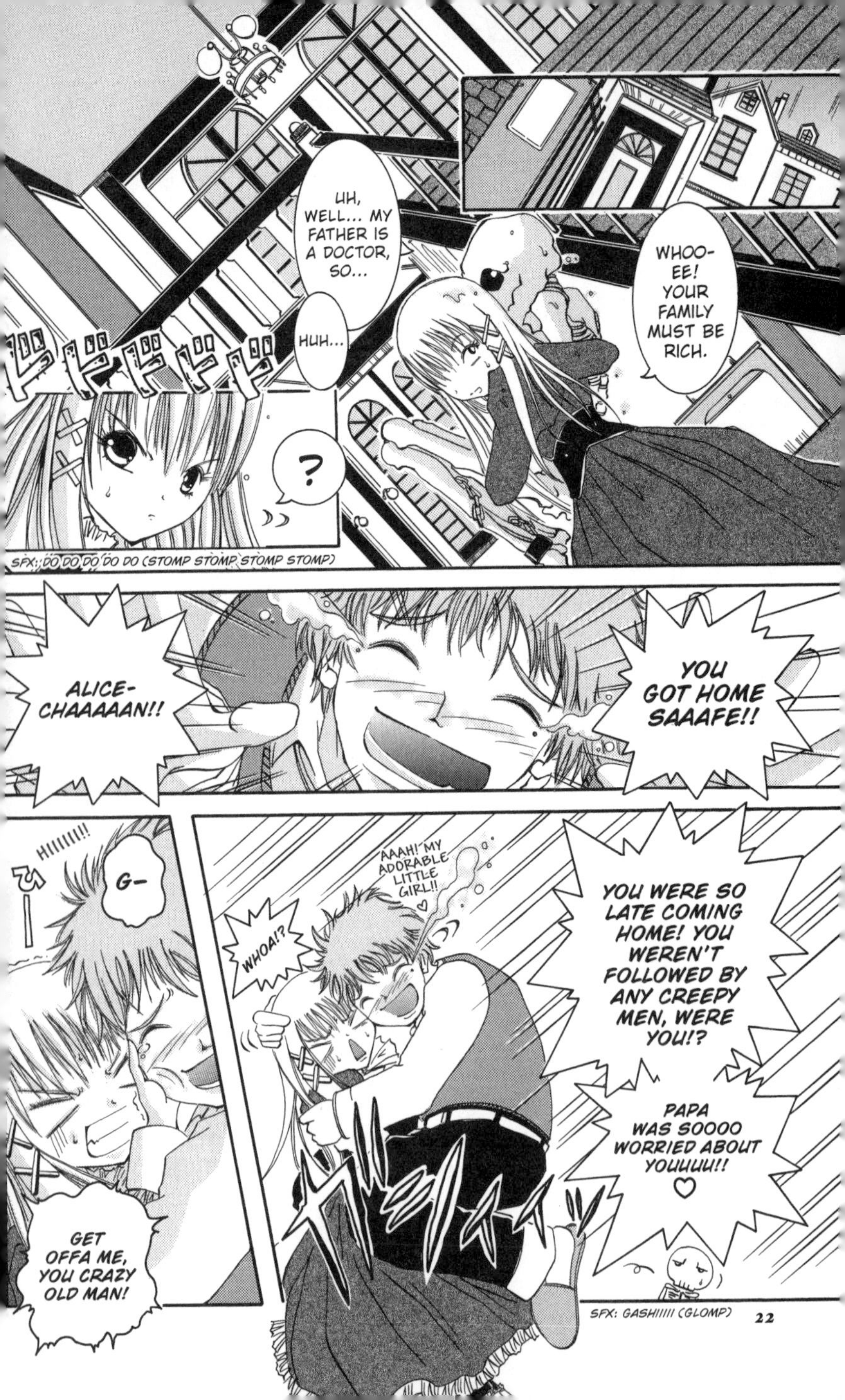
WHOO-EE! YOUR FAMILY MUST BE RICH.
UH, WELL... MY FATHER IS A DOCTOR, SO...
HUH...
?
SFX: DO DO DO DO DO (STOMP STOMP STOMP STOMP)
YOU GOT HOME SAAAFE!!
ALICE-CHAAAAAN!!
YOU WERE SO LATE COMING HOME! YOU WEREN'T FOLLOWED BY ANY CREEPY MEN, WERE YOU!?
AAAH! MY ADORABLE LITTLE GIRL!! ♡
WHOA!?
PAPA WAS SOOOO WORRIED ABOUT YOUUUU!! ♡
SFX: GASHIIIII (GLOMP)
HIIIIII!!
G-
GET OFFA ME, YOU CRAZY OLD MAN!

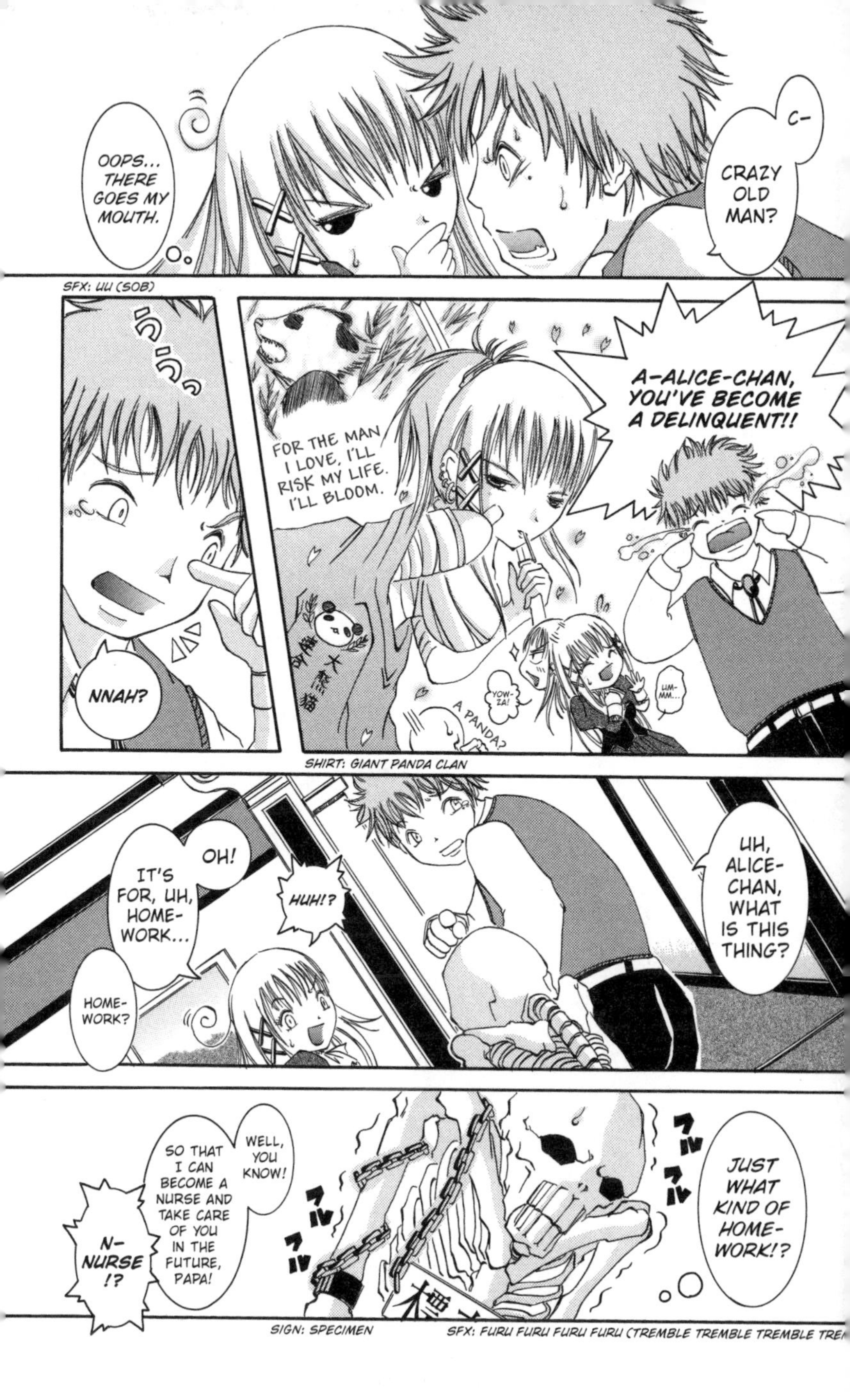
C– CRAZY OLD MAN?
OOPS... THERE GOES MY MOUTH.
SFX: UU (SOB)
A–ALICE-CHAN, YOU'VE BECOME A DELINQUENT!!
FOR THE MAN I LOVE, I'LL RISK MY LIFE. I'LL BLOOM.
UMM...
YOW-ZA!
A PANDA?
SHIRT: GIANT PANDA CLAN
NNAH?
UH, ALICE-CHAN, WHAT IS THIS THING?
HUH!?
OH! IT'S FOR, UH, HOME-WORK...
HOME-WORK?
JUST WHAT KIND OF HOME-WORK!?
WELL, YOU KNOW!
SO THAT I CAN BECOME A NURSE AND TAKE CARE OF YOU IN THE FUTURE, PAPA!
N–NURSE!?
SIGN: SPECIMEN
SFX: FURU FURU FURU FURU (TREMBLE TREMBLE TREMBLE TRE

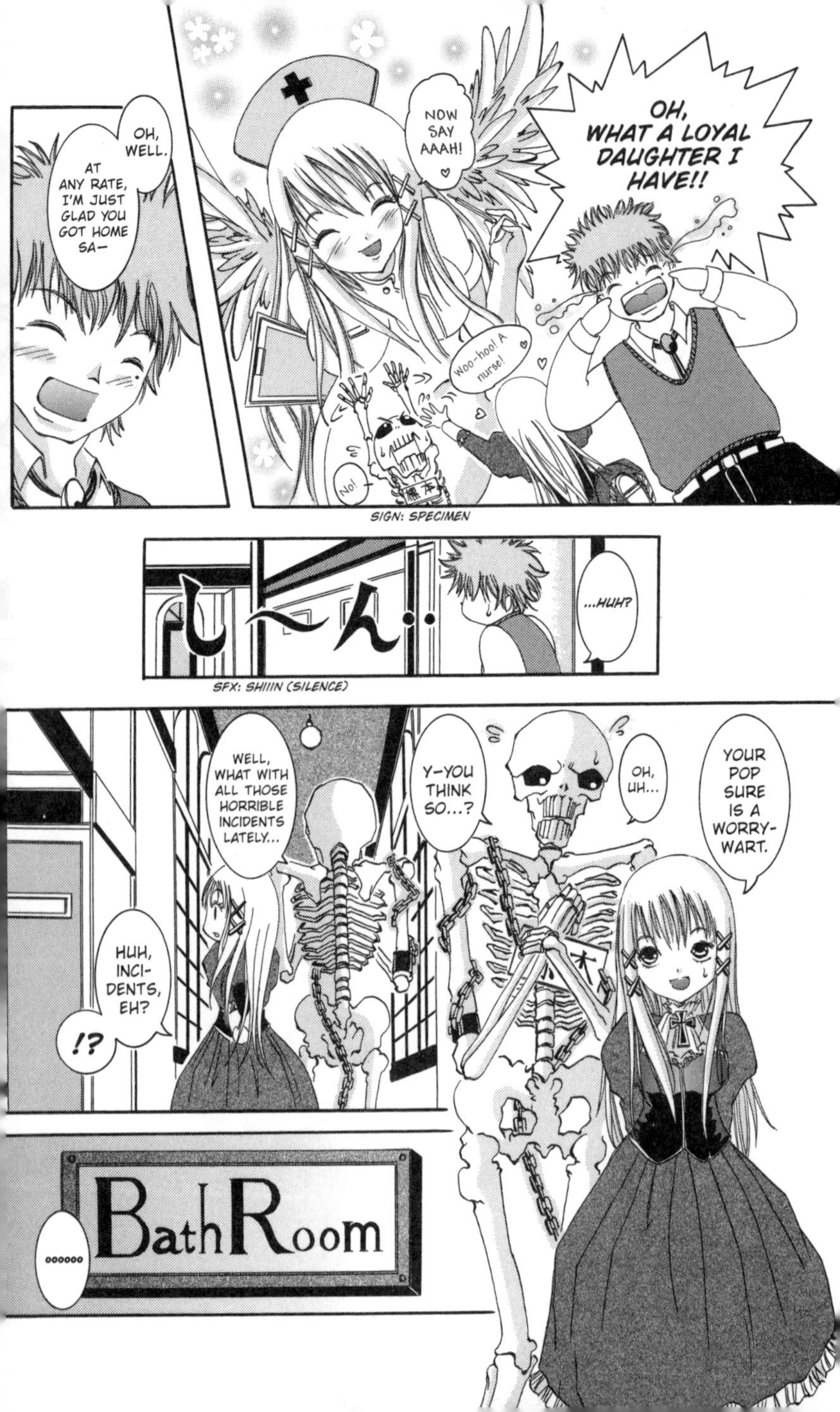
OH, WHAT A LOYAL DAUGHTER I HAVE!!
NOW SAY AAAH! ♡
Woo-hoo! A nurse! ♡
No!
SIGN: SPECIMEN
OH, WELL.
AT ANY RATE, I'M JUST GLAD YOU GOT HOME SA—
...HUH?
しーん..
SFX: SHIIIN (SILENCE)
YOUR POP SURE IS A WORRY-WART.
OH, UH...
Y-YOU THINK SO...?
WELL, WHAT WITH ALL THOSE HORRIBLE INCIDENTS LATELY...
HUH, INCI-DENTS, EH?
!?
BathRoom
oooooo

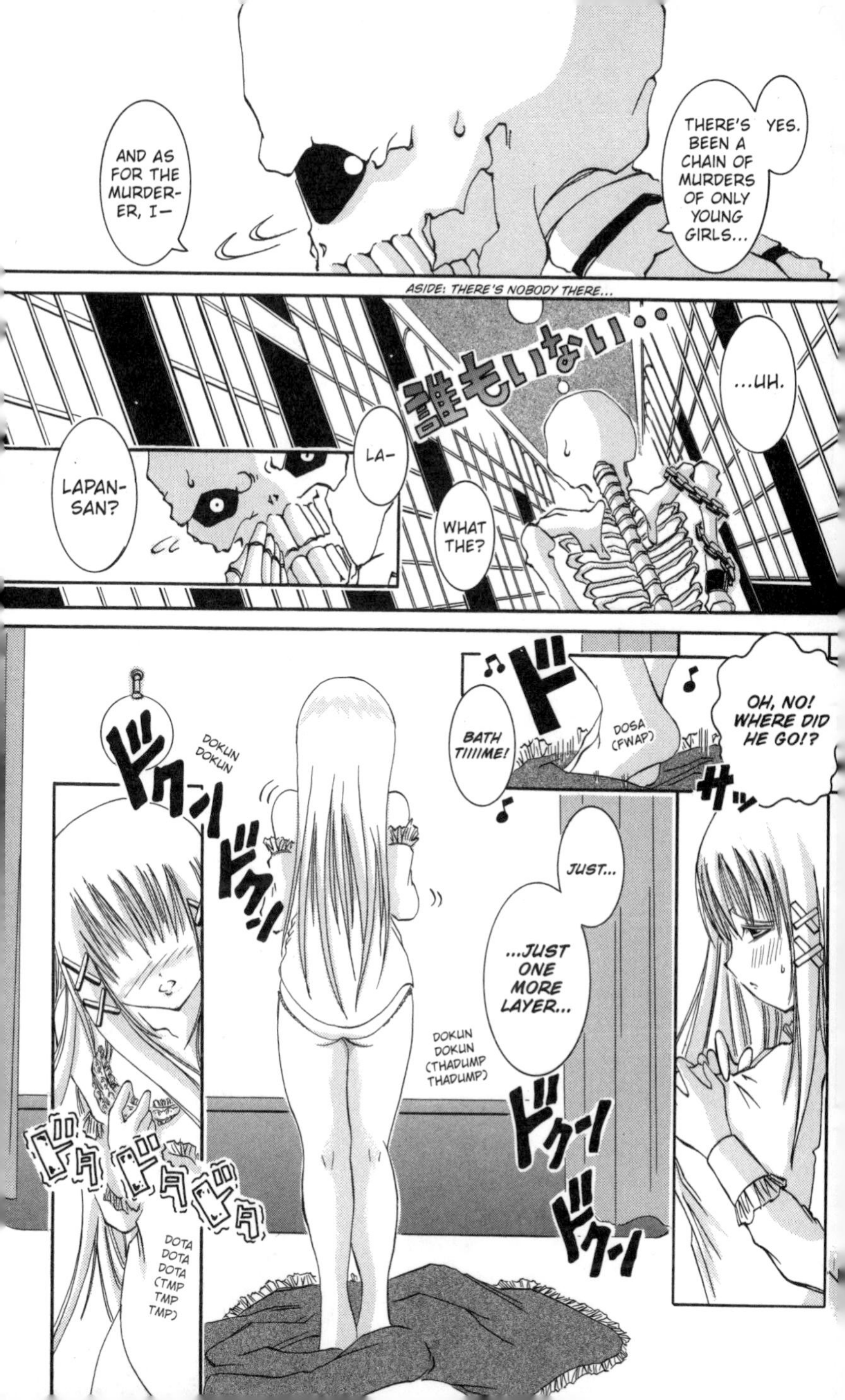
YES.
THERE'S BEEN A CHAIN OF MURDERS OF ONLY YOUNG GIRLS...
AND AS FOR THE MURDERER, I—
ASIDE: THERE'S NOBODY THERE...
誰もいない..
...UH.
WHAT THE?
LA-
LAPAN-SAN?
OH, NO! WHERE DID HE GO!?
サッ
ド
DOSA (FWAP)
BATH TIIIIME!
JUST...
...JUST ONE MORE LAYER...
ドクーン ドクーン
DOKUN DOKUN (THADUMP THADUMP)
ドクン ドクン
DOKUN DOKUN
ドタドタドタ
DOTA DOTA DOTA (TMP TMP TMP)

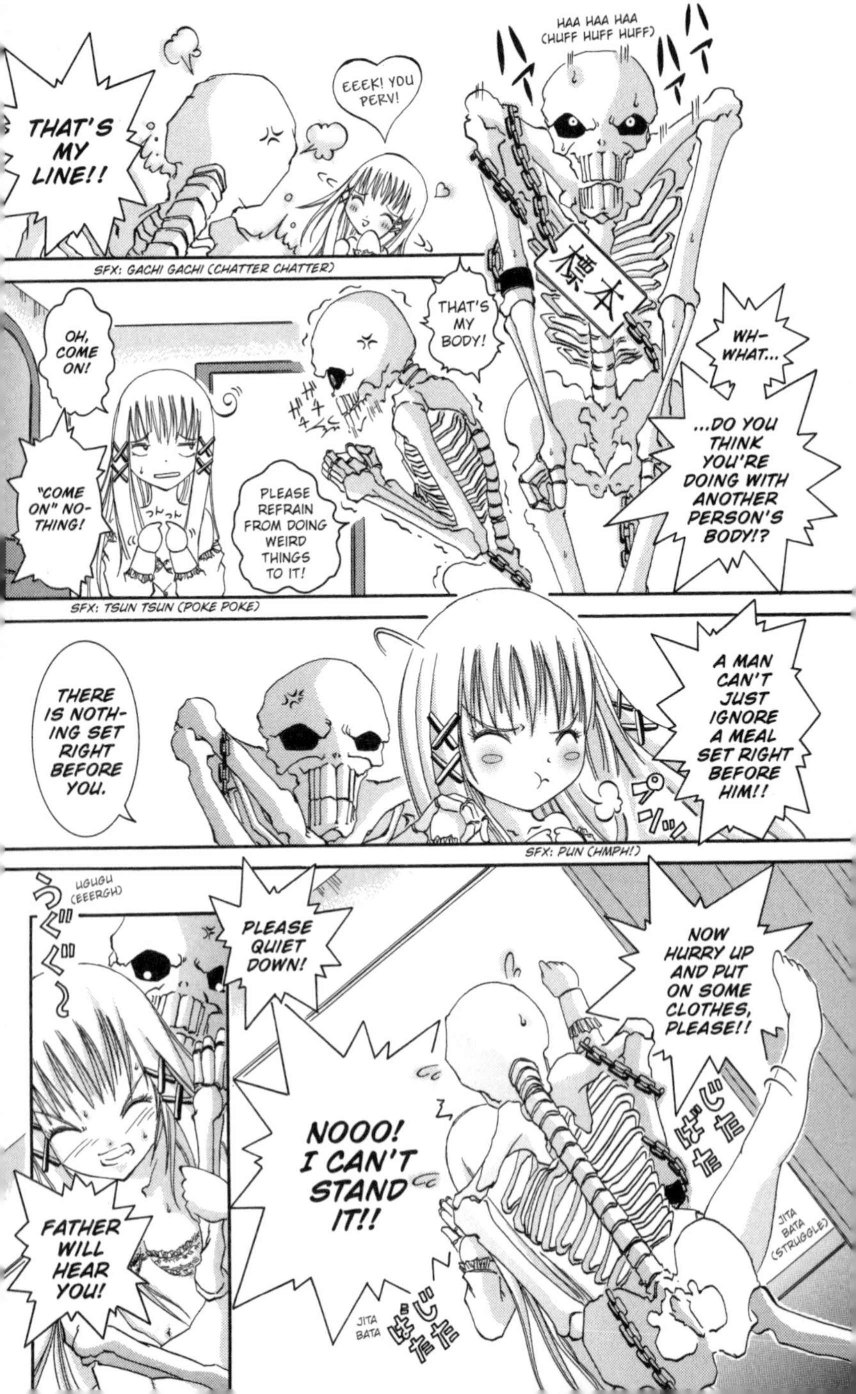
HAA HAA HAA (HUFF HUFF HUFF)
標本
WH-WHAT...
...DO YOU THINK YOU'RE DOING WITH ANOTHER PERSON'S BODY!?
EEEK! YOU PERV!
THAT'S MY LINE!!
SFX: GACHI GACHI (CHATTER CHATTER)
THAT'S MY BODY!
OH, COME ON!
PLEASE REFRAIN FROM DOING WEIRD THINGS TO IT!
"COME ON" NO-THING!
SFX: TSUN TSUN (POKE POKE)
A MAN CAN'T JUST IGNORE A MEAL SET RIGHT BEFORE HIM!!
THERE IS NOTH-ING SET RIGHT BEFORE YOU.
SFX: PUN (HMPH!)
NOW HURRY UP AND PUT ON SOME CLOTHES, PLEASE!!
JITA BATA (STRUGGLE)
NOOO! I CAN'T STAND IT!!
JITA BATA
UGUGU (EEERGH)
PLEASE QUIET DOWN!
FATHER WILL HEAR YOU!

SFX: DOSA (CRASH)

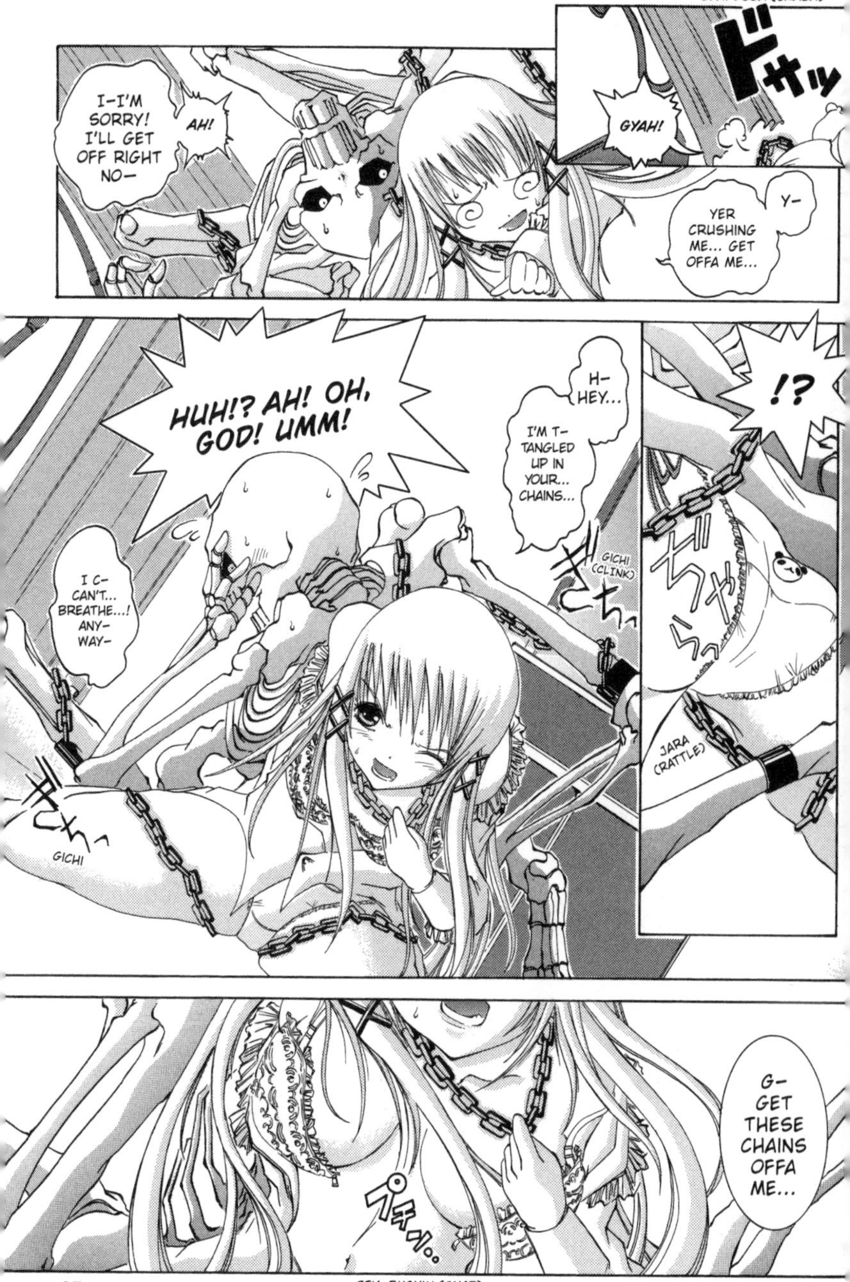
GYAH!
Y-
YER CRUSHING ME... GET OFFA ME...
AH!
I-I'M SORRY! I'LL GET OFF RIGHT NO—
!?
JARA (RATTLE)
H-HEY...
I'M T-TANGLED UP IN YOUR... CHAINS...
GICHI (CLINK)
HUH!? AH! OH, GOD! UMM!
I C-CAN'T... BREATHE...! ANYWAY-
GICHI
G-GET THESE CHAINS OFFA ME...

SFX: PUCHIN (SNAP)

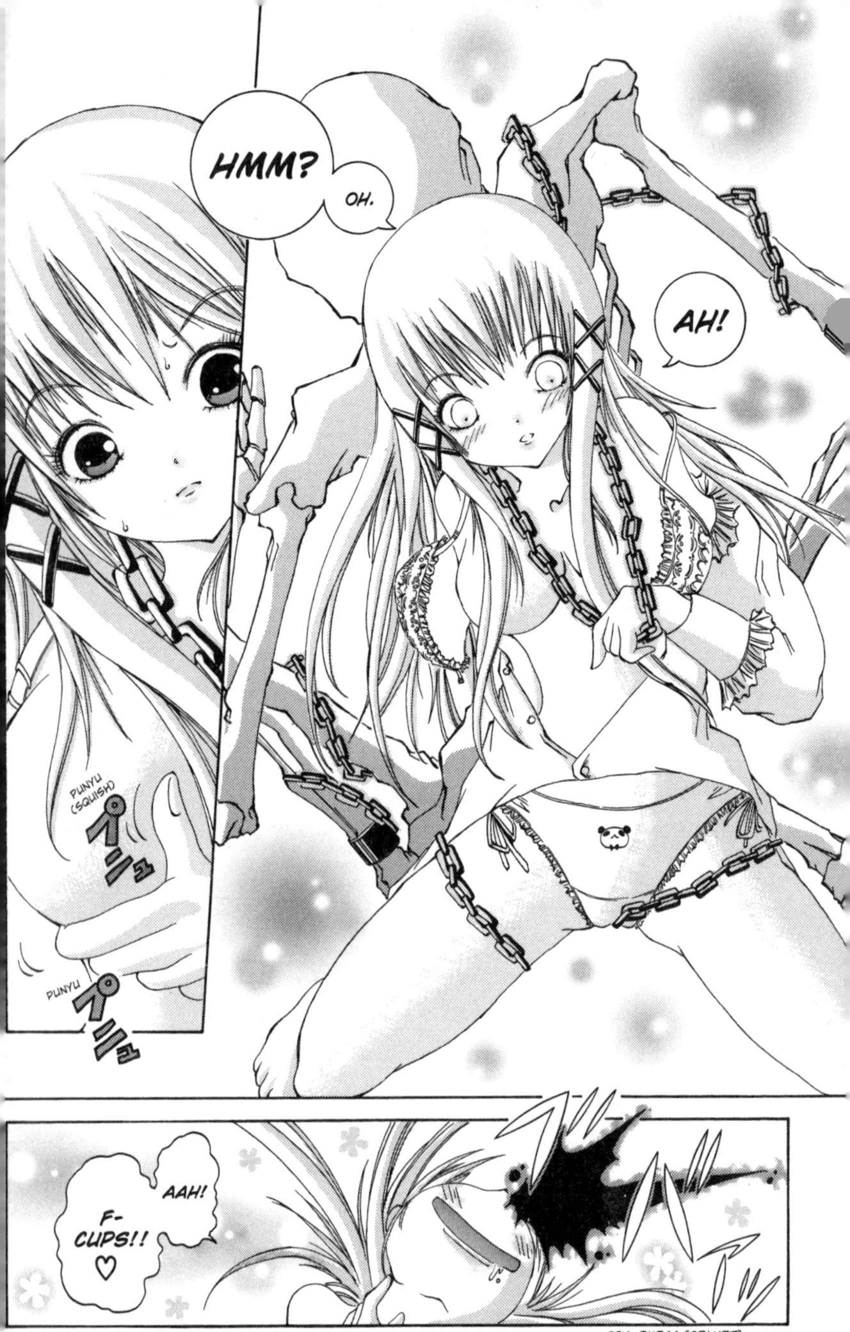
HMM?
OH.
AH!
PUNYU (SQUISH)
PUNYU
AAH! F-CUPS!! ♡

SFX: BUBAA (SPLURT)

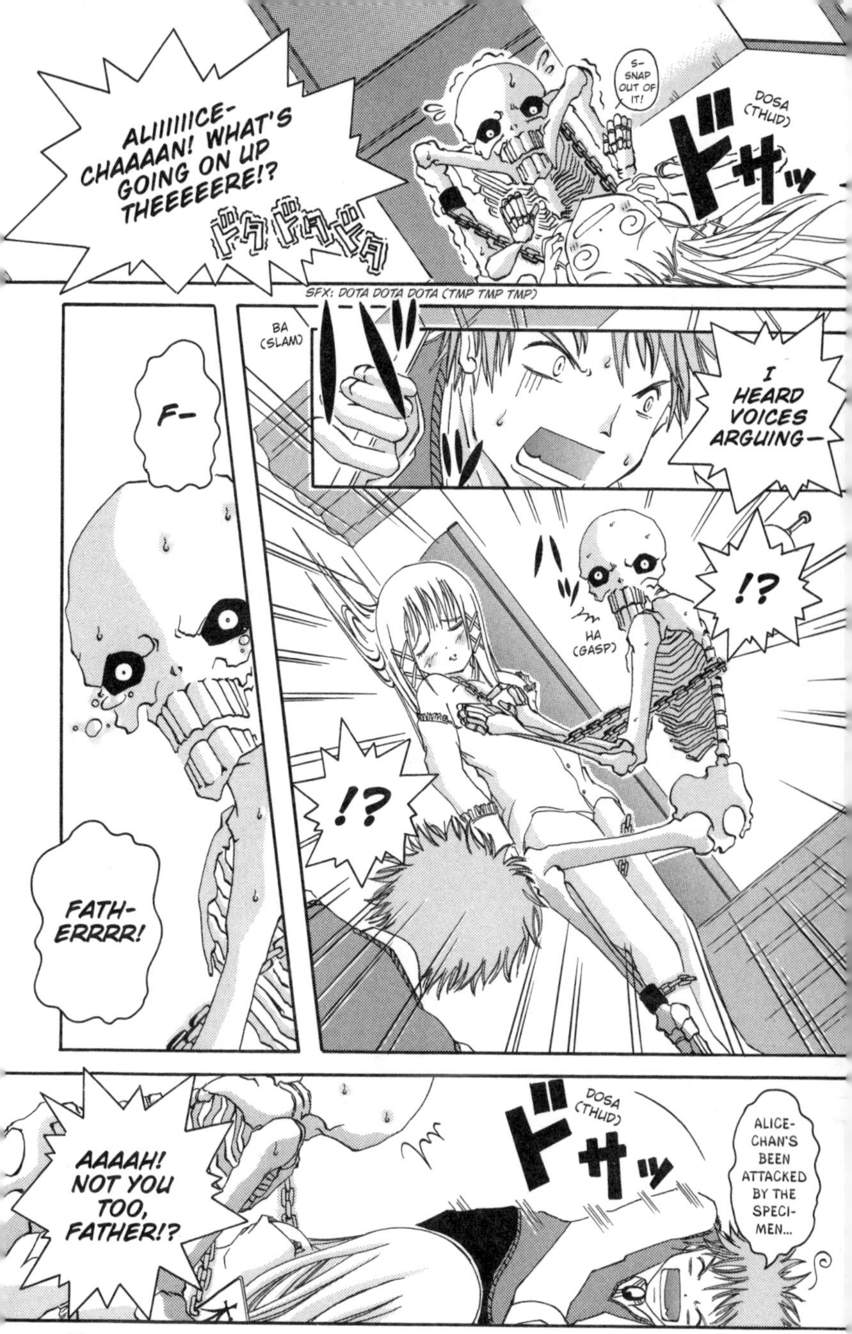
S-SNAP OUT OF IT!
DOSA (THUD)
ドサッ
ALIIIIICE-CHAAAAN! WHAT'S GOING ON UP THEEEEERE!?
SFX: DOTA DOTA DOTA (TMP TMP TMP)
BA (SLAM)
I HEARD VOICES ARGUING—
!?
HA (GASP)
!?
F-
FATH-ERRRR!
ALICE-CHAN'S BEEN ATTACKED BY THE SPECI-MEN...
DOSA (THUD)
ドサッ
AAAAH! NOT YOU TOO, FATHER!?

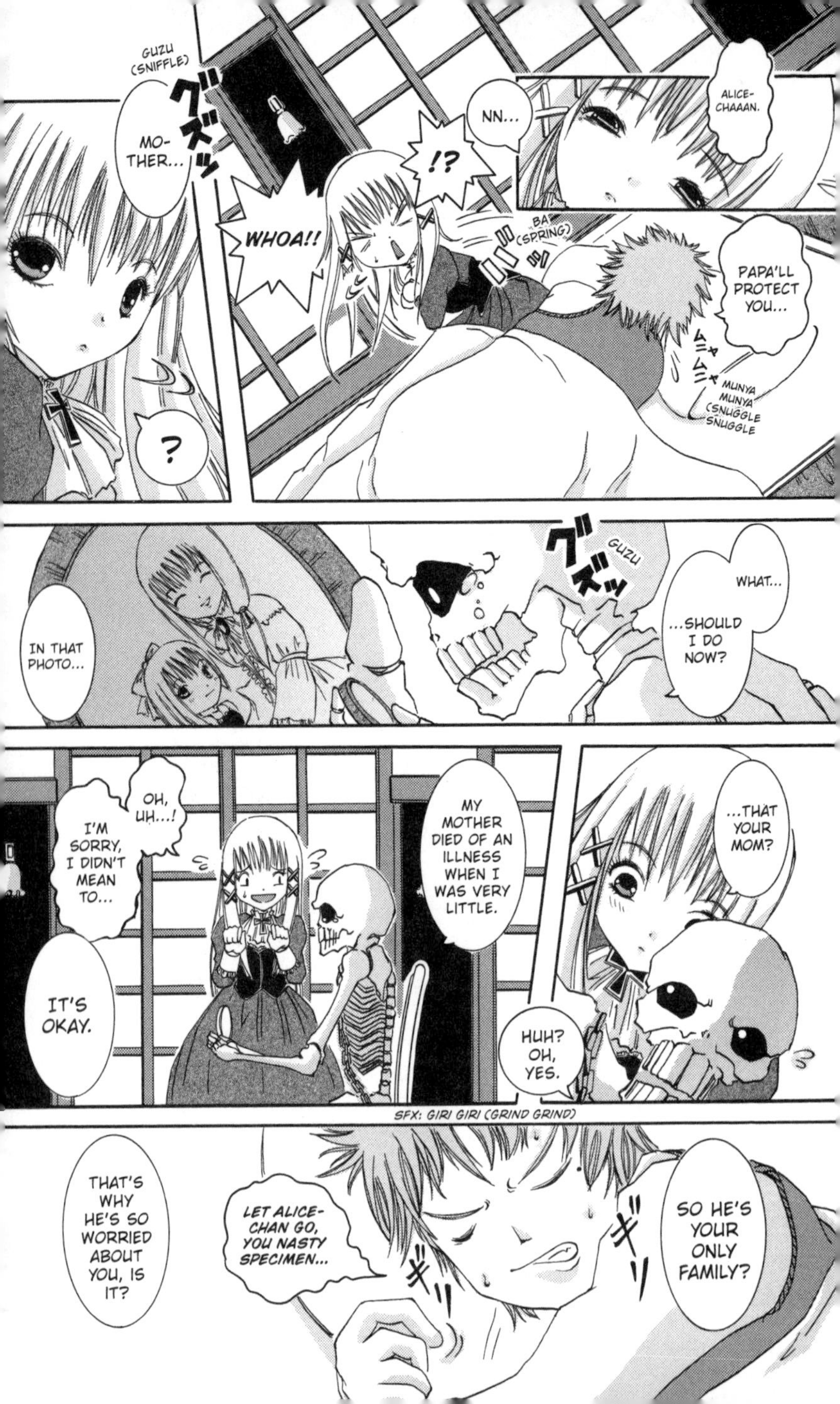
ALICE-CHAAAN.
NN...
PAPA'LL PROTECT YOU...
MUNYA MUNYA (SNUGGLE SNUGGLE)
!?
BA (SPRING)
WHOA!!
GUZU (SNIFFLE)
MO-THER...
?
GUZU
WHAT...
...SHOULD I DO NOW?
IN THAT PHOTO...
...THAT YOUR MOM?
HUH? OH, YES.
MY MOTHER DIED OF AN ILLNESS WHEN I WAS VERY LITTLE.
OH, UH...!
I'M SORRY, I DIDN'T MEAN TO...
IT'S OKAY.
SFX: GIRI GIRI (GRIND GRIND)
SO HE'S YOUR ONLY FAMILY?
LET ALICE-CHAN GO, YOU NASTY SPECIMEN...
THAT'S WHY HE'S SO WORRIED ABOUT YOU, IS IT?

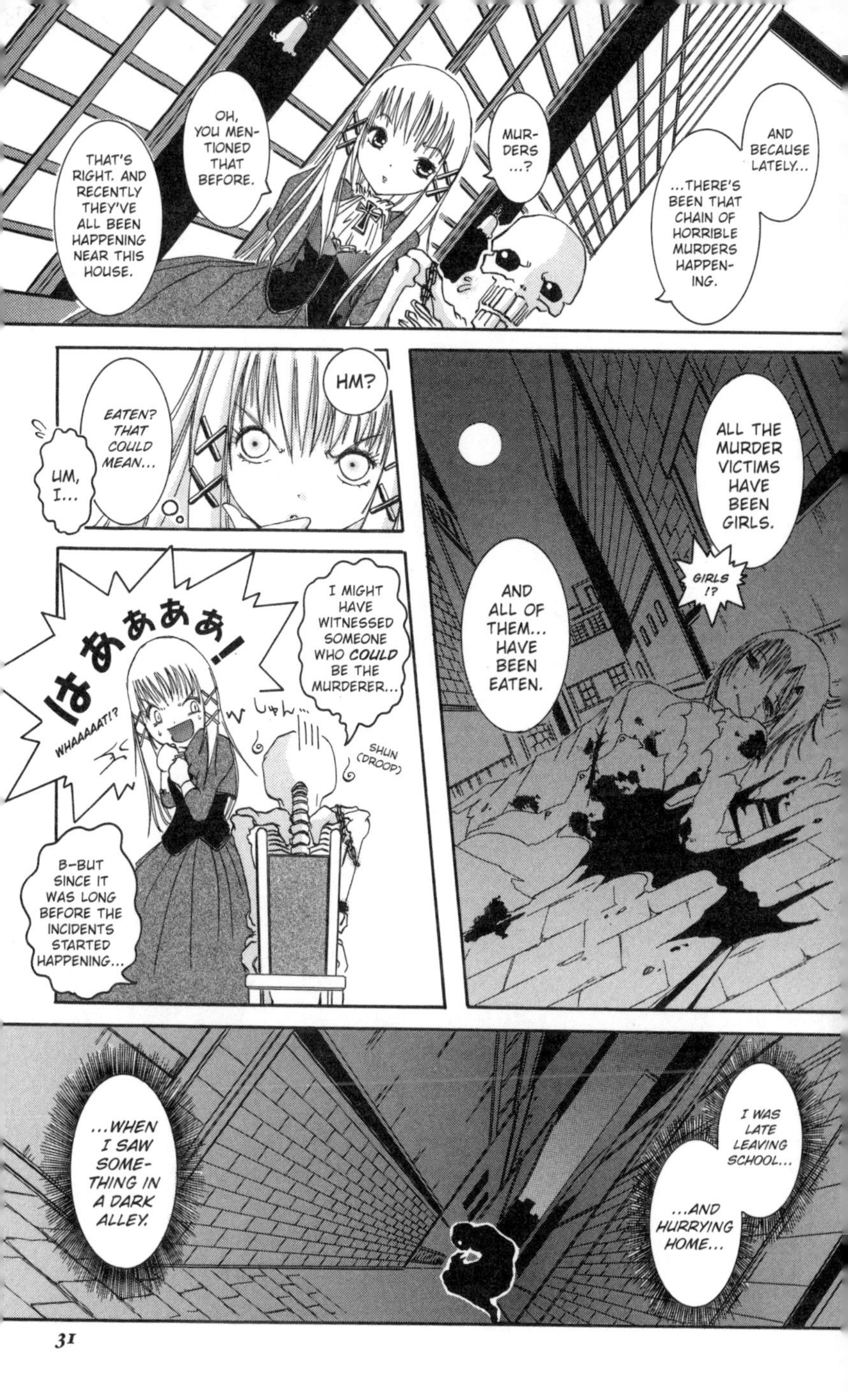
AND BECAUSE LATELY...
...THERE'S BEEN THAT CHAIN OF HORRIBLE MURDERS HAPPENING.
MURDERS...?
OH, YOU MENTIONED THAT BEFORE.
THAT'S RIGHT. AND RECENTLY THEY'VE ALL BEEN HAPPENING NEAR THIS HOUSE.
ALL THE MURDER VICTIMS HAVE BEEN GIRLS.
GIRLS!?
AND ALL OF THEM... HAVE BEEN EATEN.
HM?
EATEN? THAT COULD MEAN...
UM, I...
I MIGHT HAVE WITNESSED SOMEONE WHO *COULD* BE THE MURDERER...
しゅん...
SHUN (DROOP)
はあああぁ!
WHAAAAAT!?
B-BUT SINCE IT WAS LONG BEFORE THE INCIDENTS STARTED HAPPENING...
I WAS LATE LEAVING SCHOOL...
...AND HURRYING HOME...
...WHEN I SAW SOMETHING IN A DARK ALLEY.

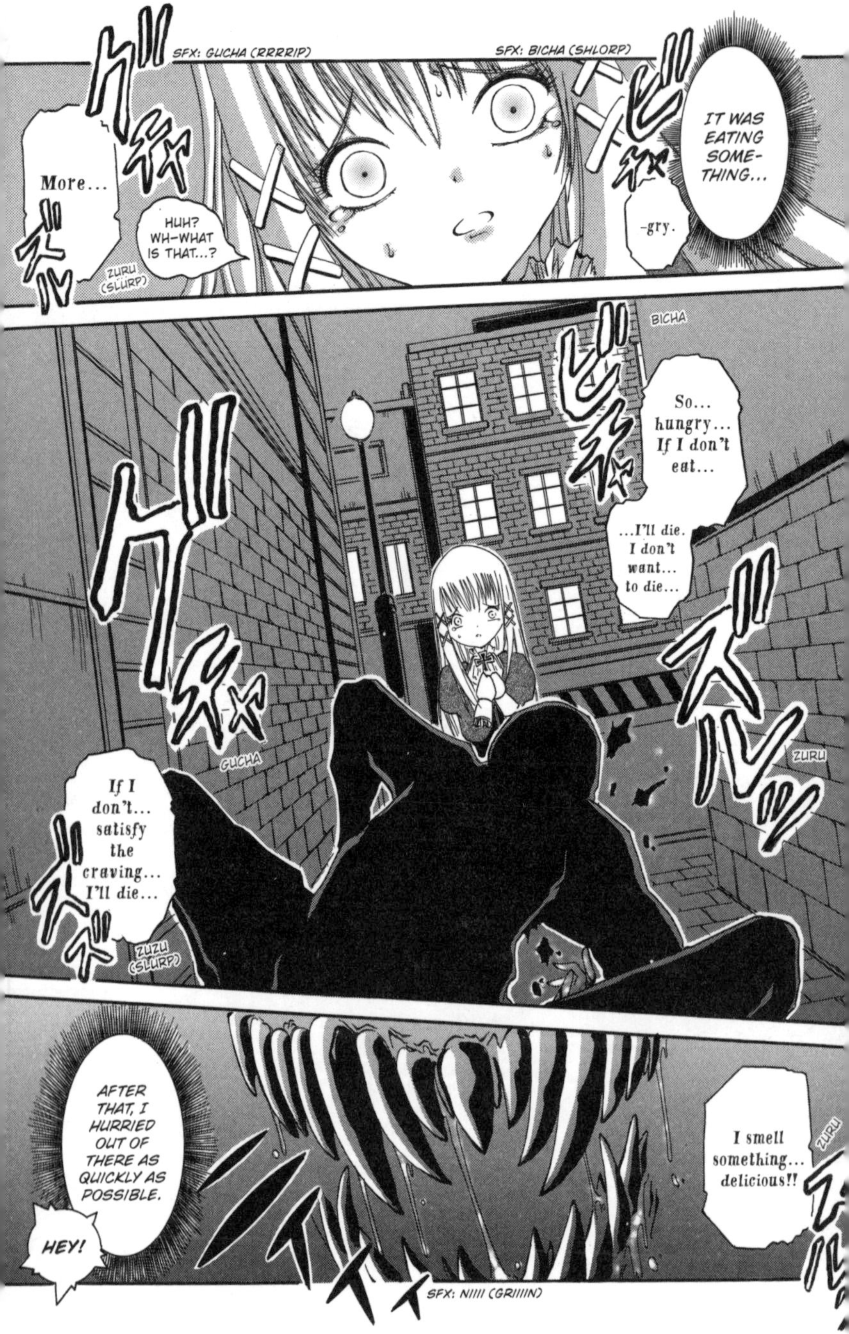
SFX: BICHA (SHLORP)
IT WAS EATING SOMETHING...
-gry.
HUH? WH-WHAT IS THAT...?
More...
SFX: GUCHA (RRRRIP)
ZURU (SLURP)
BICHA
So... hungry... If I don't eat...
...I'll die. I don't want... to die...
ZURU
GUCHA
If I don't... satisfy the craving... I'll die...
ZUZU (SLURP)
ZURU
I smell something... delicious!!
AFTER THAT, I HURRIED OUT OF THERE AS QUICKLY AS POSSIBLE.
HEY!
SFX: NIIII (GRIIIIN)

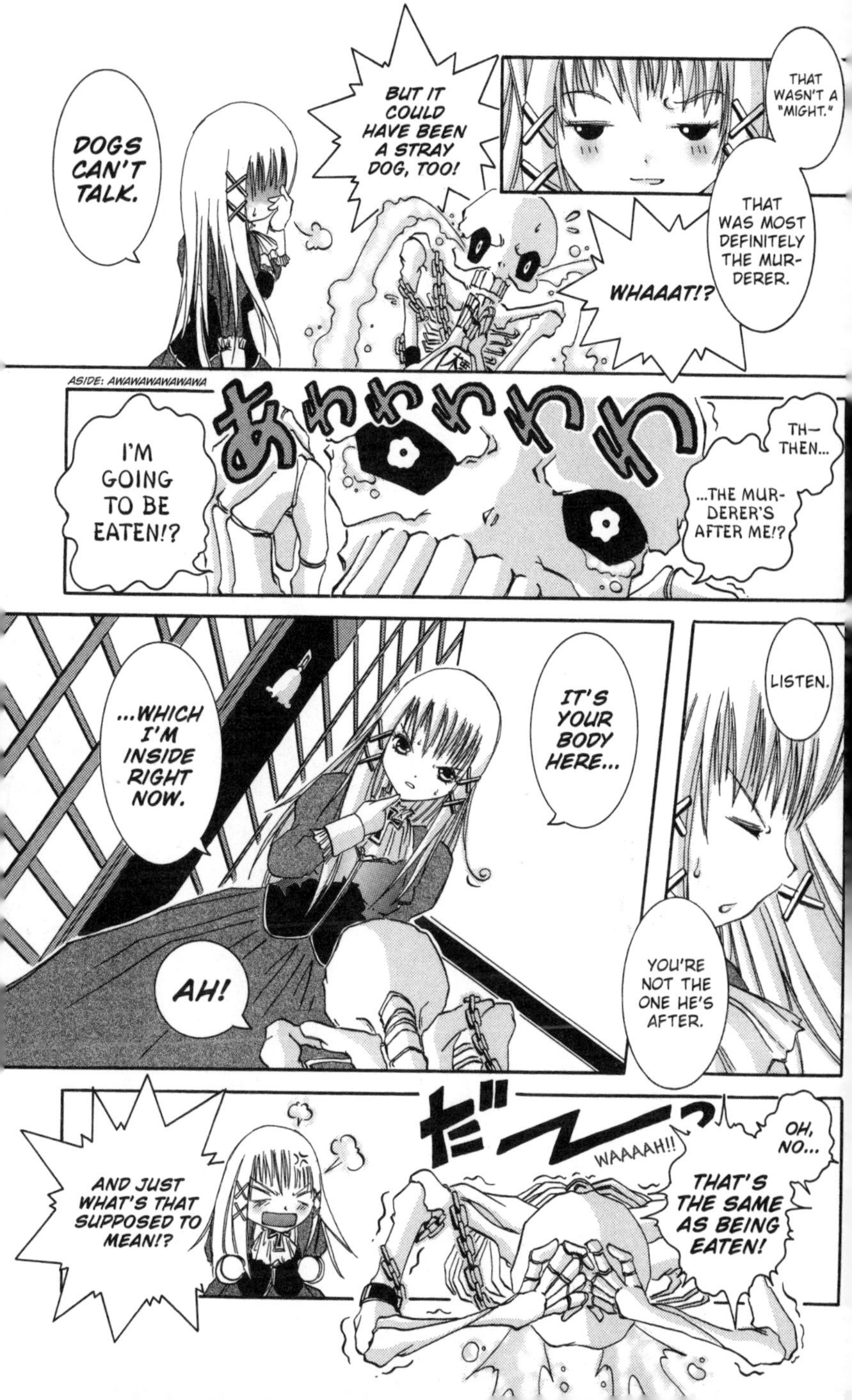

THAT WASN'T A "MIGHT."
THAT WAS MOST DEFINITELY THE MURDERER.
WHAAAT!?
BUT IT COULD HAVE BEEN A STRAY DOG, TOO!
DOGS CAN'T TALK.
ASIDE: AWAWAWAWAWAWA
あわわわわわ
TH— THEN...
...THE MURDERER'S AFTER ME!?
I'M GOING TO BE EATEN!?
LISTEN.
YOU'RE NOT THE ONE HE'S AFTER.
IT'S YOUR BODY HERE...
...WHICH I'M INSIDE RIGHT NOW.
AH!
OH, NO...
THAT'S THE SAME AS BEING EATEN!
だーっ
WAAAAH!!
AND JUST WHAT'S THAT SUPPOSED TO MEAN!?

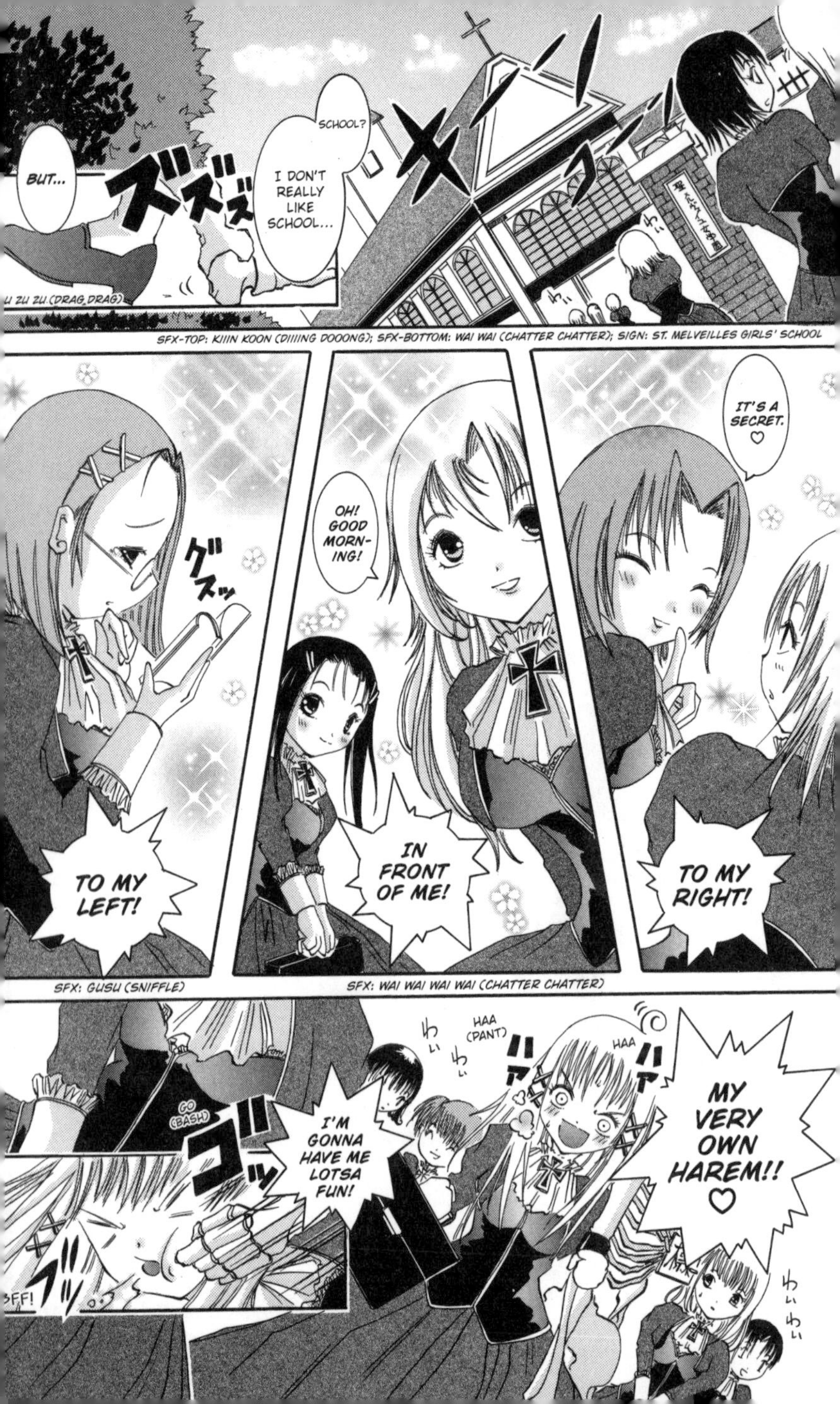
SCHOOL?
I DON'T REALLY LIKE SCHOOL...
BUT...
ZU ZU (DRAG DRAG)
SFX-TOP: KIIIN KOON (DIIIING DOOONG); SFX-BOTTOM: WAI WAI (CHATTER CHATTER); SIGN: ST. MELVEILLES GIRLS' SCHOOL
IT'S A SECRET. ♡
TO MY RIGHT!
OH! GOOD MORNING!
IN FRONT OF ME!
TO MY LEFT!
SFX: GUSU (SNIFFLE)
SFX: WAI WAI WAI WAI (CHATTER CHATTER)
MY VERY OWN HAREM!! ♡
HAA (PANT)
HAA
I'M GONNA HAVE ME LOTSA FUN!
GO (BASH)

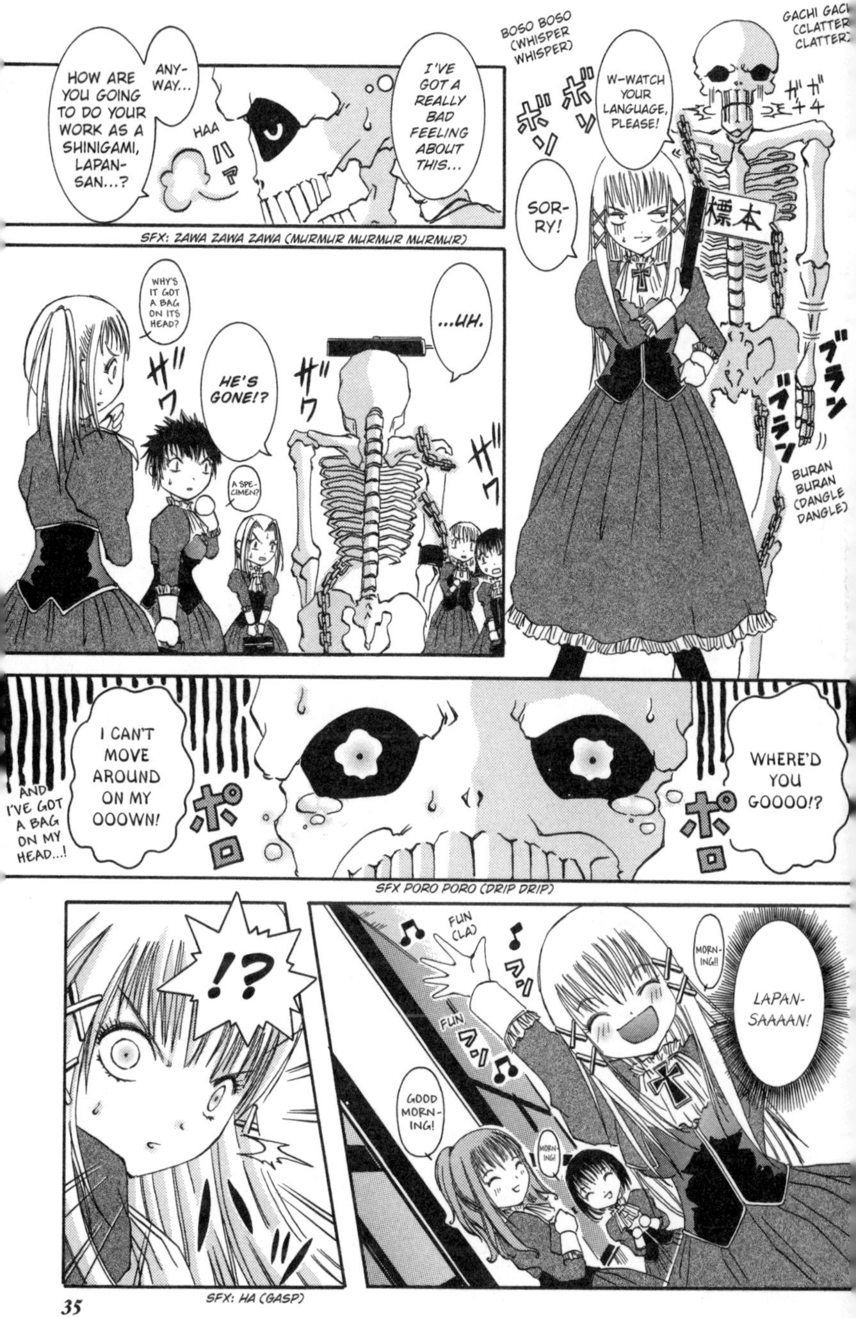
BOSO BOSO (WHISPER WHISPER)
GACHI GAC (CLATTER CLATTER)
W-WATCH YOUR LANGUAGE, PLEASE!
SORRY!
標本
BURAN BURAN (DANGLE DANGLE)
I'VE GOT A REALLY BAD FEELING ABOUT THIS...
HAA
ANYWAY...
HOW ARE YOU GOING TO DO YOUR WORK AS A SHINIGAMI, LAPAN-SAN...?
SFX: ZAWA ZAWA ZAWA (MURMUR MURMUR MURMUR)
...UH.
HE'S GONE!?
A SPECIMEN?
WHY'S IT GOT A BAG ON ITS HEAD?
WHERE'D YOU GOOOO!?
I CAN'T MOVE AROUND ON MY OOOWN!
AND I'VE GOT A BAG ON MY HEAD...!
SFX PORO PORO (DRIP DRIP)
LAPAN-SAAAAN!
MORNING!!
FUN (LA)
FUN
GOOD MORNING!
MORNING!
!?
SFX: HA (GASP)

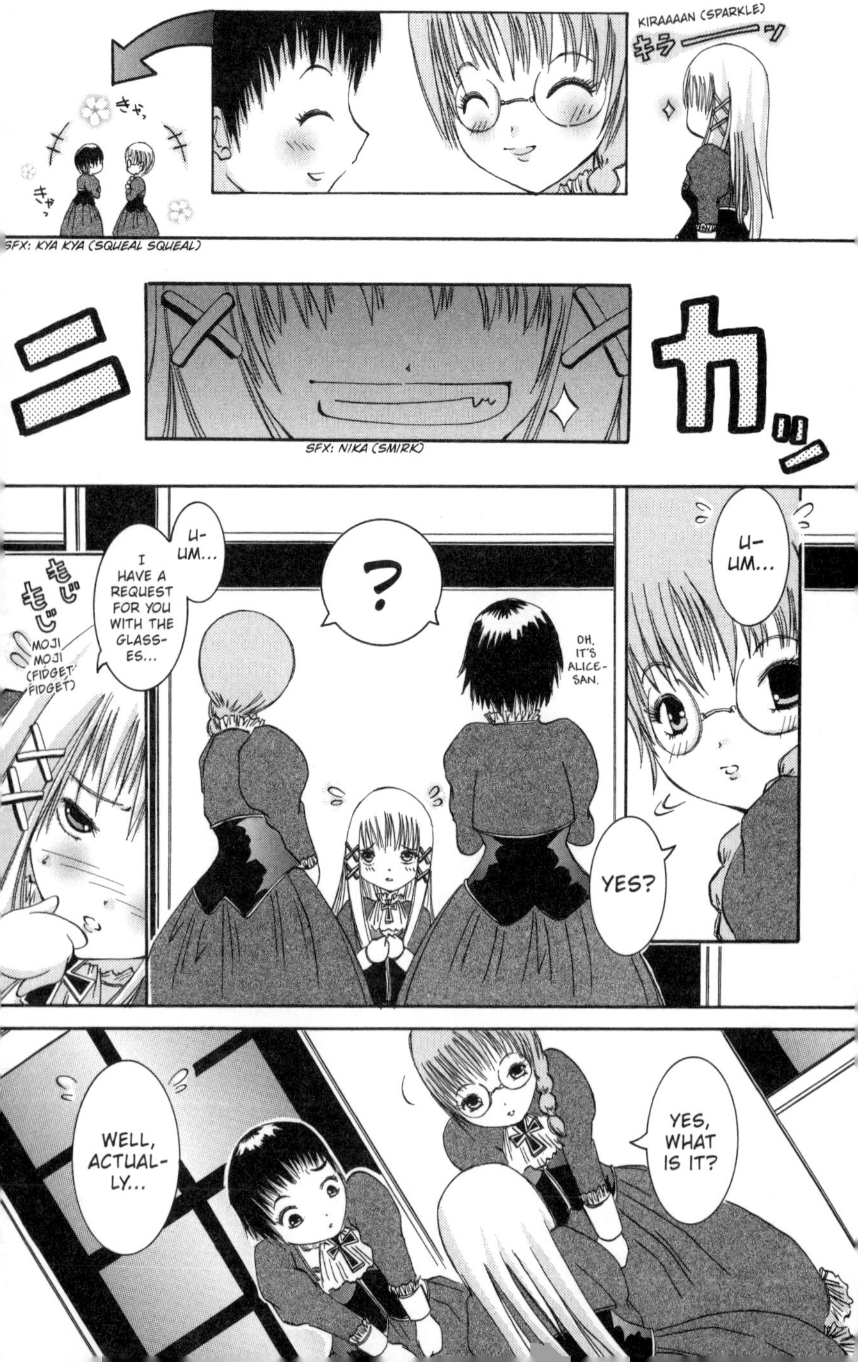
KIRAAAAN (SPARKLE)
キラーーッ
きゃっ
きゃっ
SFX: KYA KYA (SQUEAL SQUEAL)
ニカッ
SFX: NIKA (SMIRK)
U-UM...
YES?
?
OH, IT'S ALICE-SAN.
U-UM...
I HAVE A REQUEST FOR YOU WITH THE GLASSES...
もじもじ
MOJI MOJI (FIDGET FIDGET)
YES, WHAT IS IT?
WELL, ACTUAL-LY...

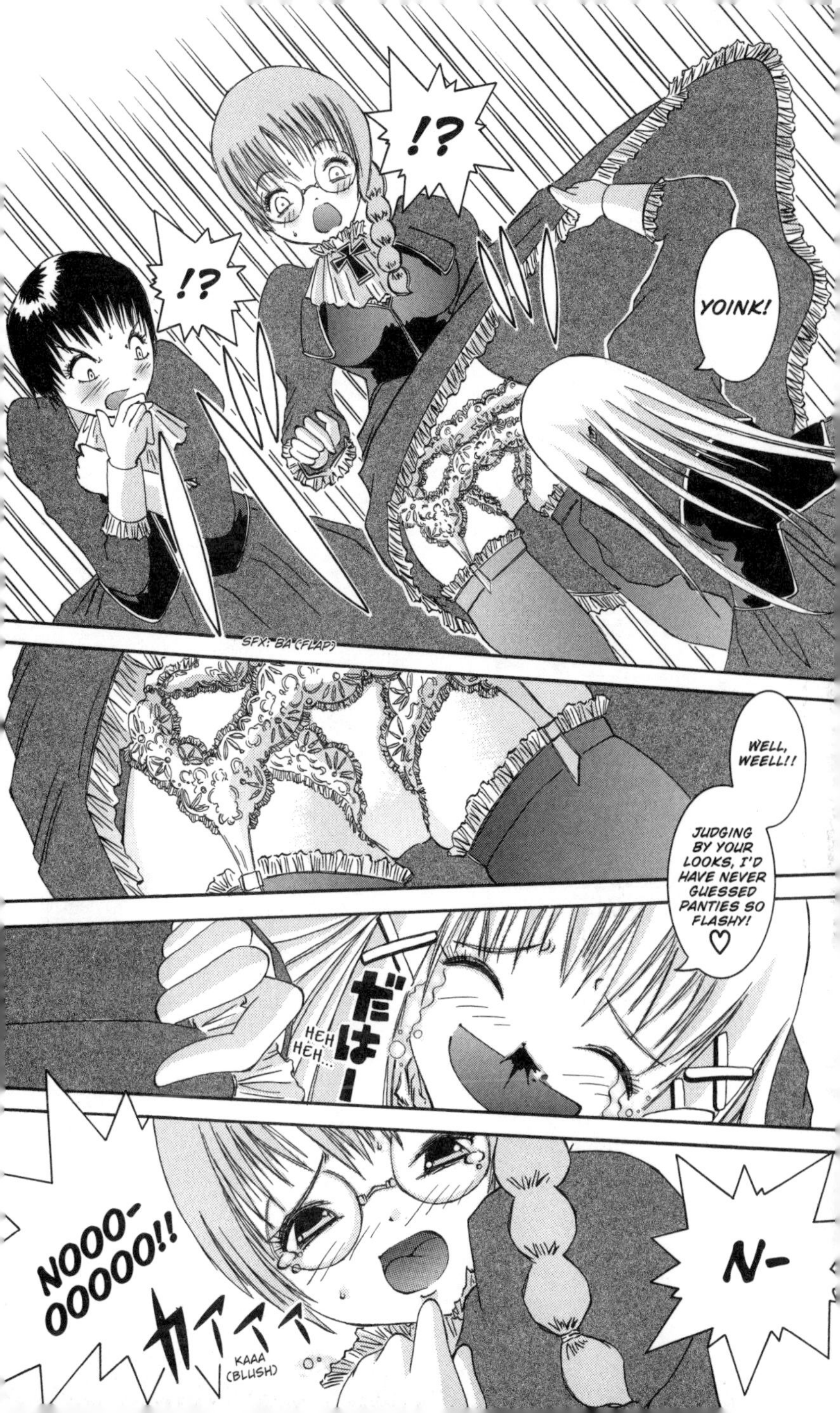
YOINK!
!?
!?
SFX: BA (FLAP)
WELL, WEELL!!
JUDGING BY YOUR LOOKS, I'D HAVE NEVER GUESSED PANTIES SO FLASHY! ♡
だはー
HEH HEH...
N-
NOOO-OOOOO!!
KAAA (BLUSH)

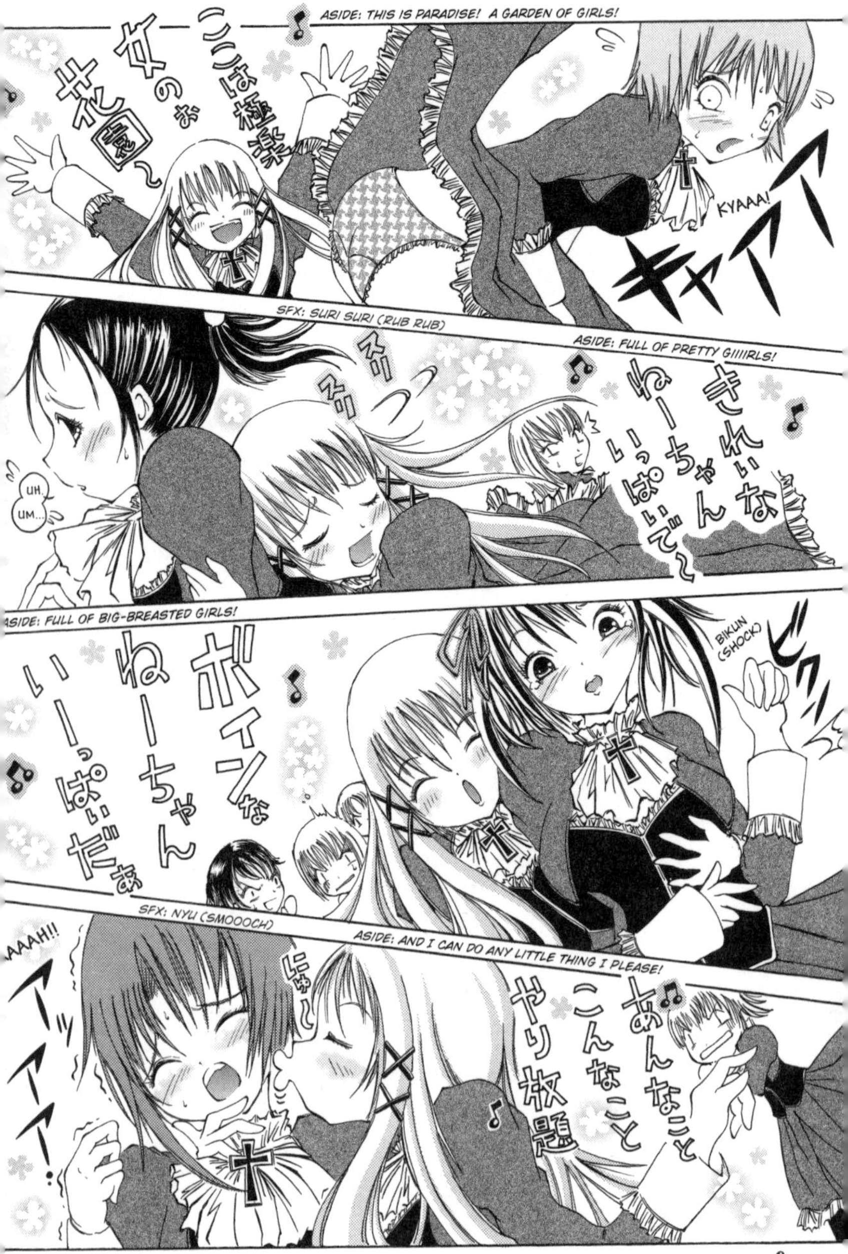
KYAAA!
キャアア
ASIDE: THIS IS PARADISE! A GARDEN OF GIRLS!
ここは極楽 女のぉ 花園～
ASIDE: FULL OF PRETTY GIIIIRLS!
きれいな ねーちゃん いっぱいでぇ～
SFX: SURI SURI (RUB RUB)
スリ スリ
UH, UM...
BIKUN (SHOCK)
ビクッ
ASIDE: FULL OF BIG-BREASTED GIRLS!
ボインな ねーちゃん いーっぱいだぁ
ASIDE: AND I CAN DO ANY LITTLE THING I PLEASE!
あんなこと こんなこと やり放題
SFX: NYU (SMOOOCH)
にゅ～
AAAH!!
アーッ アーー!

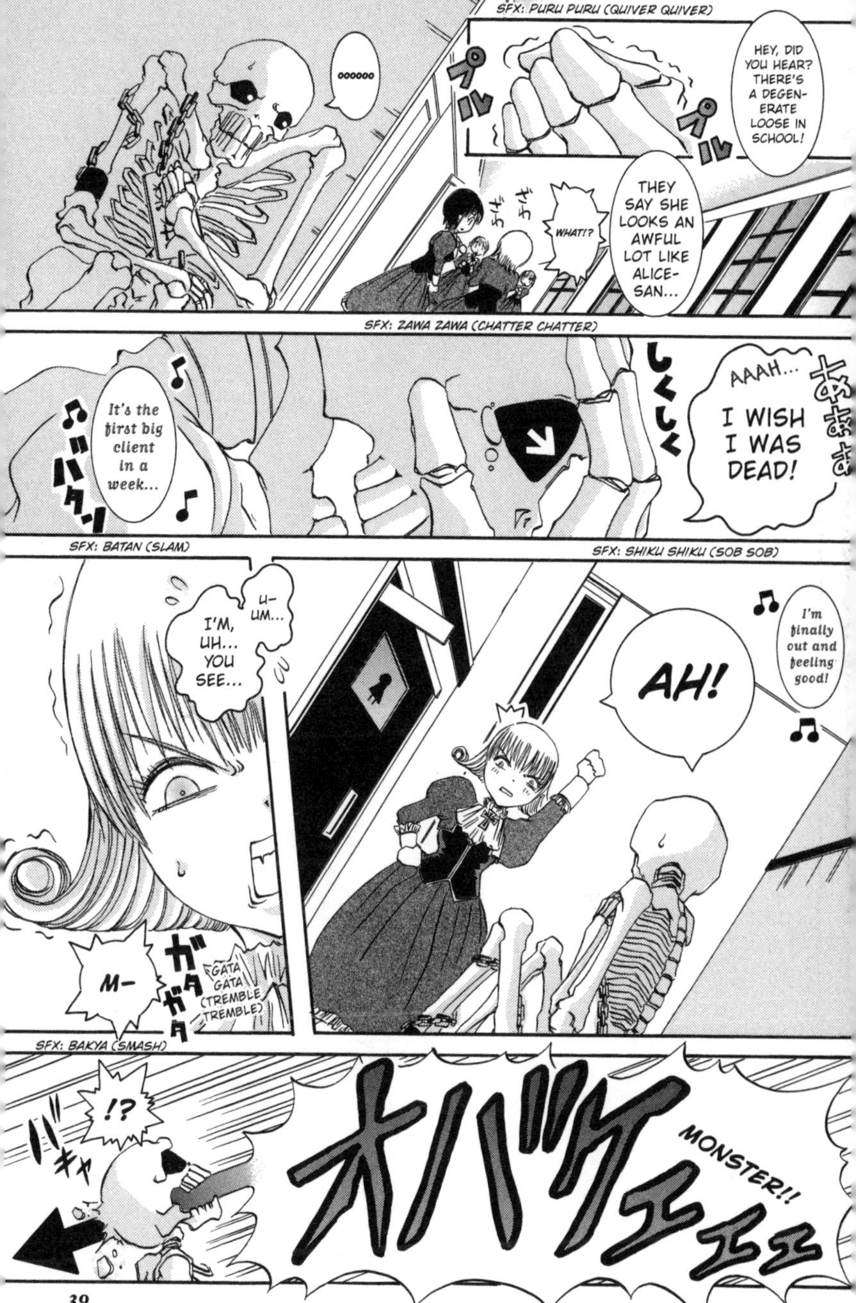
SFX: PURU PURU (QUIVER QUIVER)
HEY, DID YOU HEAR? THERE'S A DEGEN-ERATE LOOSE IN SCHOOL!
THEY SAY SHE LOOKS AN AWFUL LOT LIKE ALICE-SAN...
WHAT!?
SFX: ZAWA ZAWA (CHATTER CHATTER)
......
AAAH... I WISH I WAS DEAD!
SFX: SHIKU SHIKU (SOB SOB)
It's the first big client in a week...
SFX: BATAN (SLAM)
I'm finally out and feeling good!
AH!
U-UM...
I'M, UH... YOU SEE...
M-
GATA GATA (TREMBLE TREMBLE)
MONSTER!!
!?
SFX: BAKYA (SMASH)

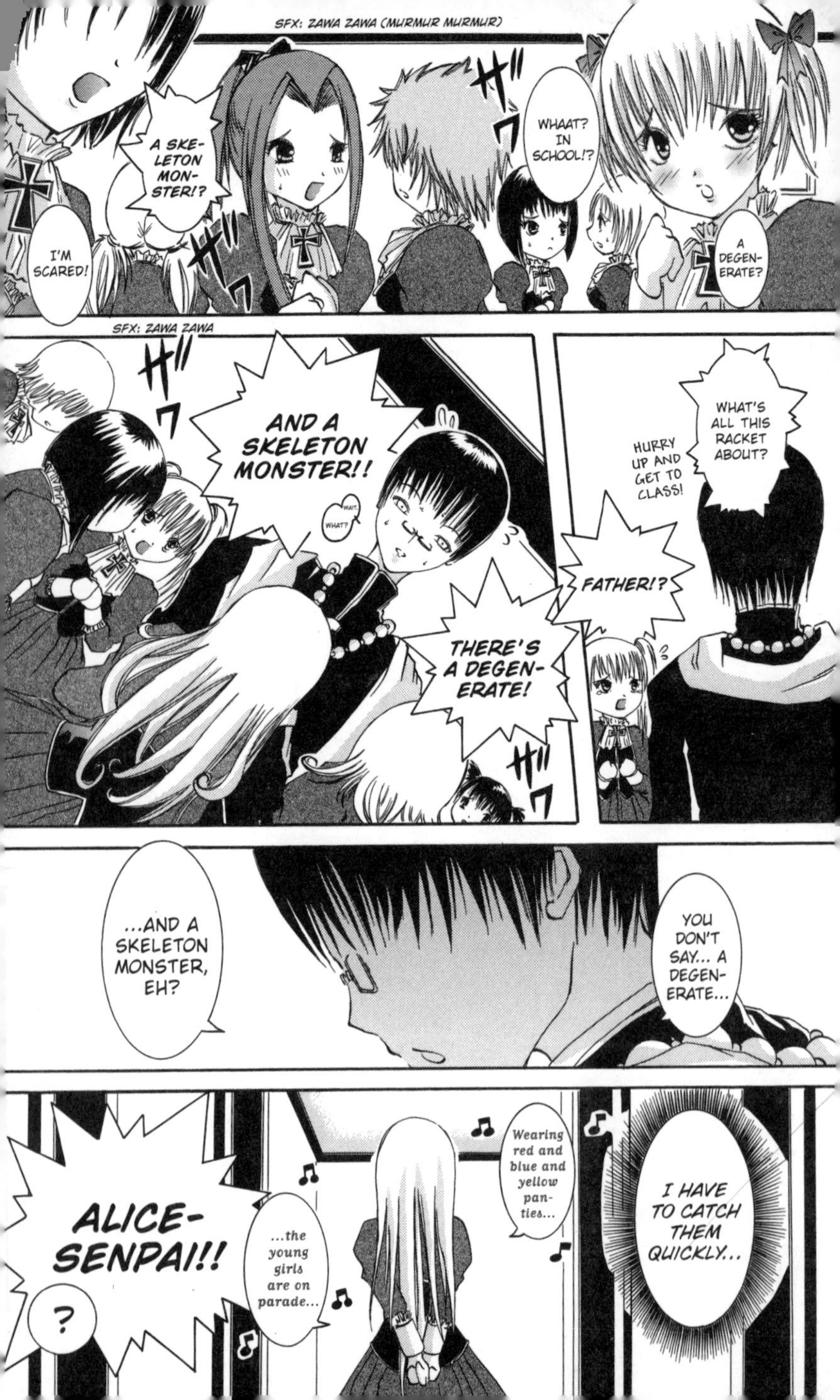
SFX: ZAWA ZAWA (MURMUR MURMUR)
A DEGENERATE?
WHAAT? IN SCHOOL!?
A SKELETON MONSTER!?
I'M SCARED!
WHAT'S ALL THIS RACKET ABOUT?
HURRY UP AND GET TO CLASS!
FATHER!?
SFX: ZAWA ZAWA
AND A SKELETON MONSTER!!
WAIT, WHAT?
THERE'S A DEGENERATE!
YOU DON'T SAY... A DEGENERATE...
...AND A SKELETON MONSTER, EH?
I HAVE TO CATCH THEM QUICKLY...
Wearing red and blue and yellow panties...
...the young girls are on parade...
ALICE-SENPAI!!
?

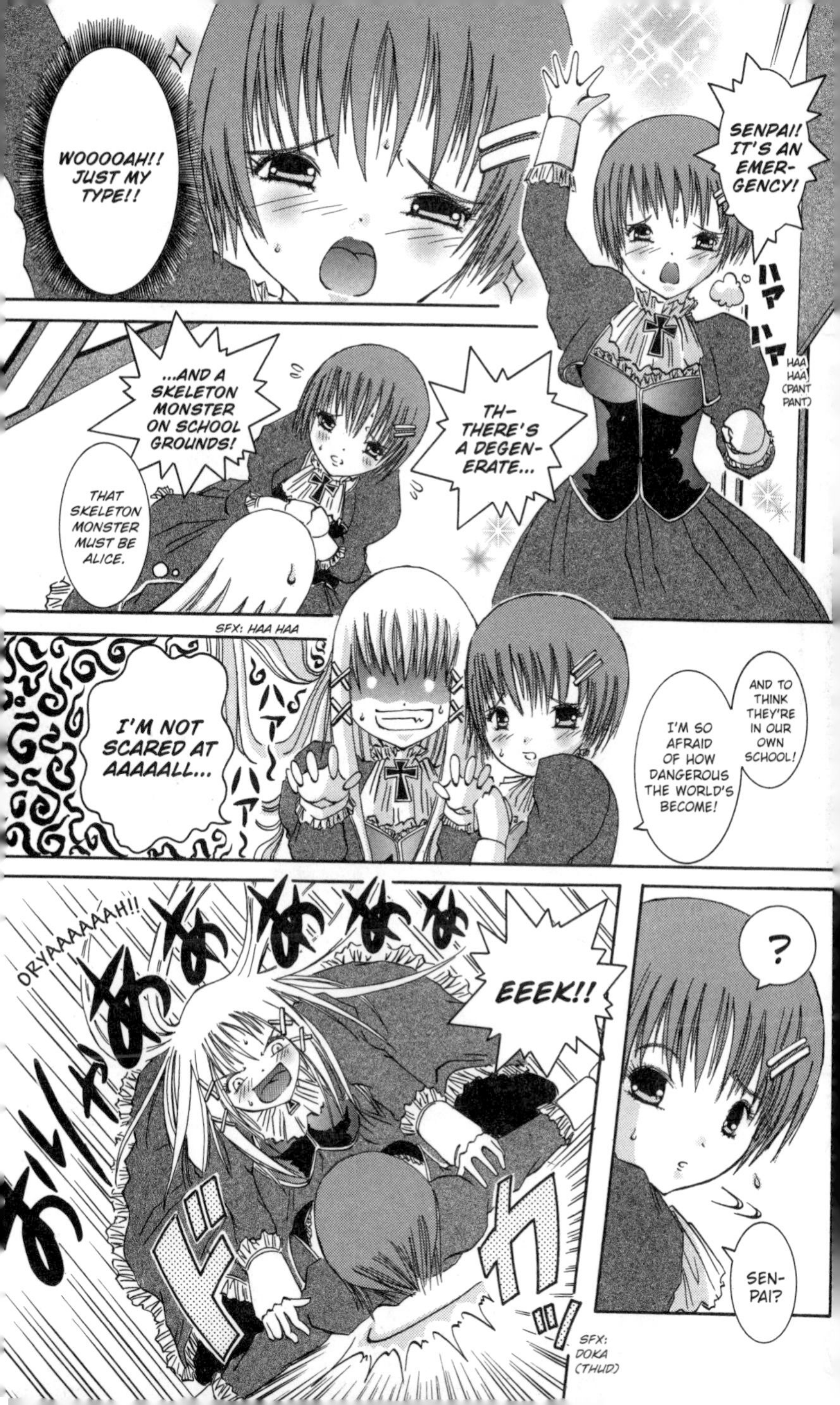
WOOOOAH!! JUST MY TYPE!!
SENPAI! IT'S AN EMER-GENCY!
ハア ハア
HAA HAA (PANT PANT)
TH-THERE'S A DEGEN-ERATE...
...AND A SKELETON MONSTER ON SCHOOL GROUNDS!
THAT SKELETON MONSTER MUST BE ALICE.
SFX: HAA HAA
AND TO THINK THEY'RE IN OUR OWN SCHOOL!
I'M SO AFRAID OF HOW DANGEROUS THE WORLD'S BECOME!
I'M NOT SCARED AT AAAAALL...
ハア ハア
?
SEN-PAI?
EEEK!!
ORYAAAAAAH!!
SFX: DOKA (THUD)

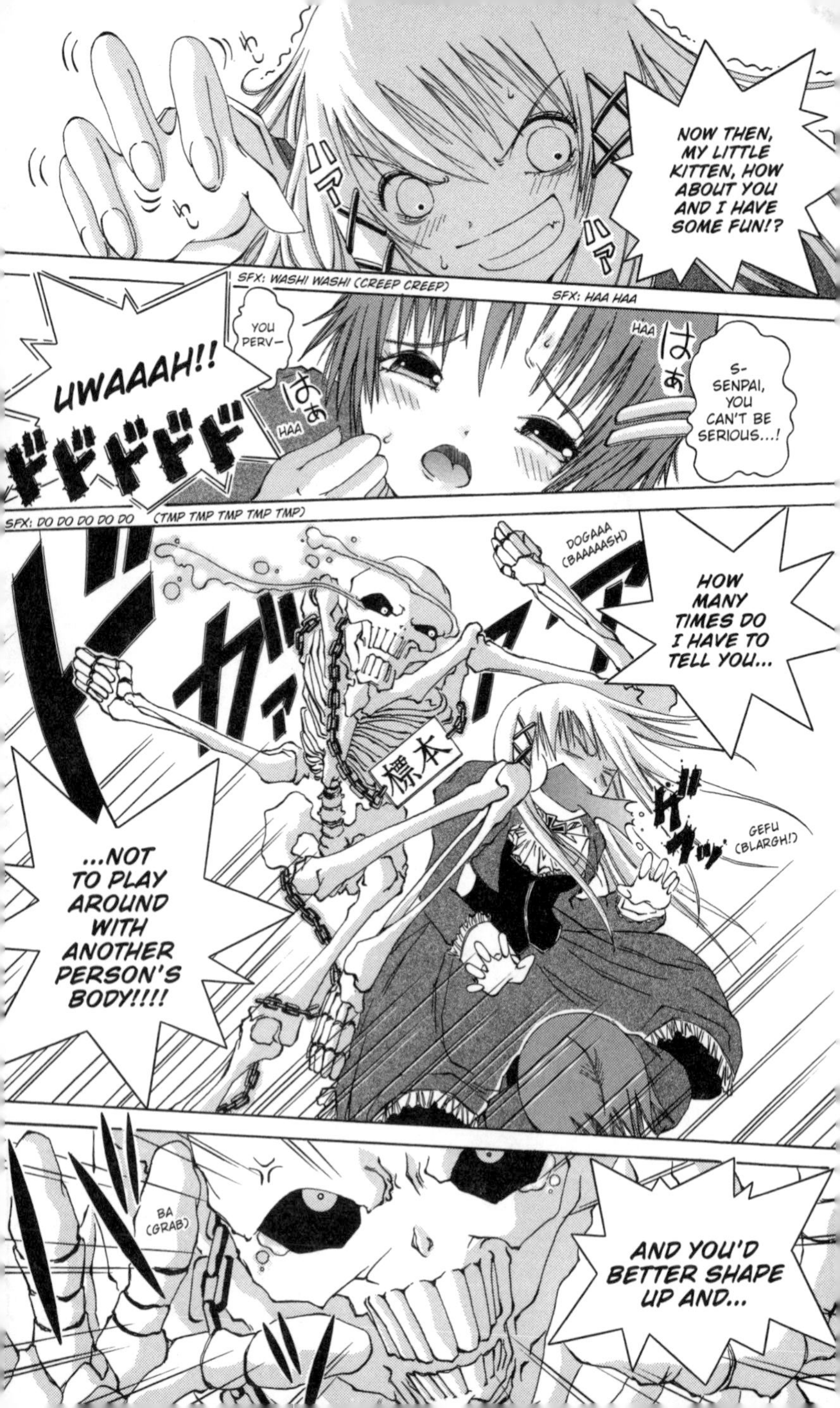
NOW THEN, MY LITTLE KITTEN, HOW ABOUT YOU AND I HAVE SOME FUN!?
ハァ ハァ
SFX: HAA HAA
SFX: WASHI WASHI (CREEP CREEP)
S-SENPAI, YOU CAN'T BE SERIOUS...!
HAA はぁ
YOU PERV—
はぁ HAA
UWAAAH!!
ドドドドド
SFX: DO DO DO DO DO (TMP TMP TMP TMP TMP)
HOW MANY TIMES DO I HAVE TO TELL YOU...
DOGAAA (BAAAAASH)
標本
GEFU (BLARGH!)
...NOT TO PLAY AROUND WITH ANOTHER PERSON'S BODY!!!!
AND YOU'D BETTER SHAPE UP AND...
BA (GRAB)

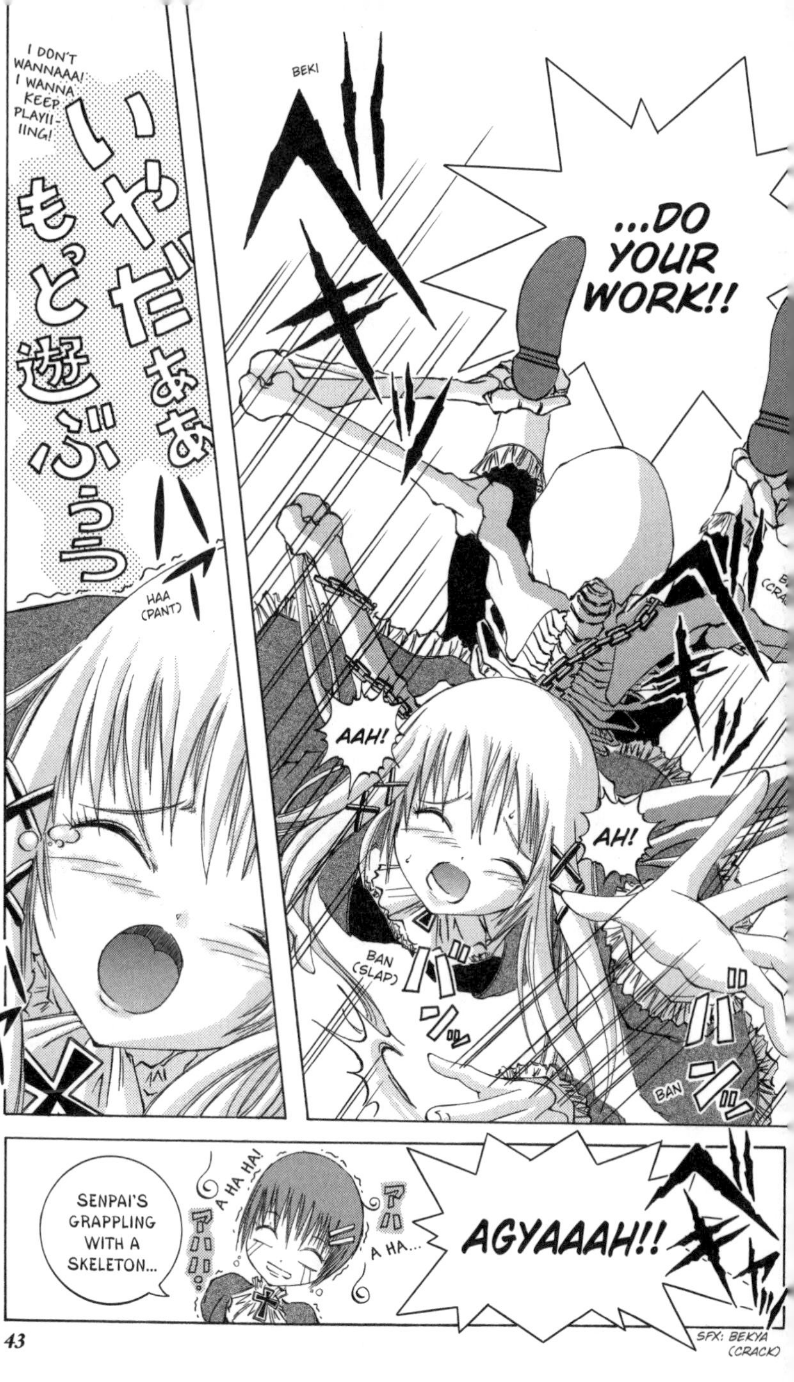
BEKI
...DO YOUR WORK!!
AAH!
AH!
BAN (SLAP)
BAN
I DON'T WANNAAA! I WANNA KEEP PLAYII-IING!
いやだぁぁ もっと遊ぶぅぅ
HAA (PANT)
HAA
AGYAAAH!!
A HA HA!
A HA...
SENPAI'S GRAPPLING WITH A SKELETON...
SFX: BEKYA (CRACK)

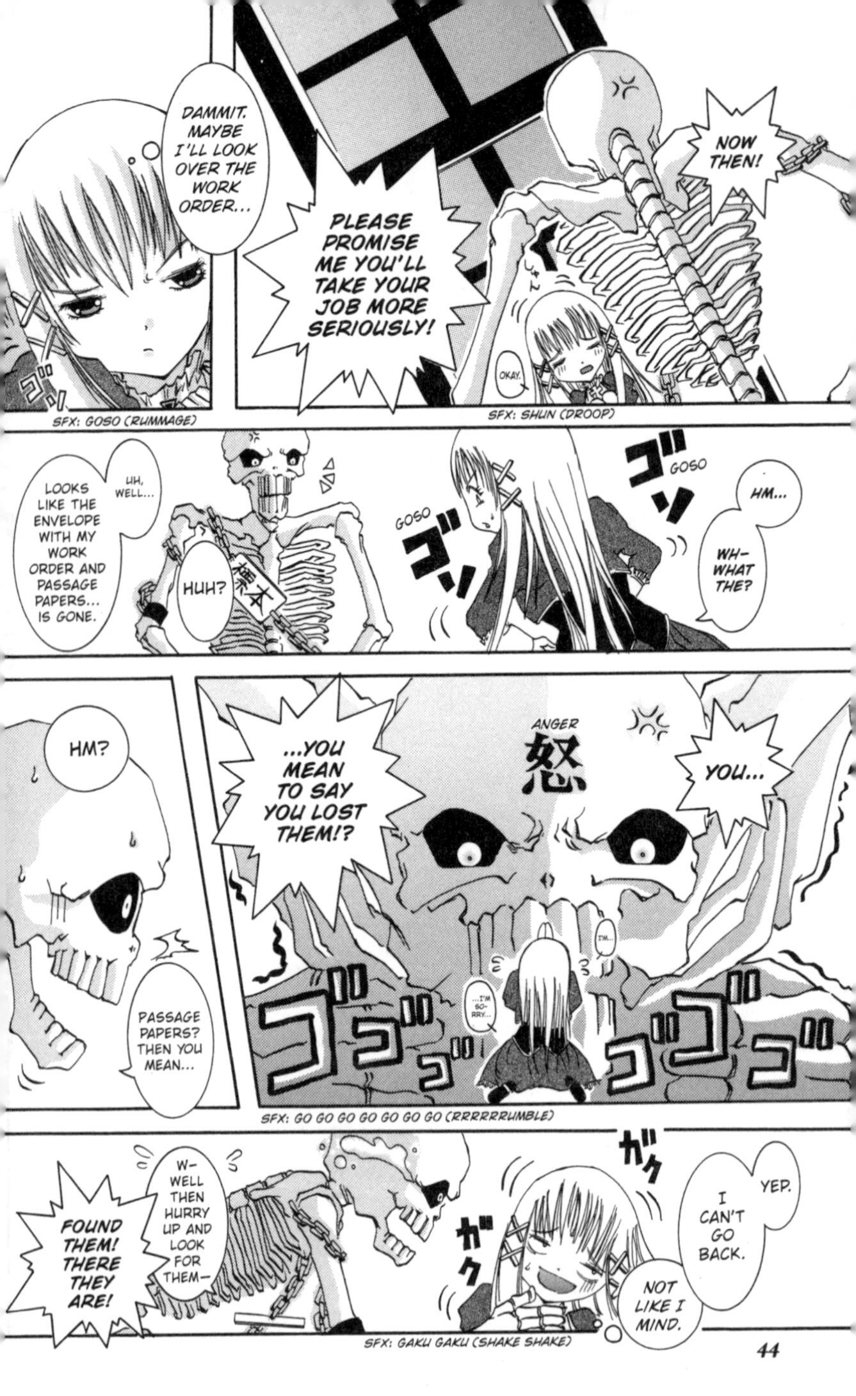
NOW THEN!
PLEASE PROMISE ME YOU'LL TAKE YOUR JOB MORE SERIOUSLY!
OKAY.
SFX: SHUN (DROOP)
DAMMIT. MAYBE I'LL LOOK OVER THE WORK ORDER...
SFX: GOSO (RUMMAGE)
HM...
WH-WHAT THE?
ゴソ GOSO
ゴソ GOSO
UH, WELL...
LOOKS LIKE THE ENVELOPE WITH MY WORK ORDER AND PASSAGE PAPERS... IS GONE.
標本
HUH?
YOU...
ANGER
怒
...YOU MEAN TO SAY YOU LOST THEM!?
I'M...
...I'M SO-RRY...
SFX: GO GO GO GO GO GO GO (RRRRRRUMBLE)
HM?
PASSAGE PAPERS? THEN YOU MEAN...
ガク
ガク
YEP.
I CAN'T GO BACK.
NOT LIKE I MIND.
W-WELL THEN HURRY UP AND LOOK FOR THEM—
FOUND THEM! THERE THEY ARE!
SFX: GAKU GAKU (SHAKE SHAKE)

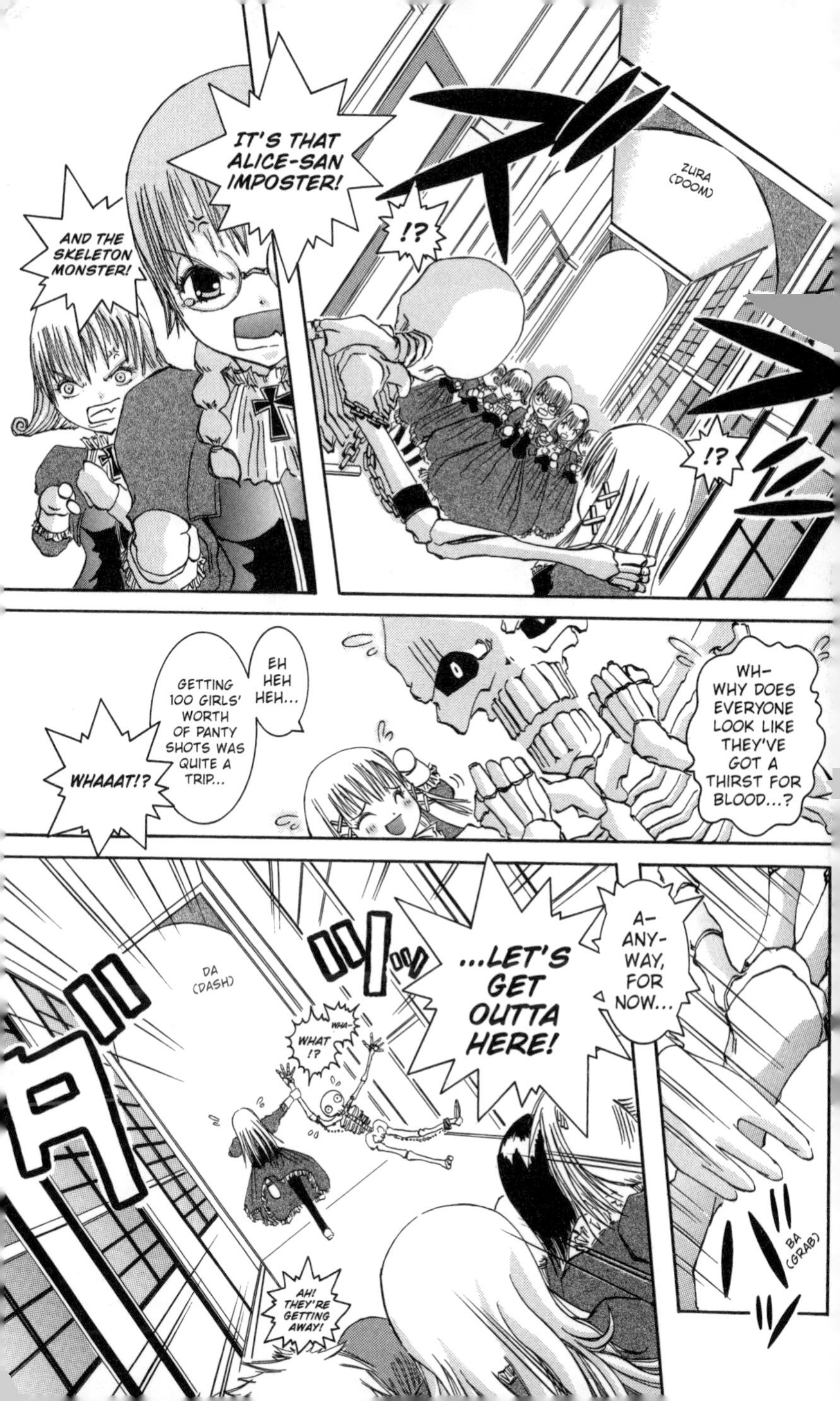
ZURA (DOOM)
!?
!?
IT'S THAT ALICE-SAN IMPOSTER!
AND THE SKELETON MONSTER!
WH- WHY DOES EVERYONE LOOK LIKE THEY'VE GOT A THIRST FOR BLOOD...?
EH HEH HEH...
GETTING 100 GIRLS' WORTH OF PANTY SHOTS WAS QUITE A TRIP...
WHAAAT!?
A- ANYWAY, FOR NOW...
...LET'S GET OUTTA HERE!
BA (GRAB)
DA (DASH)
WHA-
WHAT !?
AH! THEY'RE GETTING AWAY!

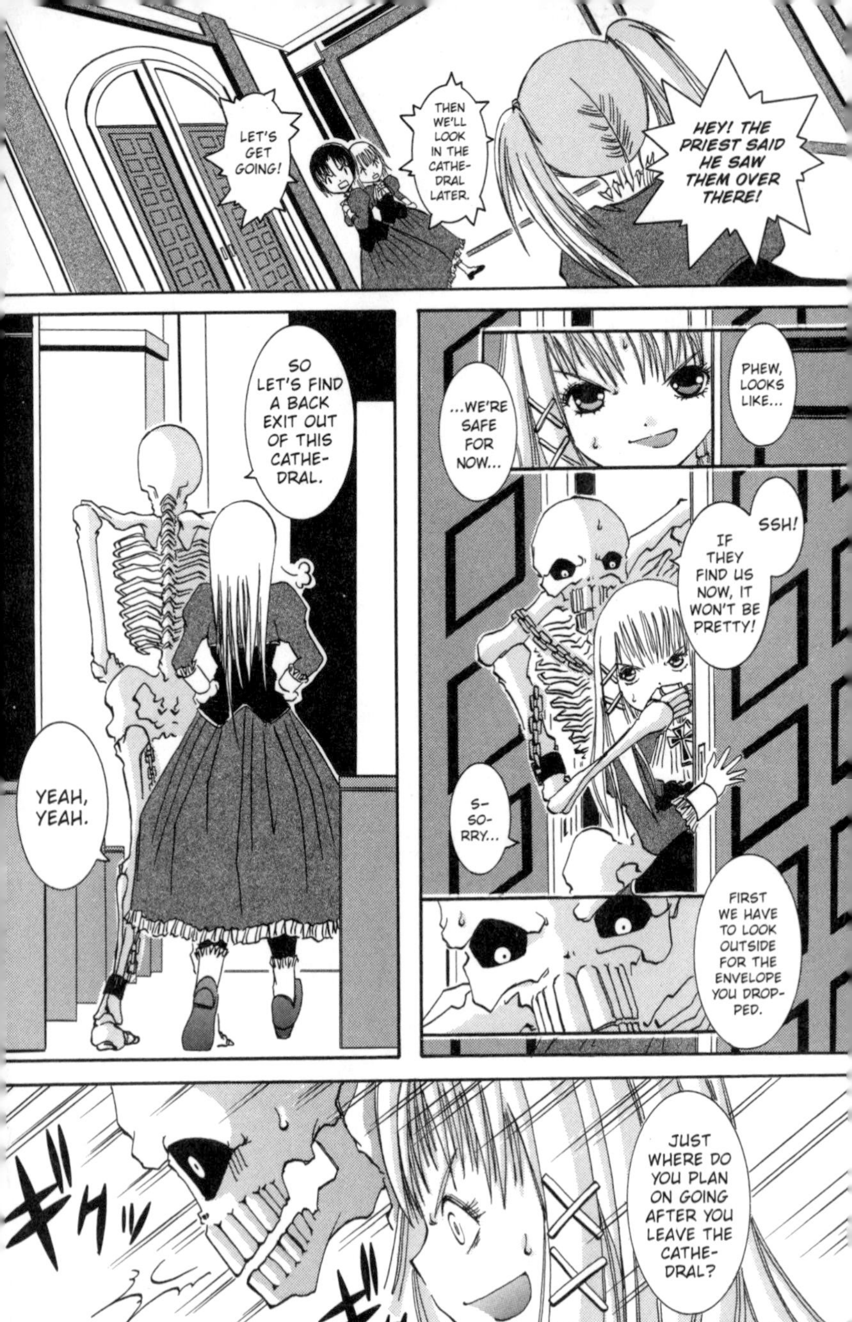
HEY! THE PRIEST SAID HE SAW THEM OVER THERE!
THEN WE'LL LOOK IN THE CATHE-DRAL LATER.
LET'S GET GOING!
PHEW, LOOKS LIKE...
...WE'RE SAFE FOR NOW...
SSH!
IF THEY FIND US NOW, IT WON'T BE PRETTY!
S-SO-RRY...
FIRST WE HAVE TO LOOK OUTSIDE FOR THE ENVELOPE YOU DROP-PED.
SO LET'S FIND A BACK EXIT OUT OF THIS CATHE-DRAL.
YEAH, YEAH.
JUST WHERE DO YOU PLAN ON GOING AFTER YOU LEAVE THE CATHE-DRAL?

SFX: GIKU GIKU (FREEZE FREEZE)

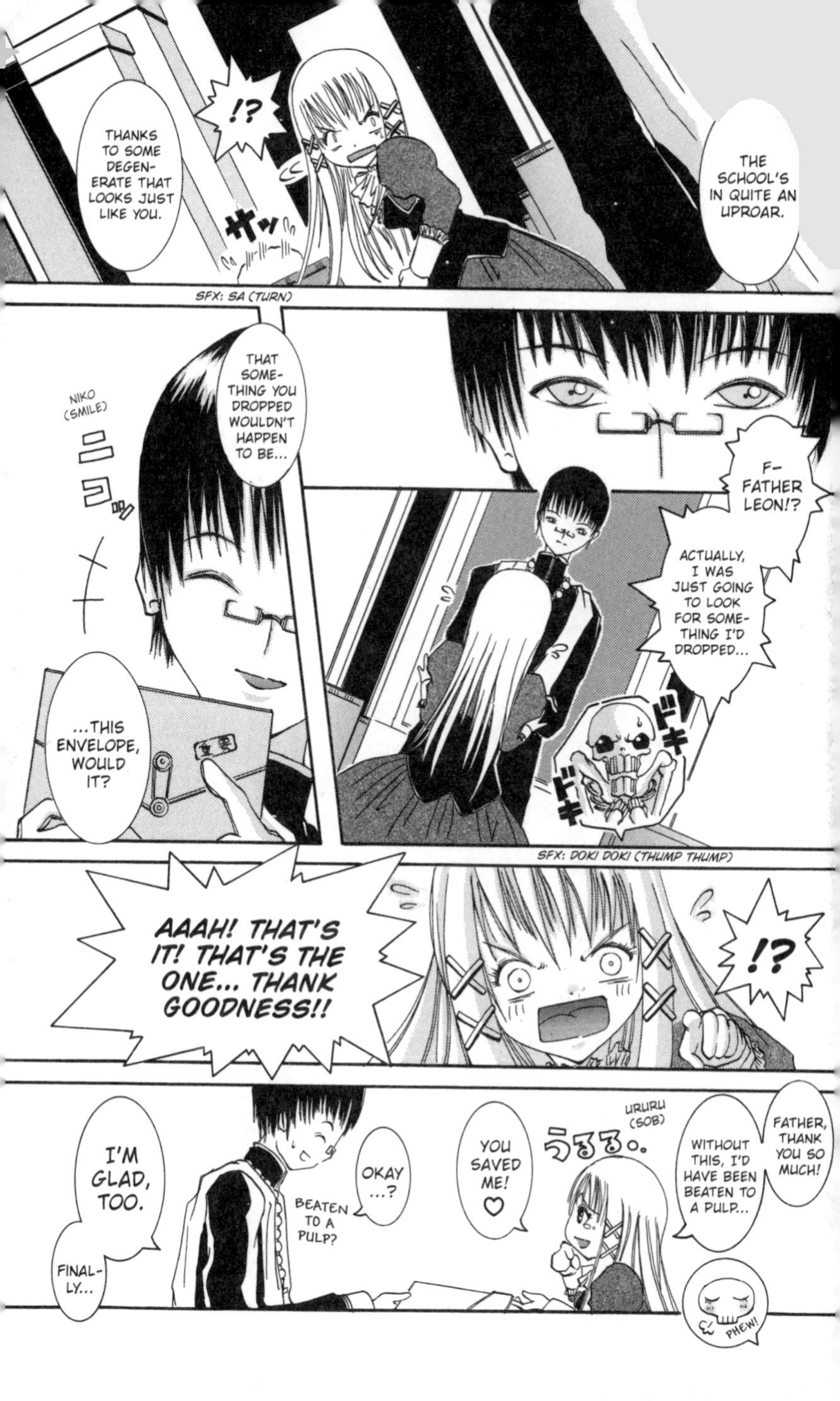

THE SCHOOL'S IN QUITE AN UPROAR.
!?
THANKS TO SOME DEGEN-ERATE THAT LOOKS JUST LIKE YOU.
SFX: SA (TURN)
F-FATHER LEON!?
ACTUALLY, I WAS JUST GOING TO LOOK FOR SOME-THING I'D DROPPED...
SFX: DOKI DOKI (THUMP THUMP)
THAT SOME-THING YOU DROPPED WOULDN'T HAPPEN TO BE...
NIKO (SMILE)
...THIS ENVELOPE, WOULD IT?
!?
AAAH! THAT'S IT! THAT'S THE ONE... THANK GOODNESS!!
FATHER, THANK YOU SO MUCH!
WITHOUT THIS, I'D HAVE BEEN BEATEN TO A PULP...
URURU (SOB)
YOU SAVED ME! ♡
PHEW!
OKAY ...?
BEATEN TO A PULP?
I'M GLAD, TOO.
FINAL-LY...

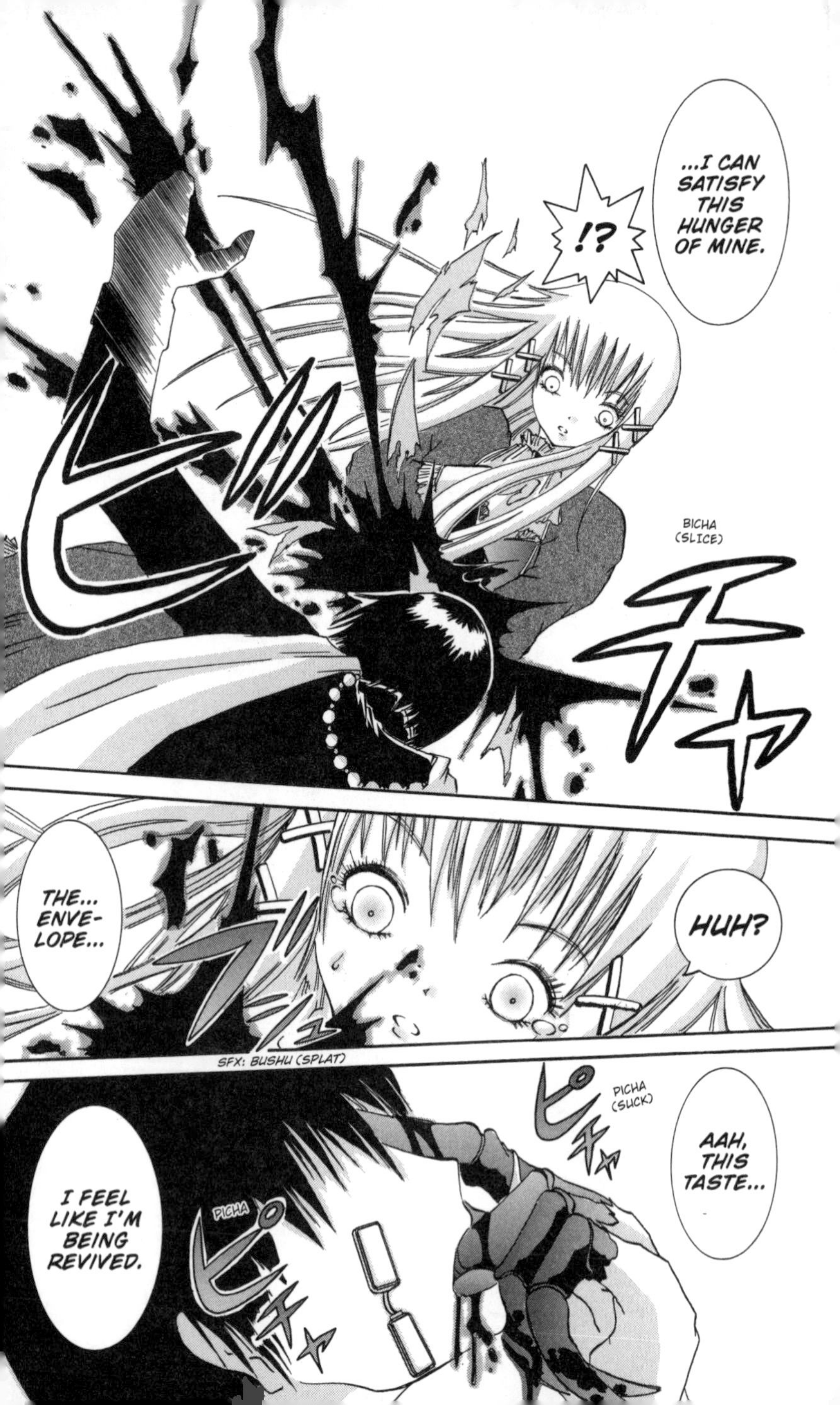
...I CAN SATISFY THIS HUNGER OF MINE.
!?
BICHA (SLICE)
HUH?
THE... ENVE-LOPE...
SFX: BUSHU (SPLAT)
PICHA (SUCK)
AAH, THIS TASTE...
PICHA
I FEEL LIKE I'M BEING REVIVED.

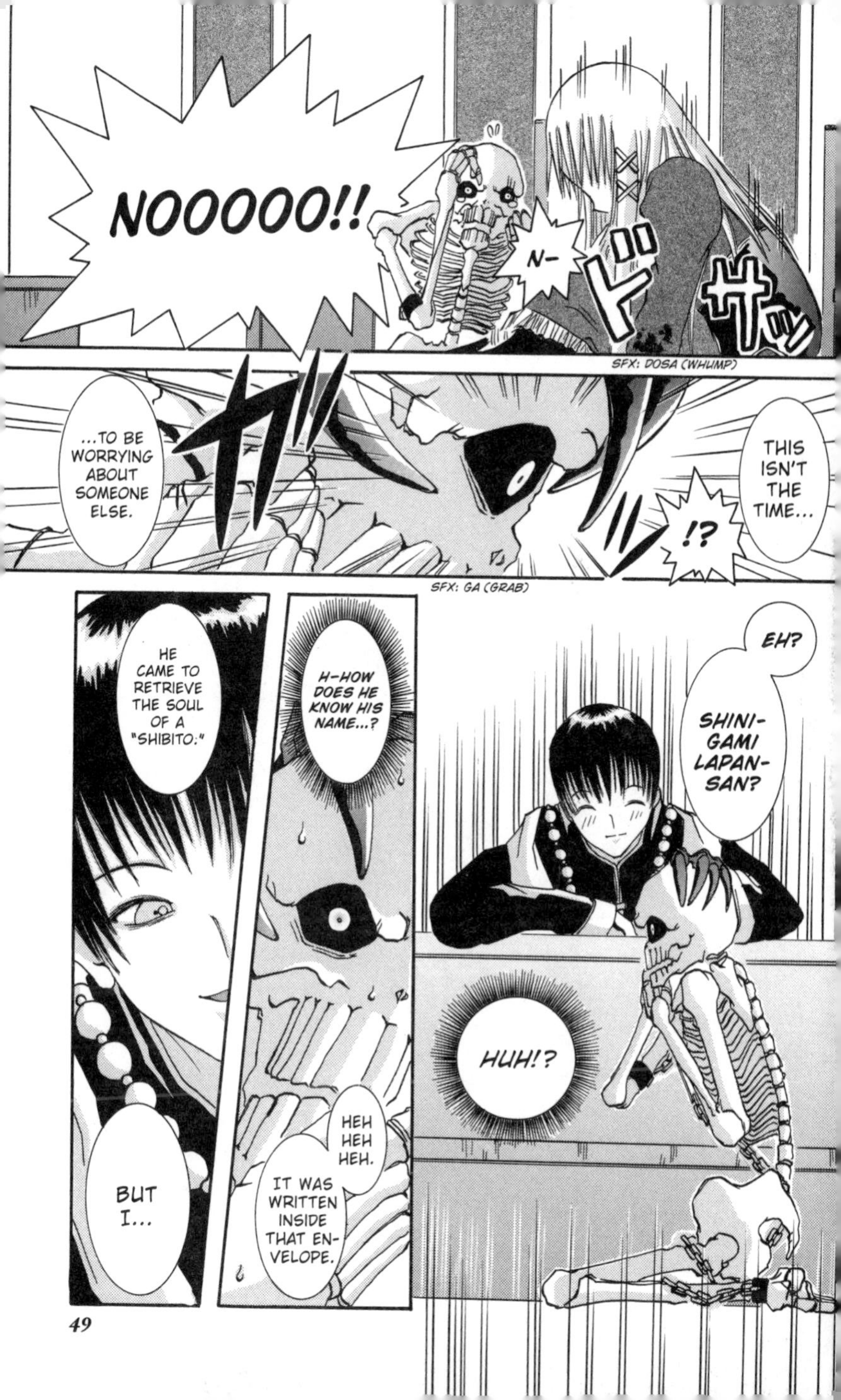
NOOOOO!!
N-
SFX: DOSA (WHUMP)
THIS ISN'T THE TIME...
!?
...TO BE WORRYING ABOUT SOMEONE ELSE.
SFX: GA (GRAB)
EH?
SHINI-GAMI LAPAN-SAN?
HUH!?
H-HOW DOES HE KNOW HIS NAME...?
HEH HEH HEH.
IT WAS WRITTEN INSIDE THAT EN-VELOPE.
HE CAME TO RETRIEVE THE SOUL OF A "SHIBITO."
BUT I...

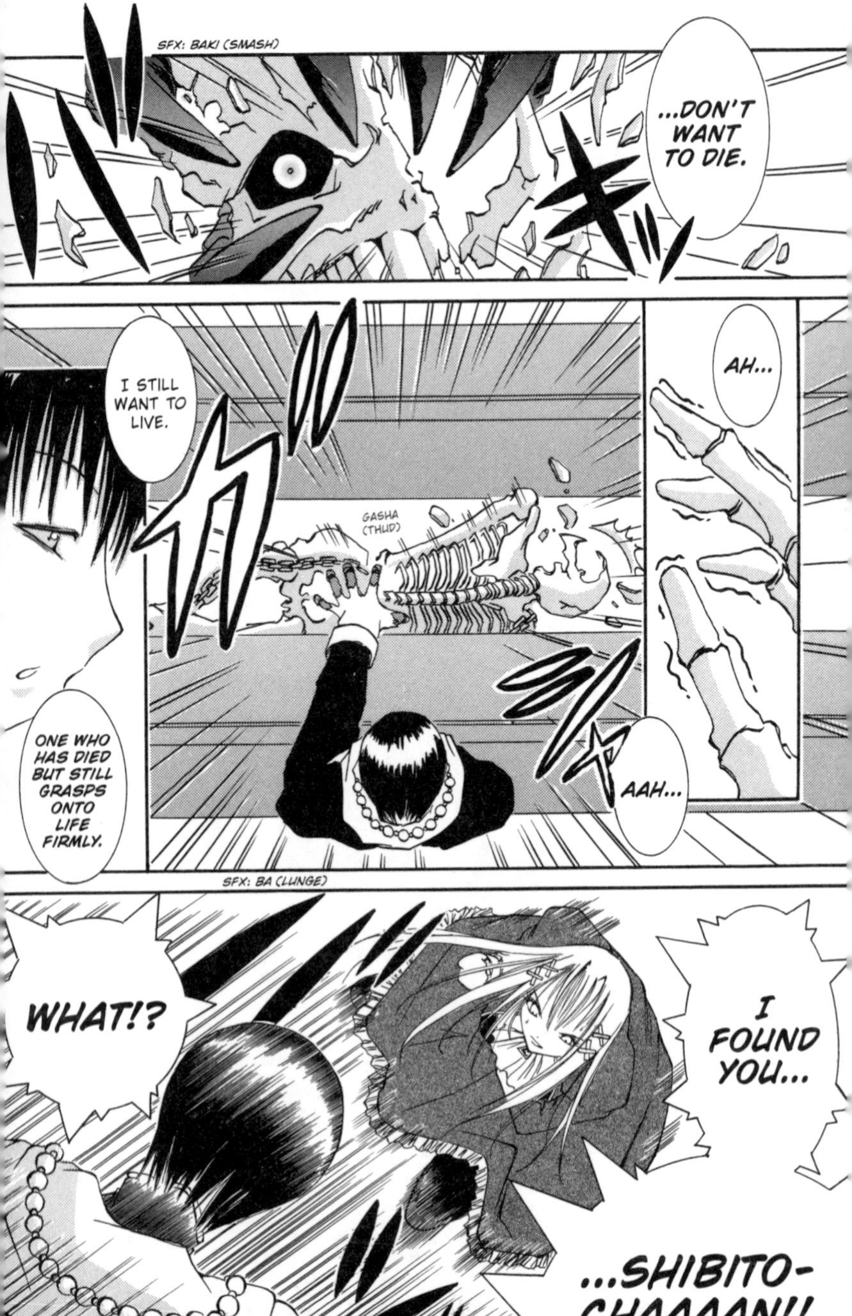
...DON'T WANT TO DIE.
SFX: BAKI (SMASH)
AH...
AAH...
I STILL WANT TO LIVE.
GASHA (THUD)
ONE WHO HAS DIED BUT STILL GRASPS ONTO LIFE FIRMLY.
SFX: BA (LUNGE)
I FOUND YOU...
...SHIBITO-CHAAAAN!!
WHAT!?

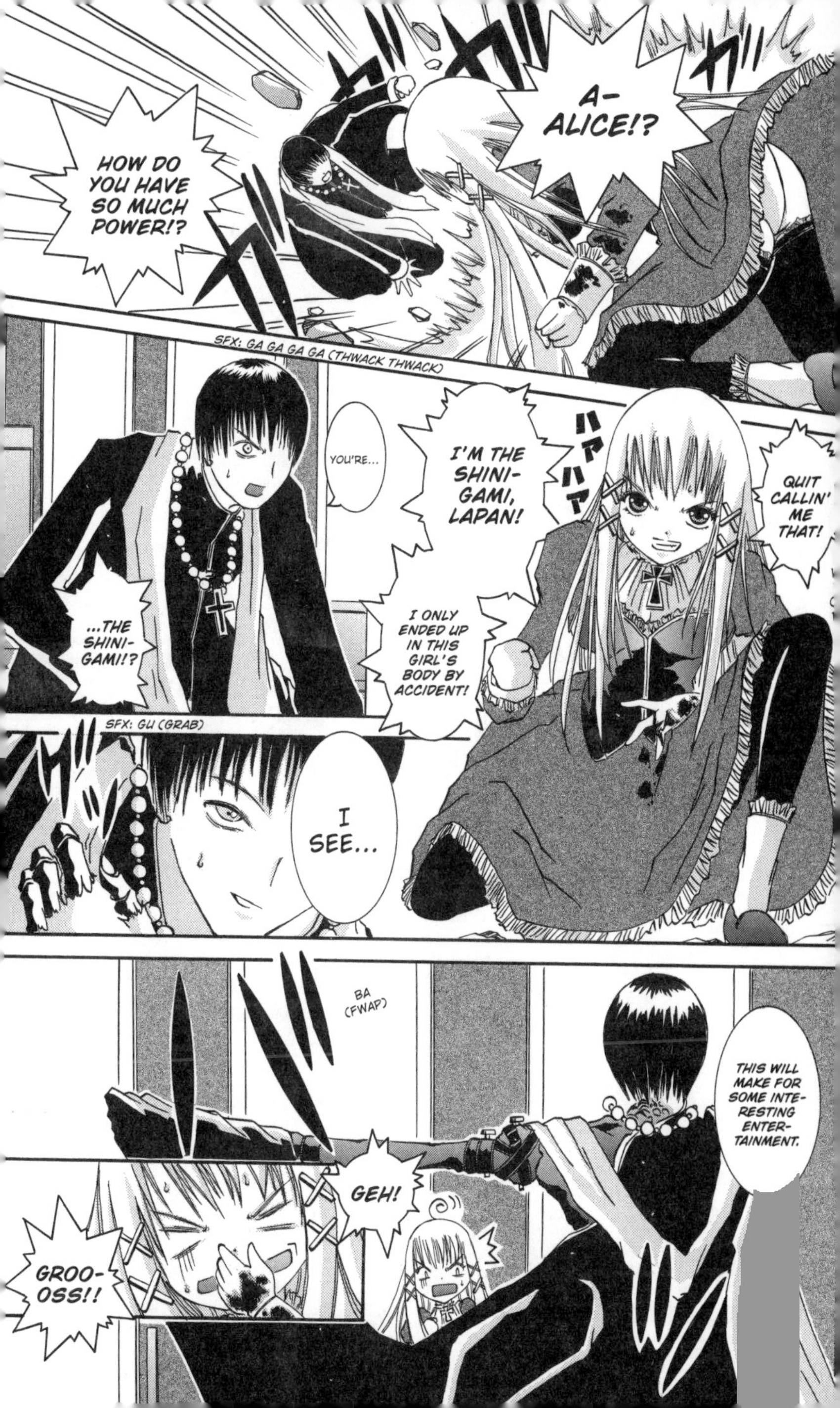
A- ALICE!?
HOW DO YOU HAVE SO MUCH POWER!?
SFX: GA GA GA GA (THWACK THWACK)
QUIT CALLIN' ME THAT!
YOU'RE...
I'M THE SHINI-GAMI, LAPAN!
...THE SHINI-GAMI!?
I ONLY ENDED UP IN THIS GIRL'S BODY BY ACCIDENT!
SFX: GU (GRAB)
I SEE...
BA (FWAP)
THIS WILL MAKE FOR SOME INTE-RESTING ENTER-TAINMENT.
GEH!
GROO-OSS!!

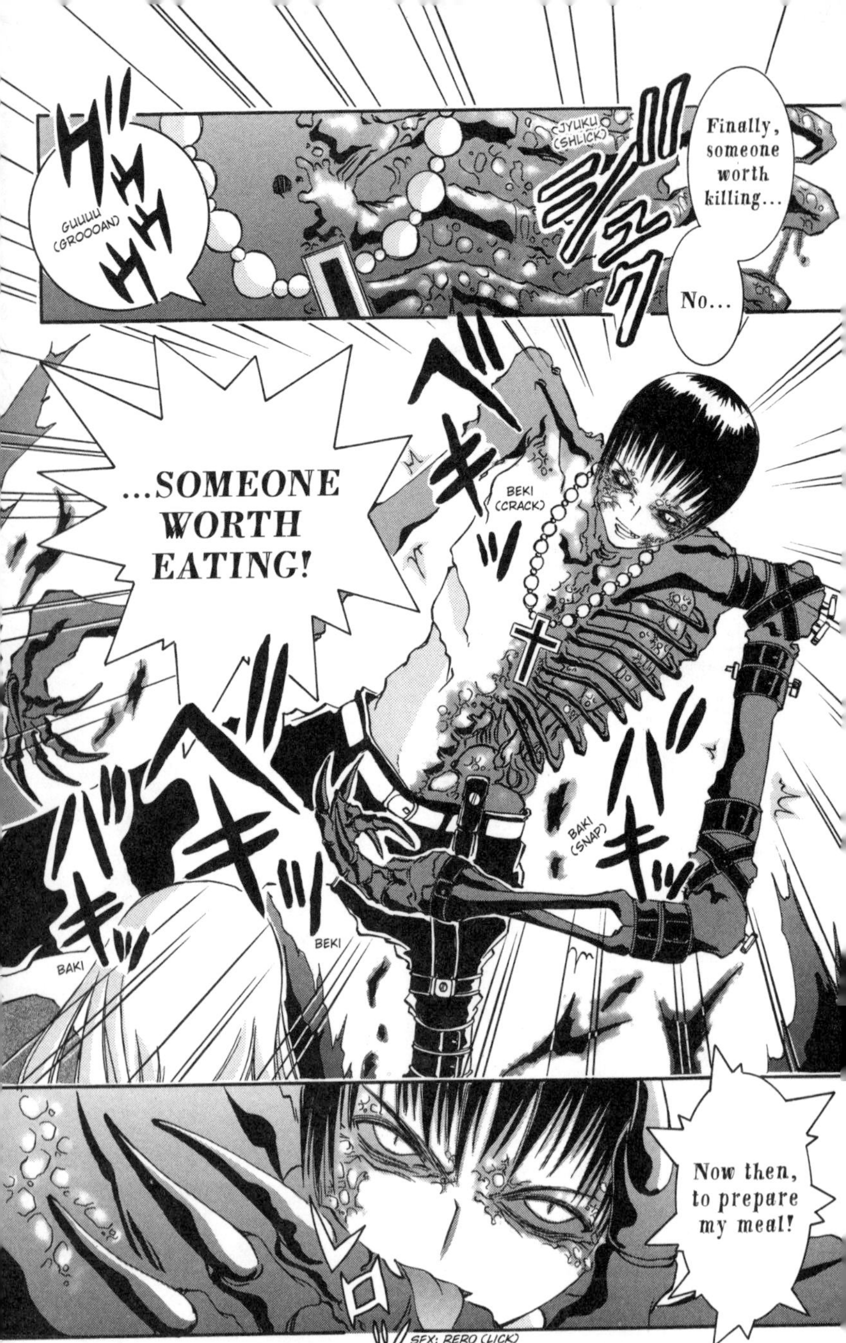
Finally, someone worth killing...
No...
JYUKU (SHLICK)
GUUUU (GROOOAN)
...SOMEONE WORTH EATING!
BEKI (CRACK)
BAKI (SNAP)
BEKI
BAKI
Now then, to prepare my meal!
SFX: RERO (LICK)

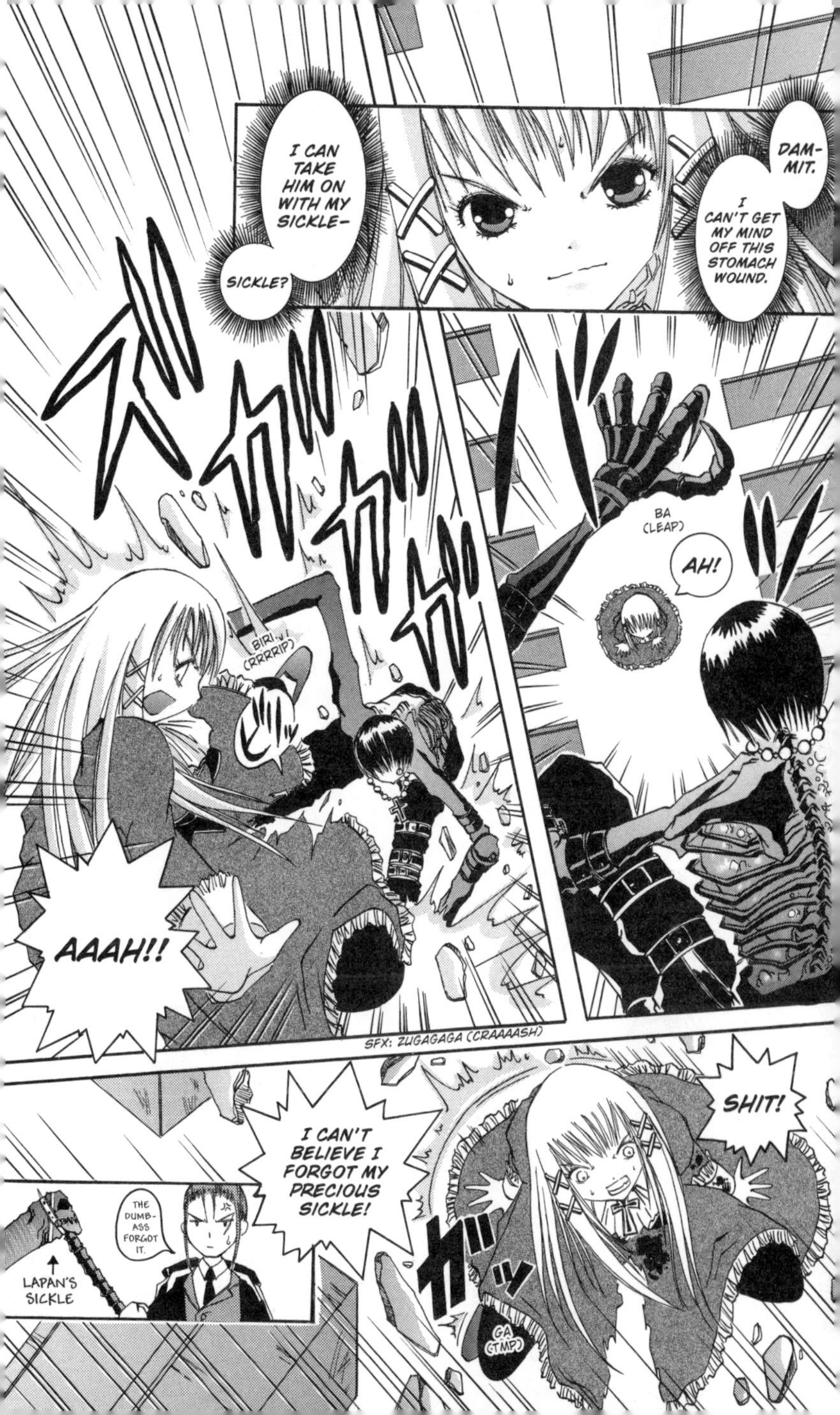
DAM-MIT.
I CAN'T GET MY MIND OFF THIS STOMACH WOUND.
I CAN TAKE HIM ON WITH MY SICKLE-
SICKLE?
BA (LEAP)
AH!
BIRI (RRRRIP)
AAAH!!
SFX: ZUGAGAGA (CRAAAASH)
SHIT!
I CAN'T BELIEVE I FORGOT MY PRECIOUS SICKLE!
GA (TMP)
THE DUMB-ASS FORGOT IT.
LAPAN'S SICKLE

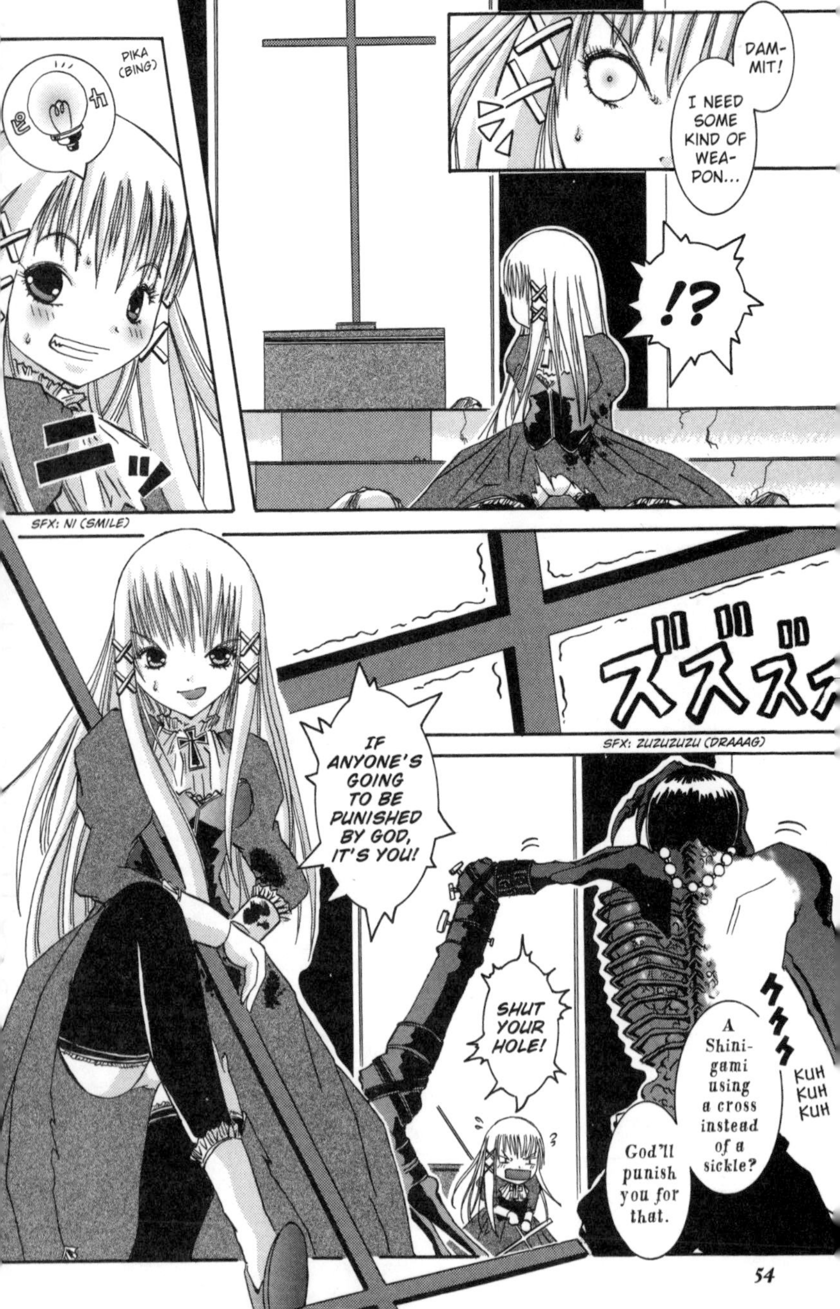
DAM-MIT!
I NEED SOME KIND OF WEA-PON...
!?
PIKA (BING)
SFX: NI (SMILE)
SFX: ZUZUZUZU (DRAAAG)
KUH KUH KUH
A Shinigami using a cross instead of a sickle?
God'll punish you for that.
SHUT YOUR HOLE!
IF ANYONE'S GOING TO BE PUNISHED BY GOD, IT'S YOU!

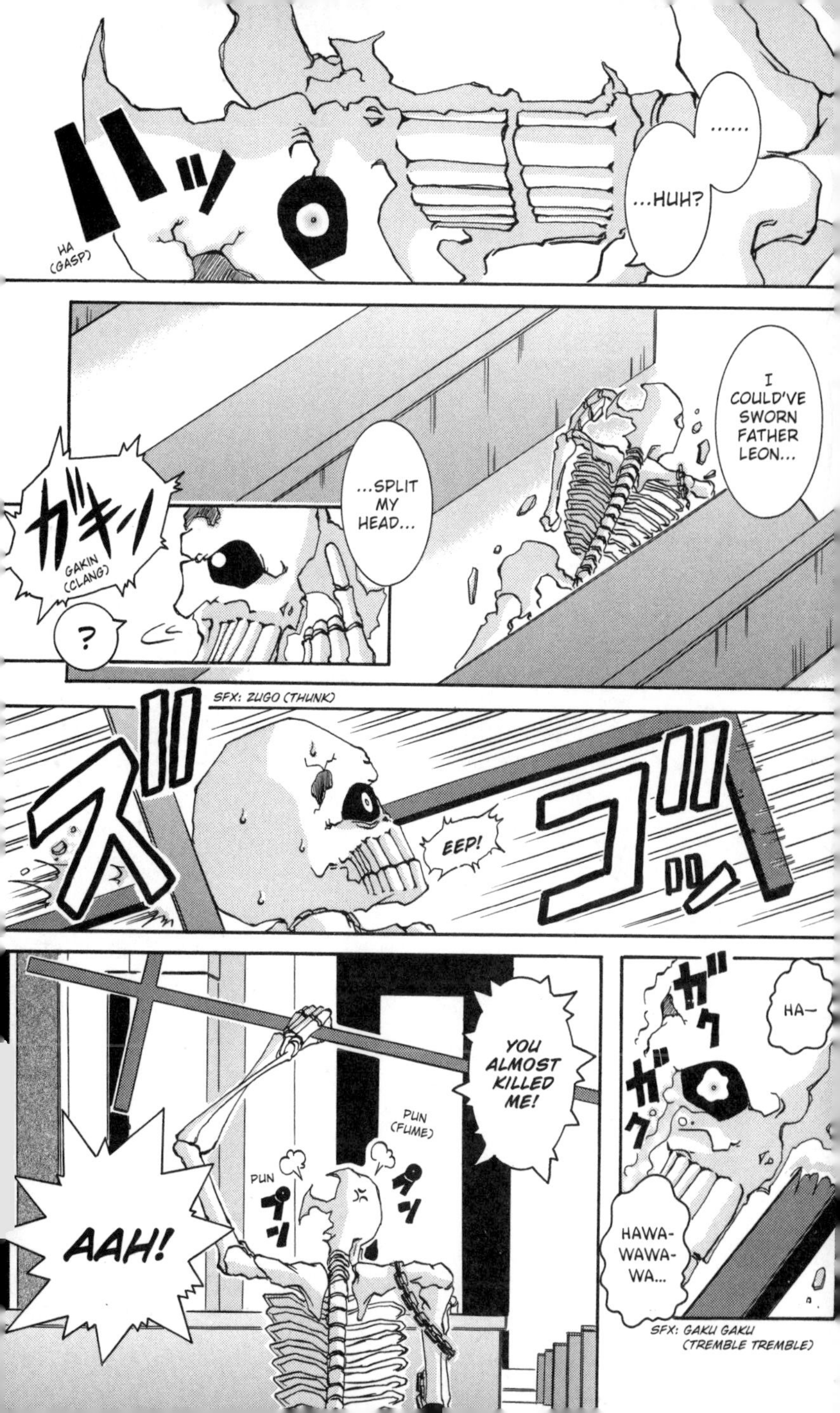

......
...HUH?
ハッ
HA (GASP)
I COULD'VE SWORN FATHER LEON...
...SPLIT MY HEAD...
ガキンッ
GAKIN (CLANG)
?
SFX: ZUGO (THUNK)
ズゴッ
EEP!
HA—
ガクガク
HAWA-WAWA-WA...
SFX: GAKU GAKU (TREMBLE TREMBLE)
YOU ALMOST KILLED ME!
PUN (FUME)
プンッ
PUN
プンッ
AAH!

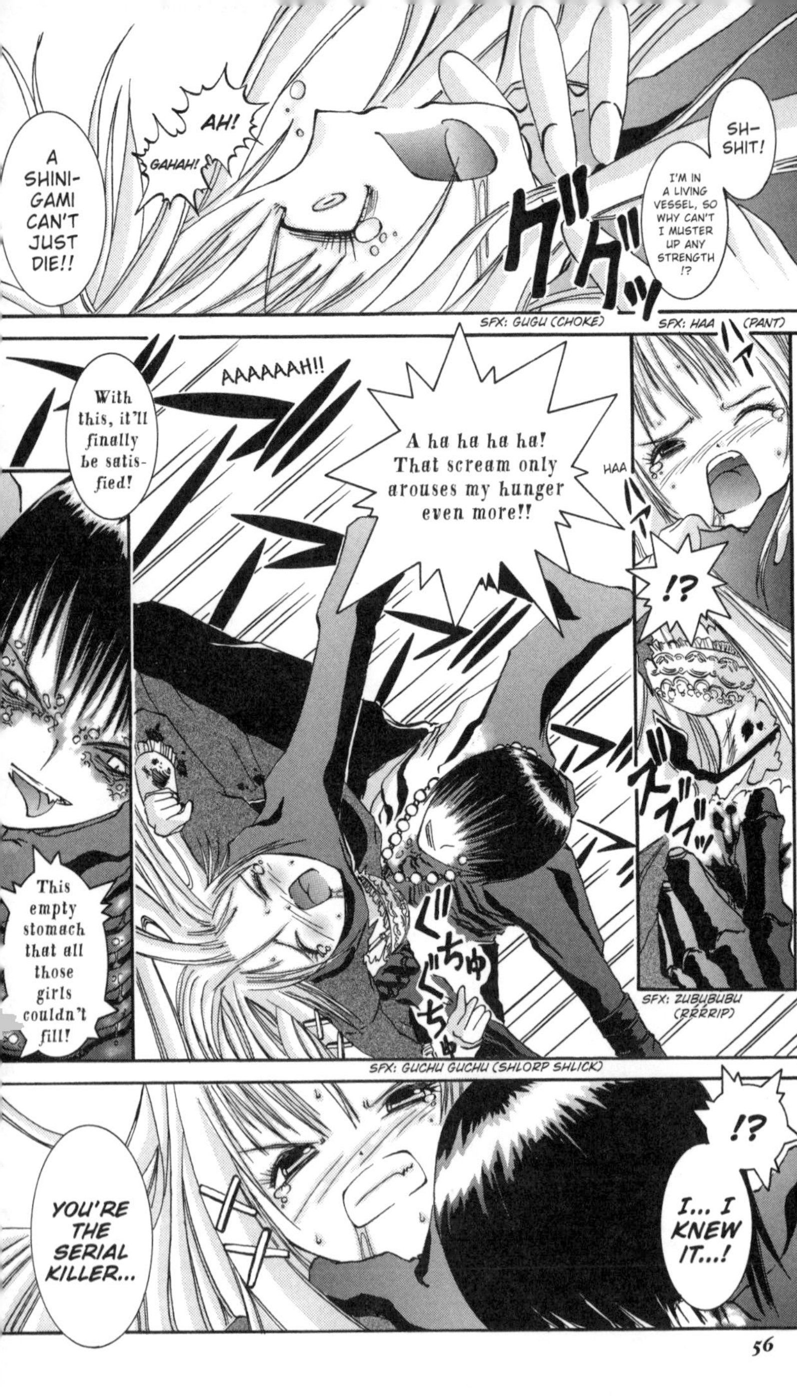
SH— SHIT!
I'M IN A LIVING VESSEL, SO WHY CAN'T I MUSTER UP ANY STRENGTH!?
SFX: GUGU (CHOKE)
AH! GAHAH!
A SHINIGAMI CAN'T JUST DIE!!
SFX: HAA (PANT)
HAA
!?
SFX: ZUBUBUBU (RRRRIP)
A ha ha ha ha! That scream only arouses my hunger even more!!
AAAAAAH!!
With this, it'll finally be satisfied!
This empty stomach that all those girls couldn't fill!
SFX: GUCHU GUCHU (SHLORP SHLICK)
!?
I... I KNEW IT...!
YOU'RE THE SERIAL KILLER...

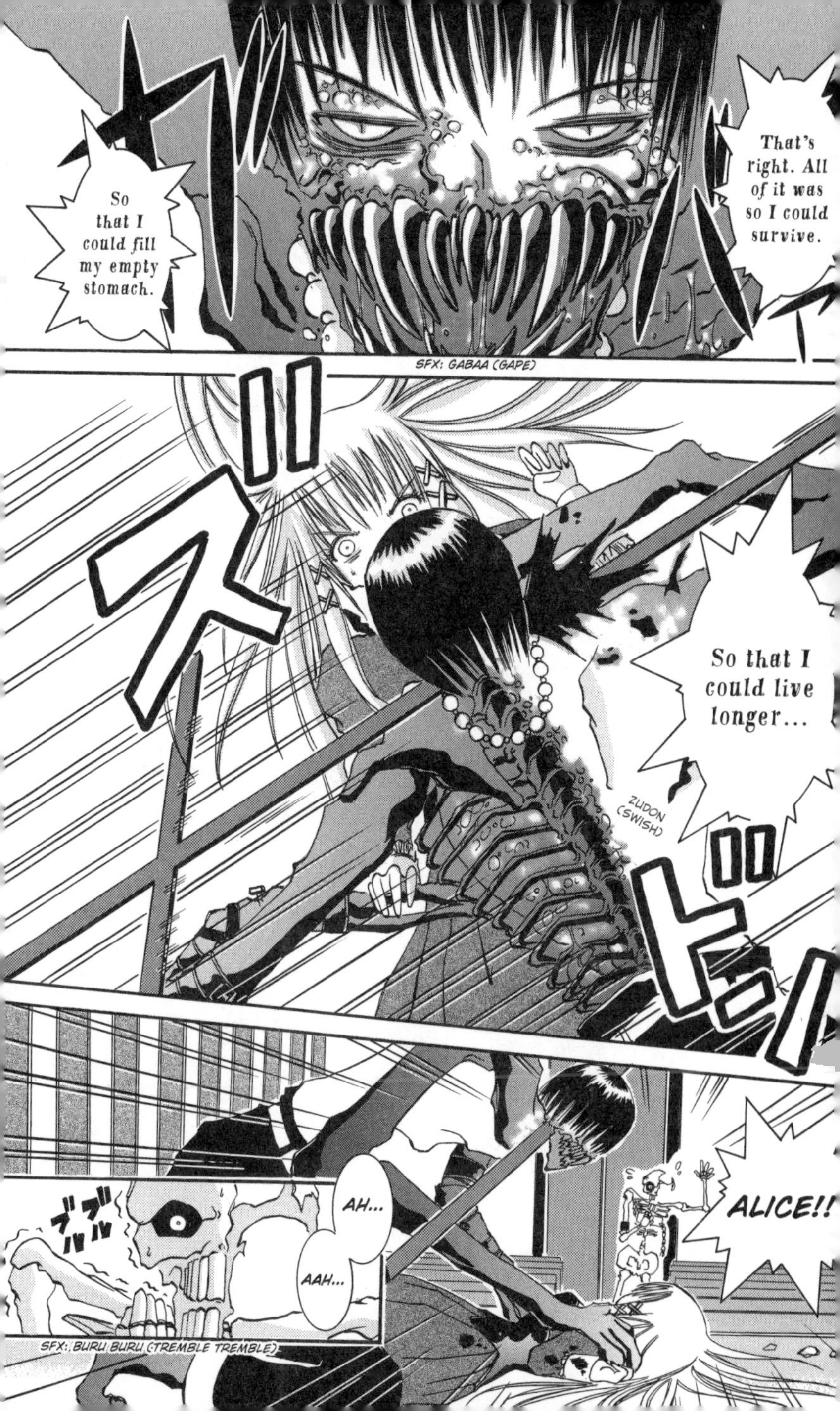
That's right. All of it was so I could survive.
So that I could fill my empty stomach.
SFX: GABAA (GAPE)
So that I could live longer...
ZUDON (SWISH)
ALICE!!
AH...
AAH...
SFX: BURU BURU (TREMBLE TREMBLE)

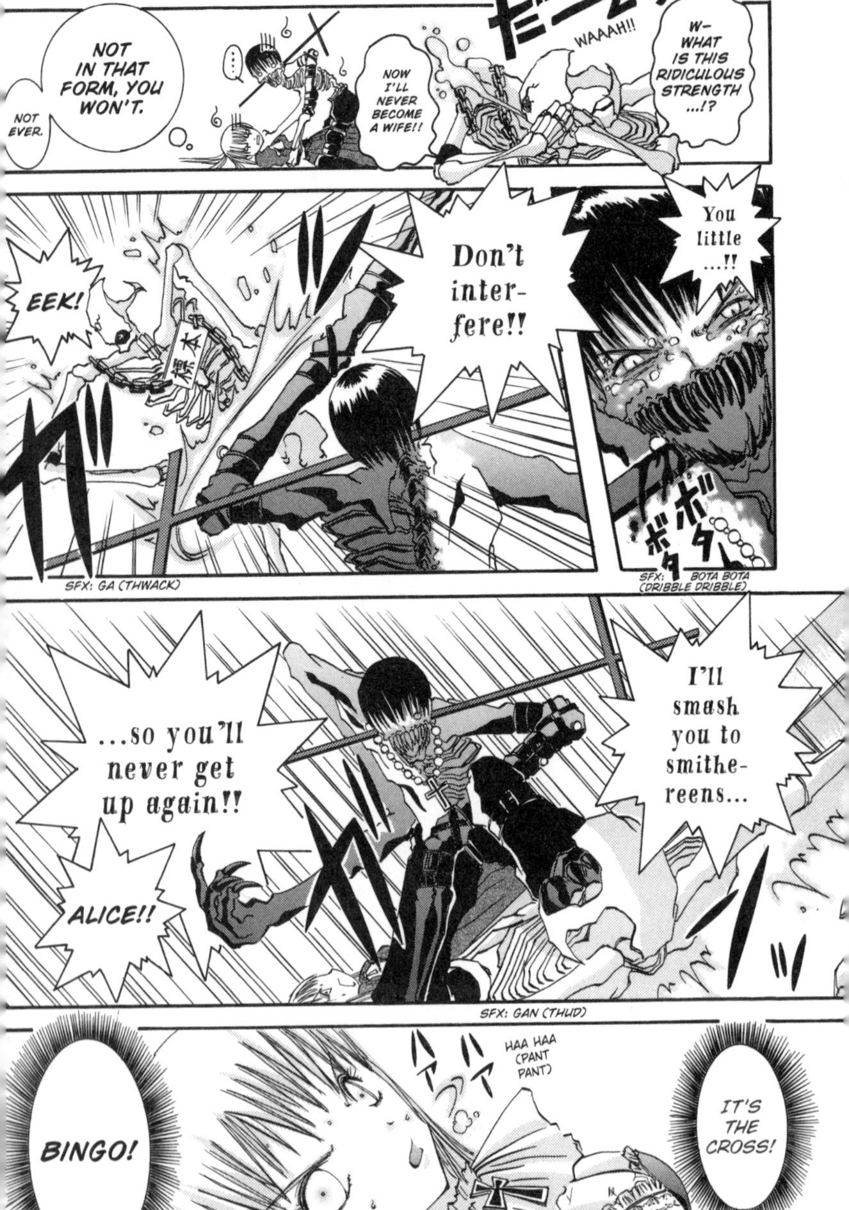
W- WHAT IS THIS RIDICULOUS STRENGTH ...!?
WAAAH!!
NOW I'LL NEVER BECOME A WIFE!!
NOT IN THAT FORM, YOU WON'T.
NOT EVER.
You little ...!!
SFX: BOTA BOTA (DRIBBLE DRIBBLE)
Don't interfere!!
EEK!
SFX: GA (THWACK)
I'll smash you to smithereens...
...so you'll never get up again!!
ALICE!!
SFX: GAN (THUD)
IT'S THE CROSS!
HAA HAA (PANT PANT)
BINGO!

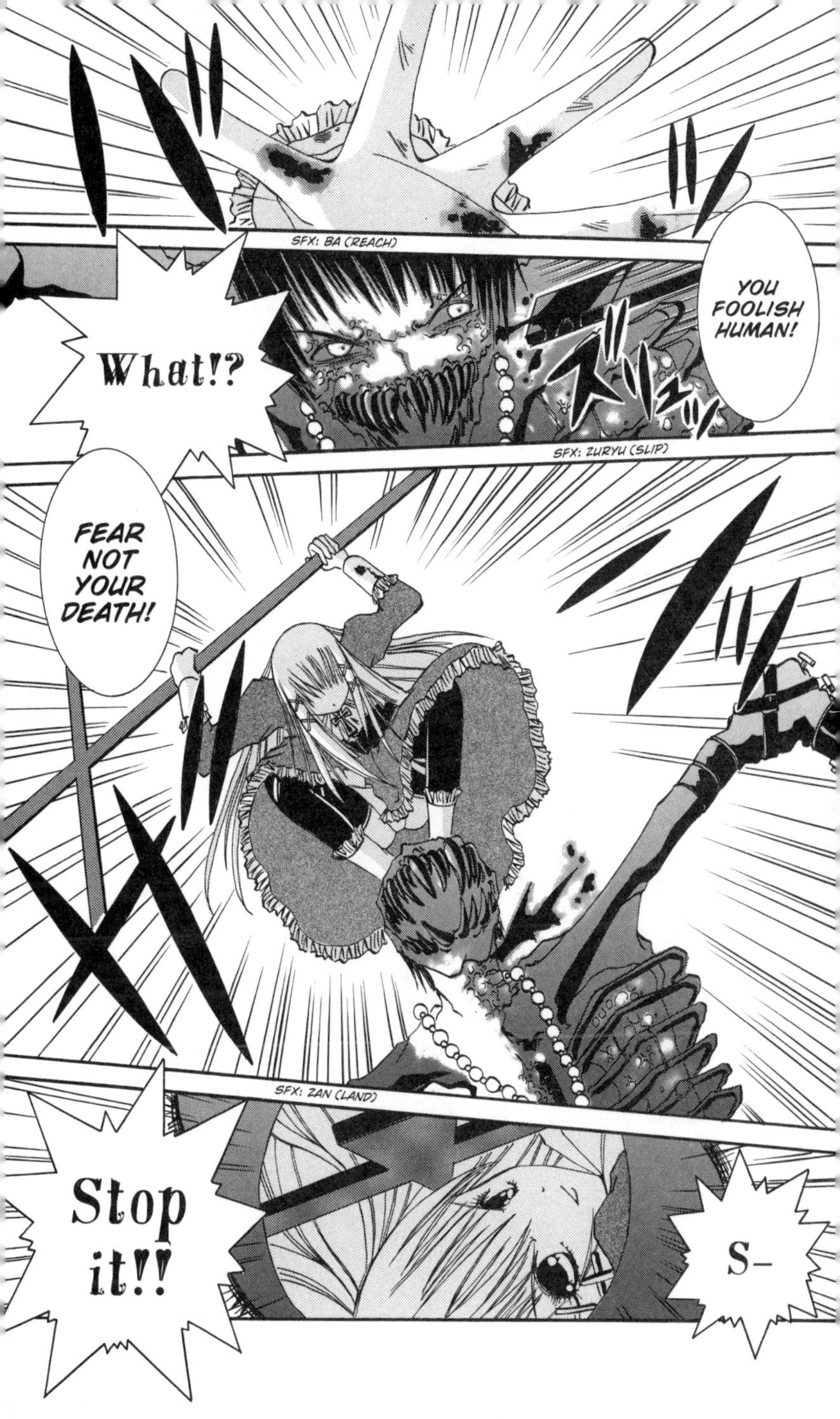
SFX: BA (REACH)
YOU FOOLISH HUMAN!
SFX: ZURYU (SLIP)
What!?
FEAR NOT YOUR DEATH!
SFX: ZAN (LAND)
S-
Stop it!!

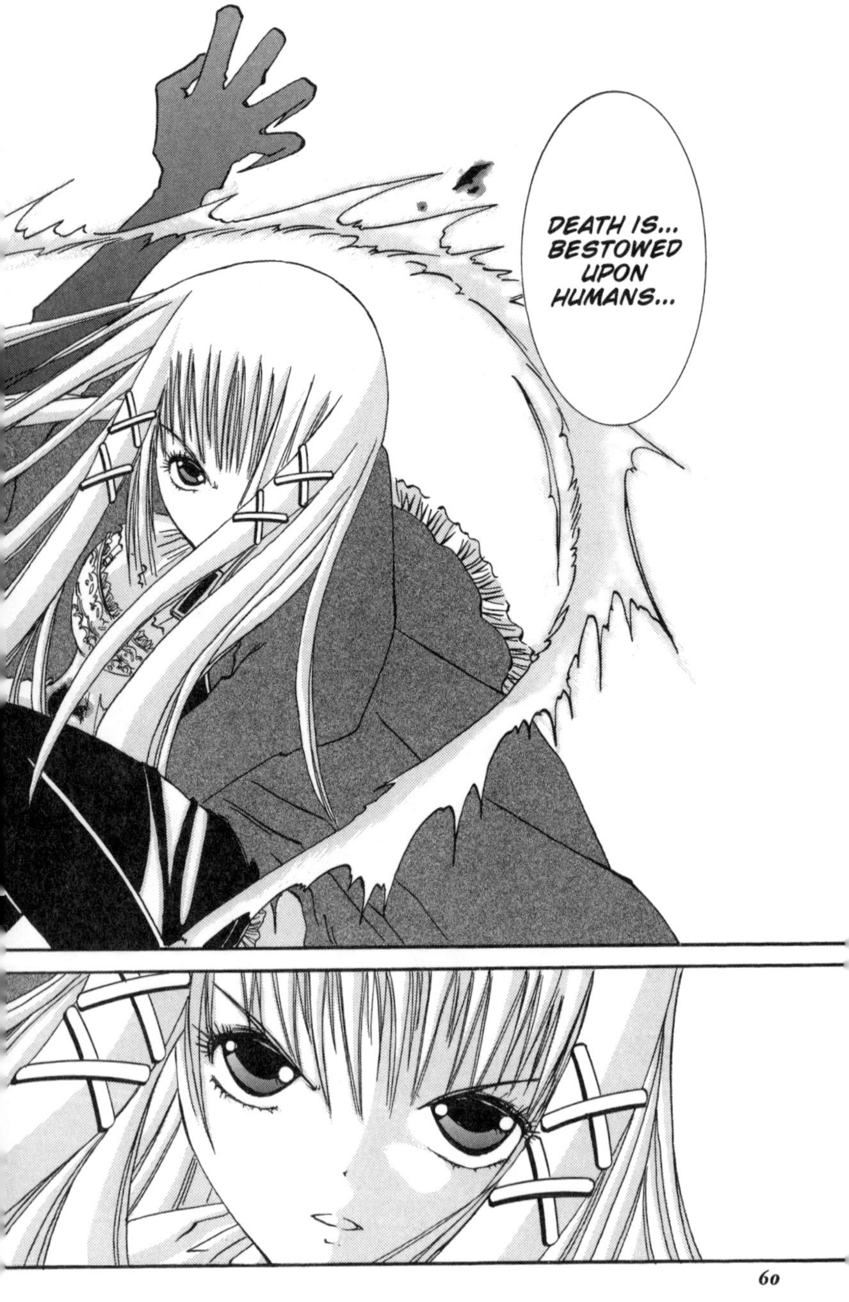
DEATH IS... BESTOWED UPON HUMANS...

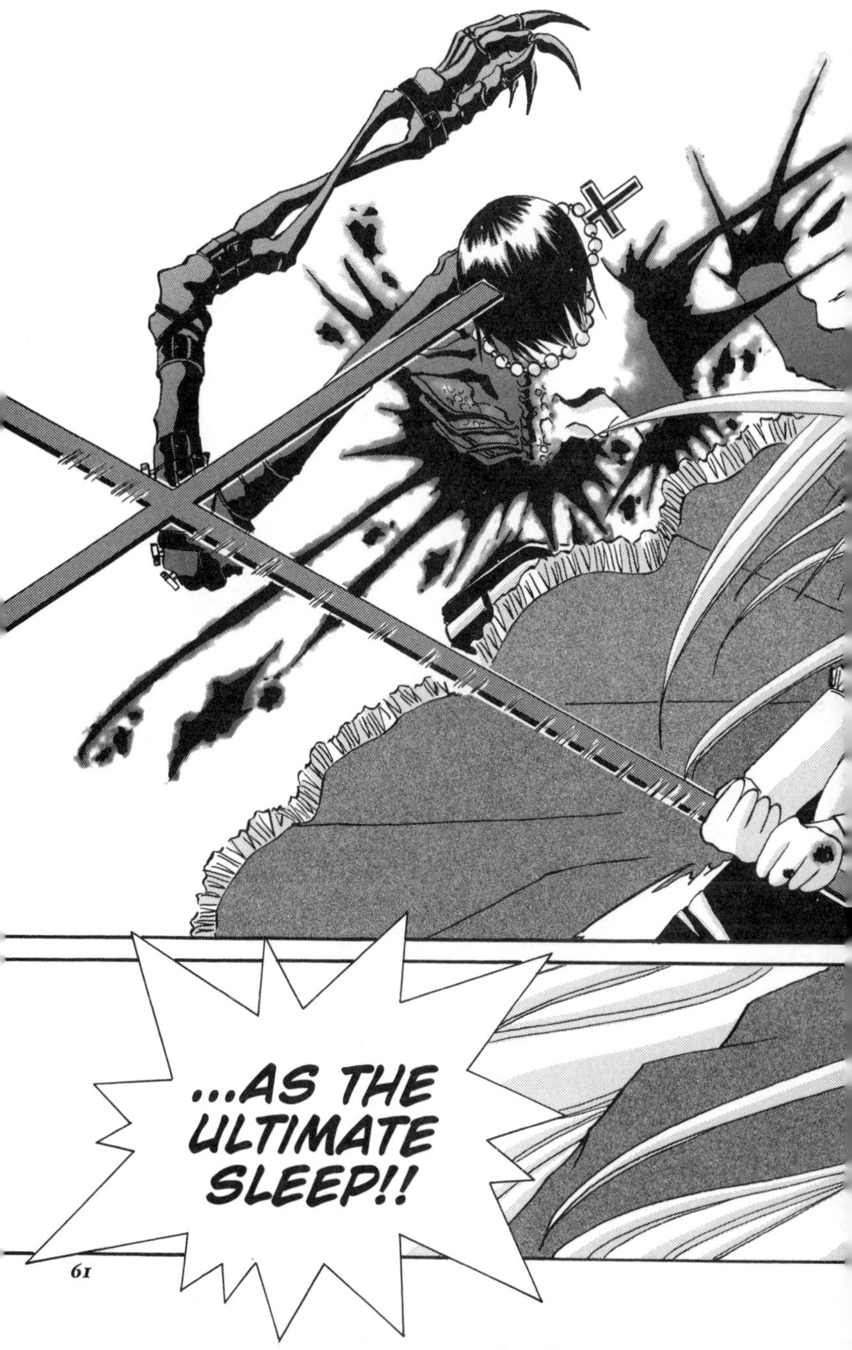
...AS THE ULTIMATE SLEEP!!

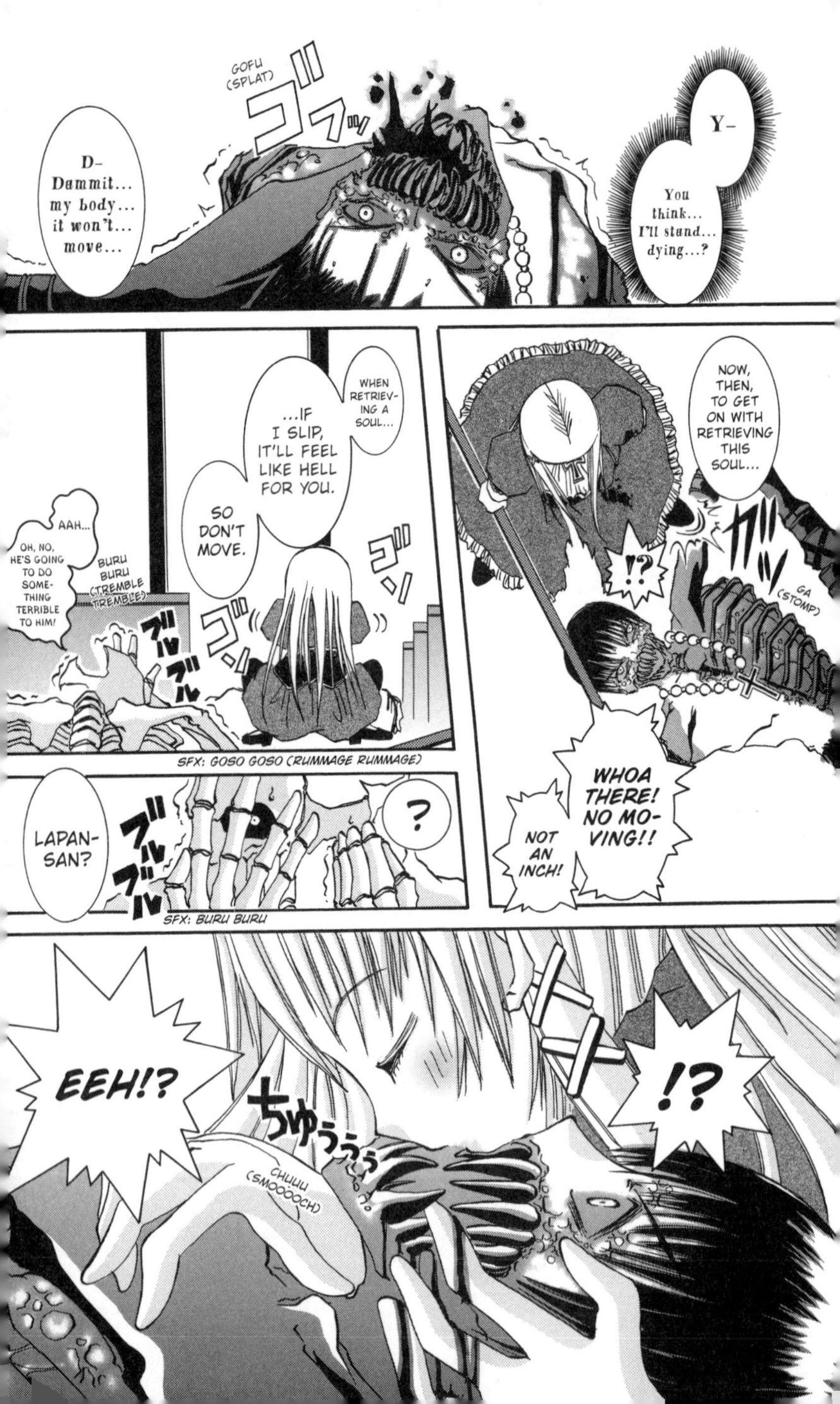
Y–
You think... I'll stand... dying...?
GOFU (SPLAT)
D– Dammit... my body... it won't... move...
NOW, THEN, TO GET ON WITH RETRIEVING THIS SOUL...
!?
GA (STOMP)
WHOA THERE! NO MO-VING!!
NOT AN INCH!
WHEN RETRIEV-ING A SOUL...
...IF I SLIP, IT'LL FEEL LIKE HELL FOR YOU.
SO DON'T MOVE.
BURU BURU (TREMBLE TREMBLE)
AAH...
OH, NO, HE'S GOING TO DO SOME-THING TERRIBLE TO HIM!
SFX: GOSO GOSO (RUMMAGE RUMMAGE)
?
LAPAN-SAN?
SFX: BURU BURU
!?
CHUUU (SMOOOOCH)
EEH!?

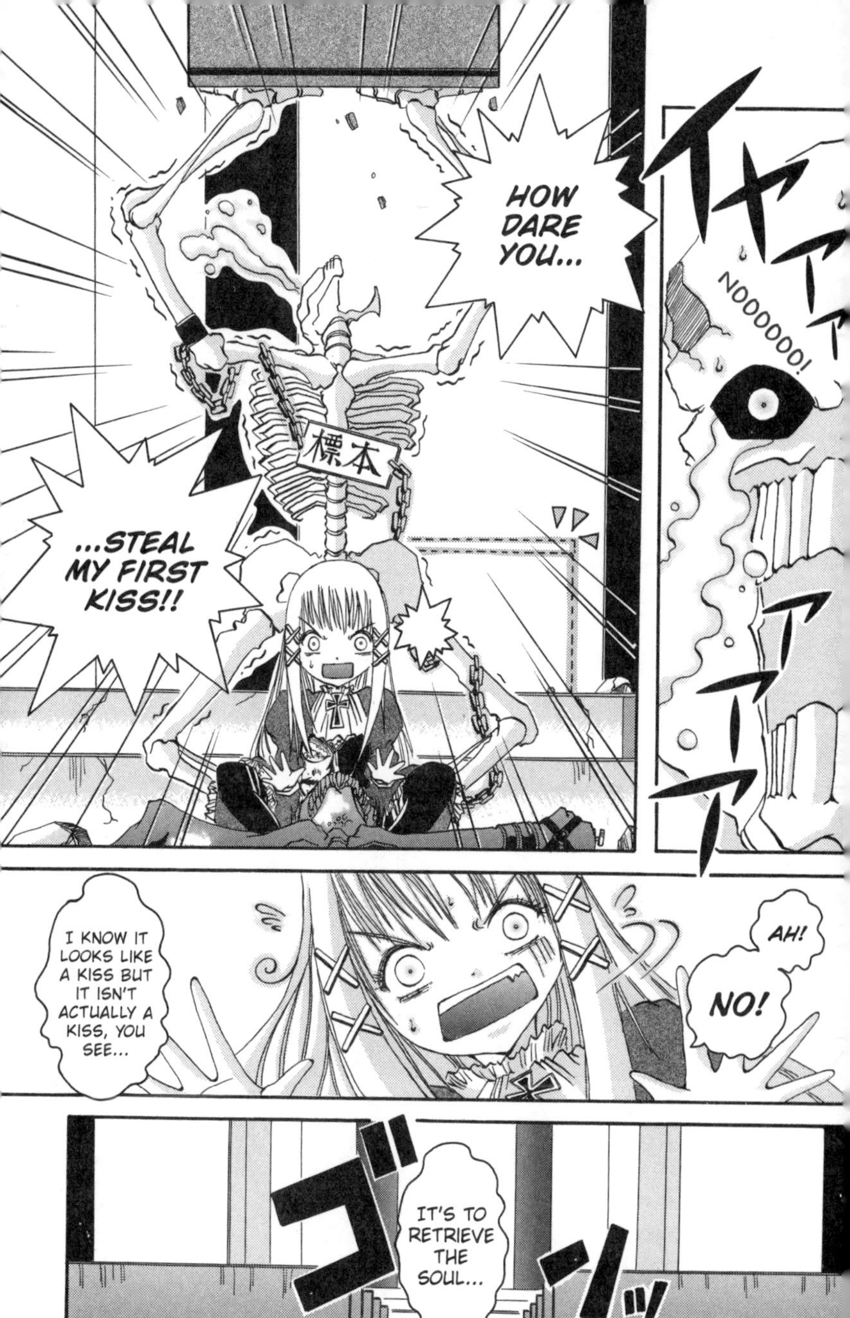

NOOOOOO!
HOW DARE YOU...
標本
...STEAL MY FIRST KISS!!
AH!
NO!
I KNOW IT LOOKS LIKE A KISS BUT IT ISN'T ACTUALLY A KISS, YOU SEE...
ゴッ
IT'S TO RETRIEVE THE SOUL...

SFX: GON (BANG)

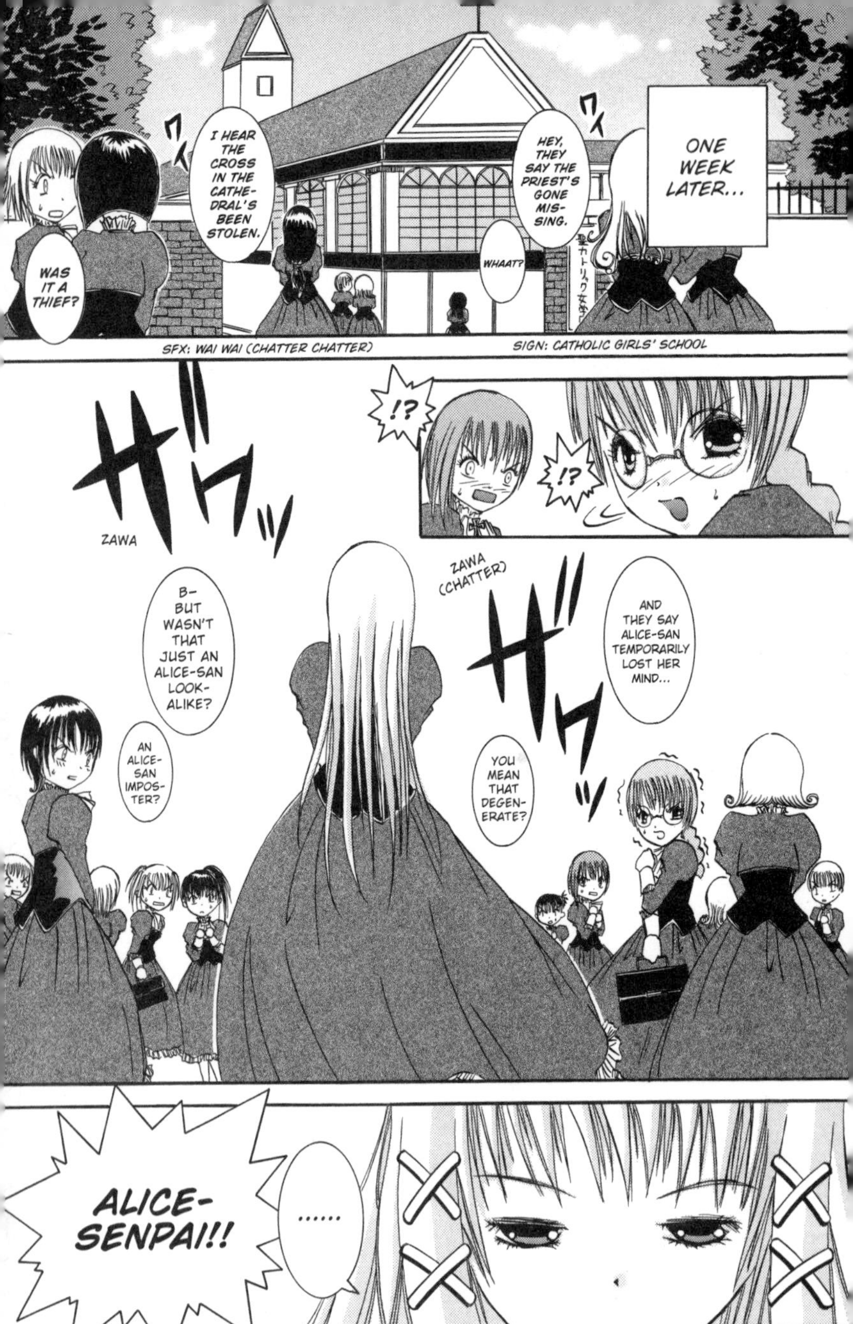
ONE WEEK LATER...
HEY, THEY SAY THE PRIEST'S GONE MIS-SING.
WHAAT?
I HEAR THE CROSS IN THE CATHE-DRAL'S BEEN STOLEN.
WAS IT A THIEF?
SIGN: CATHOLIC GIRLS' SCHOOL
SFX: WAI WAI (CHATTER CHATTER)
!?
!?
ZAWA
AND THEY SAY ALICE-SAN TEMPORARILY LOST HER MIND...
ZAWA (CHATTER)
B-BUT WASN'T THAT JUST AN ALICE-SAN LOOK-ALIKE?
YOU MEAN THAT DEGEN-ERATE?
AN ALICE-SAN IMPOS-TER?
......
ALICE-SENPAI!!

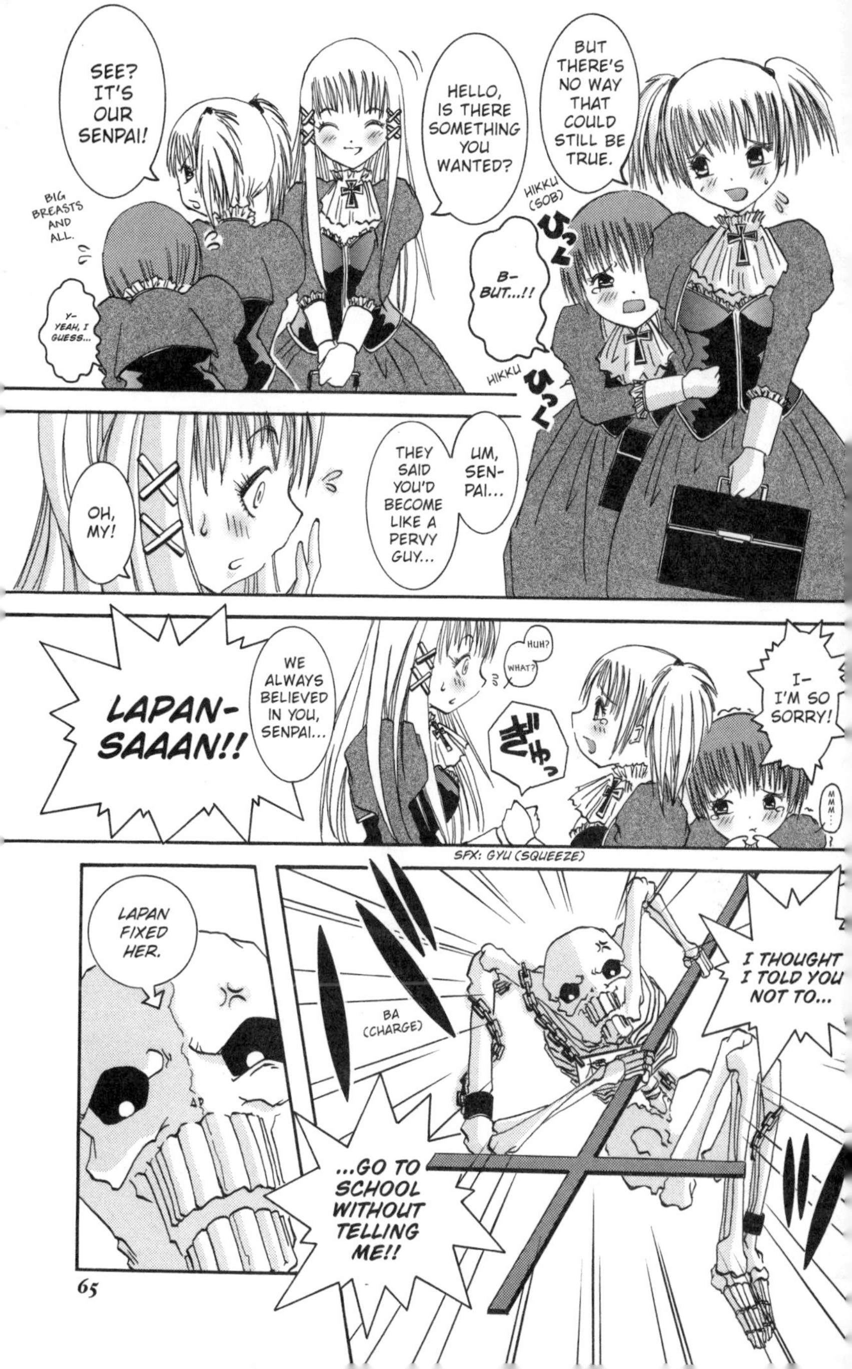
BUT THERE'S NO WAY THAT COULD STILL BE TRUE.
HIKKU (SOB)
ひっく
B-BUT...!!
HIKKU
ひっく
HELLO, IS THERE SOMETHING YOU WANTED?
SEE? IT'S OUR SENPAI!
BIG BREASTS AND ALL.
Y-YEAH, I GUESS...
UM, SENPAI...
THEY SAID YOU'D BECOME LIKE A PERVY GUY...
OH, MY!
I-I'M SO SORRY!
MMM...
HUH?
WHAT?
ぎゅっ
WE ALWAYS BELIEVED IN YOU, SENPAI...
LAPAN-SAAAN!!
SFX: GYU (SQUEEZE)
I THOUGHT I TOLD YOU NOT TO...
BA (CHARGE)
...GO TO SCHOOL WITHOUT TELLING ME!!
LAPAN FIXED HER.

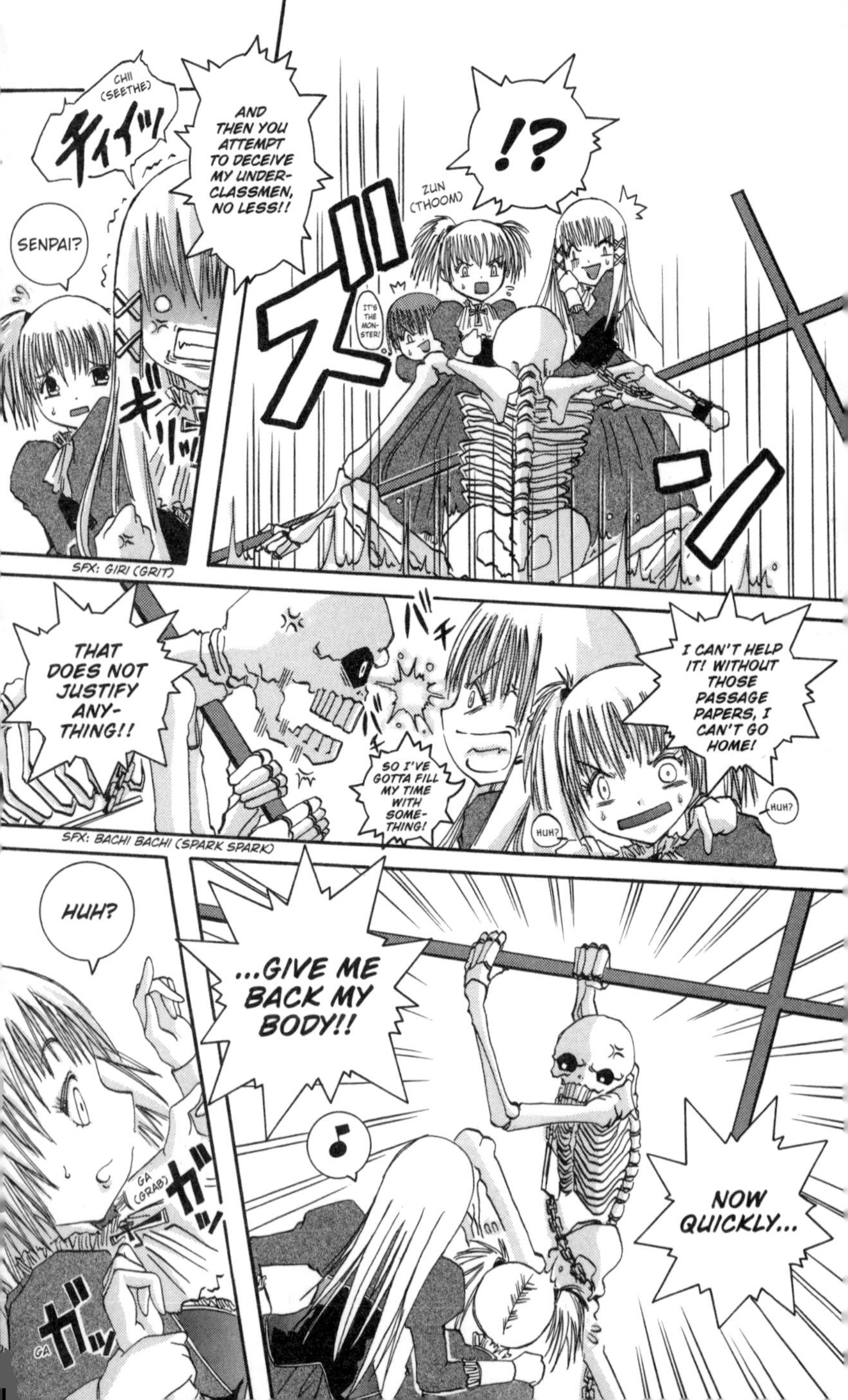
!?
ZUN (THOOM)
IT'S THE MONSTER!
AND THEN YOU ATTEMPT TO DECEIVE MY UNDER-CLASSMEN, NO LESS!!
CHII (SEETHE)
SENPAI?
SFX: GIRI (GRIT)
I CAN'T HELP IT! WITHOUT THOSE PASSAGE PAPERS, I CAN'T GO HOME!
HUH?
HUH?
SO I'VE GOTTA FILL MY TIME WITH SOME-THING!
THAT DOES NOT JUSTIFY ANY-THING!!
SFX: BACHI BACHI (SPARK SPARK)
NOW QUICKLY...
...GIVE ME BACK MY BODY!!
HUH?
GA (GRAB)
GA

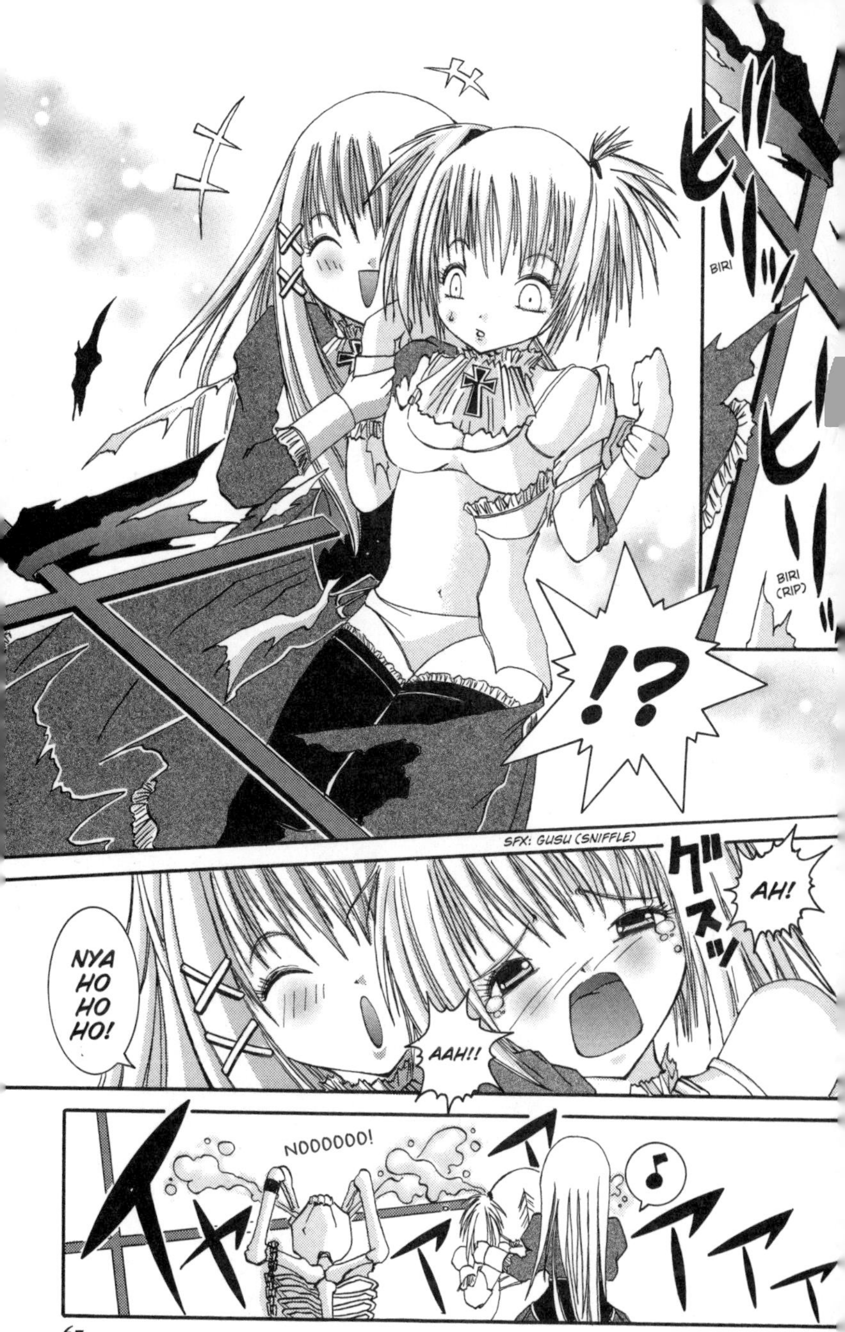
BIRI
BIRI (RIP)
!?
SFX: GUSU (SNIFFLE)
AH!
NYA HO HO HO!
AAH!!
NOOOOOO!

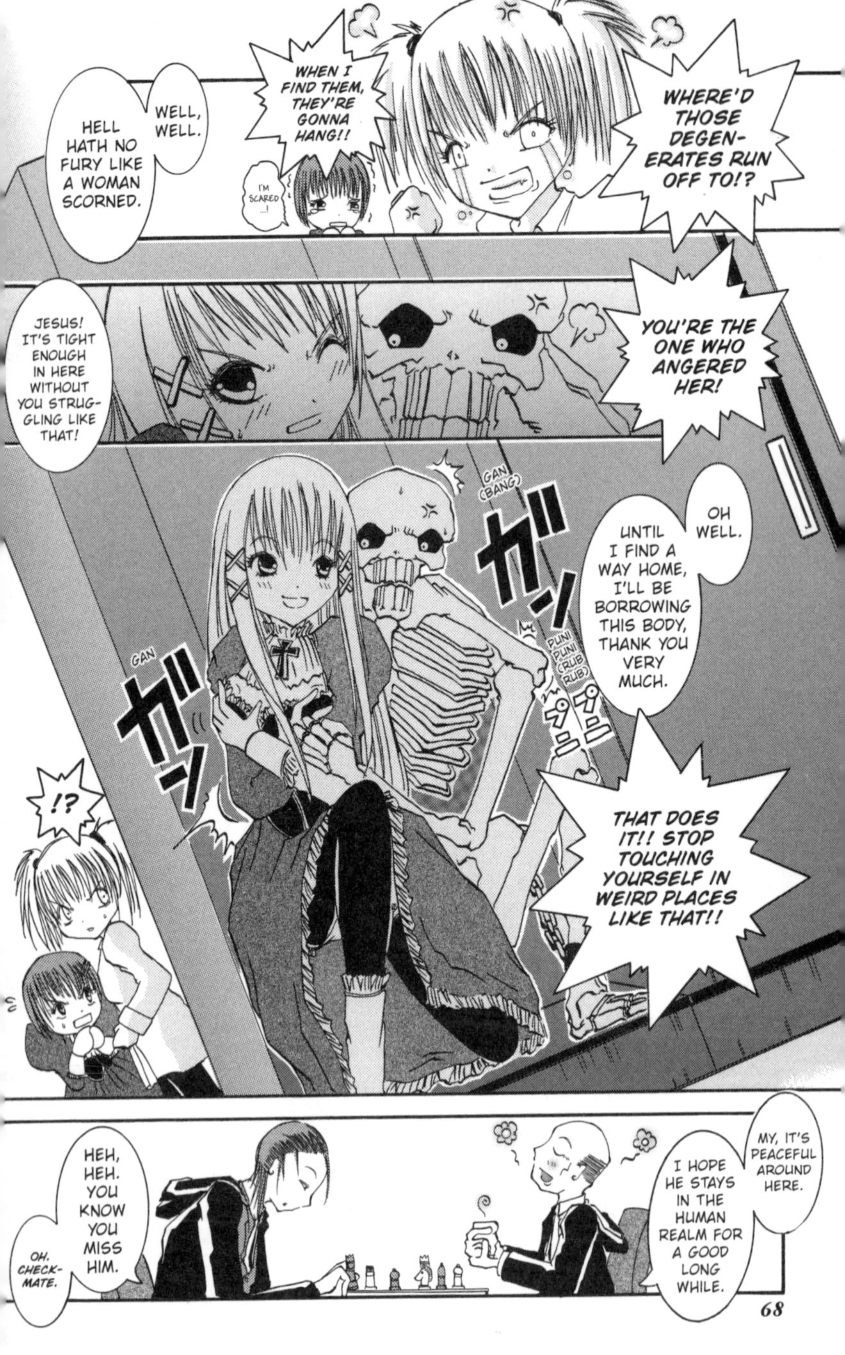
WHERE'D THOSE DEGENERATES RUN OFF TO!?
WHEN I FIND THEM, THEY'RE GONNA HANG!!
I'M SCARED ...!
WELL, WELL.
HELL HATH NO FURY LIKE A WOMAN SCORNED.
YOU'RE THE ONE WHO ANGERED HER!
JESUS! IT'S TIGHT ENOUGH IN HERE WITHOUT YOU STRUGGLING LIKE THAT!
GAN (BANG)
OH WELL.
UNTIL I FIND A WAY HOME, I'LL BE BORROWING THIS BODY, THANK YOU VERY MUCH.
PUNI PUNI (RUB RUB)
THAT DOES IT!! STOP TOUCHING YOURSELF IN WEIRD PLACES LIKE THAT!!
GAN
!?
MY, IT'S PEACEFUL AROUND HERE.
I HOPE HE STAYS IN THE HUMAN REALM FOR A GOOD LONG WHILE.
HEH, HEH. YOU KNOW YOU MISS HIM.
OH. CHECKMATE.

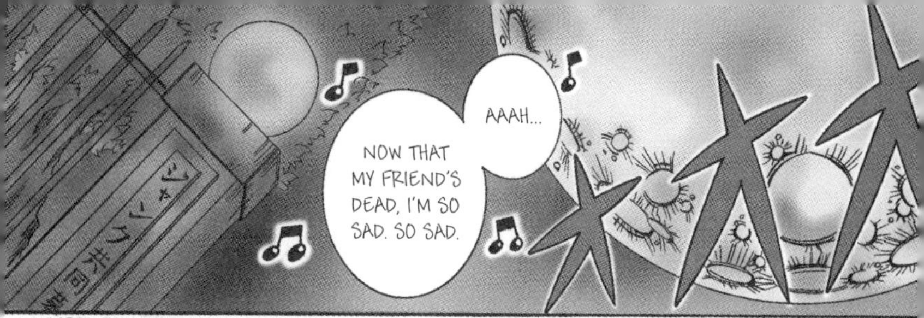
AAAH...
NOW THAT MY FRIEND'S DEAD, I'M SO SAD. SO SAD.
ジャンク共同墓

LABEL: JUNK ASSOCIATION CEMETERY

SFX: OOOO (HOOOOWL)

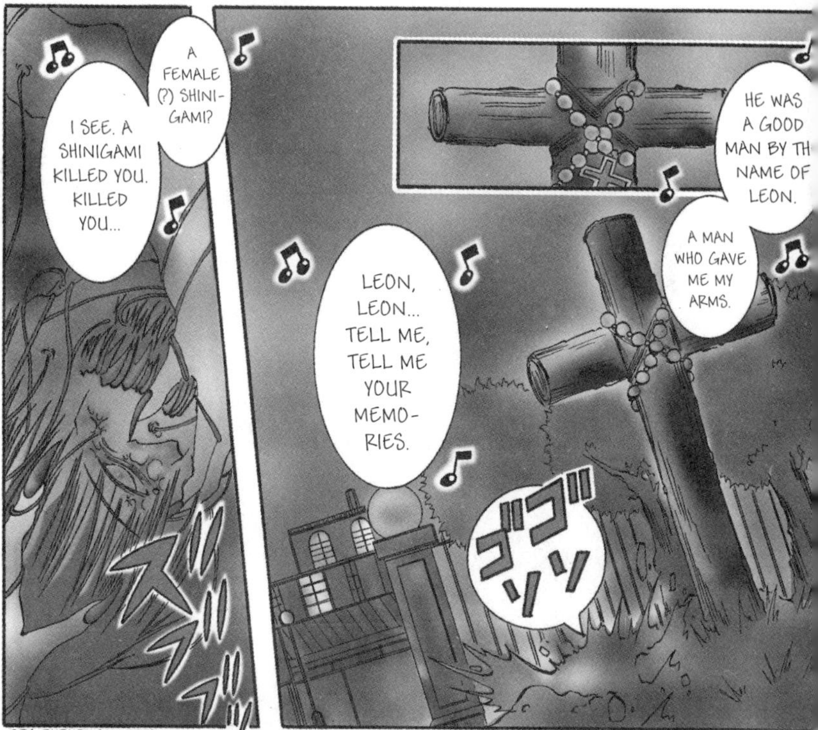
HE WAS A GOOD MAN BY TH NAME OF LEON.
A MAN WHO GAVE ME MY ARMS.
LEON, LEON... TELL ME, TELL ME YOUR MEMO- RIES.
ゴソゴソ
A FEMALE (?) SHINI- GAMI?
I SEE. A SHINIGAMI KILLED YOU. KILLED YOU...
ズブブ

SFX: GOSO GOSO (RUMMAGE RUMMAGE)

SFX: ZUBUBU (SHLORP)

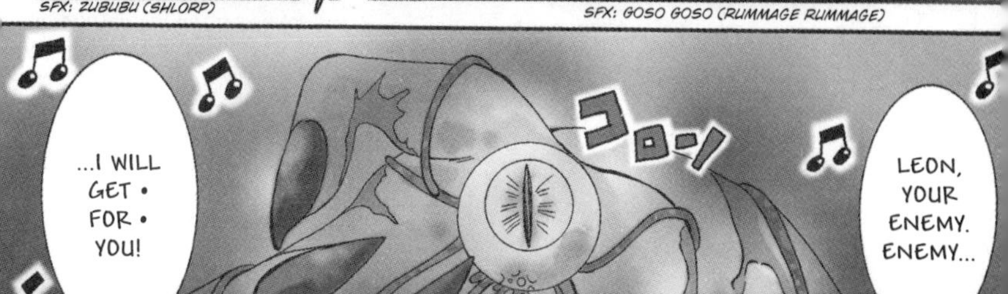
LEON, YOUR ENEMY. ENEMY...
コローン
...I WILL GET • FOR • YOU!

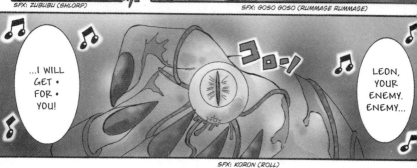

SFX: KORON (ROLL)

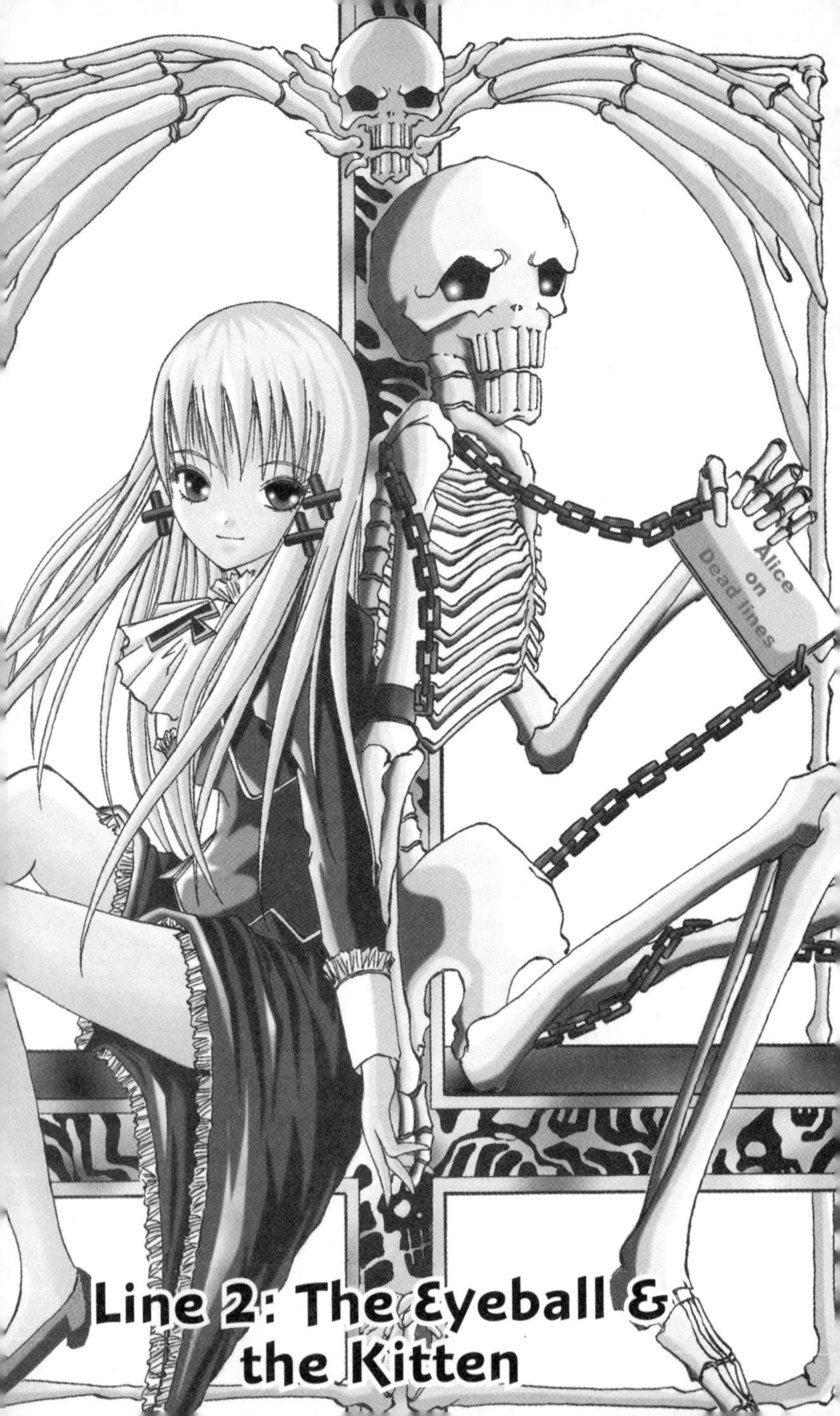
Alice on Dead lines

Line 2: The Eyeball & the Kitten

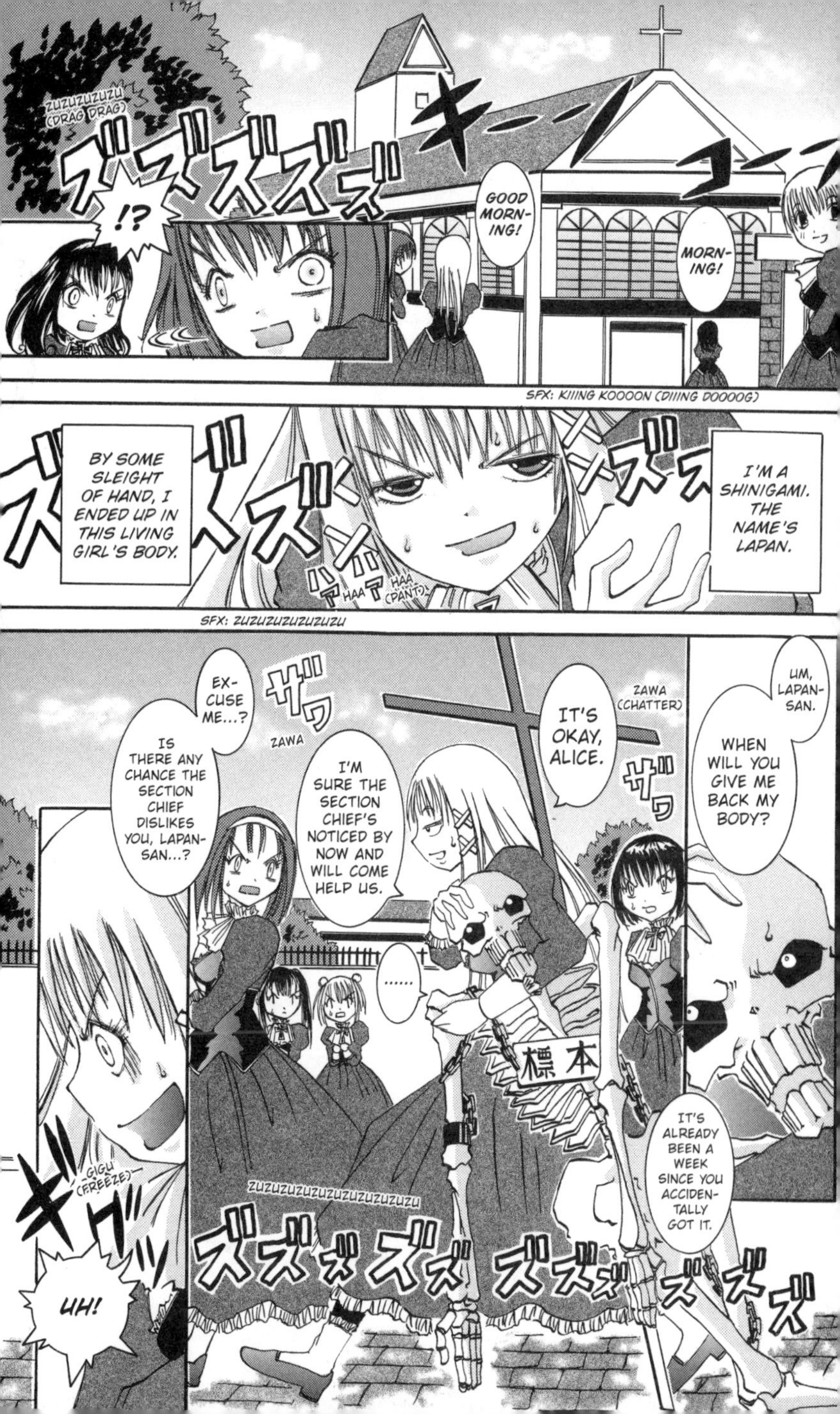
MORN-ING!
GOOD MORN-ING!
SFX: KIIING KOOOON (DIIING DOOOOG)
ZUZUZUZUZU (DRAG DRAG)
!?
I'M A SHINIGAMI. THE NAME'S LAPAN.
BY SOME SLEIGHT OF HAND, I ENDED UP IN THIS LIVING GIRL'S BODY.
HAA HAA (PANT)
SFX: ZUZUZUZUZUZUZU
UM, LAPAN-SAN.
WHEN WILL YOU GIVE ME BACK MY BODY?
IT'S ALREADY BEEN A WEEK SINCE YOU ACCIDEN-TALLY GOT IT.
ZAWA (CHATTER)
IT'S OKAY, ALICE.
I'M SURE THE SECTION CHIEF'S NOTICED BY NOW AND WILL COME HELP US.
ZAWA
EX-CUSE ME...?
IS THERE ANY CHANCE THE SECTION CHIEF DISLIKES YOU, LAPAN-SAN...?
......
標本
ZUZUZUZUZUZUZUZUZUZUZU
GIGU (FREEZE)
UH!

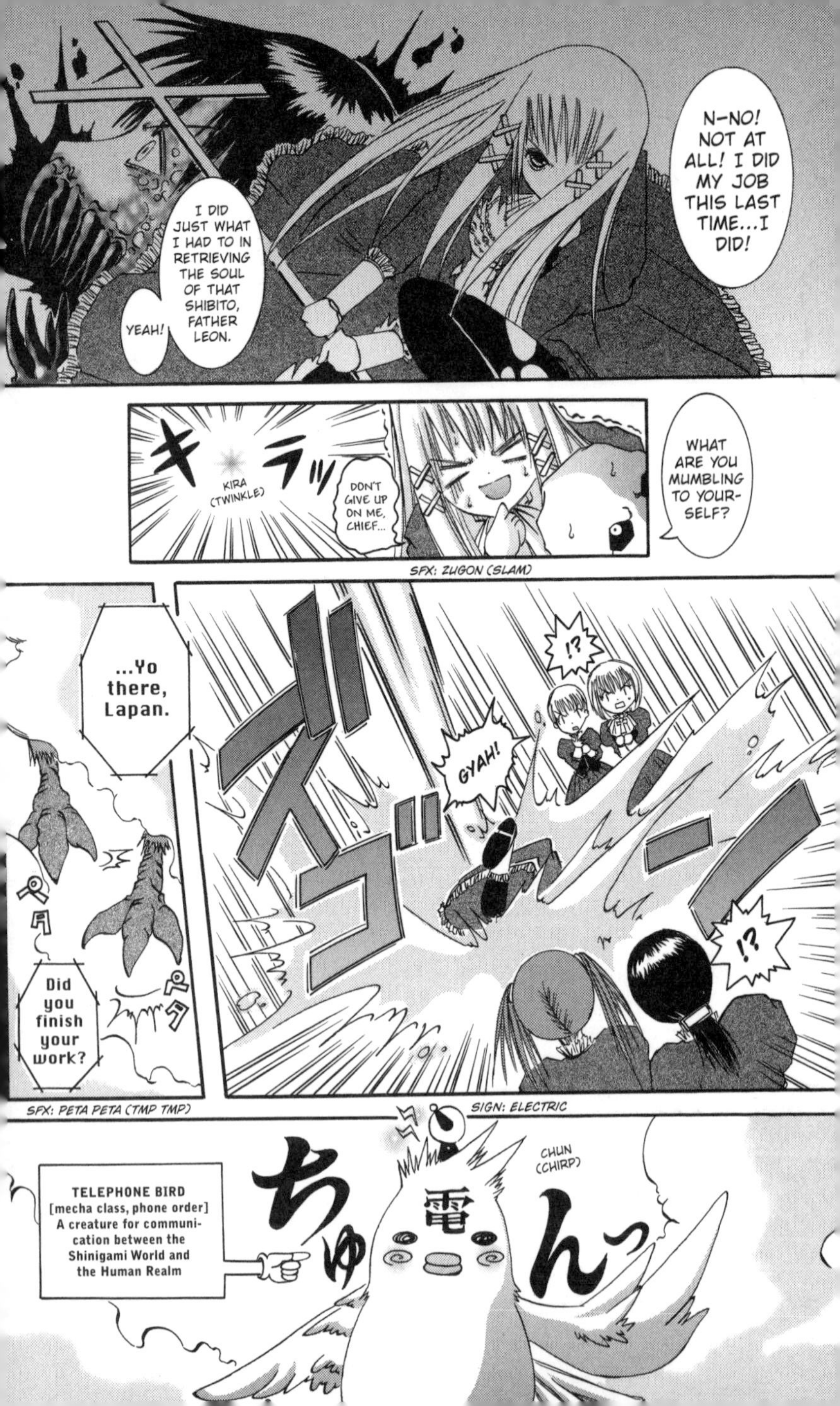
N-NO! NOT AT ALL! I DID MY JOB THIS LAST TIME...I DID!
I DID JUST WHAT I HAD TO IN RETRIEVING THE SOUL OF THAT SHIBITO, FATHER LEON.
YEAH!
WHAT ARE YOU MUMBLING TO YOUR-SELF?
DON'T GIVE UP ON ME, CHIEF...
KIRA (TWINKLE)
SFX: ZUGON (SLAM)
!?
GYAH!
!?
...Yo there, Lapan.
Did you finish your work?
SIGN: ELECTRIC
SFX: PETA PETA (TMP TMP)
CHUN (CHIRP)
ちゅんっ
電
TELEPHONE BIRD
[mecha class, phone order]
A creature for communication between the Shinigami World and the Human Realm

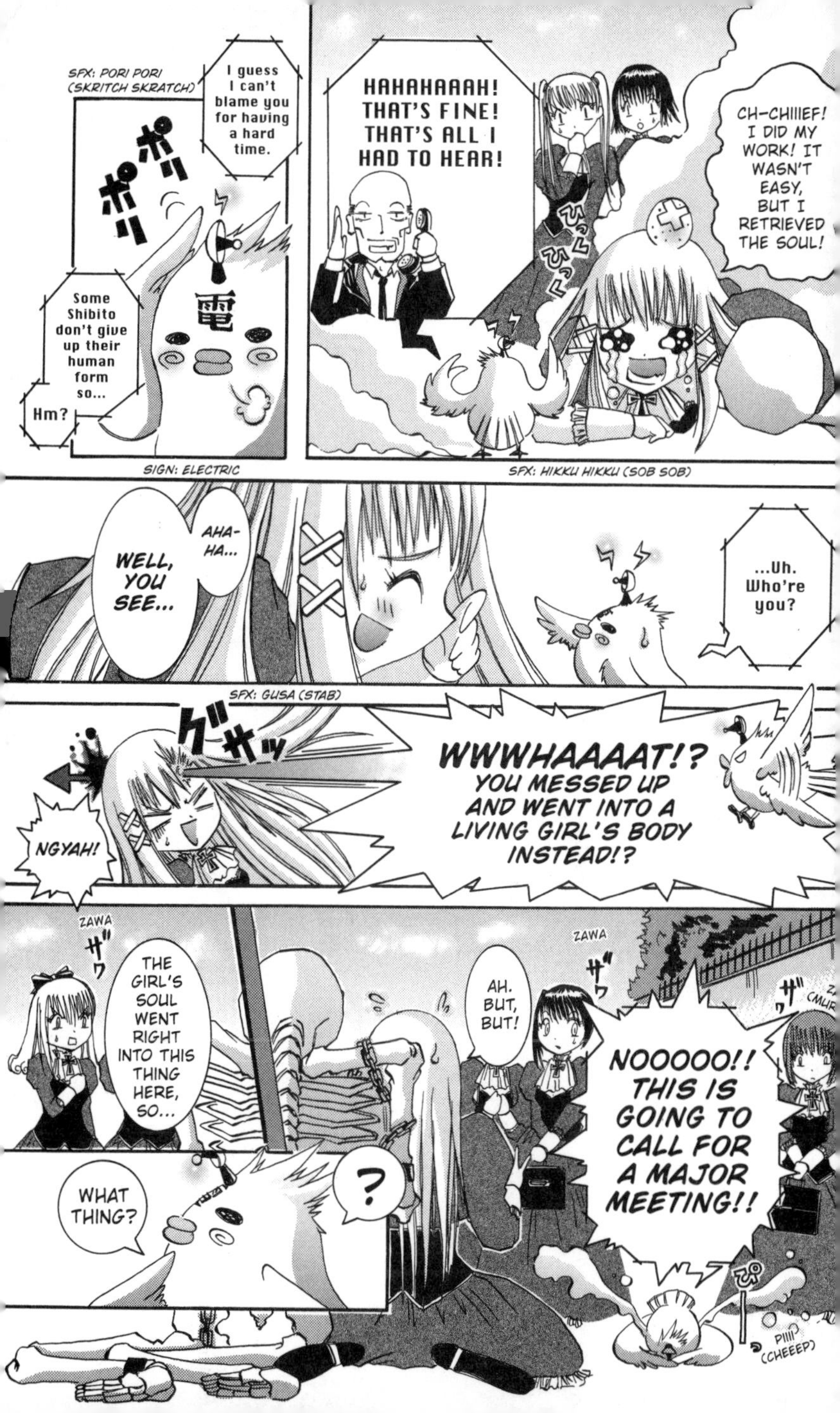
CH-CHIIIEF! I DID MY WORK! IT WASN'T EASY, BUT I RETRIEVED THE SOUL!
HAHAHAAAH! THAT'S FINE! THAT'S ALL I HAD TO HEAR!
SFX: HIKKU HIKKU (SOB SOB)
I guess I can't blame you for having a hard time.
SFX: PORI PORI (SKRITCH SKRATCH)
電
Some Shibito don't give up their human form so...
Hm?
SIGN: ELECTRIC
...Uh. Who're you?
AHA-HA...
WELL, YOU SEE...
SFX: GUSA (STAB)
WWWHAAAAT!? YOU MESSED UP AND WENT INTO A LIVING GIRL'S BODY INSTEAD!?
NGYAH!
ZAWA
NOOOOO!! THIS IS GOING TO CALL FOR A MAJOR MEETING!!
ZAWA
AH. BUT, BUT!
THE GIRL'S SOUL WENT RIGHT INTO THIS THING HERE, SO...
ZAWA
?
WHAT THING?
PIIII (CHEEEP)

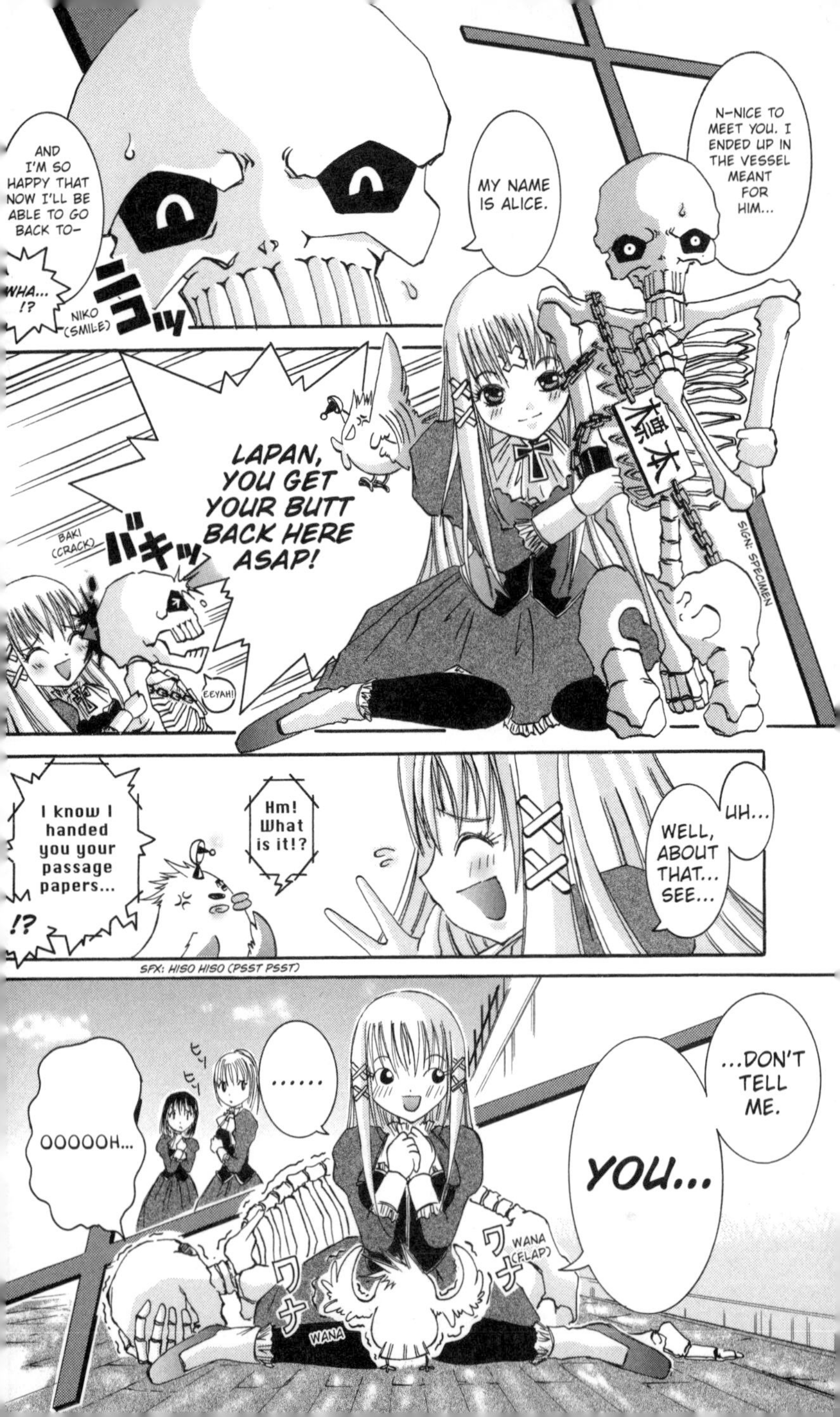
N-NICE TO MEET YOU. I ENDED UP IN THE VESSEL MEANT FOR HIM...
MY NAME IS ALICE.
SIGN: SPECIMEN
AND I'M SO HAPPY THAT NOW I'LL BE ABLE TO GO BACK TO-
WHA... !?
NIKO (SMILE)
LAPAN, YOU GET YOUR BUTT BACK HERE ASAP!
BAKI (CRACK)
EEYAH!
UH...
WELL, ABOUT THAT... SEE...
Hm! What is it!?
I know I handed you your passage papers...
!?
SFX: HISO HISO (PSST PSST)
...DON'T TELL ME.
YOU...
WANA (FLAP)
......
OOOOOH...
WANA

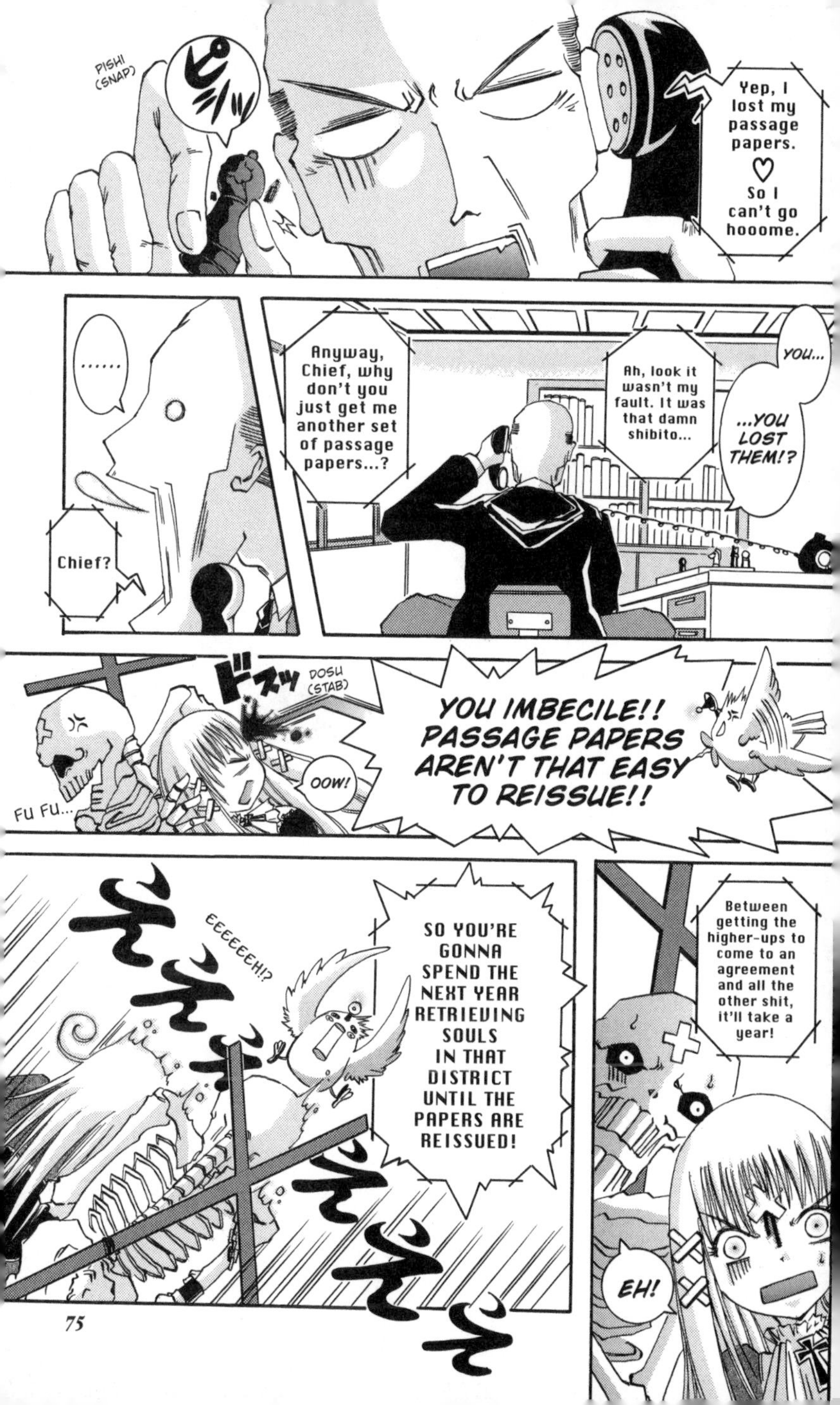

Yep, I lost my passage papers. ♡ So I can't go hooome.
PISHI (SNAP)
YOU... ...YOU LOST THEM!?
Ah, look it wasn't my fault. It was that damn shibito...
Anyway, Chief, why don't you just get me another set of passage papers...?
......
Chief?
YOU IMBECILE!! PASSAGE PAPERS AREN'T THAT EASY TO REISSUE!!
DOSU (STAB)
OOW!
FU FU...
Between getting the higher-ups to come to an agreement and all the other shit, it'll take a year!
EH!
SO YOU'RE GONNA SPEND THE NEXT YEAR RETRIEVING SOULS IN THAT DISTRICT UNTIL THE PAPERS ARE REISSUED!
EEEEEEH!?

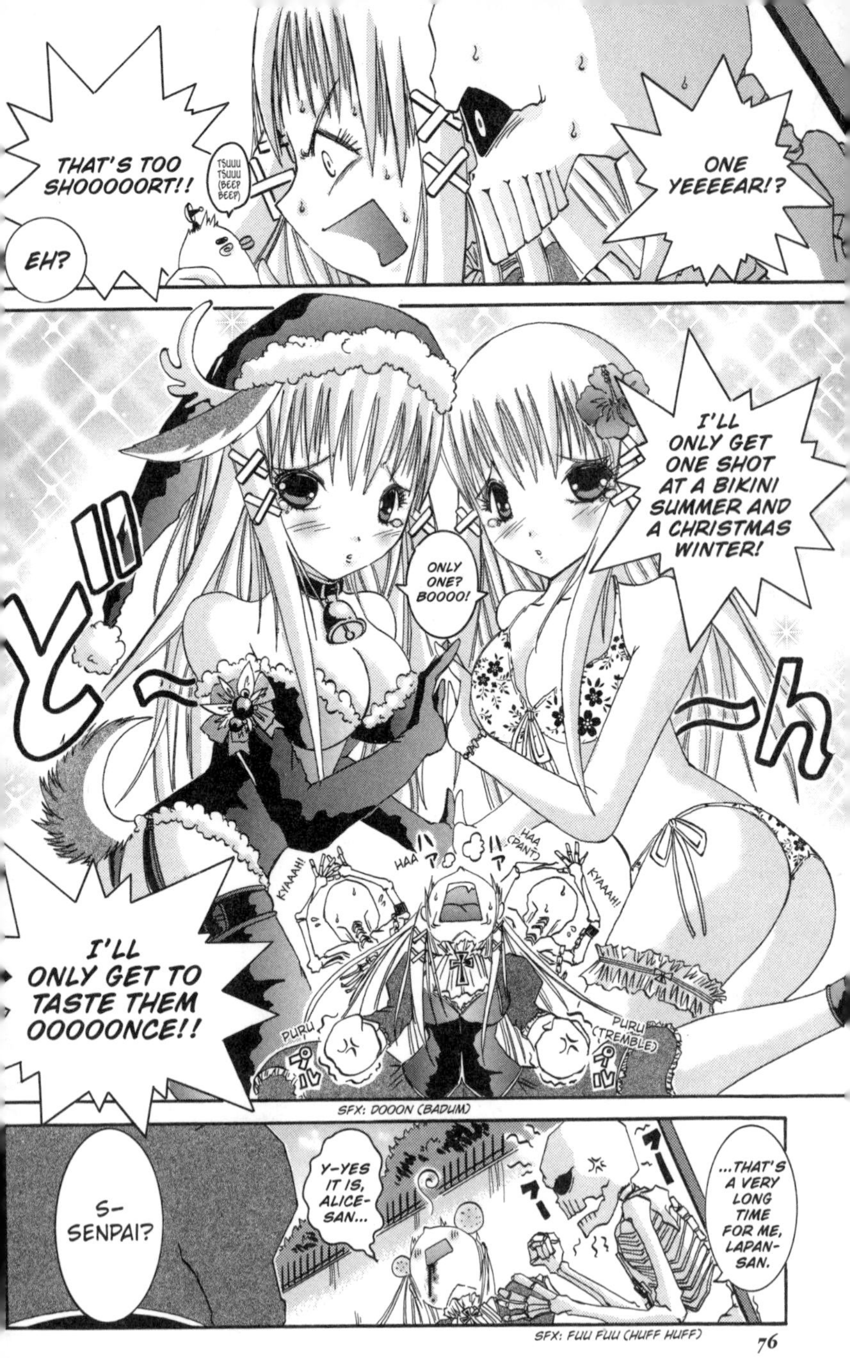
ONE YEEEEAR!?
THAT'S TOO SHOOOOORT!!
TSUUU TSUUU (BEEP BEEP)
EH?
I'LL ONLY GET ONE SHOT AT A BIKINI SUMMER AND A CHRISTMAS WINTER!
ONLY ONE? BOOOO!
HAA (PANT)
KYAAAH!
HAA
KYAAAH!
I'LL ONLY GET TO TASTE THEM OOOOONCE!!
PURU (TREMBLE)
PURU
SFX: DOOON (BADUM)
...THAT'S A VERY LONG TIME FOR ME, LAPAN-SAN.
Y-YES IT IS, ALICE-SAN...
S-SENPAI?
SFX: FUU FUU (HUFF HUFF)

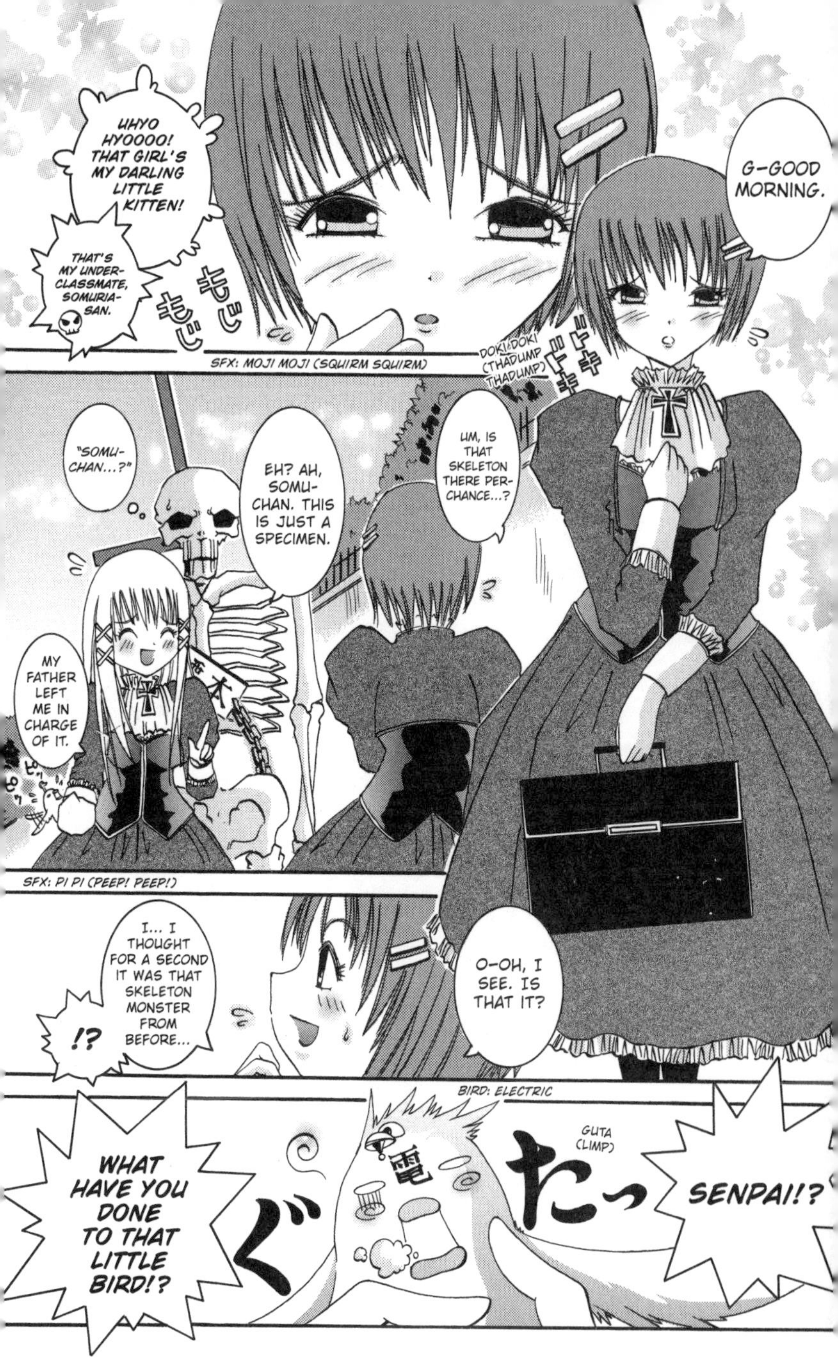
G-GOOD MORNING.
UHYO HYOOOO! THAT GIRL'S MY DARLING LITTLE KITTEN!
THAT'S MY UNDER-CLASSMATE, SOMURIA-SAN.
もじもじ
SFX: MOJI MOJI (SQUIRM SQUIRM)
ドキドキ
DOKI DOKI (THADUMP THADUMP)
UM, IS THAT SKELETON THERE PER-CHANCE...?
EH? AH, SOMU-CHAN. THIS IS JUST A SPECIMEN.
"SOMU-CHAN...?"
MY FATHER LEFT ME IN CHARGE OF IT.
SFX: PI PI (PEEP! PEEP!)
O-OH, I SEE. IS THAT IT?
I... I THOUGHT FOR A SECOND IT WAS THAT SKELETON MONSTER FROM BEFORE...
!?
SENPAI!?
ぐ
たっ
GUTA (LIMP)
電
BIRD: ELECTRIC
WHAT HAVE YOU DONE TO THAT LITTLE BIRD!?

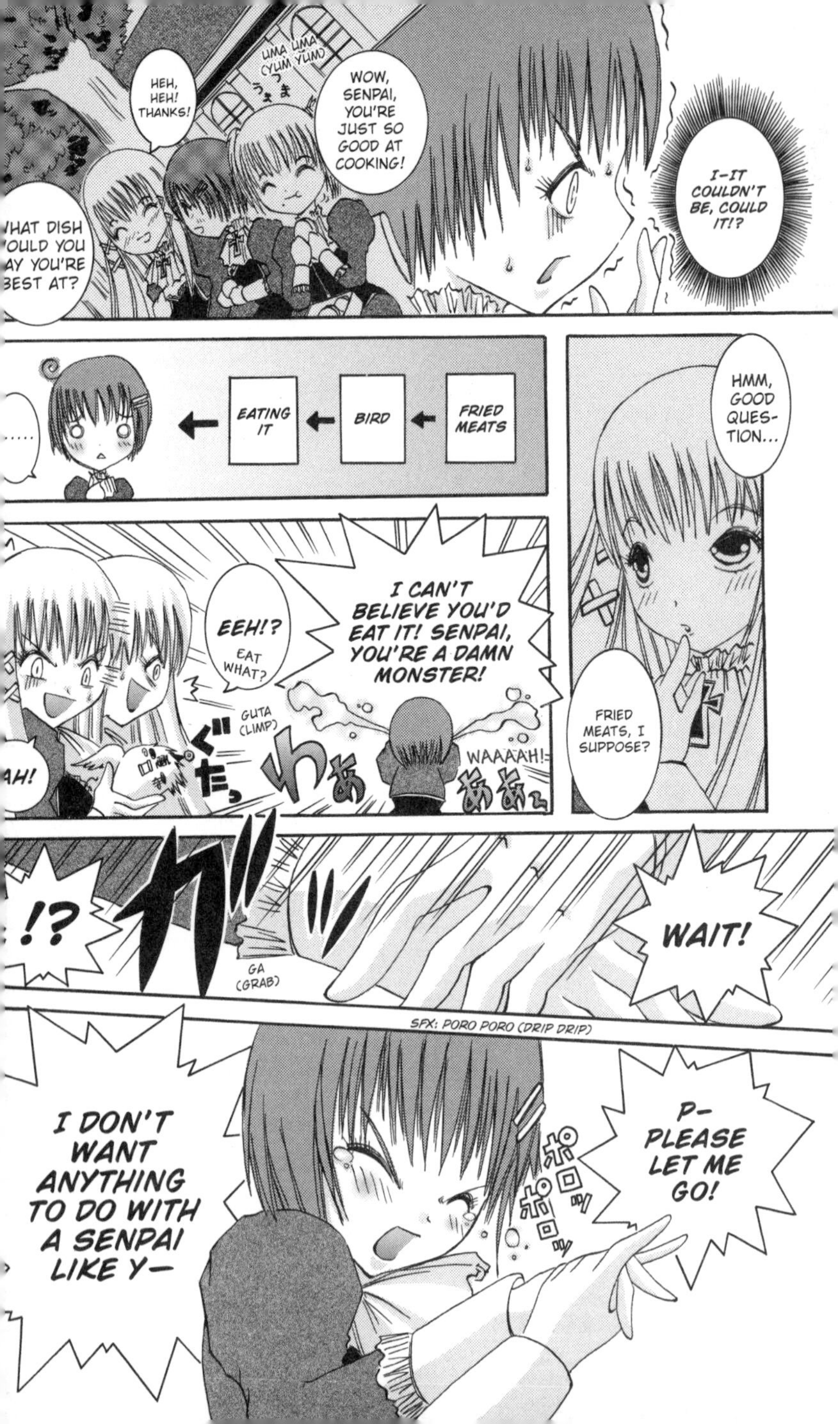

I-IT COULDN'T BE, COULD IT!?
WOW, SENPAI, YOU'RE JUST SO GOOD AT COOKING!
UMA UMA (YUM YUM)
HEH, HEH! THANKS!
HAT DISH OULD YOU AY YOU'RE BEST AT?
HMM, GOOD QUES-TION...
FRIED MEATS, I SUPPOSE?
FRIED MEATS
BIRD
EATING IT
.....
I CAN'T BELIEVE YOU'D EAT IT! SENPAI, YOU'RE A DAMN MONSTER!
WAAAAH!
EEH!? EAT WHAT?
GUTA (LIMP)
AH!
WAIT!
GA (GRAB)
!?
SFX: PORO PORO (DRIP DRIP)
P-PLEASE LET ME GO!
I DON'T WANT ANYTHING TO DO WITH A SENPAI LIKE Y—

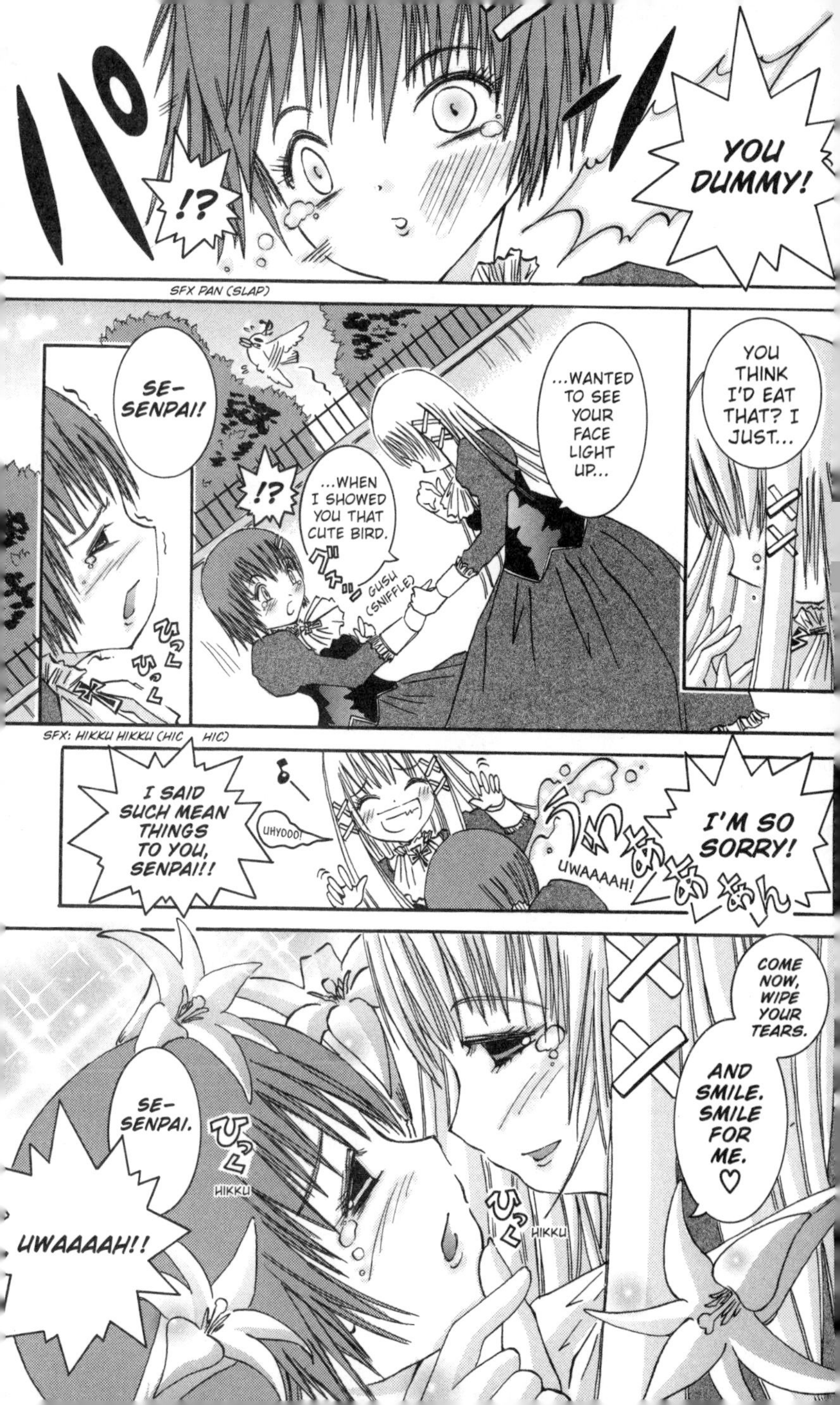
YOU DUMMY!
!?
SFX PAN (SLAP)
YOU THINK I'D EAT THAT? I JUST...
...WANTED TO SEE YOUR FACE LIGHT UP...
...WHEN I SHOWED YOU THAT CUTE BIRD.
GUSU (SNIFFLE)
!?
SE-SENPAI!
SFX: HIKKU HIKKU (HIC HIC)
I'M SO SORRY!
UWAAAAH!
UHYOOO!
I SAID SUCH MEAN THINGS TO YOU, SENPAI!!
COME NOW, WIPE YOUR TEARS.
AND SMILE. SMILE FOR ME. ♡
HIKKU
SE-SENPAI.
HIKKU
UWAAAAH!!

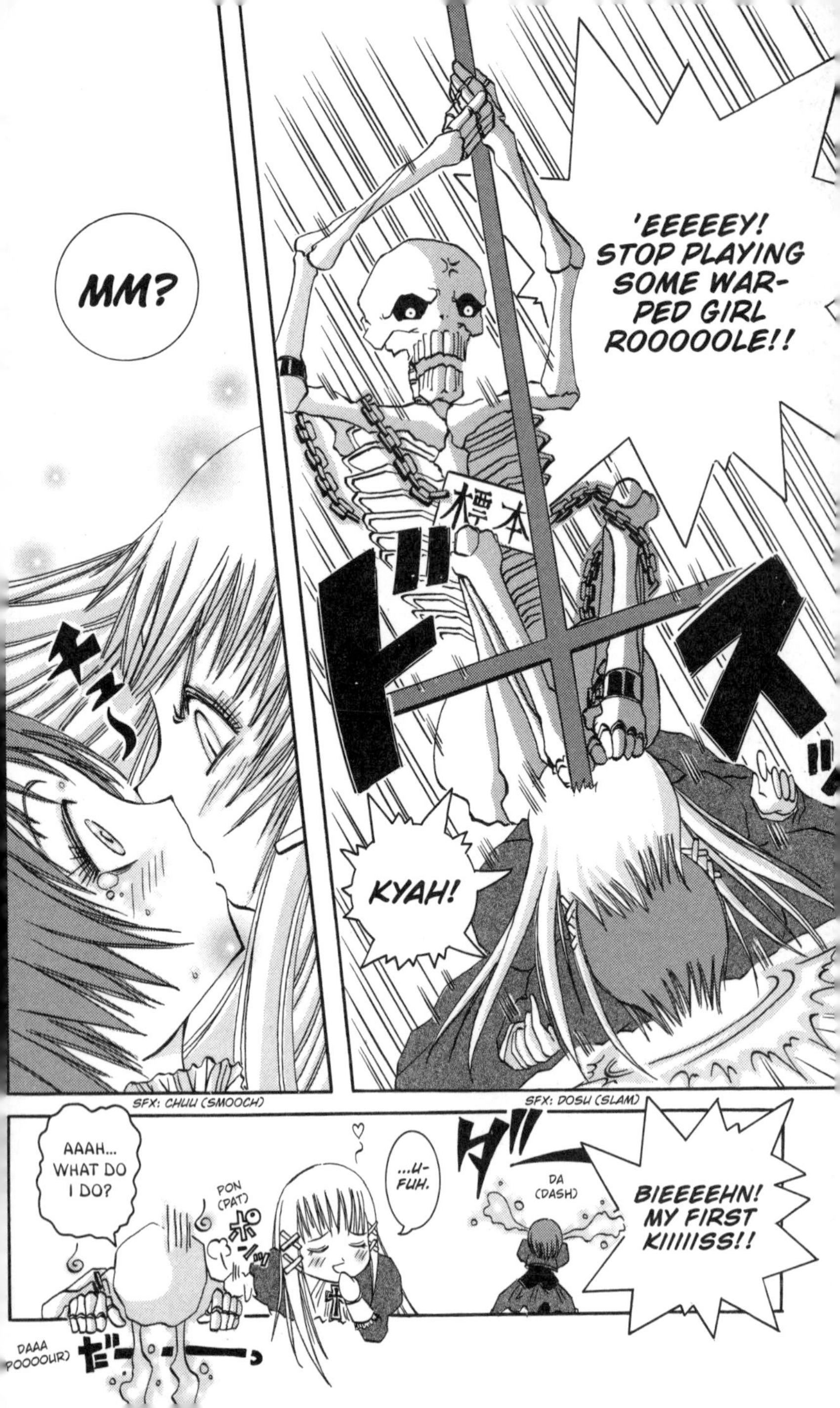
'EEEEEY! STOP PLAYING SOME WAR-PED GIRL ROOOOOLE!!
KYAH!
SFX: DOSU (SLAM)
MM?
SFX: CHUU (SMOOCH)
BIEEEEHN! MY FIRST KIIIIISS!!
DA (DASH)
...U-FUH.
PON (PAT)
AAAH... WHAT DO I DO?
DAAA POOOOUR)

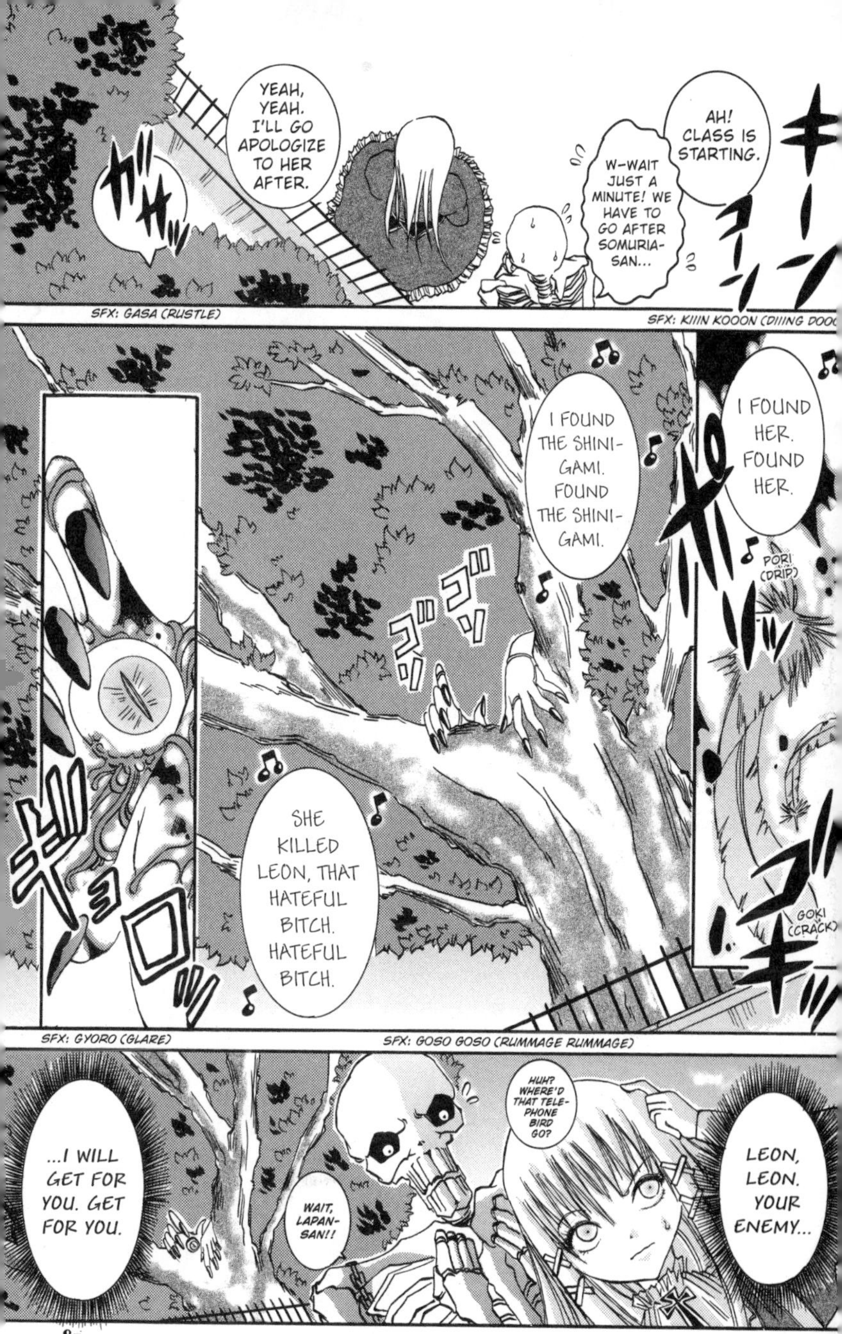
AH! CLASS IS STARTING.
W-WAIT JUST A MINUTE! WE HAVE TO GO AFTER SOMURIA-SAN...
YEAH, YEAH. I'LL GO APOLOGIZE TO HER AFTER.
SFX: KIIN KOOON (DIIING DOO
SFX: GASA (RUSTLE)
I FOUND HER. FOUND HER.
PORI (DRIP)
GOKI (CRACK)
I FOUND THE SHINI-GAMI. FOUND THE SHINI-GAMI.
SHE KILLED LEON, THAT HATEFUL BITCH. HATEFUL BITCH.
SFX: GOSO GOSO (RUMMAGE RUMMAGE)
SFX: GYORO (GLARE)
LEON, LEON. YOUR ENEMY...
HUH? WHERE'D THAT TELE-PHONE BIRD GO?
WAIT, LAPAN-SAN!!
...I WILL GET FOR YOU. GET FOR YOU.

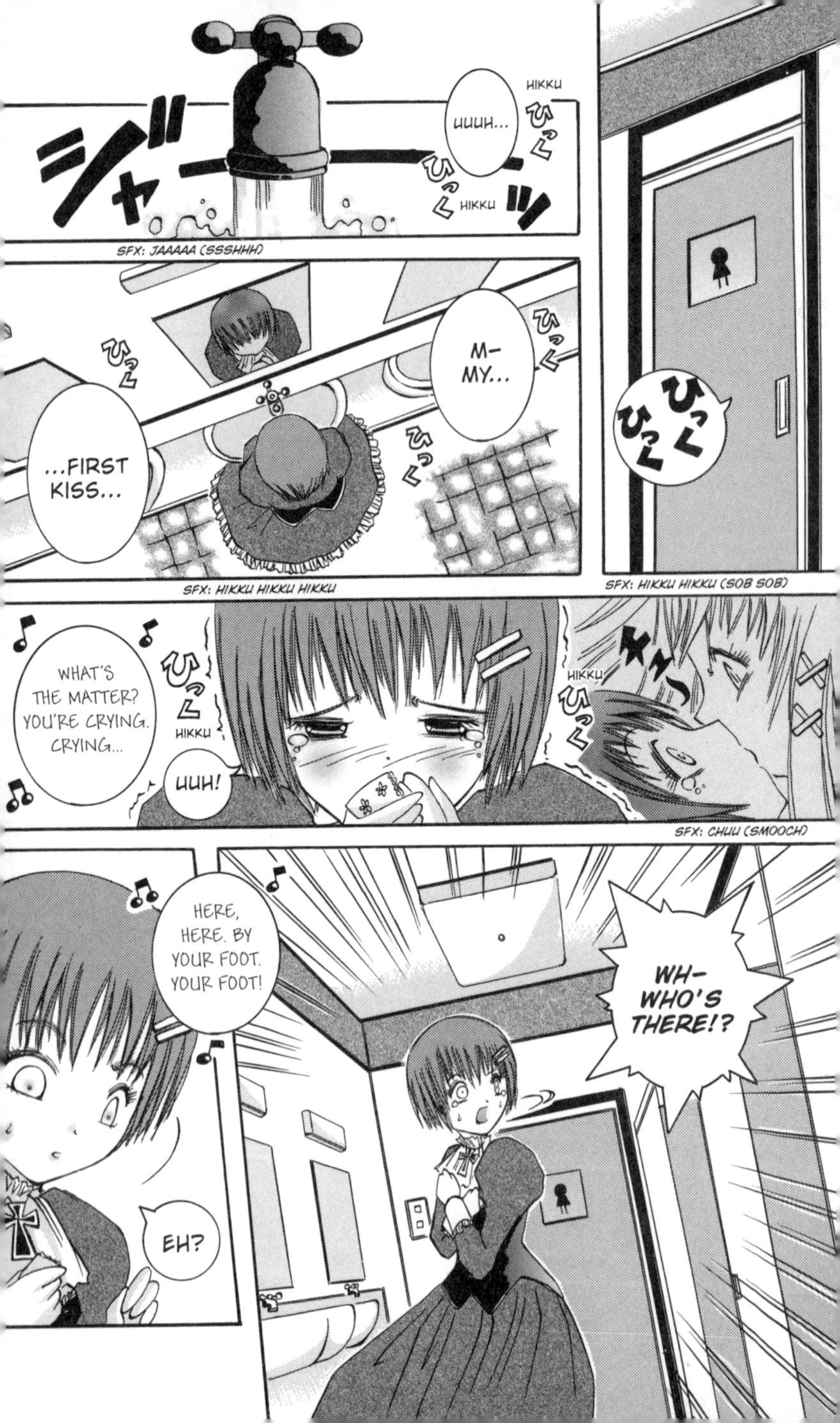
ひっく ひっく
SFX: HIKKU HIKKU (SOB SOB)
HIKKU
UUUH...
HIKKU
SFX: JAAAAA (SSSHHH)
M-MY...
...FIRST KISS...
SFX: HIKKU HIKKU HIKKU
HIKKU
SFX: CHUU (SMOOCH)
HIKKU
UUH!
WHAT'S THE MATTER? YOU'RE CRYING. CRYING...
WH- WHO'S THERE!?
HERE, HERE. BY YOUR FOOT. YOUR FOOT!
EH?

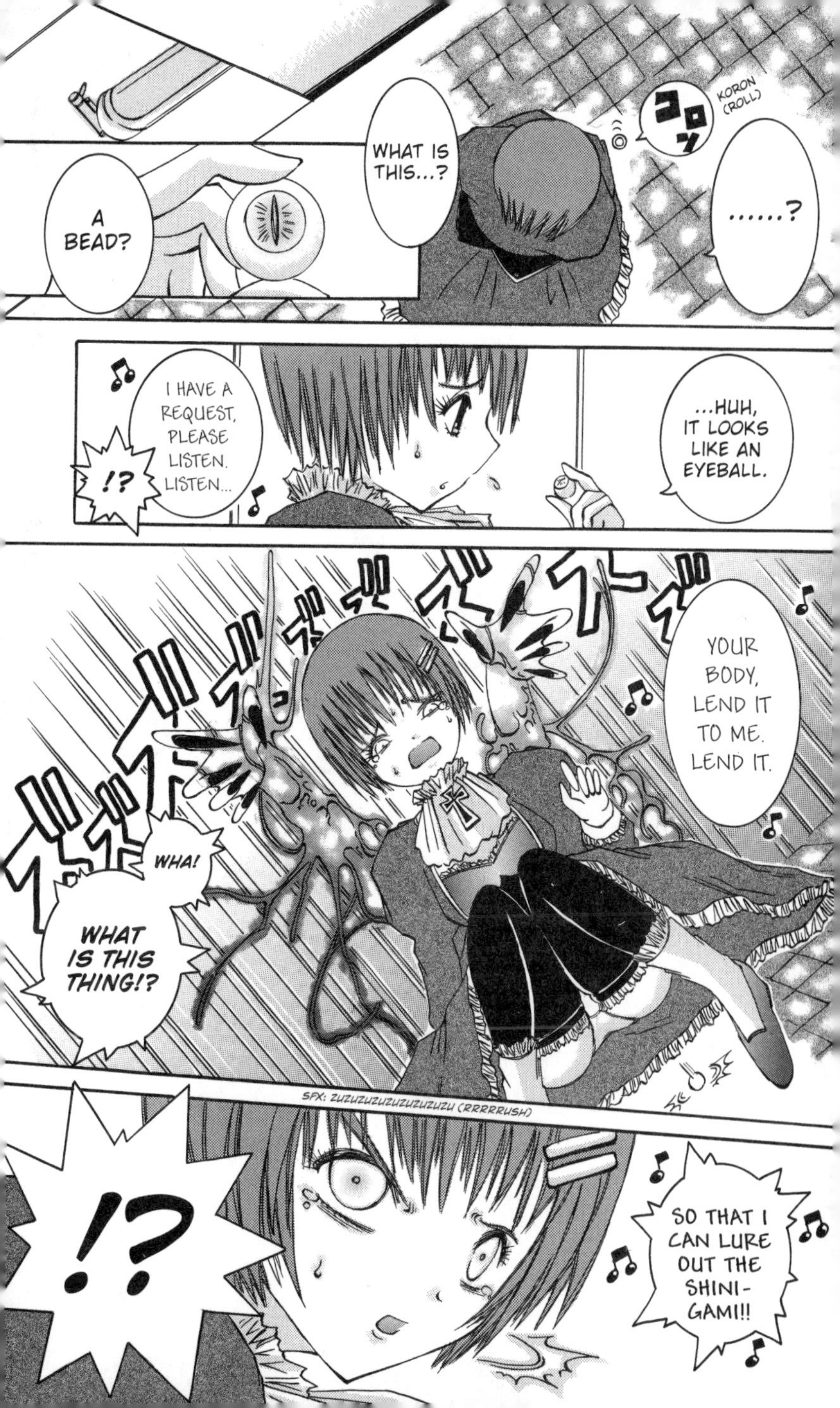
コロッ
KORON (ROLL)
......?
WHAT IS THIS...?
A BEAD?
...HUH, IT LOOKS LIKE AN EYEBALL.
I HAVE A REQUEST, PLEASE LISTEN. LISTEN...
!?
YOUR BODY, LEND IT TO ME. LEND IT.
WHA!
WHAT IS THIS THING!?
SFX: ZUZUZUZUZUZUZUZUZU (RRRRRUSH)
SO THAT I CAN LURE OUT THE SHINI-GAMI!!
!?

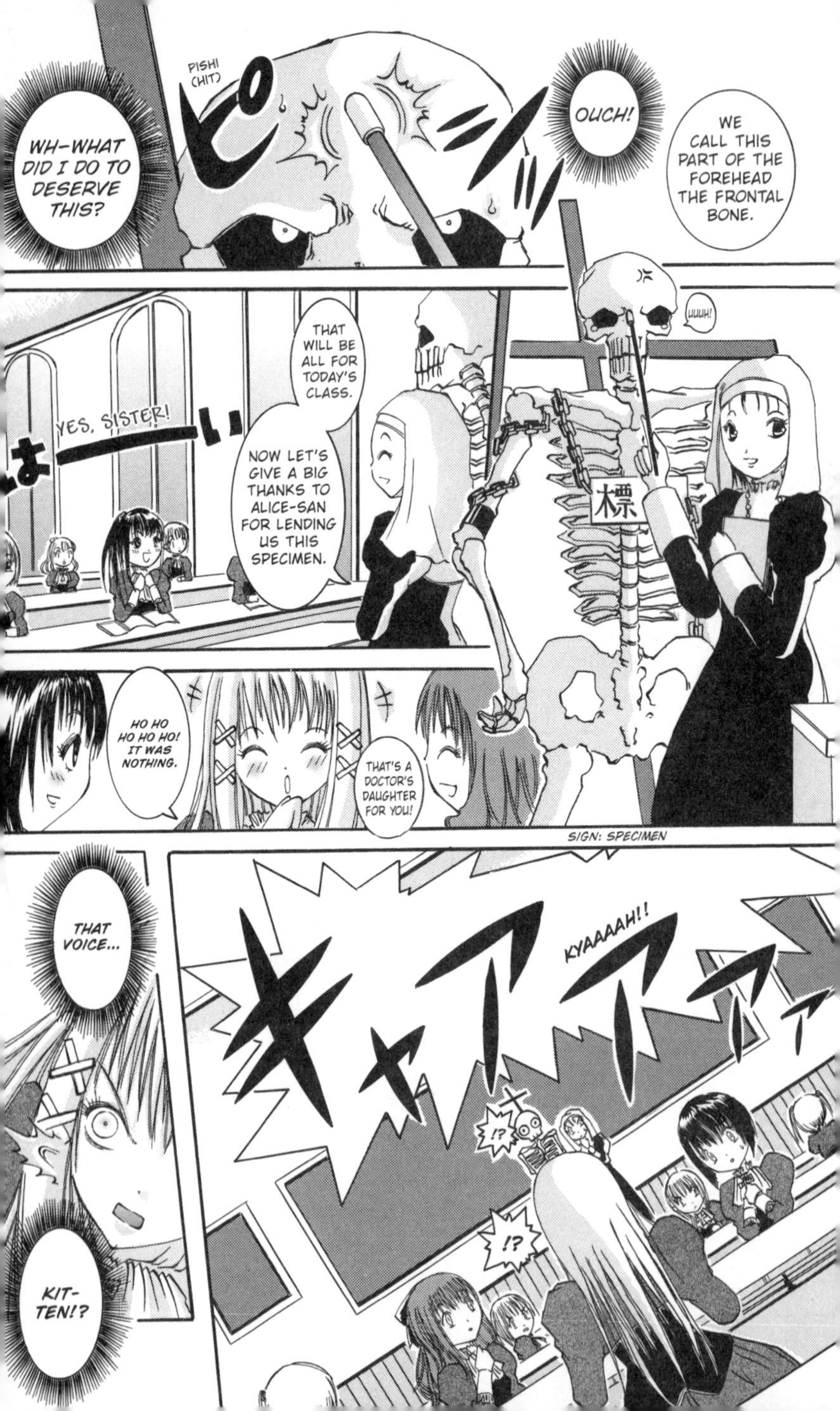
WE CALL THIS PART OF THE FOREHEAD THE FRONTAL BONE.
OUCH!
PISHI (HIT)
WH-WHAT DID I DO TO DESERVE THIS?
UUUH!
THAT WILL BE ALL FOR TODAY'S CLASS.
NOW LET'S GIVE A BIG THANKS TO ALICE-SAN FOR LENDING US THIS SPECIMEN.
YES, SISTER!
THAT'S A DOCTOR'S DAUGHTER FOR YOU!
HO HO HO HO HO! IT WAS NOTHING.
SIGN: SPECIMEN
KYAAAAH!!
!?
!?
THAT VOICE...
KIT-TEN!?

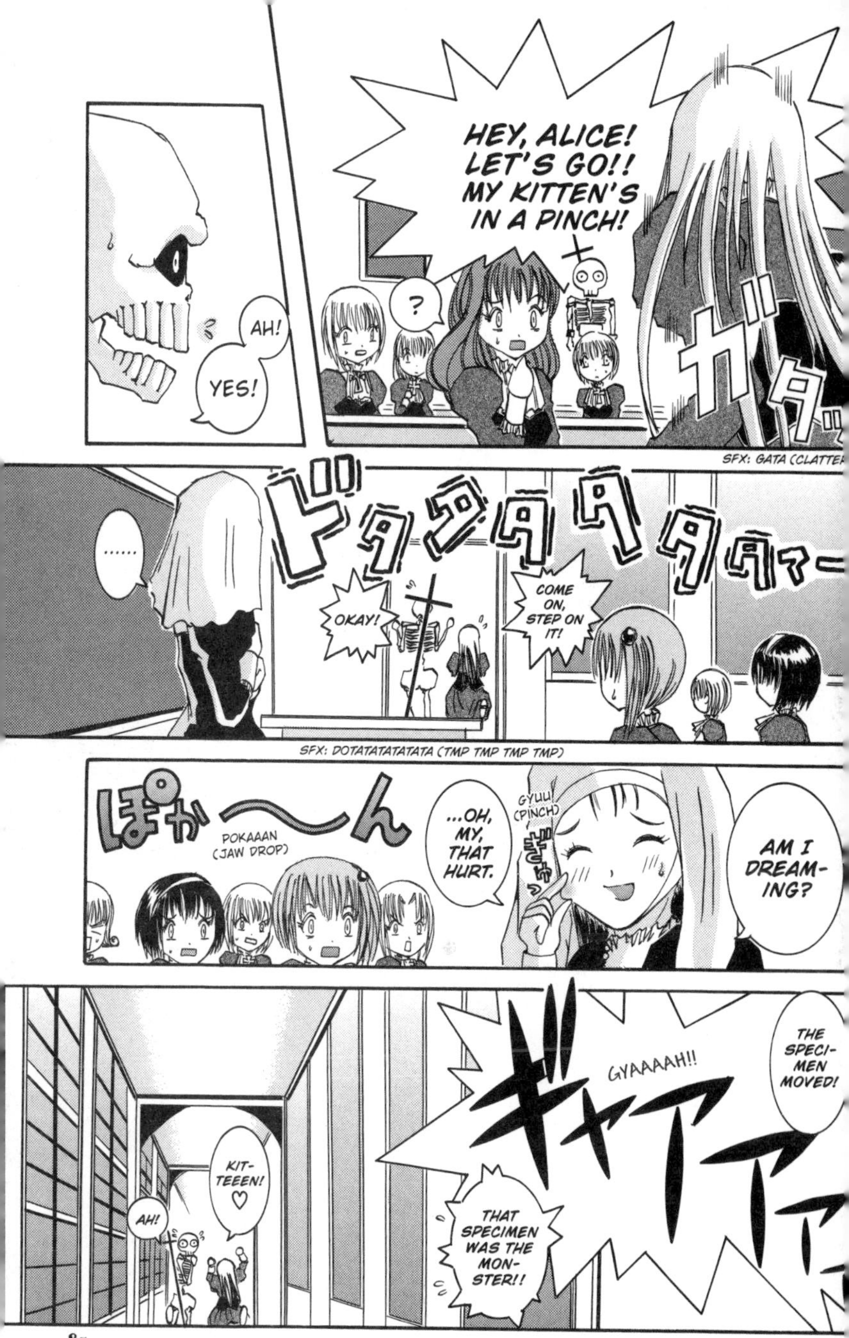
HEY, ALICE! LET'S GO!! MY KITTEN'S IN A PINCH!
?
ガタッ
SFX: GATA (CLATTER
AH!
YES!
ドタタタタタタァー
COME ON, STEP ON IT!
OKAY!
......
SFX: DOTATATATATATA (TMP TMP TMP TMP)
AM I DREAM-ING?
GYUU (PINCH)
ぎゅっ
...OH, MY, THAT HURT.
ぽか〜ん
POKAAAN (JAW DROP)
THE SPECI-MEN MOVED!
GYAAAAH!!
ギャアア
THAT SPECIMEN WAS THE MON-STER!!
KIT-TEEEN! ♡
AH!

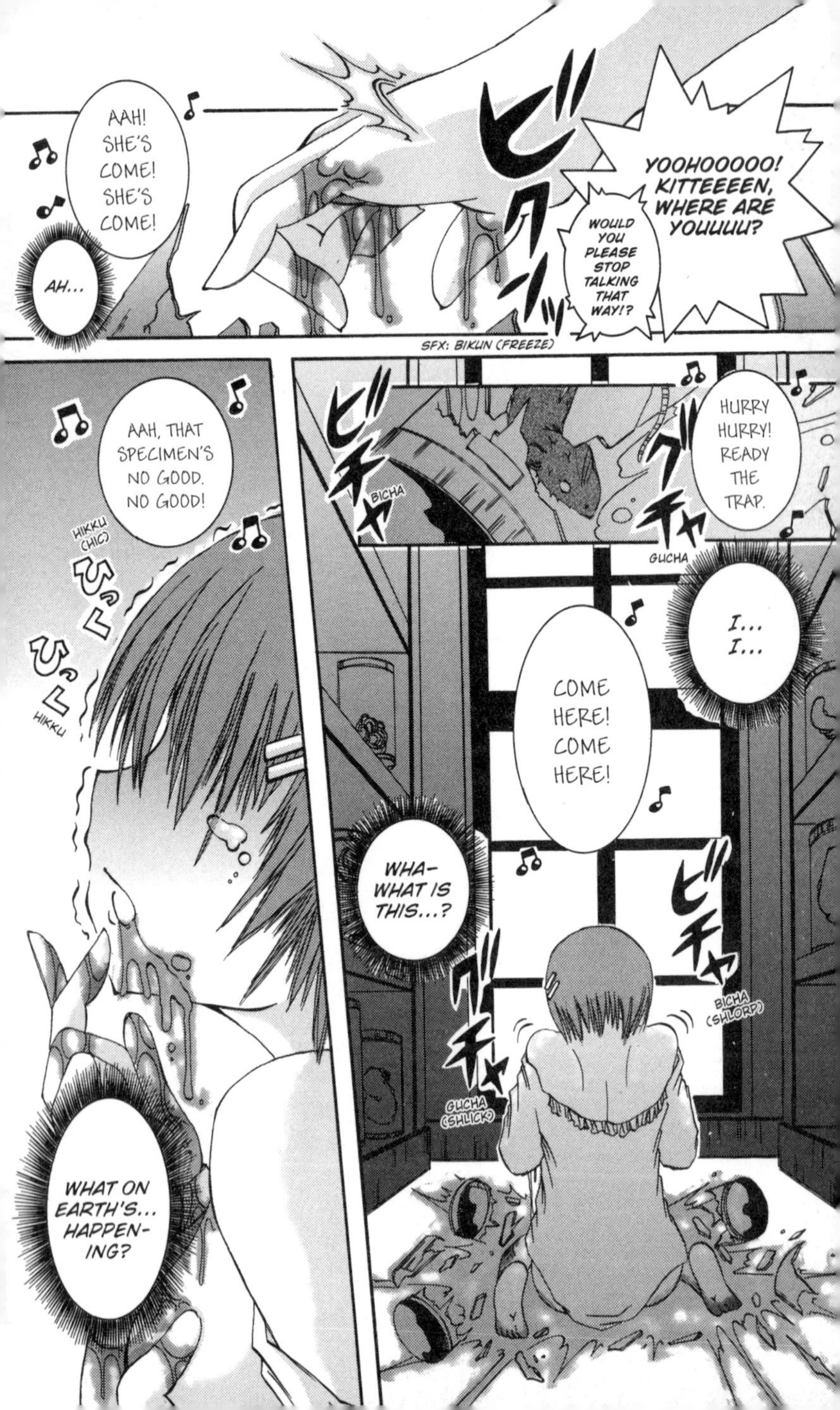
YOOHOOOOO! KITTEEEEN, WHERE ARE YOUUUUU?
WOULD YOU PLEASE STOP TALKING THAT WAY!?
AAH! SHE'S COME! SHE'S COME!
AH...
SFX: BIKUN (FREEZE)
HURRY HURRY! READY THE TRAP.
GUCHA
BICHA
I... I...
COME HERE! COME HERE!
WHA- WHAT IS THIS...?
BICHA (SHLORP)
GUCHA (SHLICK)
AAH, THAT SPECIMEN'S NO GOOD. NO GOOD!
HIKKU (HIC)
HIKKU
WHAT ON EARTH'S... HAPPENING?

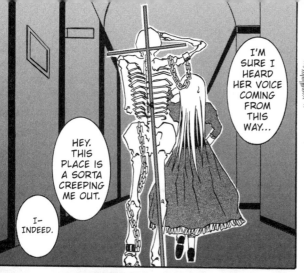

SOME-BODY!!
キョロ キョロ
SFX: KYORO KYORO (LOOK LOOK)
I'M SURE I HEARD HER VOICE COMING FROM THIS WAY...
HEY. THIS PLACE IS A SORTA CREEPING ME OUT.
I- INDEED.
THE SCIENCE LAB...
...AND PREP ROOM FULL OF SPECIMENS IN FOR-MALIN ARE HERE.
GEH!
HM?
!?
SFX: KA (FLASH)
TH- THAT'S...
...A SCHOOL UNIFORM!?

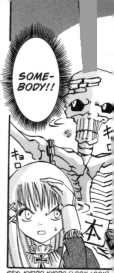

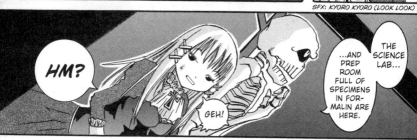

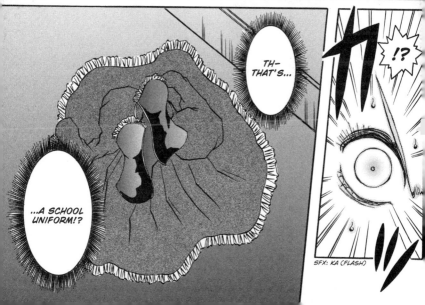

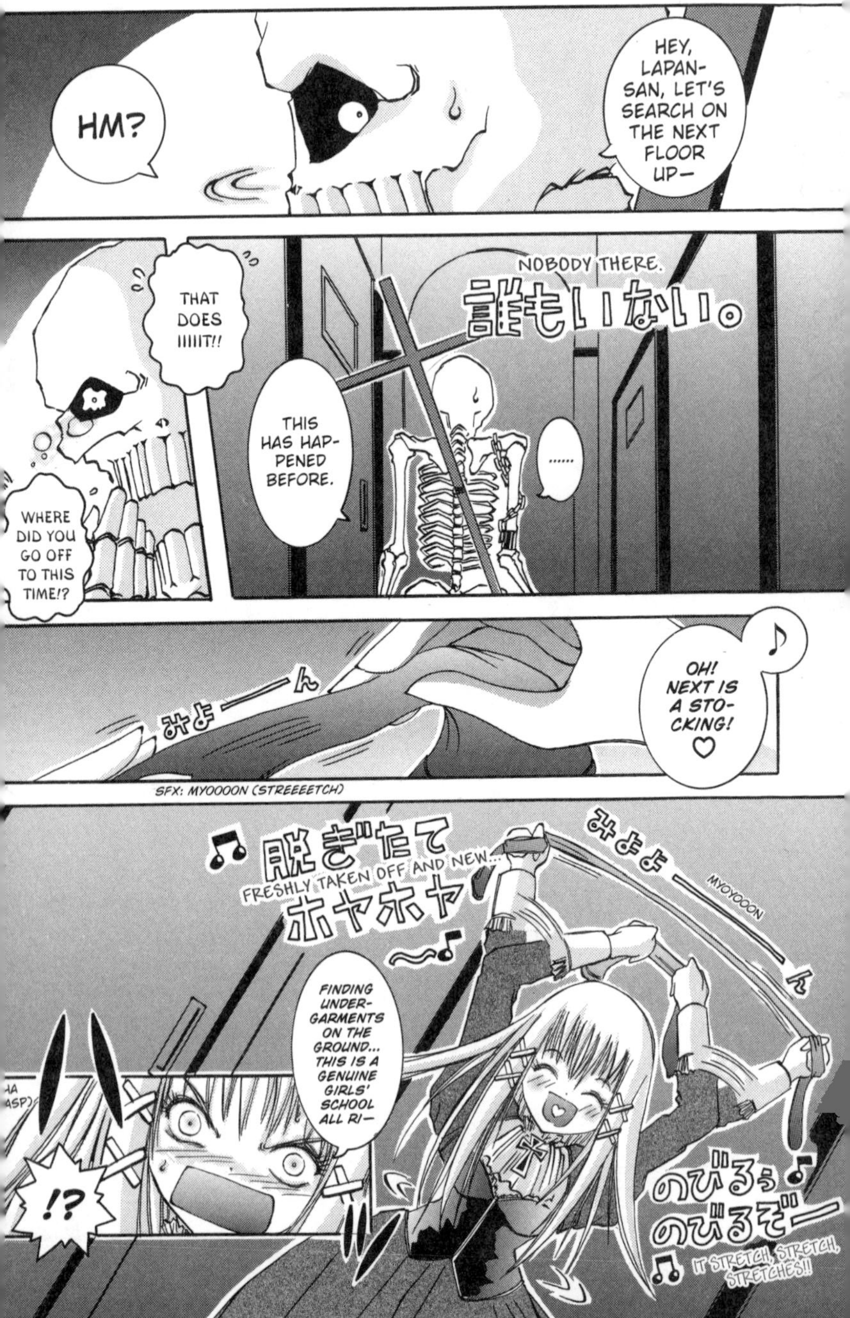
HEY, LAPAN-SAN, LET'S SEARCH ON THE NEXT FLOOR UP—
HM?
NOBODY THERE.
誰もいない。
......
THIS HAS HAPPENED BEFORE.
THAT DOES IIIIIT!!
WHERE DID YOU GO OFF TO THIS TIME!?
OH! NEXT IS A STOCKING! ♡
みよーーん
SFX: MYOOOON (STREEEETCH)
みよよーーーん
MYOYOOON
脱ぎたてホヤホヤ〜
FRESHLY TAKEN OFF AND NEW...
FINDING UNDER-GARMENTS ON THE GROUND... THIS IS A GENUINE GIRLS' SCHOOL ALL RI—
のびるぅのびるぞーー
IT STRETCH, STRETCH, STRETCHES!!
!?

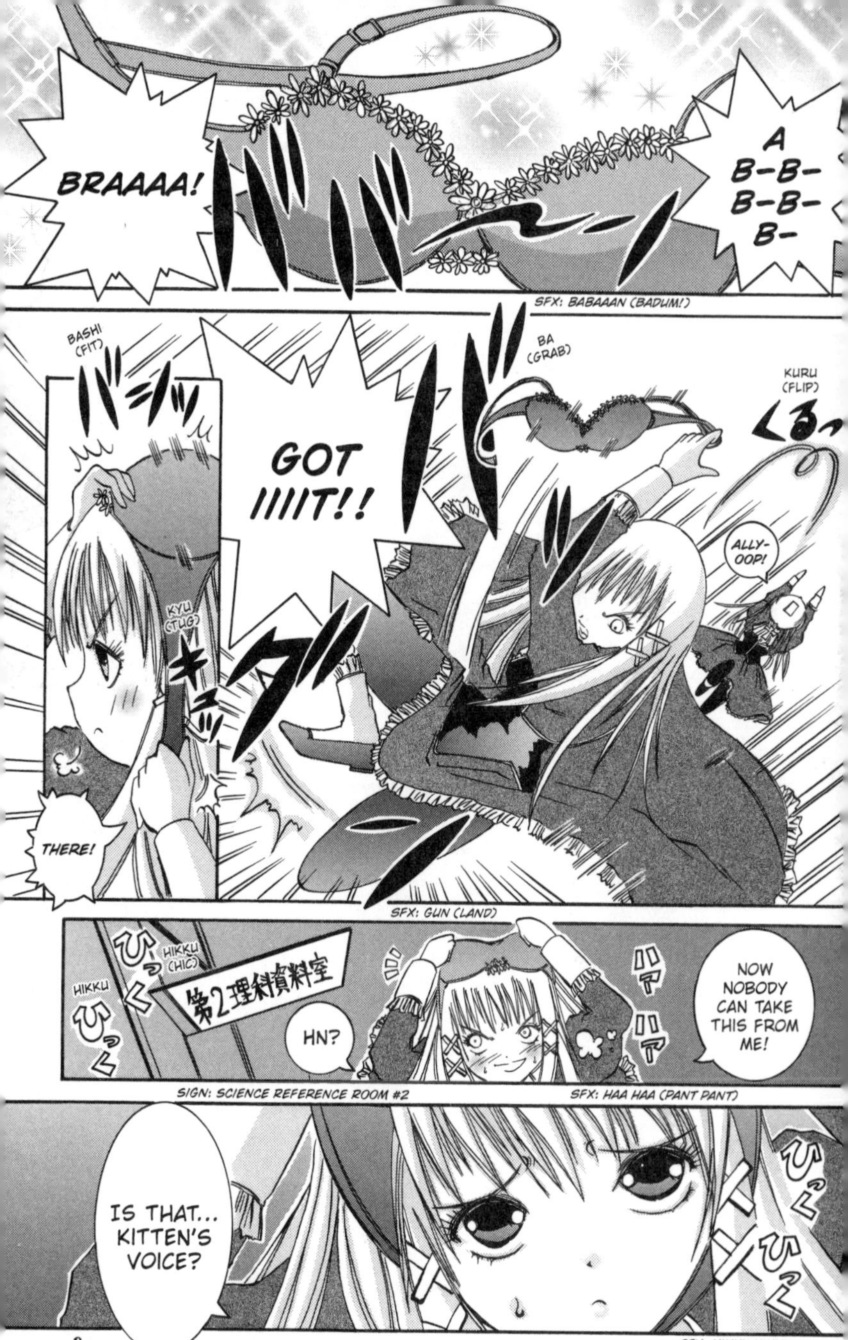
A B-B-B-B-B-
BRAAAA!
SFX: BABAAAN (BADUM!)
KURU (FLIP)
BA (GRAB)
ALLY-OOP!
GOT IIIIT!!
SFX: GUN (LAND)
BASHI (FIT)
KYU (TUG)
THERE!
NOW NOBODY CAN TAKE THIS FROM ME!
SFX: HAA HAA (PANT PANT)
HN?
第2理科資料室
SIGN: SCIENCE REFERENCE ROOM #2
HIKKU (HIC)
HIKKU
IS THAT... KITTEN'S VOICE?
SFX: HIKKU HIKKU

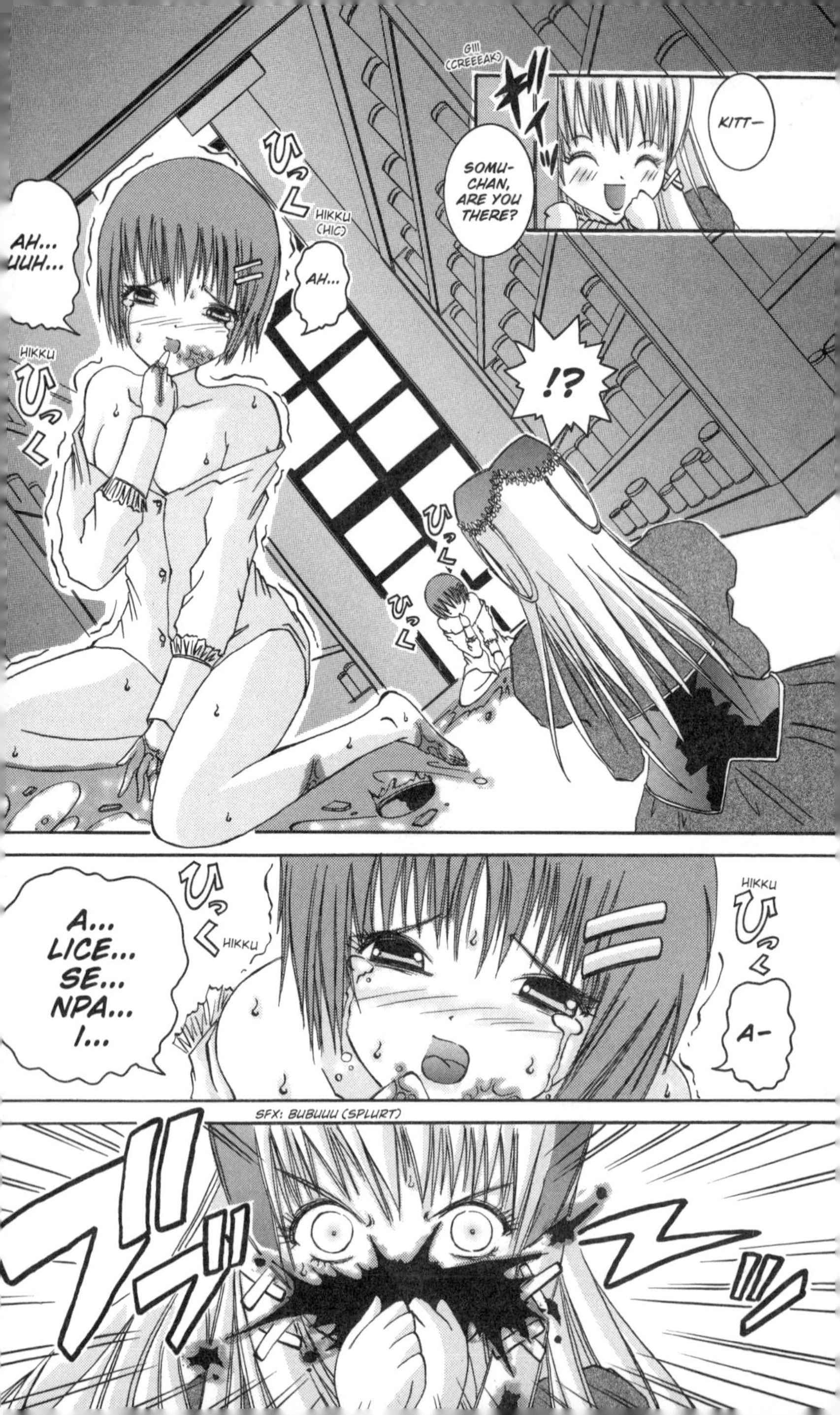

GIII (CREEEAK)
KITT—
SOMU-CHAN, ARE YOU THERE?
!?
AH...
HIKKU (HIC)
AH... UUH...
HIKKU
HIKKU
A-
HIKKU
A... LICE... SE... NPA... I...
SFX: BUBUUU (SPLURT)

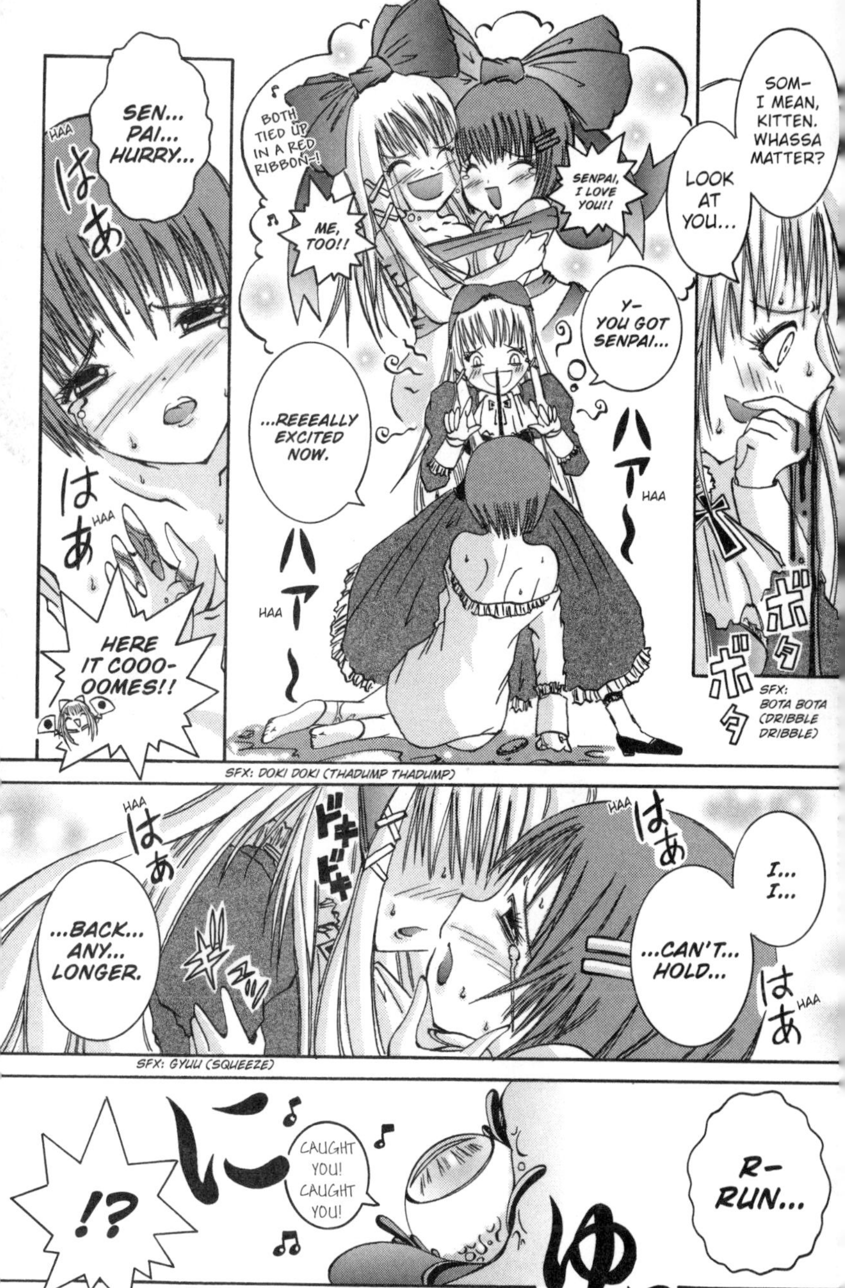
SOM–
I MEAN, KITTEN. WHASSA MATTER?
LOOK AT YOU...
ボタボタ
SFX: BOTA BOTA (DRIBBLE DRIBBLE)
SENPAI, I LOVE YOU!!
BOTH TIED UP IN A RED RIBBON~!
ME, TOO!!
Y- YOU GOT SENPAI...
...REEEALLY EXCITED NOW.
ハアー〜
HAA
ハアー〜
HAA
SFX: DOKI DOKI (THADUMP THADUMP)
はぁ
HAA
SEN... PAI... HURRY...
はぁ
HAA
HERE IT COOOO-OOMES!!
HAA
はぁ
I... I...
...CAN'T... HOLD...
はぁ
HAA
ドキドキ
HAA
はぁ
...BACK... ANY... LONGER.
SFX: GYUU (SQUEEZE)
R–RUN...
にゅっ
CAUGHT YOU! CAUGHT YOU!
!?
SFX: NIYU (WRIGGLE)

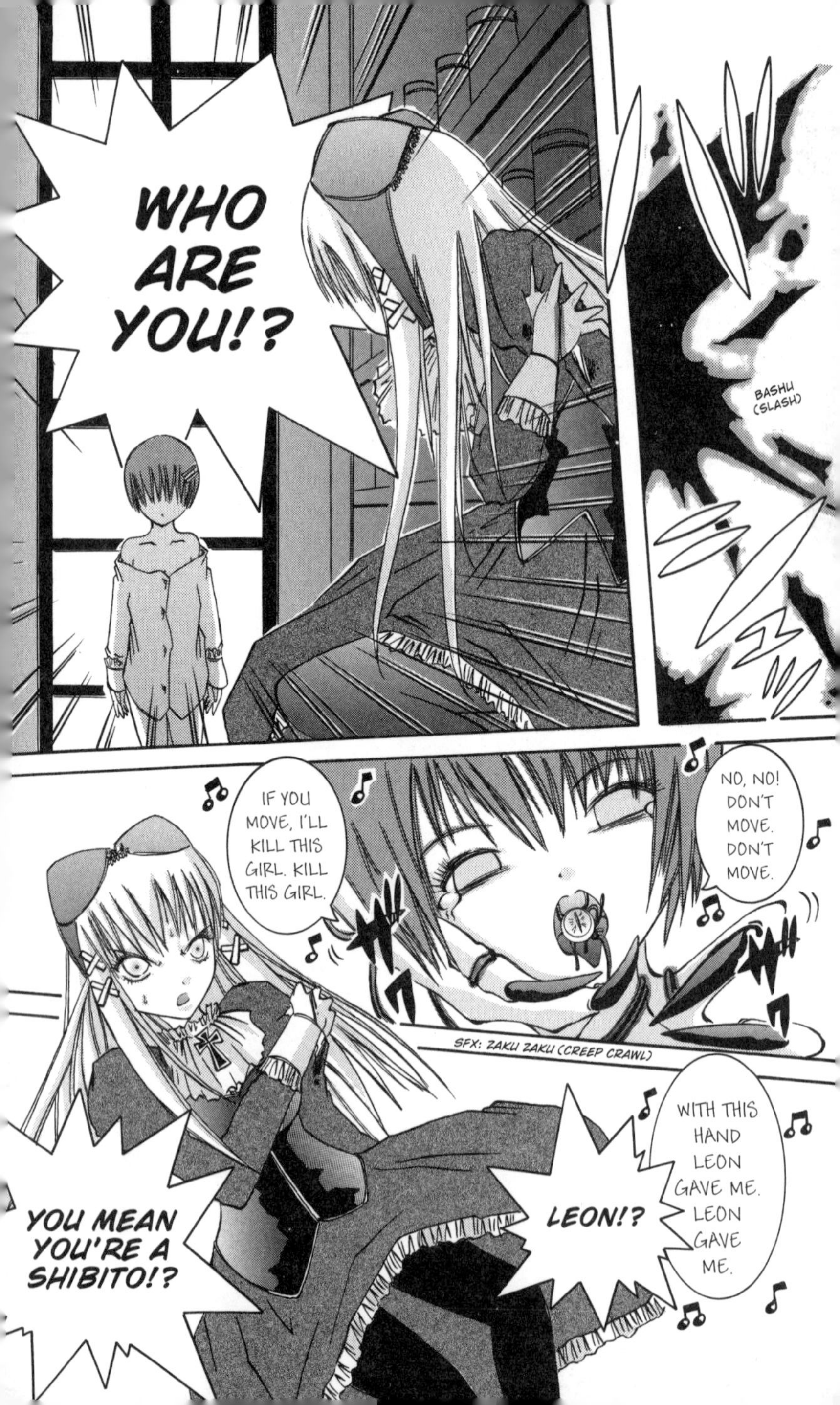
BASHU (SLASH)
WHO ARE YOU!?
NO, NO! DON'T MOVE. DON'T MOVE.
IF YOU MOVE, I'LL KILL THIS GIRL. KILL THIS GIRL.
SFX: ZAKU ZAKU (CREEP CRAWL)
WITH THIS HAND LEON GAVE ME. LEON GAVE ME.
LEON!?
YOU MEAN YOU'RE A SHIBITO!?

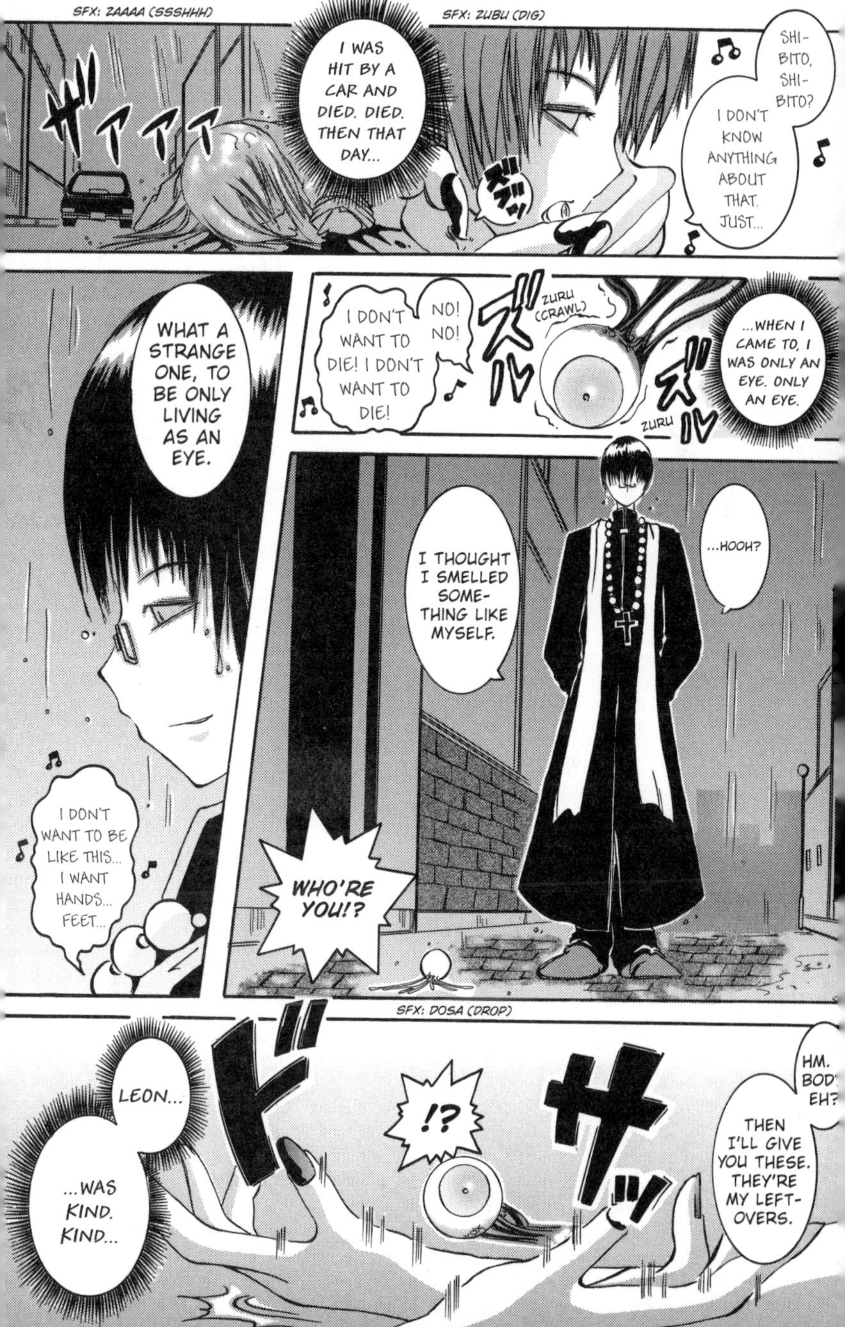
SFX: ZUBU (DIG)
SHI-BITO, SHI-BITO?
I DON'T KNOW ANYTHING ABOUT THAT. JUST...
I WAS HIT BY A CAR AND DIED. DIED. THEN THAT DAY...
SFX: ZAAAA (SSSHHH)
...WHEN I CAME TO, I WAS ONLY AN EYE. ONLY AN EYE.
ZURU
ZURU (CRAWL)
NO! NO!
I DON'T WANT TO DIE! I DON'T WANT TO DIE!
...HOOH?
I THOUGHT I SMELLED SOME-THING LIKE MYSELF.
WHO'RE YOU!?
WHAT A STRANGE ONE, TO BE ONLY LIVING AS AN EYE.
I DON'T WANT TO BE LIKE THIS... I WANT HANDS... FEET...
SFX: DOSA (DROP)
HM. BODY, EH?
THEN I'LL GIVE YOU THESE. THEY'RE MY LEFT-OVERS.
!?
LEON...
...WAS KIND. KIND...

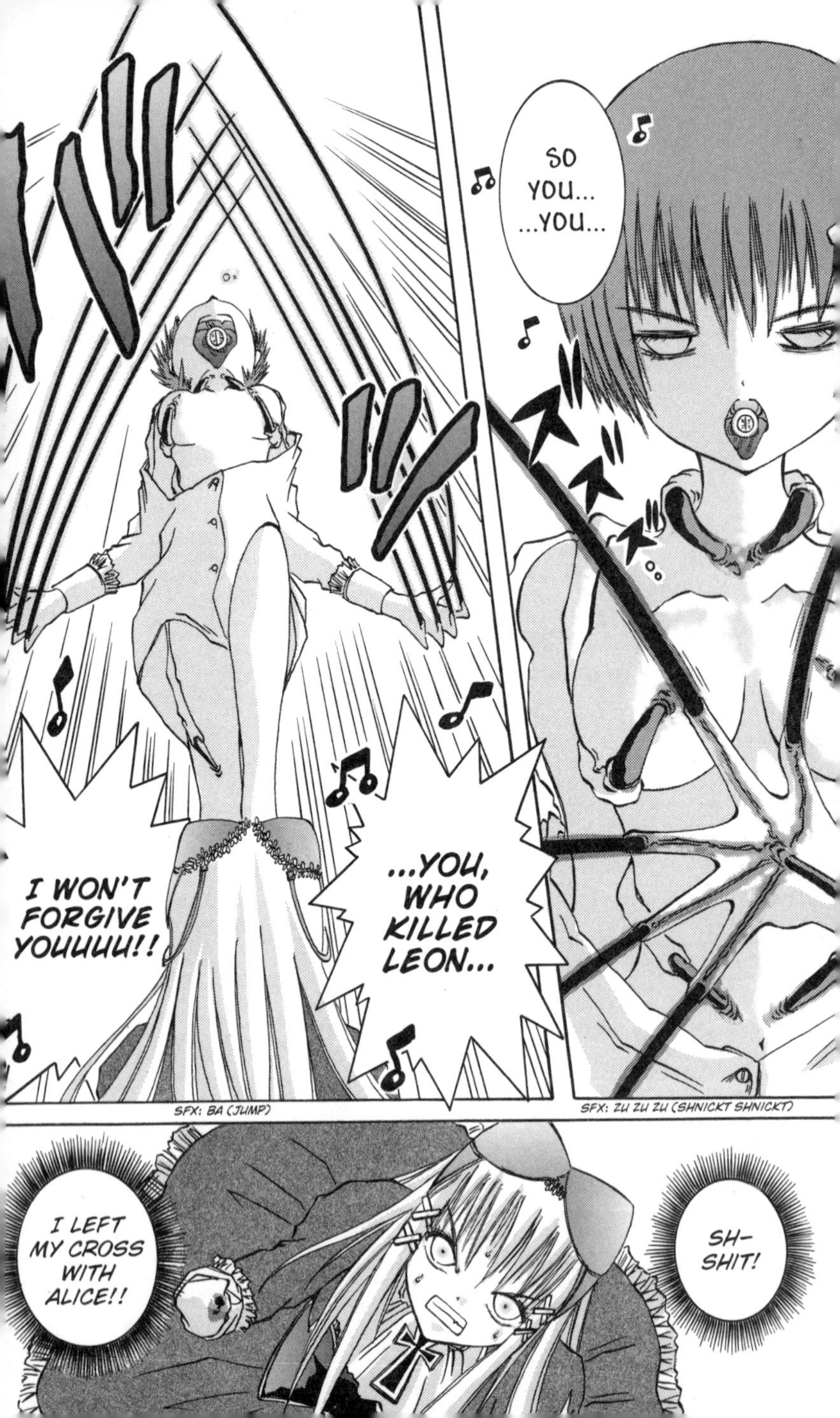
SO YOU... ...YOU...
SFX: ZU ZU ZU (SHNICKT SHNICKT)
...YOU, WHO KILLED LEON...
I WON'T FORGIVE YOUUUU!!
SFX: BA (JUMP)
SH-SHIT!
I LEFT MY CROSS WITH ALICE!!

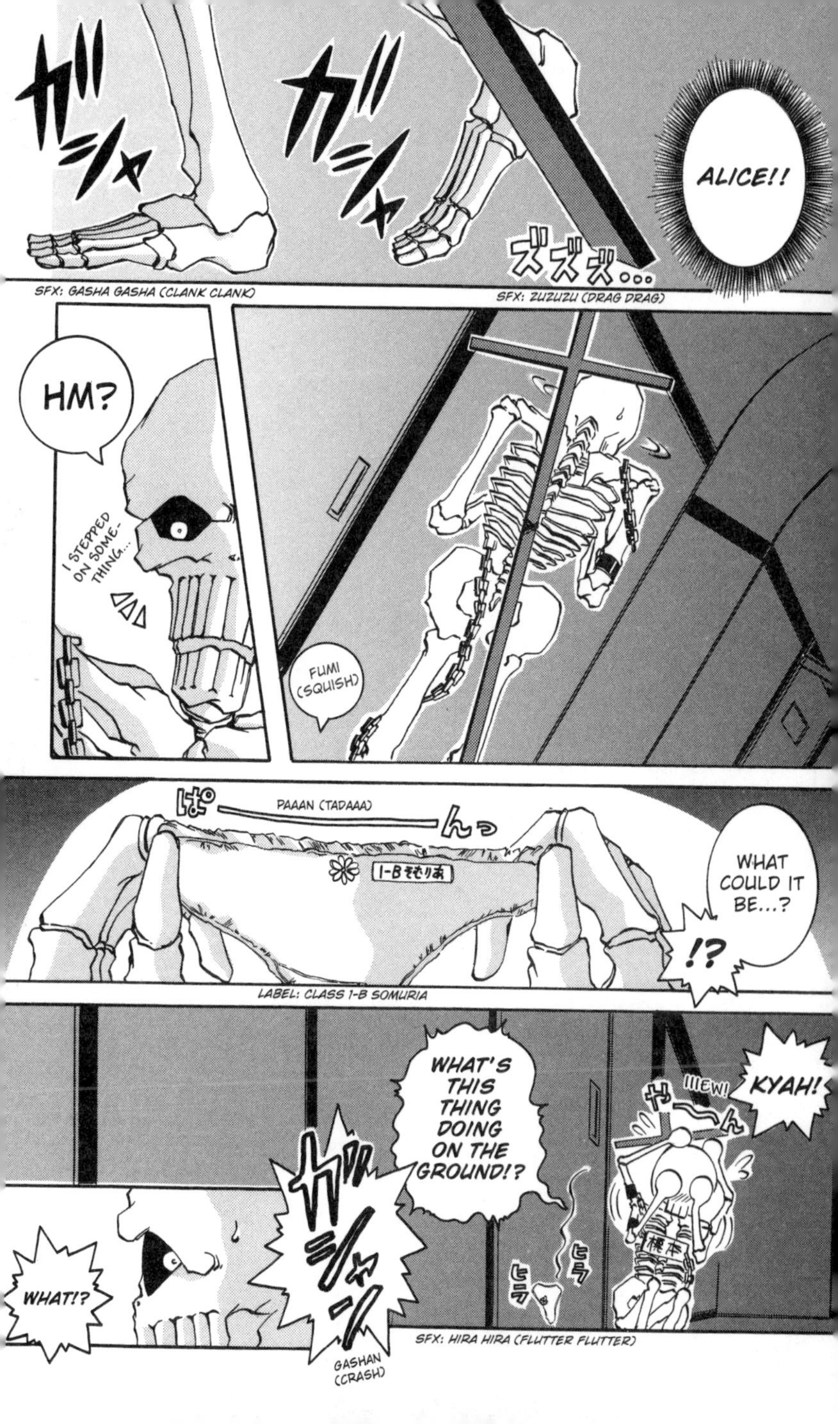
ALICE!!
ズズズ…
ガシャ
ガシャ
SFX: GASHA GASHA (CLANK CLANK)
SFX: ZUZUZU (DRAG DRAG)
FUMI (SQUISH)
HM?
I STEPPED ON SOME-THING...
ぱーんっ
PAAAN (TADAAA)
1-Bそむりあ
WHAT COULD IT BE...?
!?
LABEL: CLASS 1-B SOMURIA
KYAH!
IIIEW!
やーん
標本
ヒラ
ヒラ
SFX: HIRA HIRA (FLUTTER FLUTTER)
WHAT'S THIS THING DOING ON THE GROUND!?
ガシャーン
GASHAN (CRASH)
WHAT!?

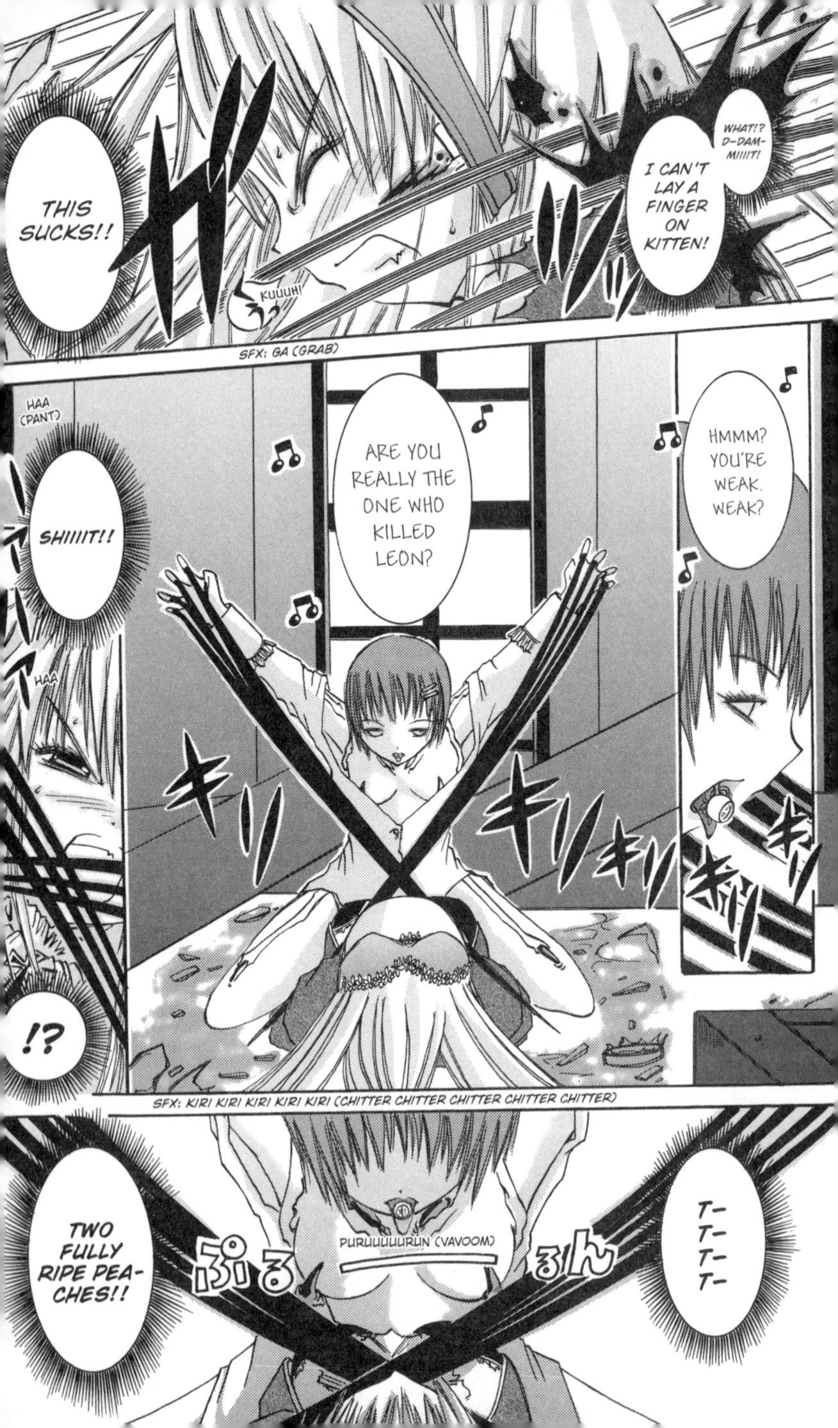
WHAT!? D-DAM-MIIIIT!
I CAN'T LAY A FINGER ON KITTEN!
KUUUH!
THIS SUCKS!!
SFX: GA (GRAB)
HMMM? YOU'RE WEAK. WEAK?
ARE YOU REALLY THE ONE WHO KILLED LEON?
HAA (PANT)
SHIIIIT!!
HAA
!?
SFX: KIRI KIRI KIRI KIRI KIRI (CHITTER CHITTER CHITTER CHITTER CHITTER)
T-T-T-T-
ぷるーるん
PURUUUUURUN (VAVOOM)
TWO FULLY RIPE PEA-CHES!!

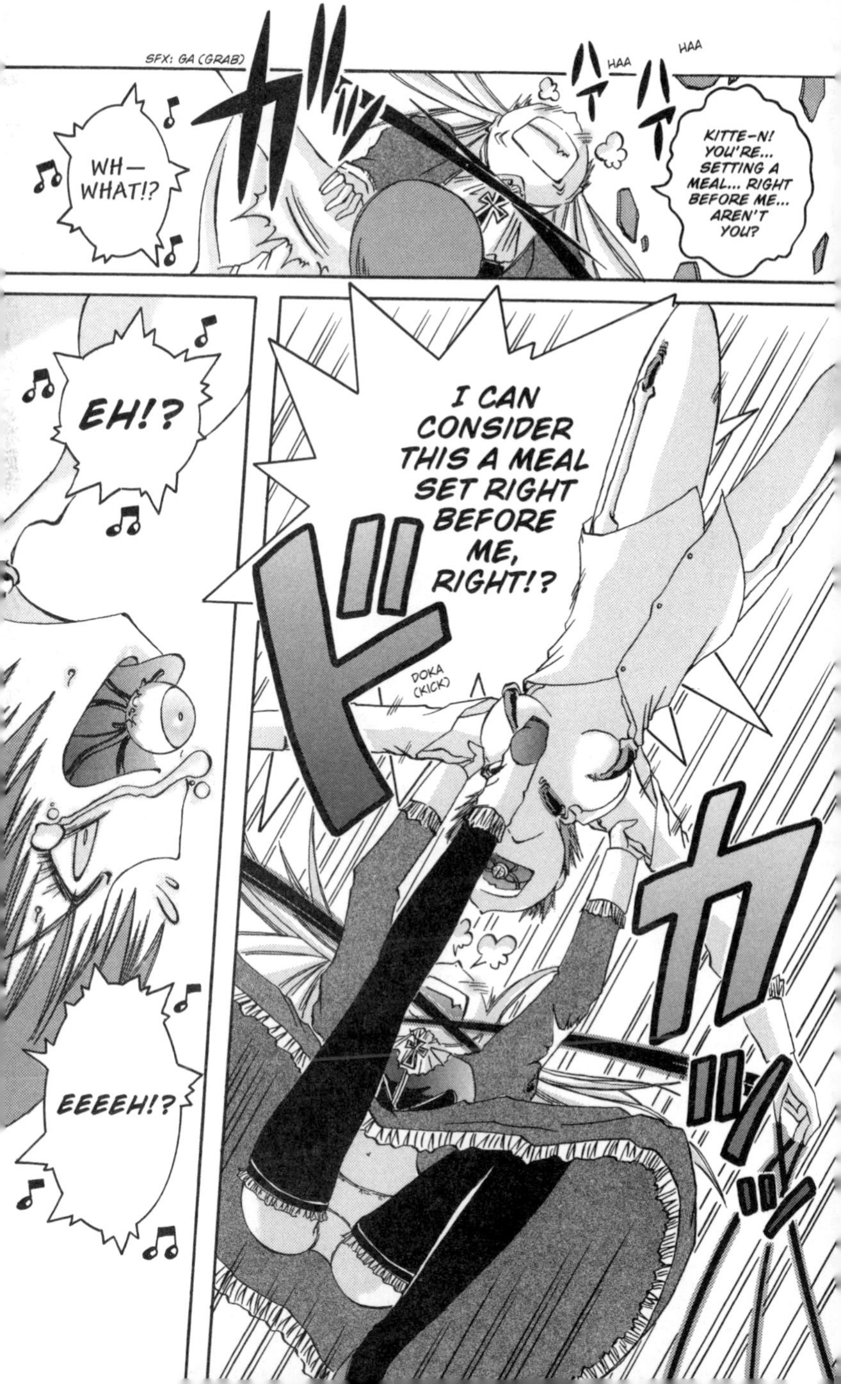
HAA
HAA
KITTE-N! YOU'RE... SETTING A MEAL... RIGHT BEFORE ME... AREN'T YOU?
SFX: GA (GRAB)
WH— WHAT!?
I CAN CONSIDER THIS A MEAL SET RIGHT BEFORE ME, RIGHT!?
DOKA (KICK)
EH!?
EEEEH!?

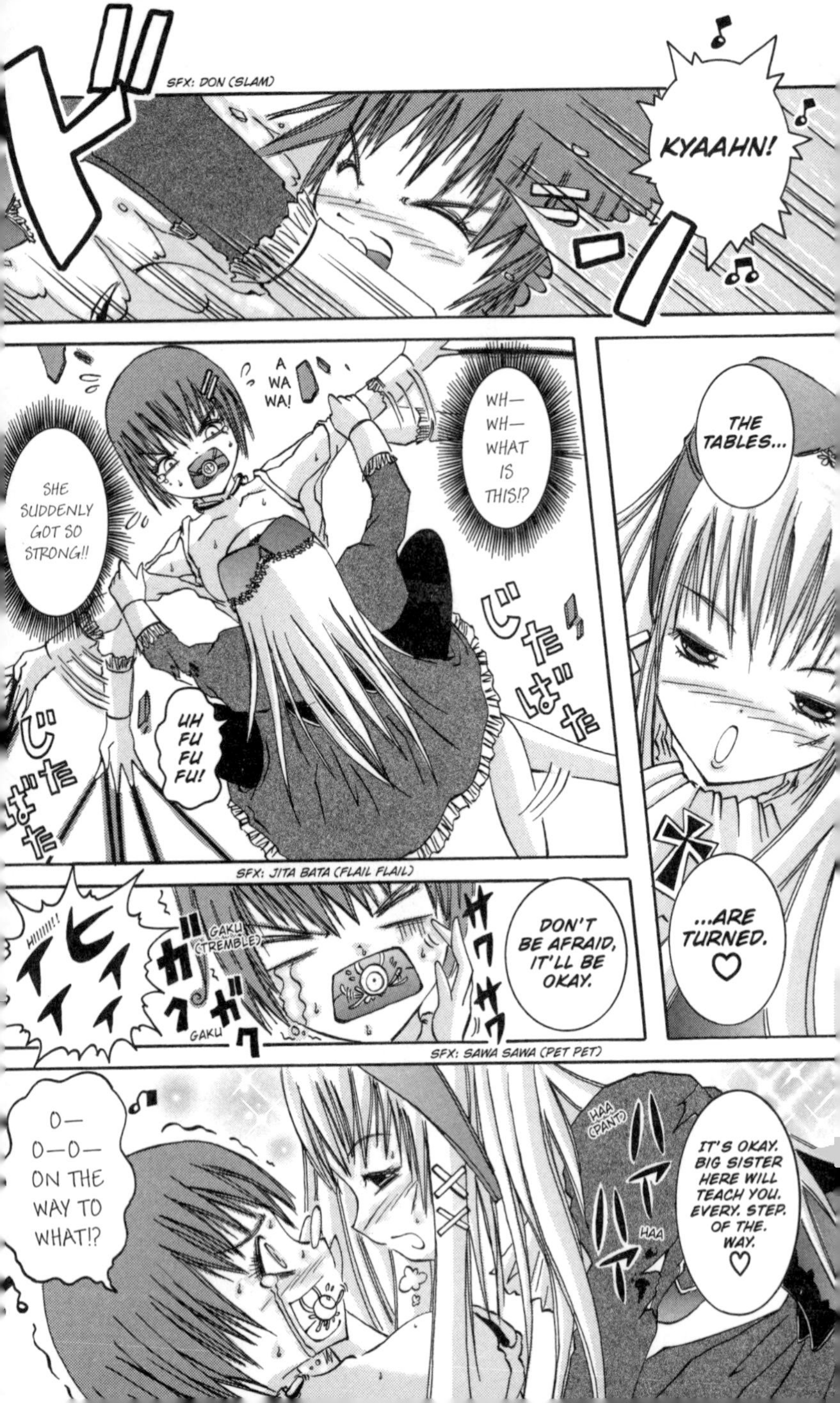
KYAAHN!
SFX: DON (SLAM)
THE TABLES...
...ARE TURNED. ♡
WH— WH— WHAT IS THIS!?
A WA WA!
SHE SUDDENLY GOT SO STRONG!!
UH FU FU FU!
SFX: JITA BATA (FLAIL FLAIL)
DON'T BE AFRAID, IT'LL BE OKAY.
GAKU (TREMBLE)
GAKU
HIIIIII!!
SFX: SAWA SAWA (PET PET)
IT'S OKAY. BIG SISTER HERE WILL TEACH YOU. EVERY. STEP. OF THE. WAY. ♡
HAA (PANT)
HAA
O— O—O— ON THE WAY TO WHAT!?

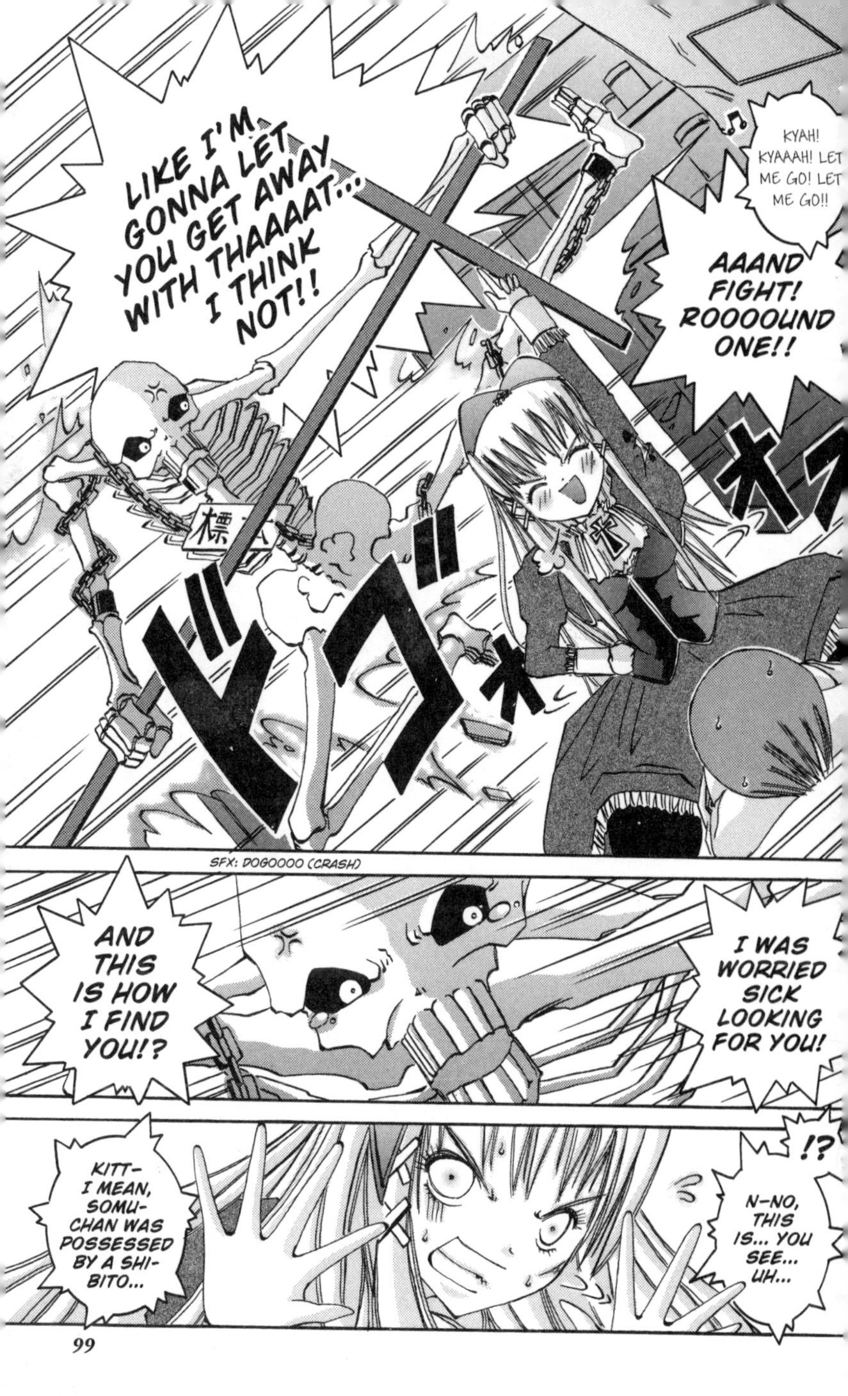
KYAH! KYAAAH! LET ME GO! LET ME GO!!
AAAND FIGHT! ROOOOUND ONE!!
LIKE I'M GONNA LET YOU GET AWAY WITH THAAAAT... I THINK NOT!!
SFX: DOGOOOO (CRASH)
I WAS WORRIED SICK LOOKING FOR YOU!
AND THIS IS HOW I FIND YOU!?
!?
N-NO, THIS IS... YOU SEE... UH...
KITT- I MEAN, SOMU-CHAN WAS POSSESSED BY A SHIBITO...

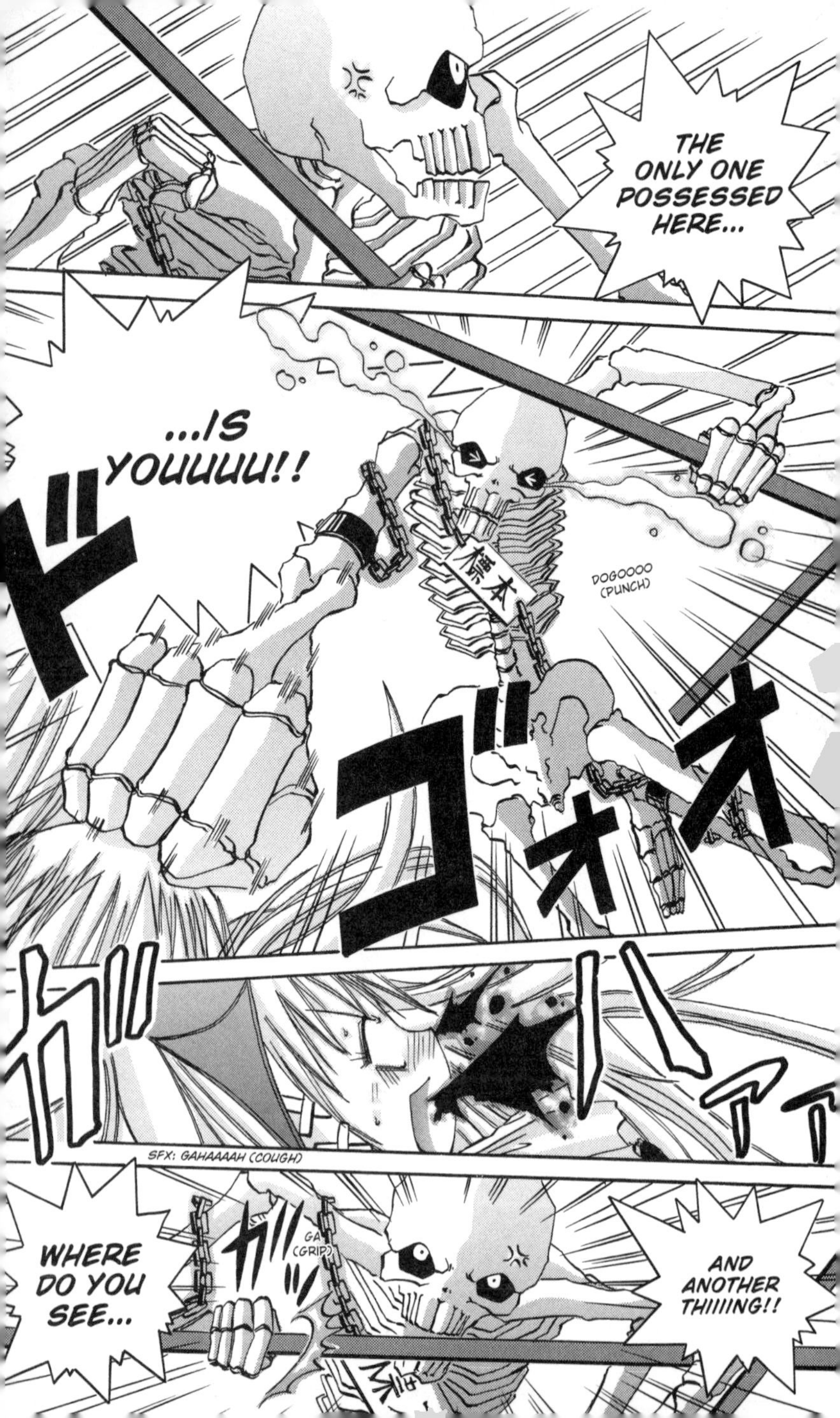
THE ONLY ONE POSSESSED HERE...
...IS YOUUUUU!!
標本
DOGOOOO (PUNCH)
SFX: GAHAAAAH (COUGH)
AND ANOTHER THIIIING!!
GA (GRIP)
WHERE DO YOU SEE...

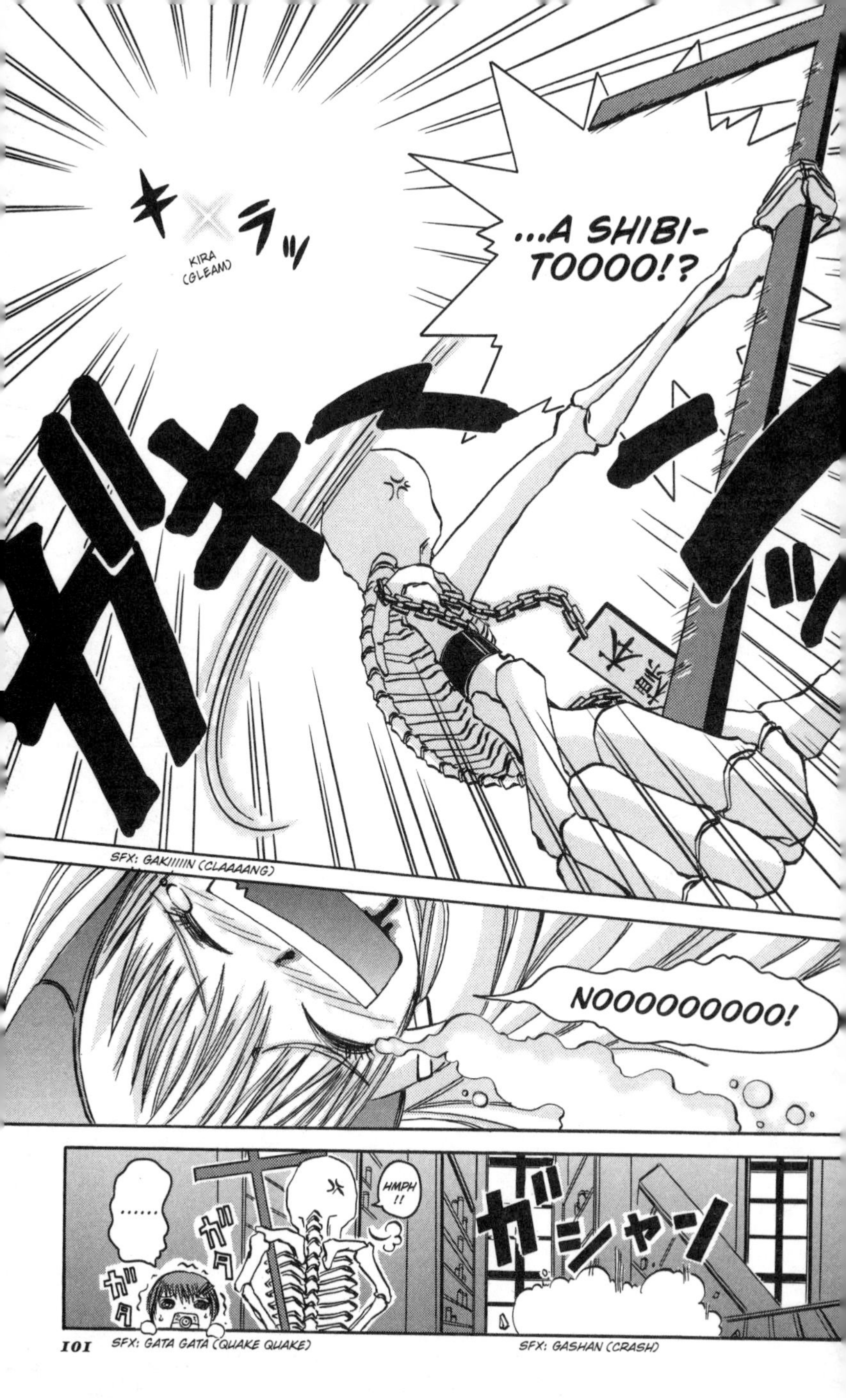
...A SHIBI-TOOOO!?
KIRA (GLEAM)
SFX: GAKIIIIIN (CLAAAANG)
NOOOOOOOOO!
SFX: GASHAN (CRASH)
HMPH !!
......
SFX: GATA GATA (QUAKE QUAKE)

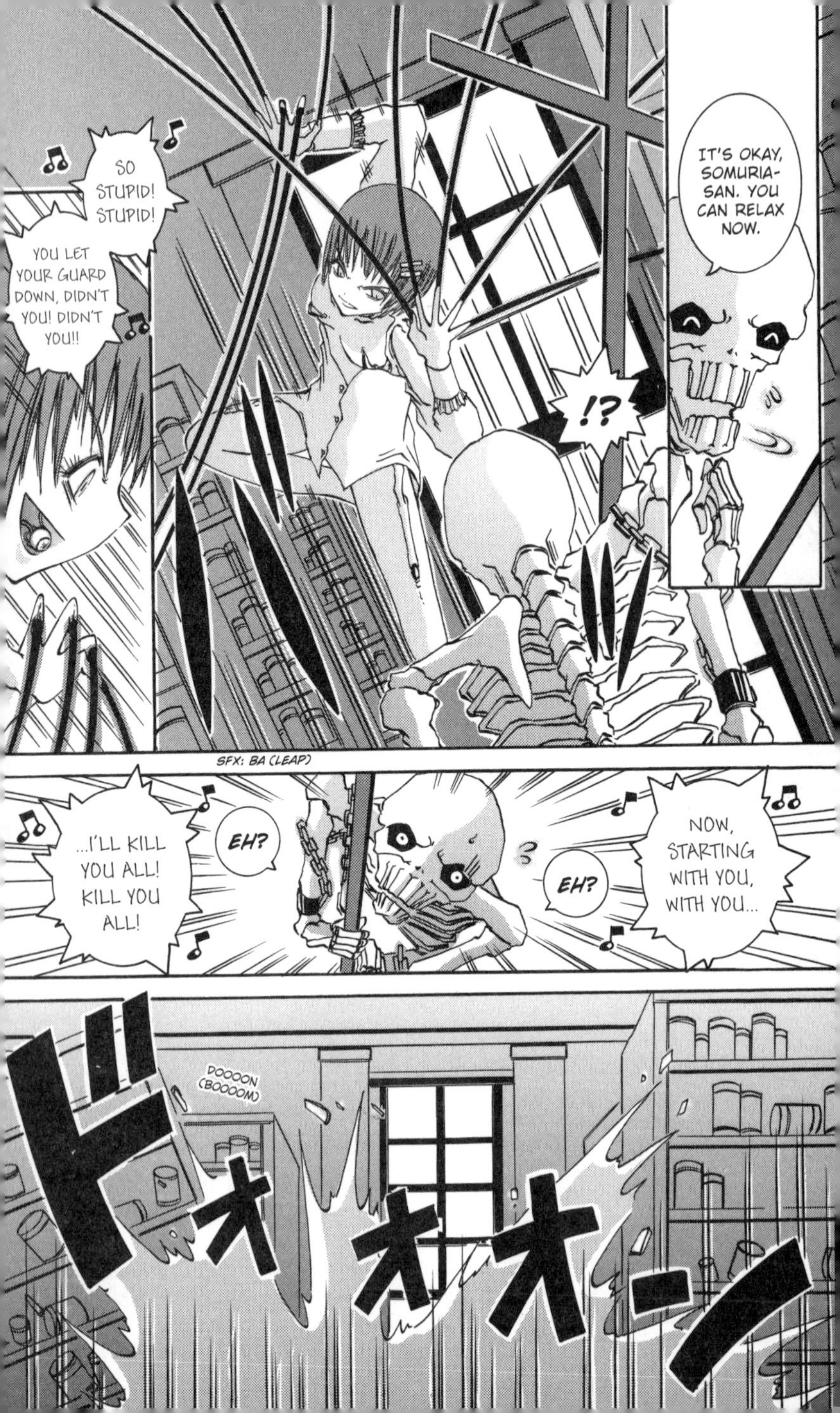
IT'S OKAY, SOMURIA-SAN. YOU CAN RELAX NOW.
!?
SO STUPID! STUPID!
YOU LET YOUR GUARD DOWN, DIDN'T YOU! DIDN'T YOU!!
SFX: BA (LEAP)
NOW, STARTING WITH YOU, WITH YOU...
EH?
EH?
...I'LL KILL YOU ALL! KILL YOU ALL!
ドオオーン
DOOOON (BOOOOM)

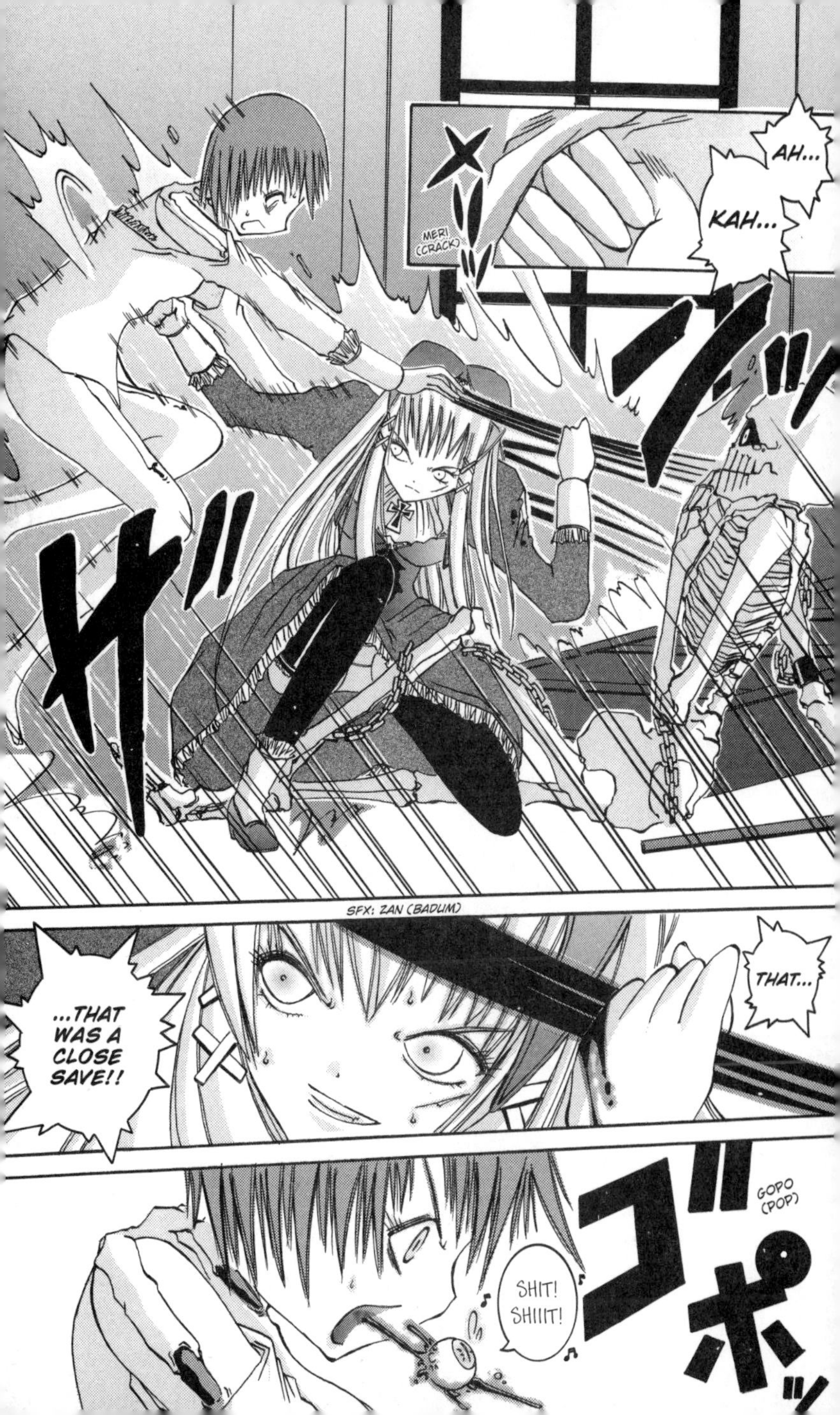
AH...
KAH...
MERI! (CRACK)
SFX: ZAN (BADUM)
THAT...
...THAT WAS A CLOSE SAVE!!
GOPO (POP)
SHIT! SHIIIT!

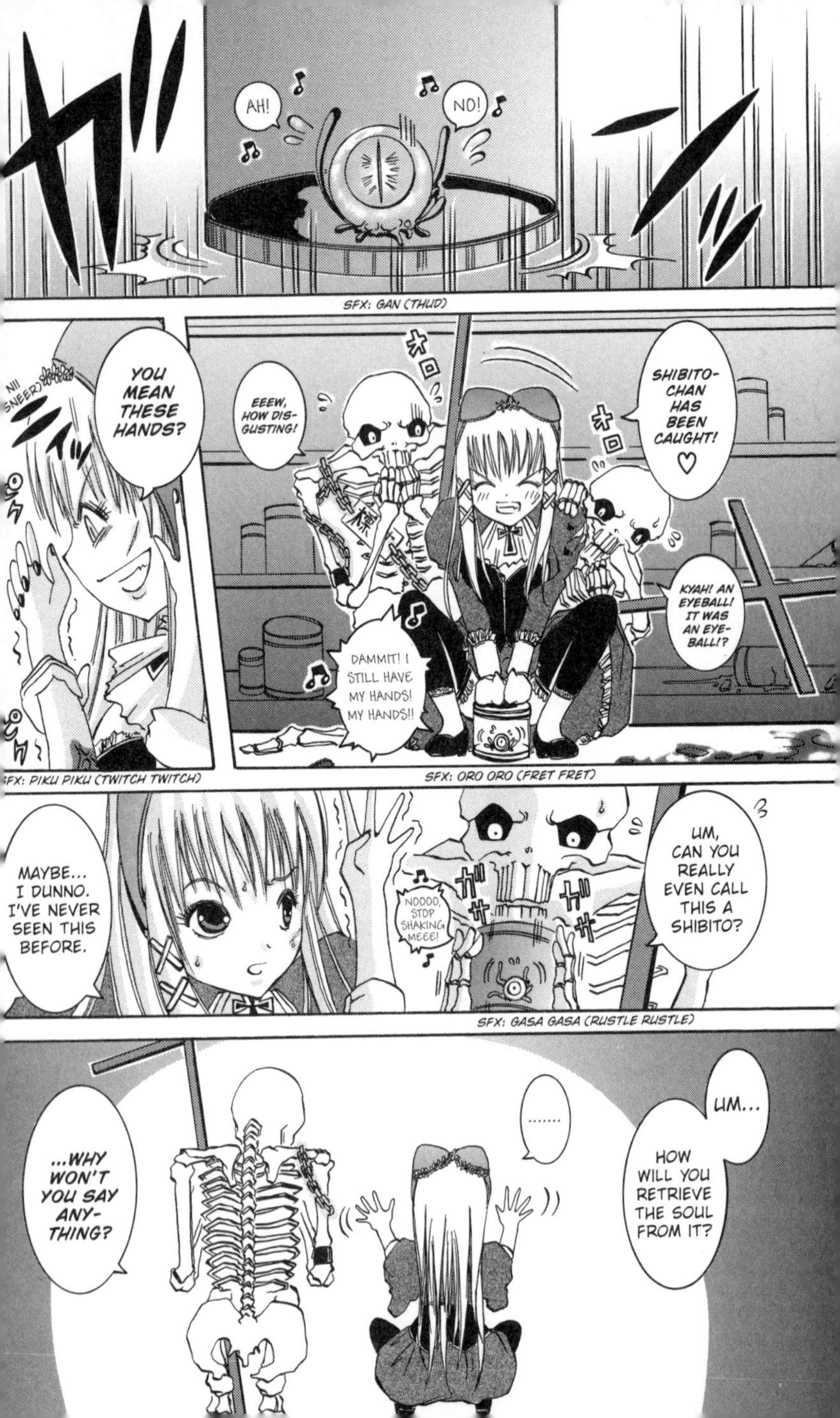
AH!
NO!
SFX: GAN (THUD)
SHIBITO-CHAN HAS BEEN CAUGHT! ♡
KYAH! AN EYEBALL! IT WAS AN EYE-BALL!?
EEEW, HOW DIS-GUSTING!
DAMMIT! I STILL HAVE MY HANDS! MY HANDS!!
SFX: ORO ORO (FRET FRET)
YOU MEAN THESE HANDS?
NII
SNEER)
SFX: PIKU PIKU (TWITCH TWITCH)
UM, CAN YOU REALLY EVEN CALL THIS A SHIBITO?
NOOOO, STOP SHAKING MEEE!
SFX: GASA GASA (RUSTLE RUSTLE)
MAYBE... I DUNNO. I'VE NEVER SEEN THIS BEFORE.
UM...
HOW WILL YOU RETRIEVE THE SOUL FROM IT?
....
...WHY WON'T YOU SAY ANY-THING?

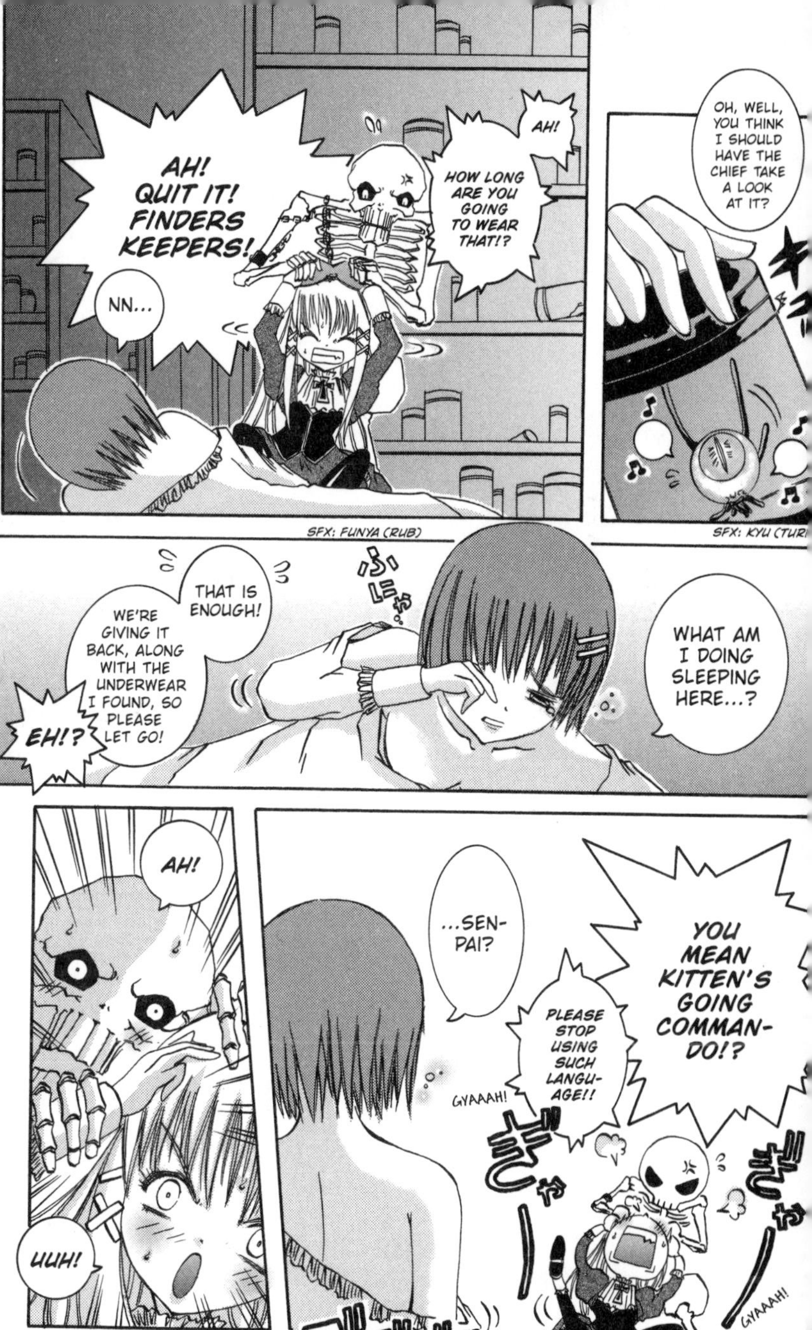
OH, WELL, YOU THINK I SHOULD HAVE THE CHIEF TAKE A LOOK AT IT?
SFX: KYU (TUR
AH!
HOW LONG ARE YOU GOING TO WEAR THAT!?
AH! QUIT IT! FINDERS KEEPERS!
NN...
SFX: FUNYA (RUB)
WHAT AM I DOING SLEEPING HERE...?
THAT IS ENOUGH!
WE'RE GIVING IT BACK, ALONG WITH THE UNDERWEAR I FOUND, SO PLEASE LET GO!
EH!?
YOU MEAN KITTEN'S GOING COMMAN-DO!?
...SEN-PAI?
PLEASE STOP USING SUCH LANGU-AGE!!
GYAAAH!
GYAAAH!
ZU ZU ZU ZU (SSSSSLIP)
AH!
UUH!

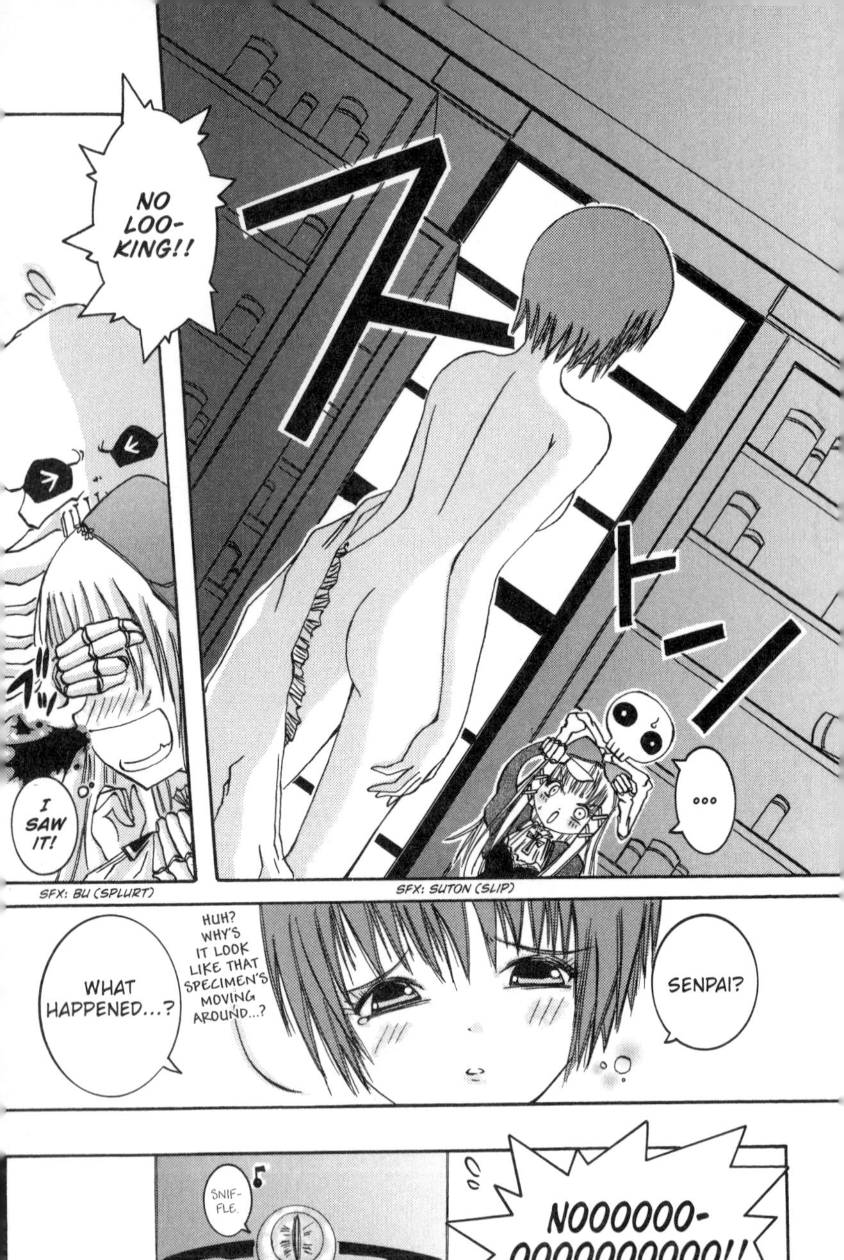
...
SFX: SUTON (SLIP)
NO LOO-KING!!
I SAW IT!
SFX: BU (SPLURT)
SENPAI?
HUH? WHY'S IT LOOK LIKE THAT SPECIMEN'S MOVING AROUND...?
WHAT HAPPENED...?
NOOOOOO-OOOOOOOOOO!!
SNIF-FLE.

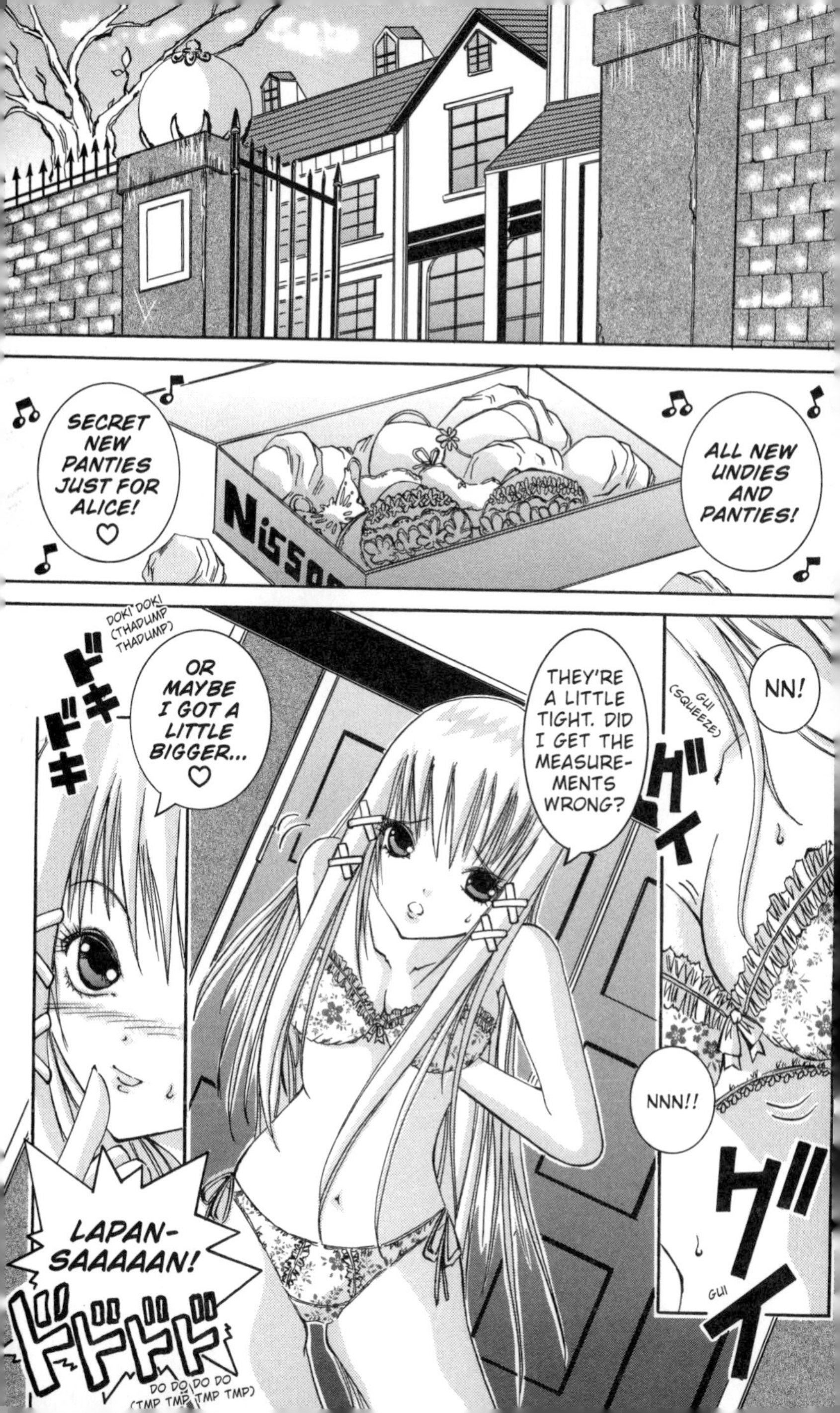
ALL NEW UNDIES AND PANTIES!
SECRET NEW PANTIES JUST FOR ALICE! ♡
NN!
GUI (SQUEEZE)
グイ
NNN!!
グイ
GUI
THEY'RE A LITTLE TIGHT. DID I GET THE MEASUREMENTS WRONG?
OR MAYBE I GOT A LITTLE BIGGER... ♡
DOKI DOKI (THADUMP THADUMP)
ドキドキ
LAPAN-SAAAAAN!
ドドドド
DO DO DO DO (TMP TMP TMP TMP)

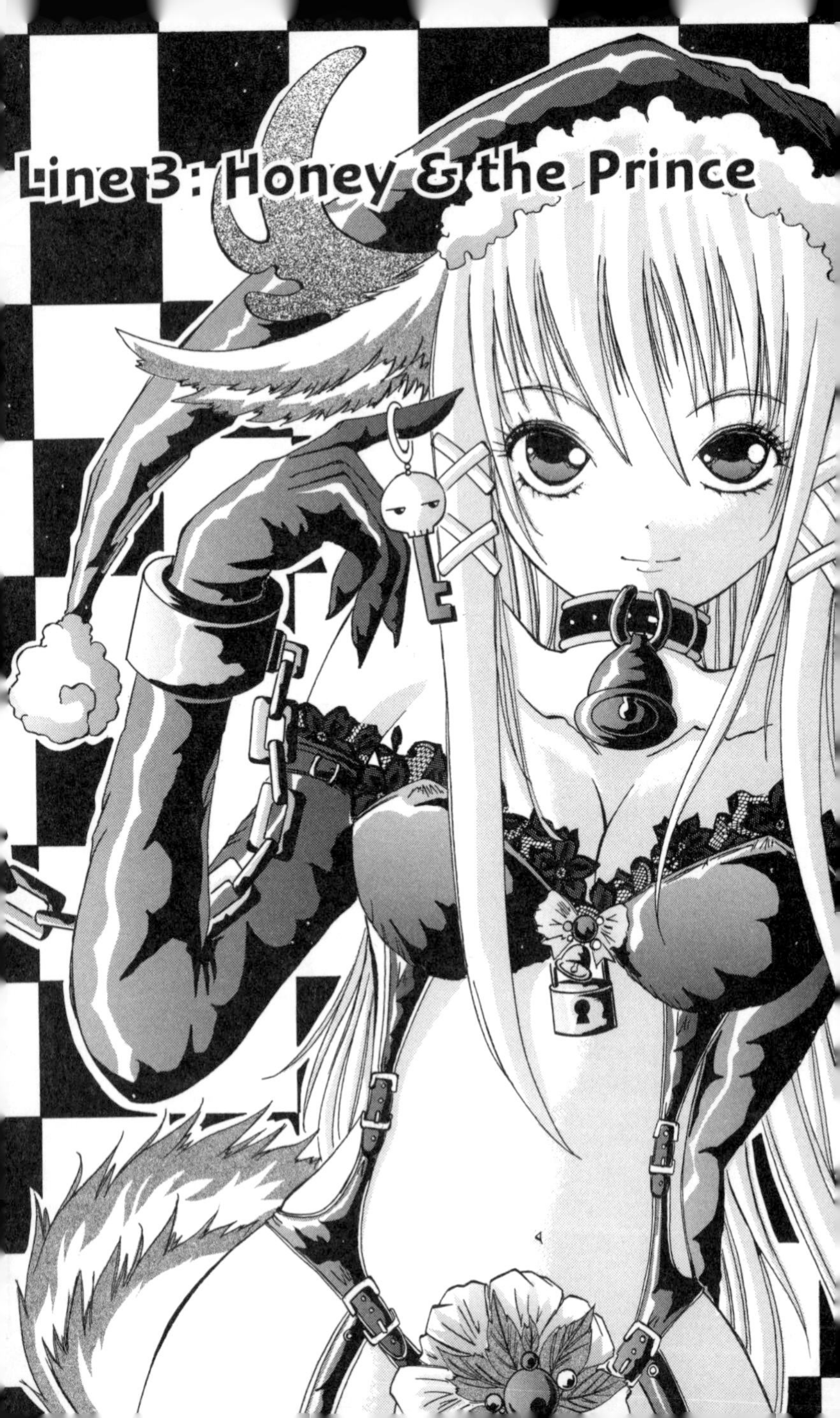
Line 3: Honey & the Prince

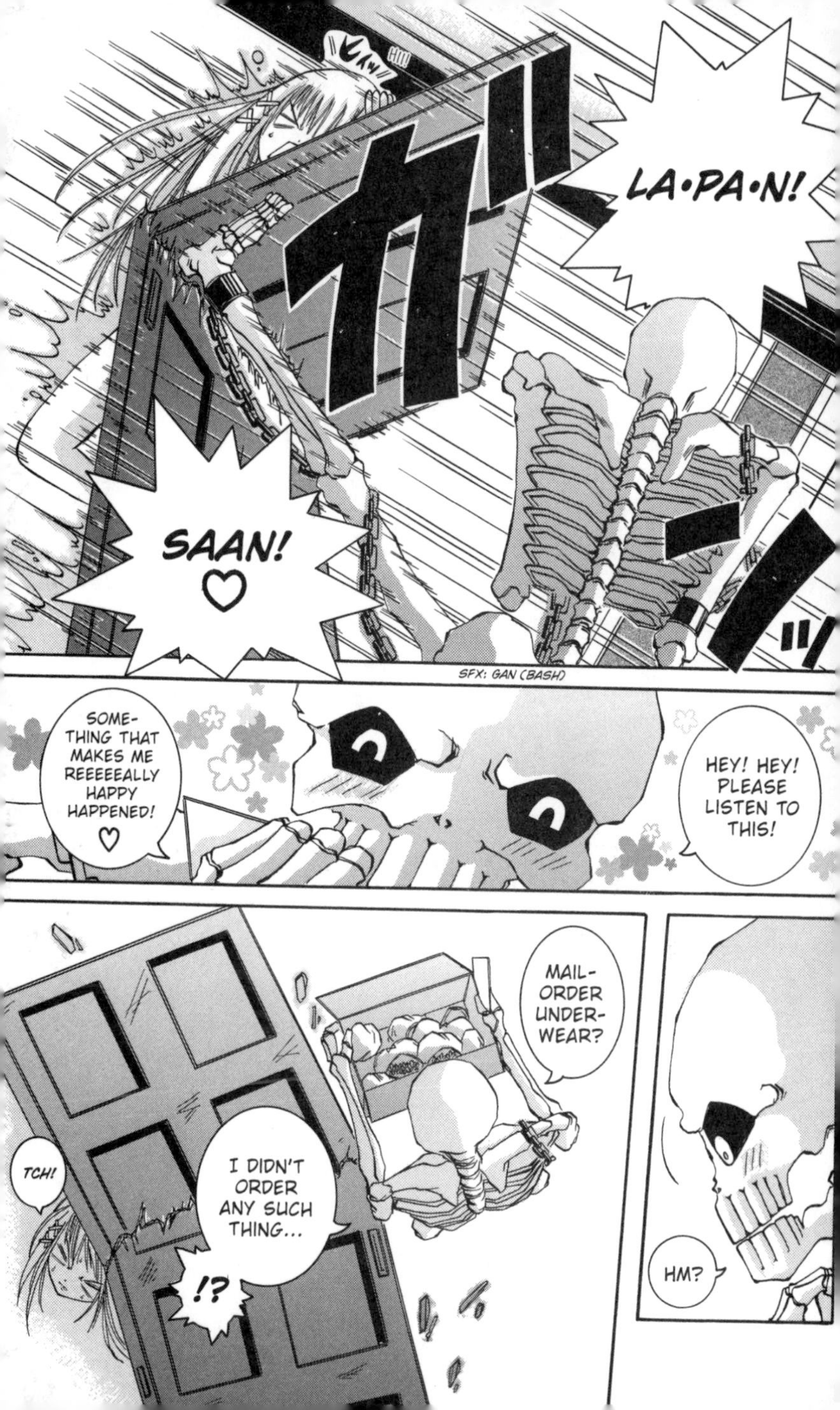
LA•PA•N!
SAAN! ♡
SFX: GAN (BASH)
HEY! HEY! PLEASE LISTEN TO THIS!
SOME-THING THAT MAKES ME REEEEEALLY HAPPY HAPPENED! ♡
HM?
MAIL-ORDER UNDER-WEAR?
I DIDN'T ORDER ANY SUCH THING...
!?
TCH!

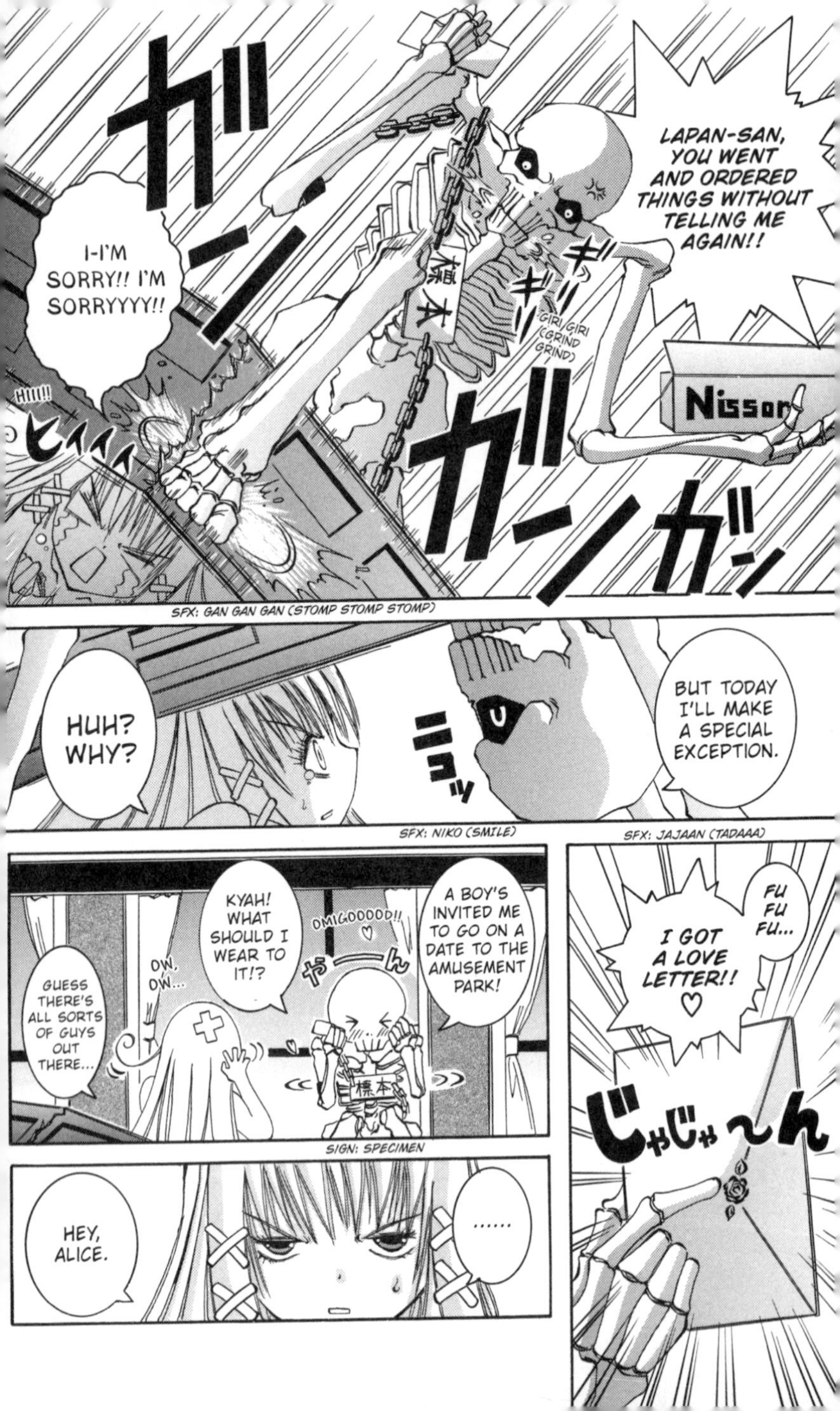

LAPAN-SAN, YOU WENT AND ORDERED THINGS WITHOUT TELLING ME AGAIN!!
GIRI GIRI (GRIND GRIND)
Nisson
標本
I-I'M SORRY!! I'M SORRYYYY!!
HIII!!
SFX: GAN GAN GAN (STOMP STOMP STOMP)
BUT TODAY I'LL MAKE A SPECIAL EXCEPTION.
HUH? WHY?
SFX: NIKO (SMILE)
SFX: JAJAAN (TADAAA)
FU FU FU...
I GOT A LOVE LETTER!! ♡
じゃじゃ～ん
A BOY'S INVITED ME TO GO ON A DATE TO THE AMUSEMENT PARK!
OMIGOOOOD!! ♡
やーん
KYAH! WHAT SHOULD I WEAR TO IT!?
OW. OW...
GUESS THERE'S ALL SORTS OF GUYS OUT THERE...
標本
SIGN: SPECIMEN
......
HEY, ALICE.

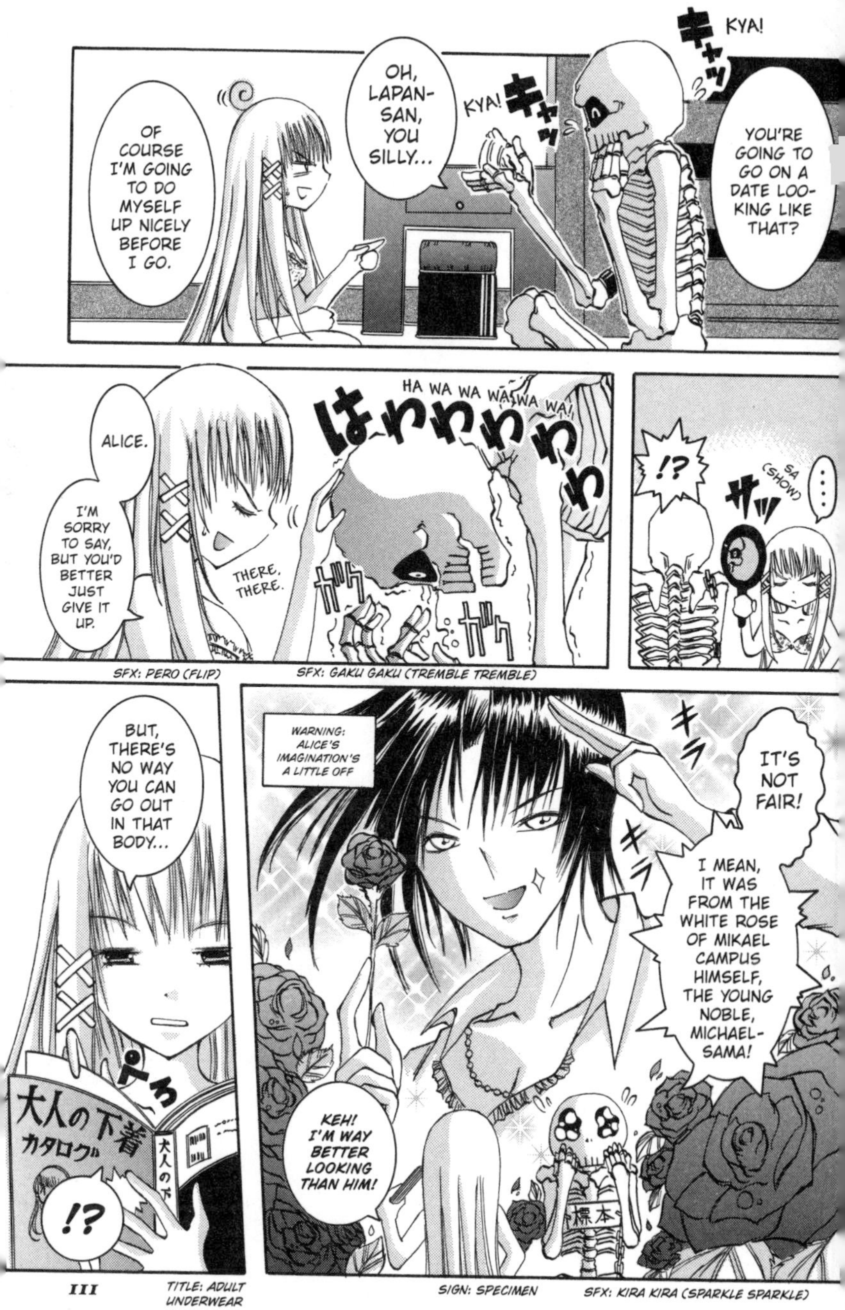
KYA!
KYA!
YOU'RE GOING TO GO ON A DATE LOO-KING LIKE THAT?
OH, LAPAN-SAN, YOU SILLY...
OF COURSE I'M GOING TO DO MYSELF UP NICELY BEFORE I GO.
!?
SA (SHOW)
...
HA WA WA WA WA WA!
ALICE.
I'M SORRY TO SAY, BUT YOU'D BETTER JUST GIVE IT UP.
THERE, THERE.
IT'S NOT FAIR!
I MEAN, IT WAS FROM THE WHITE ROSE OF MIKAEL CAMPUS HIMSELF, THE YOUNG NOBLE, MICHAEL-SAMA!
WARNING: ALICE'S IMAGINATION'S A LITTLE OFF
KEH! I'M WAY BETTER LOOKING THAN HIM!
標本
BUT, THERE'S NO WAY YOU CAN GO OUT IN THAT BODY...
大人の下着
カタログ
大人の
!?

SFX: PERO (FLIP)

SFX: GAKU GAKU (TREMBLE TREMBLE)

TITLE: ADULT UNDERWEAR CATALOGUE

SIGN: SPECIMEN

SFX: KIRA KIRA (SPARKLE SPARKLE)

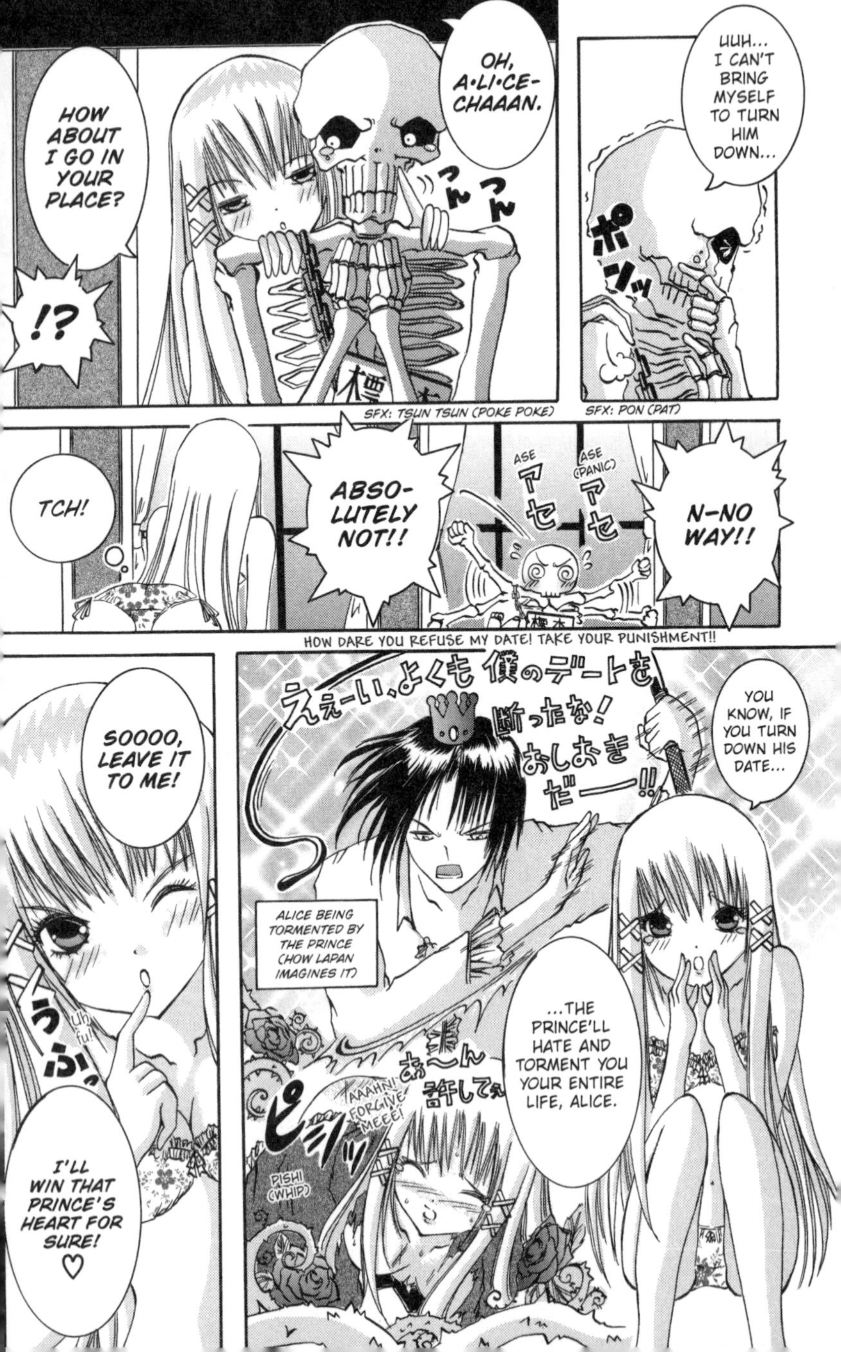
UUH... I CAN'T BRING MYSELF TO TURN HIM DOWN...
ポンッ
SFX: PON (PAT)
OH, A·LI·CE-CHAAAN.
つんつん
HOW ABOUT I GO IN YOUR PLACE?
!?
SFX: TSUN TSUN (POKE POKE)
N-NO WAY!!
ASE アセ
ASE (PANIC) アセ
ABSO-LUTELY NOT!!
TCH!
YOU KNOW, IF YOU TURN DOWN HIS DATE...
えぇーい、よくも僕のデートを断ったな！おしおきだーー!!
HOW DARE YOU REFUSE MY DATE! TAKE YOUR PUNISHMENT!!
...THE PRINCE'LL HATE AND TORMENT YOU YOUR ENTIRE LIFE, ALICE.
ALICE BEING TORMENTED BY THE PRINCE (HOW LAPAN IMAGINES IT)
あ〜ん許してぇ
AAAHN! FORGIVE MEEE!
ピシッ
PISHI (WHIP)
SOOOO, LEAVE IT TO ME!
うふっ
uh fu!
I'LL WIN THAT PRINCE'S HEART FOR SURE! ♡

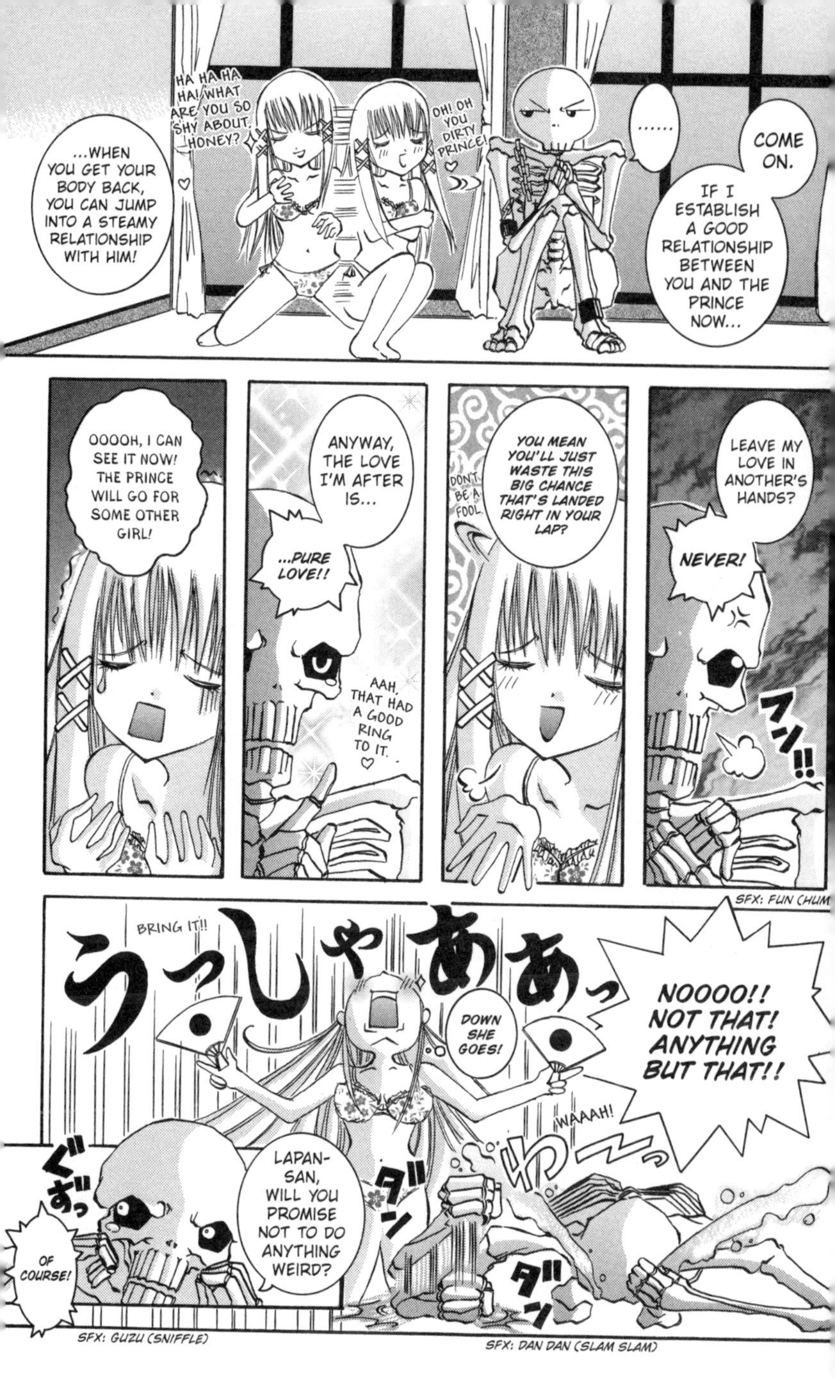
COME ON.
IF I ESTABLISH A GOOD RELATIONSHIP BETWEEN YOU AND THE PRINCE NOW...
......
OH! OH YOU DIRTY PRINCE!
HA HA HA HA! WHAT ARE YOU SO SHY ABOUT, HONEY?
...WHEN YOU GET YOUR BODY BACK, YOU CAN JUMP INTO A STEAMY RELATIONSHIP WITH HIM!
LEAVE MY LOVE IN ANOTHER'S HANDS?
NEVER!
フンッ!!
SFX: FUN (HUM
YOU MEAN YOU'LL JUST WASTE THIS BIG CHANCE THAT'S LANDED RIGHT IN YOUR LAP?
DON'T BE A FOOL.
ANYWAY, THE LOVE I'M AFTER IS...
...PURE LOVE!!
AAH, THAT HAD A GOOD RING TO IT.
OOOOH, I CAN SEE IT NOW! THE PRINCE WILL GO FOR SOME OTHER GIRL!
NOOOO!! NOT THAT! ANYTHING BUT THAT!!
うっしゃあぁっ
BRING IT!!
DOWN SHE GOES!
わ～～っ
WAAAH!
ダンッ
ダンッ
LAPAN-SAN, WILL YOU PROMISE NOT TO DO ANYTHING WEIRD?
ぐずっ
OF COURSE!
SFX: GUZU (SNIFFLE)
SFX: DAN DAN (SLAM SLAM)

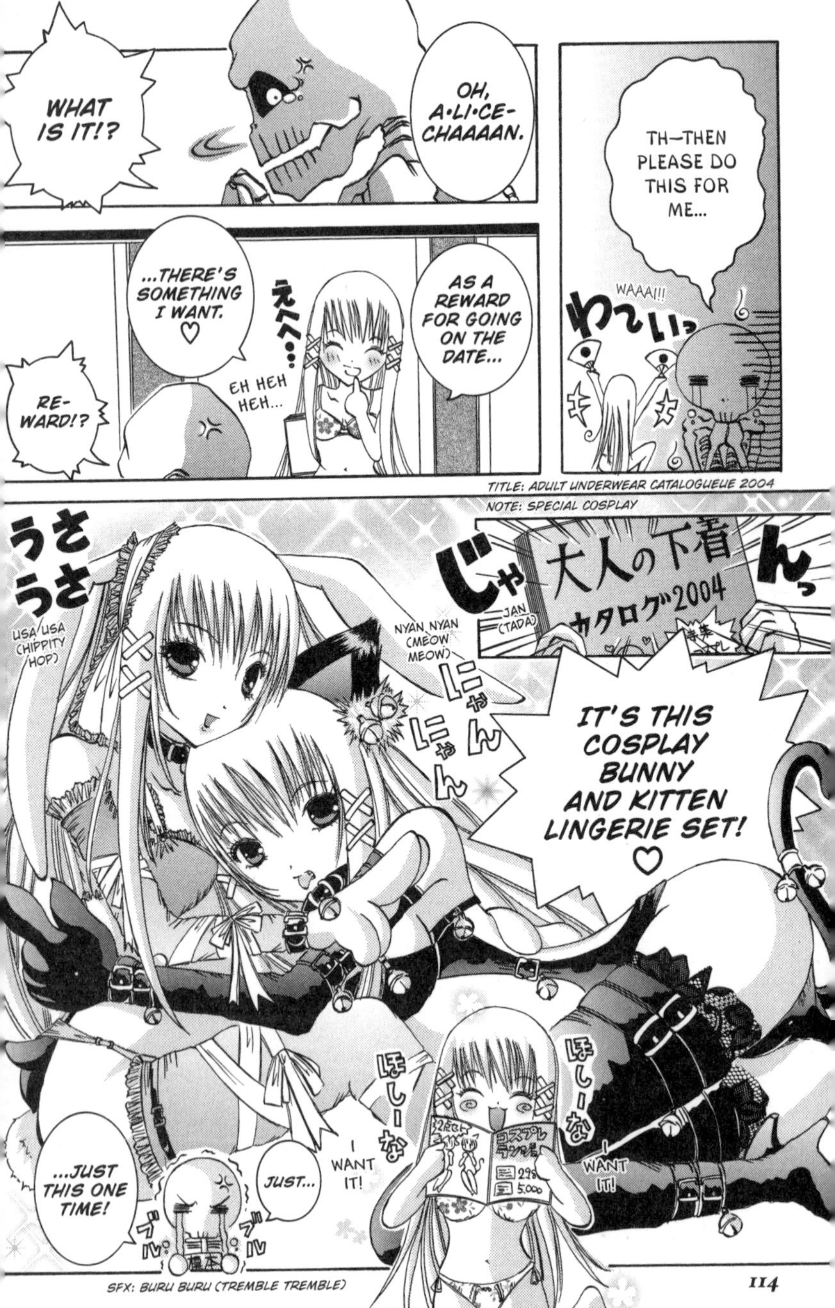
TH—THEN PLEASE DO THIS FOR ME...
わーいっ
WAAAI!!!
OH, A·LI·CE-CHAAAAN.
WHAT IS IT!?
AS A REWARD FOR GOING ON THE DATE...
えへへ…
EH HEH HEH...
...THERE'S SOMETHING I WANT. ♡
RE-WARD!?
TITLE: ADULT UNDERWEAR CATALOGUEUE 2004
NOTE: SPECIAL COSPLAY
じゃーんっ
JAN (TADA)
大人の下着
カタログ2004
うさうさ
USA USA (HIPPITY HOP)
にゃんにゃん
NYAN NYAN (MEOW MEOW)
IT'S THIS COSPLAY BUNNY AND KITTEN LINGERIE SET! ♡
ほしーな
I WANT IT!
ほしーな
I WANT IT!
JUST...
...JUST THIS ONE TIME!
ブルブル
SFX: BURU BURU (TREMBLE TREMBLE)

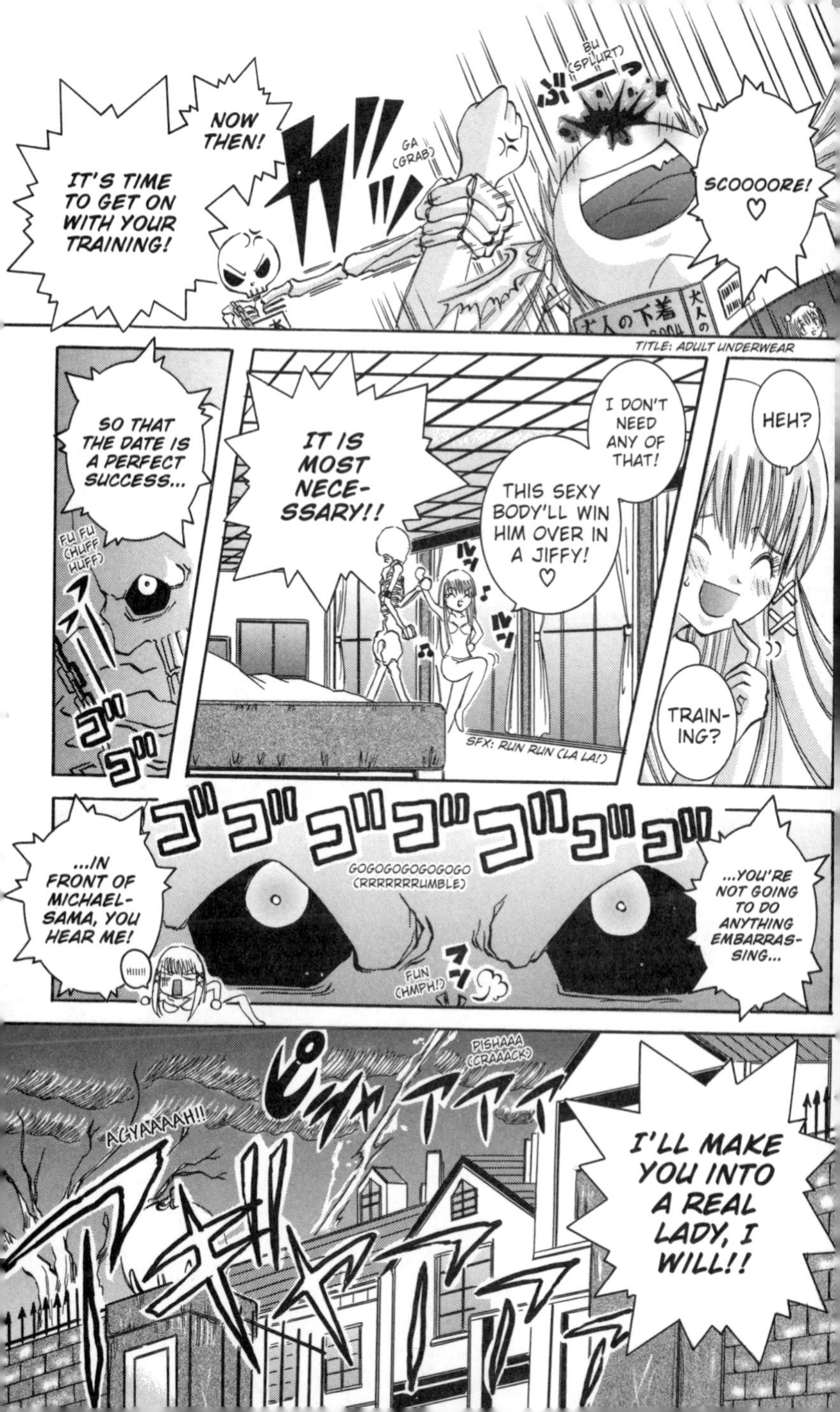
BU (SPLURT)
SCOOOORE! ♡
大人の下着
GA (GRAB)
NOW THEN!
IT'S TIME TO GET ON WITH YOUR TRAINING!
TITLE: ADULT UNDERWEAR
HEH?
TRAIN-ING?
I DON'T NEED ANY OF THAT!
THIS SEXY BODY'LL WIN HIM OVER IN A JIFFY! ♡
IT IS MOST NECE-SSARY!!
SFX: RUN RUN (LA LA!)
SO THAT THE DATE IS A PERFECT SUCCESS...
FU FU (HUFF HUFF)
...YOU'RE NOT GOING TO DO ANYTHING EMBARRAS-SING...
GOGOGOGOGOGOGO (RRRRRRRUMBLE)
FUN (HMPH!)
...IN FRONT OF MICHAEL-SAMA, YOU HEAR ME!
HI!!!!
I'LL MAKE YOU INTO A REAL LADY, I WILL!!
PISHAAA (CRAAACK)
AGYAAAAH!!

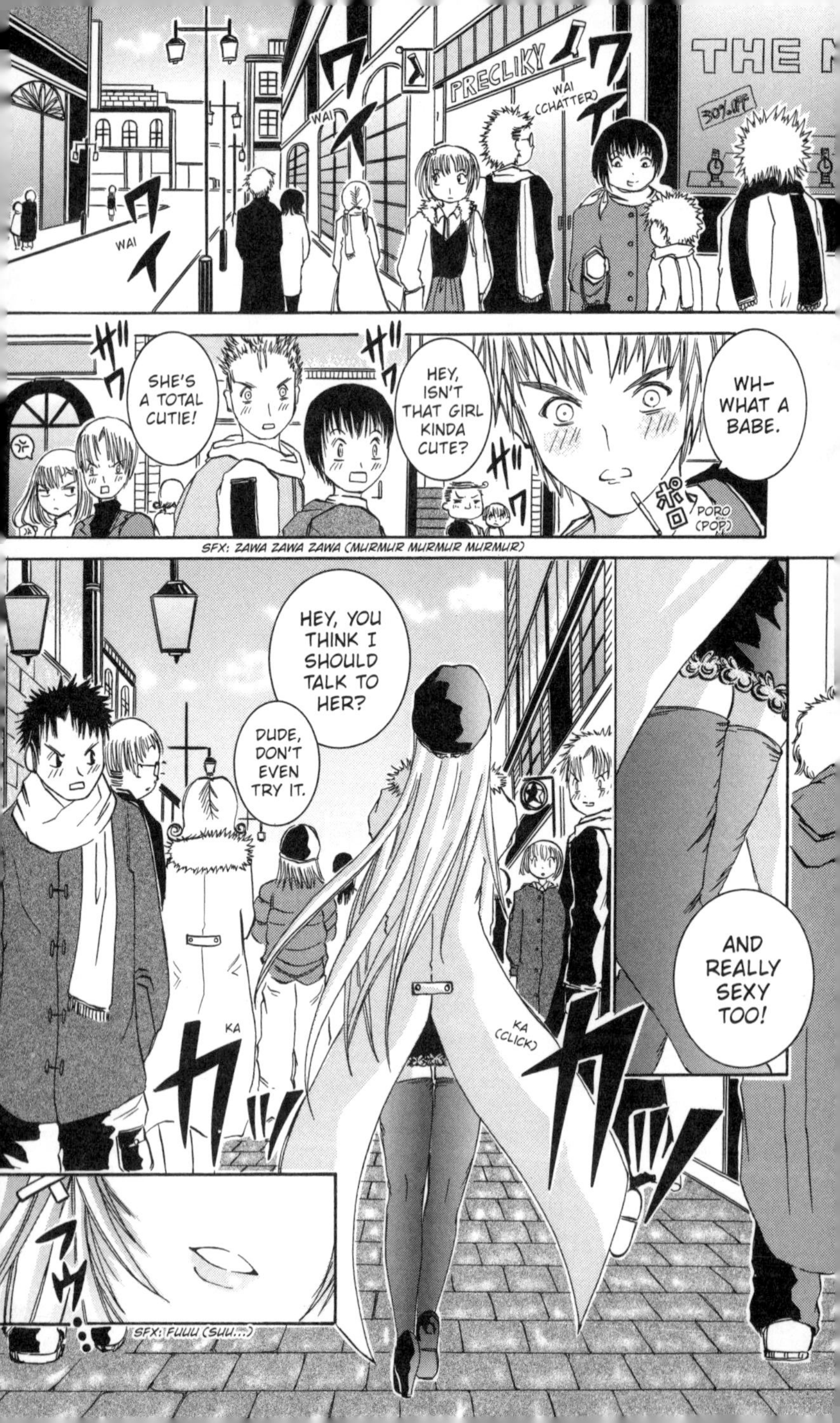
THE M
30% off
PRECLIKY
WAI (CHATTER)
WAI
WAI
WH- WHAT A BABE.
PORO (POP)
HEY, ISN'T THAT GIRL KINDA CUTE?
SHE'S A TOTAL CUTIE!
SFX: ZAWA ZAWA ZAWA (MURMUR MURMUR MURMUR)
AND REALLY SEXY TOO!
HEY, YOU THINK I SHOULD TALK TO HER?
DUDE, DON'T EVEN TRY IT.
KA (CLICK)
KA
SFX: FUUU (SUU...)

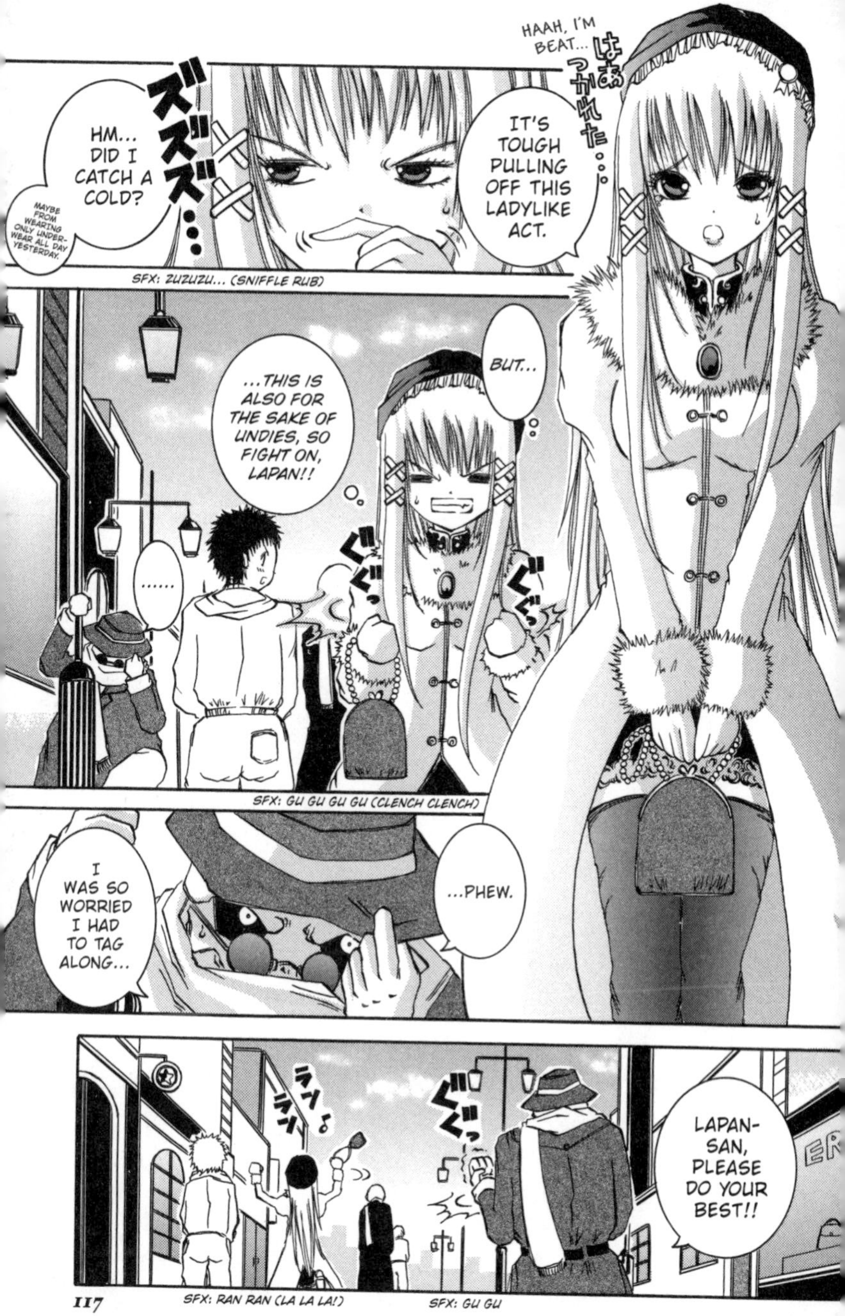
HAAH, I'M BEAT...
はあ つかれた。。。
IT'S TOUGH PULLING OFF THIS LADYLIKE ACT.
HM... DID I CATCH A COLD?
ズズズ...
MAYBE FROM WEARING ONLY UNDERWEAR ALL DAY YESTERDAY.
SFX: ZUZUZU... (SNIFFLE RUB)
BUT...
...THIS IS ALSO FOR THE SAKE OF UNDIES, SO FIGHT ON, LAPAN!!
ぐぐっ
ぐぐっ
......
SFX: GU GU GU GU (CLENCH CLENCH)
...PHEW.
I WAS SO WORRIED I HAD TO TAG ALONG...
LAPAN-SAN, PLEASE DO YOUR BEST!!
ぐぐっ
ランラン♪
SFX: RAN RAN (LA LA LA!)
SFX: GU GU

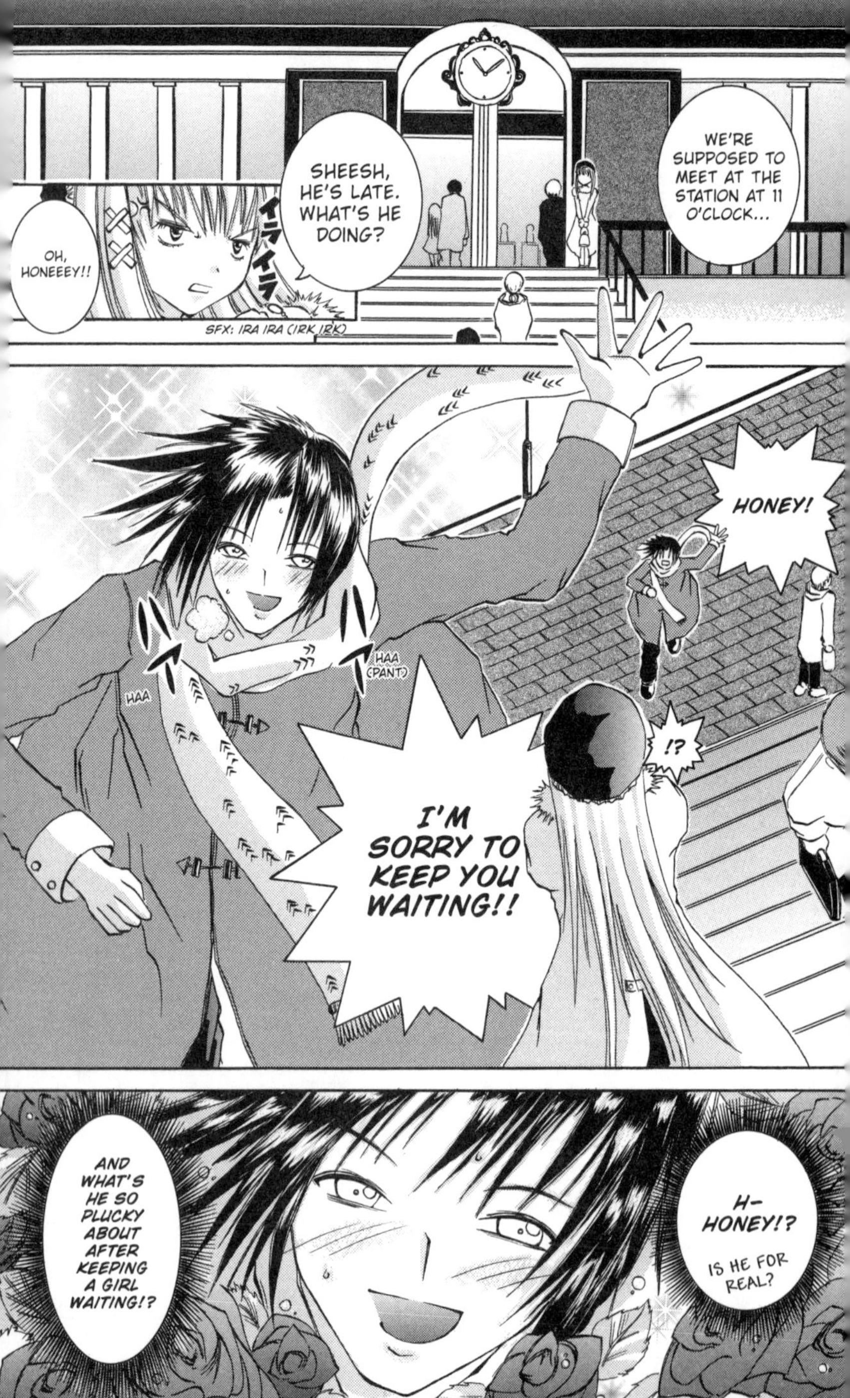
WE'RE SUPPOSED TO MEET AT THE STATION AT 11 O'CLOCK...
SHEESH, HE'S LATE. WHAT'S HE DOING?
イライラ
SFX: IRA IRA (IRK IRK)
OH, HONEEEY!!
HONEY!
!?
I'M SORRY TO KEEP YOU WAITING!!
HAA (PANT)
HAA
H-HONEY!?
IS HE FOR REAL?
AND WHAT'S HE SO PLUCKY ABOUT AFTER KEEPING A GIRL WAITING!?

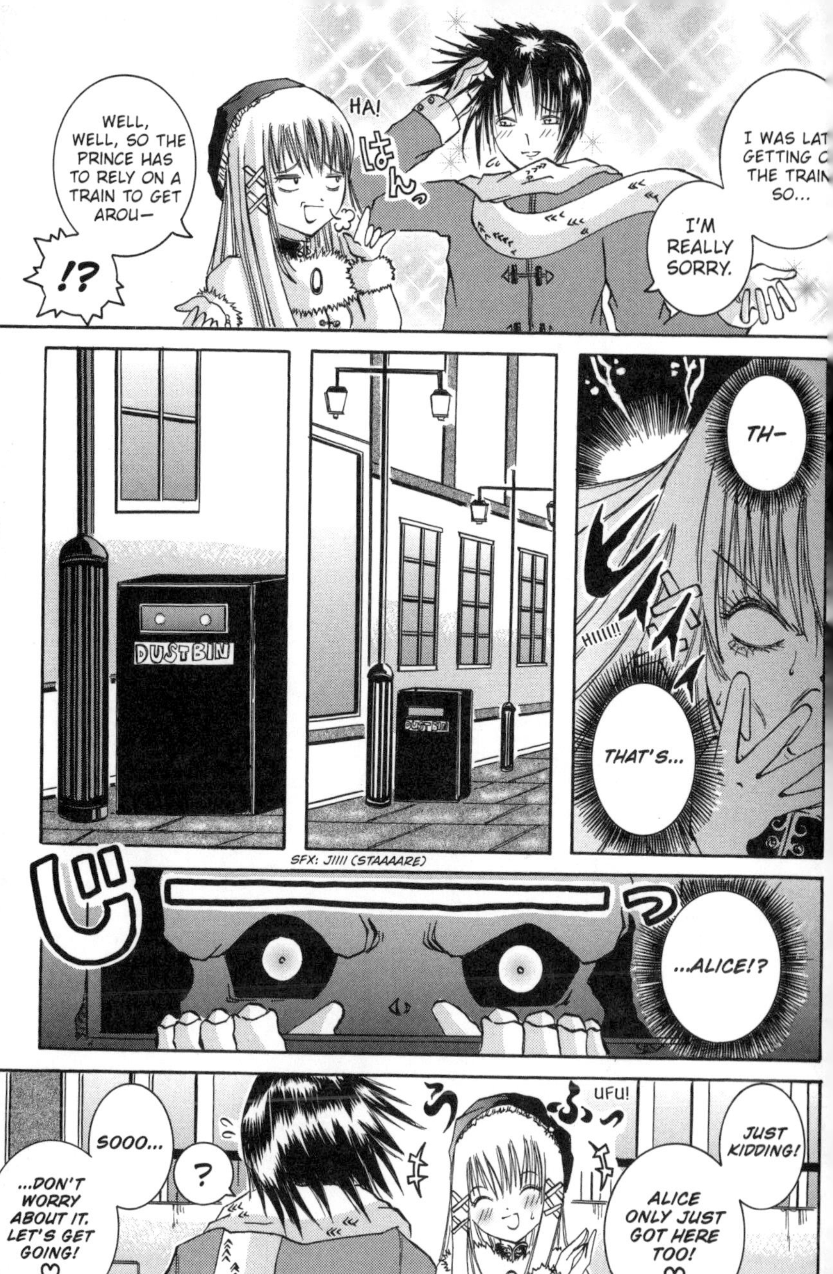
I WAS LAT GETTING C THE TRAIN SO...
I'M REALLY SORRY.
HA!
はんっ
WELL, WELL, SO THE PRINCE HAS TO RELY ON A TRAIN TO GET AROU—
!?
TH-
HIIII!!
THAT'S...
DUSTBIN
SFX: JIIII (STAAAARE)
じーっ
...ALICE!?
JUST KIDDING!
ALICE ONLY JUST GOT HERE TOO! ♡
UFU!
?
SOOO...
...DON'T WORRY ABOUT IT. LET'S GET GOING! ♡

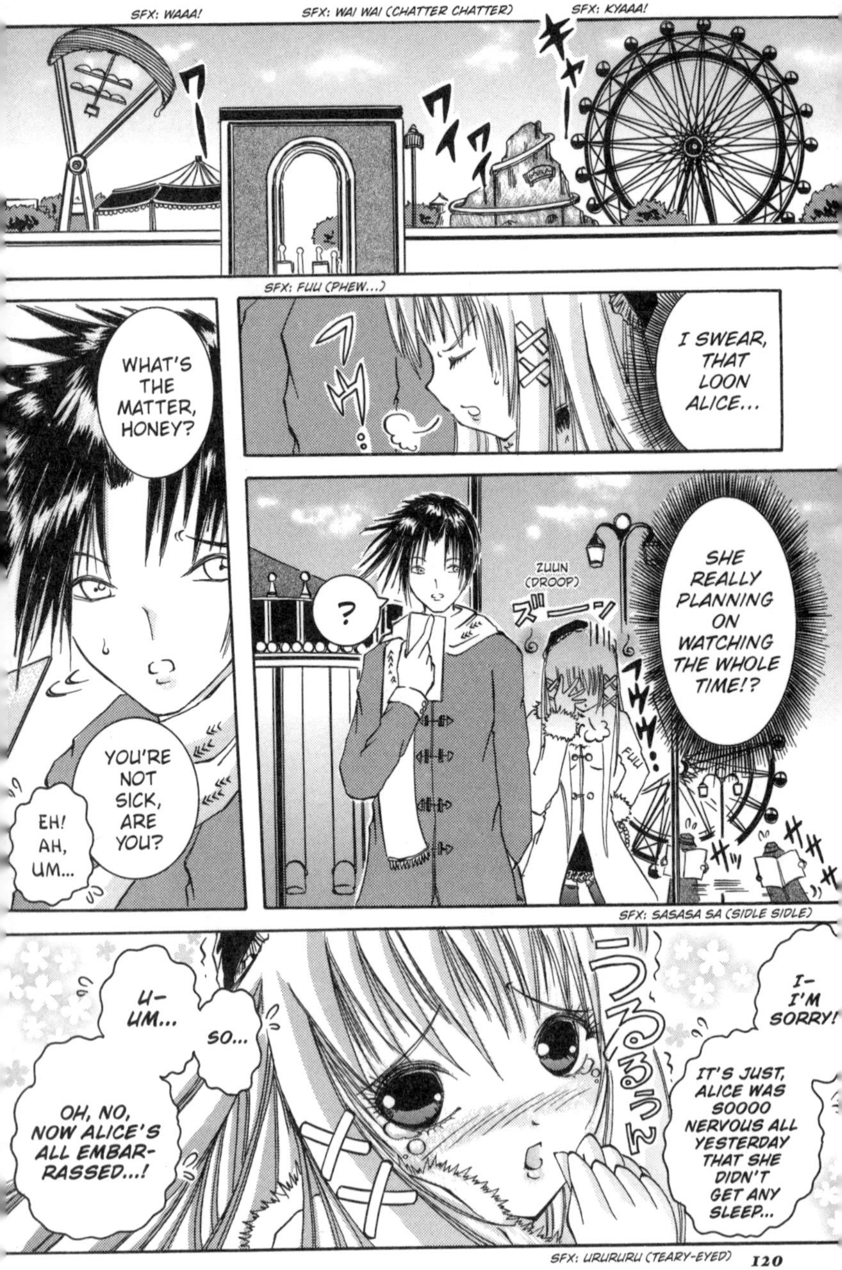
SFX: KYAAA!
SFX: WAI WAI (CHATTER CHATTER)
SFX: WAAA!
I SWEAR, THAT LOON ALICE...
SFX: FUU (PHEW...)
SHE REALLY PLANNING ON WATCHING THE WHOLE TIME!?
ZUUN (DROOP)
FUU
?
SFX: SASASA SA (SIDLE SIDLE)
WHAT'S THE MATTER, HONEY?
YOU'RE NOT SICK, ARE YOU?
EH! AH, UM...
I- I'M SORRY!
IT'S JUST, ALICE WAS SOOOO NERVOUS ALL YESTERDAY THAT SHE DIDN'T GET ANY SLEEP...
U- UM...
SO...
OH, NO, NOW ALICE'S ALL EMBARRASSED...!
SFX: URURURU (TEARY-EYED)

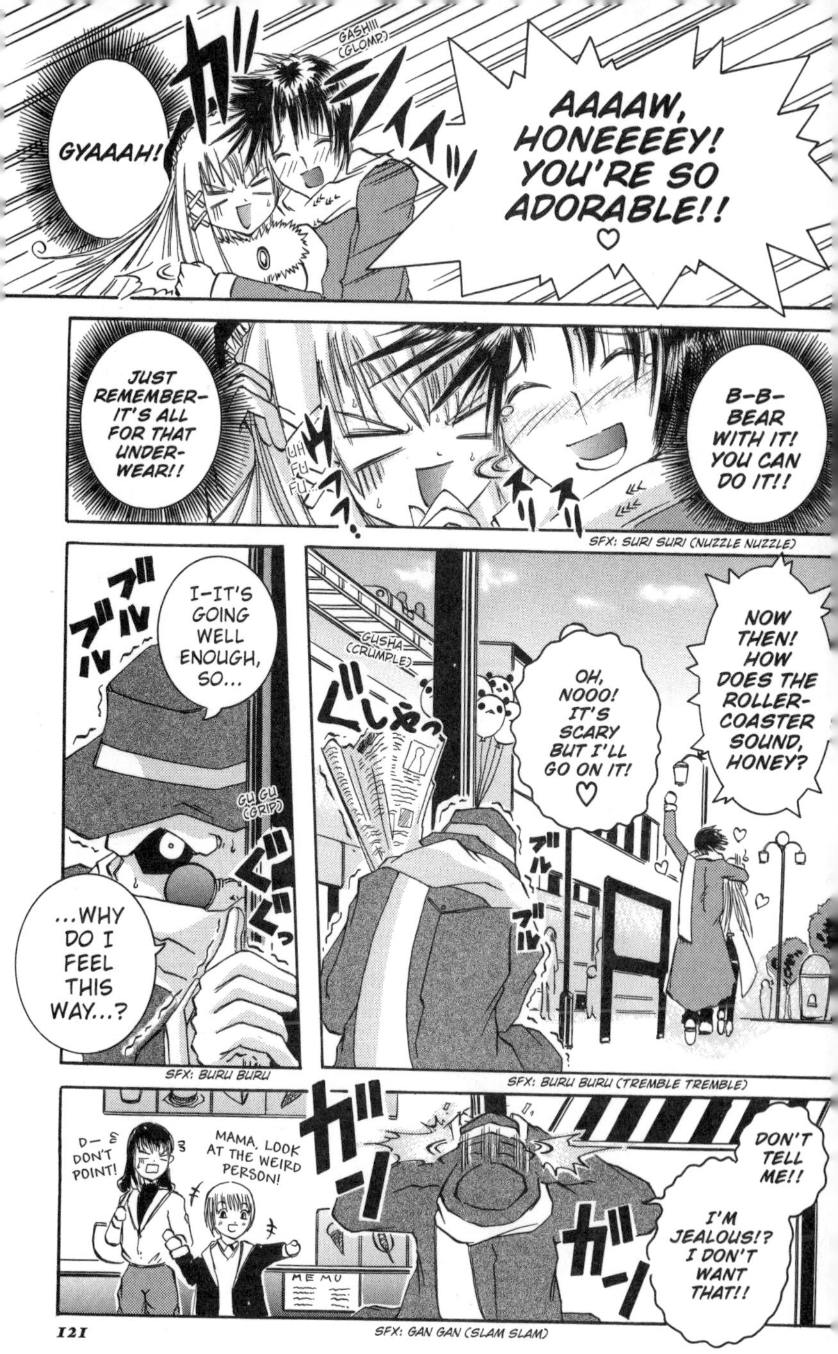
AAAAW, HONEEEEY! YOU'RE SO ADORABLE!! ♡
GASHIII (GLOMP)
GYAAAH!
B-B-BEAR WITH IT! YOU CAN DO IT!!
UH FU FU...
JUST REMEMBER- IT'S ALL FOR THAT UNDER-WEAR!!
SFX: SURI SURI (NUZZLE NUZZLE)
NOW THEN! HOW DOES THE ROLLER-COASTER SOUND, HONEY?
OH, NOOO! IT'S SCARY BUT I'LL GO ON IT! ♡
GUSHA (CRUMPLE)
SFX: BURU BURU (TREMBLE TREMBLE)
I-IT'S GOING WELL ENOUGH, SO...
GU GU (GRIP)
...WHY DO I FEEL THIS WAY...?
SFX: BURU BURU
DON'T TELL ME!!
I'M JEALOUS!? I DON'T WANT THAT!!
MAMA, LOOK AT THE WEIRD PERSON!
D- DON'T POINT!
MEMU
SFX: GAN GAN (SLAM SLAM)

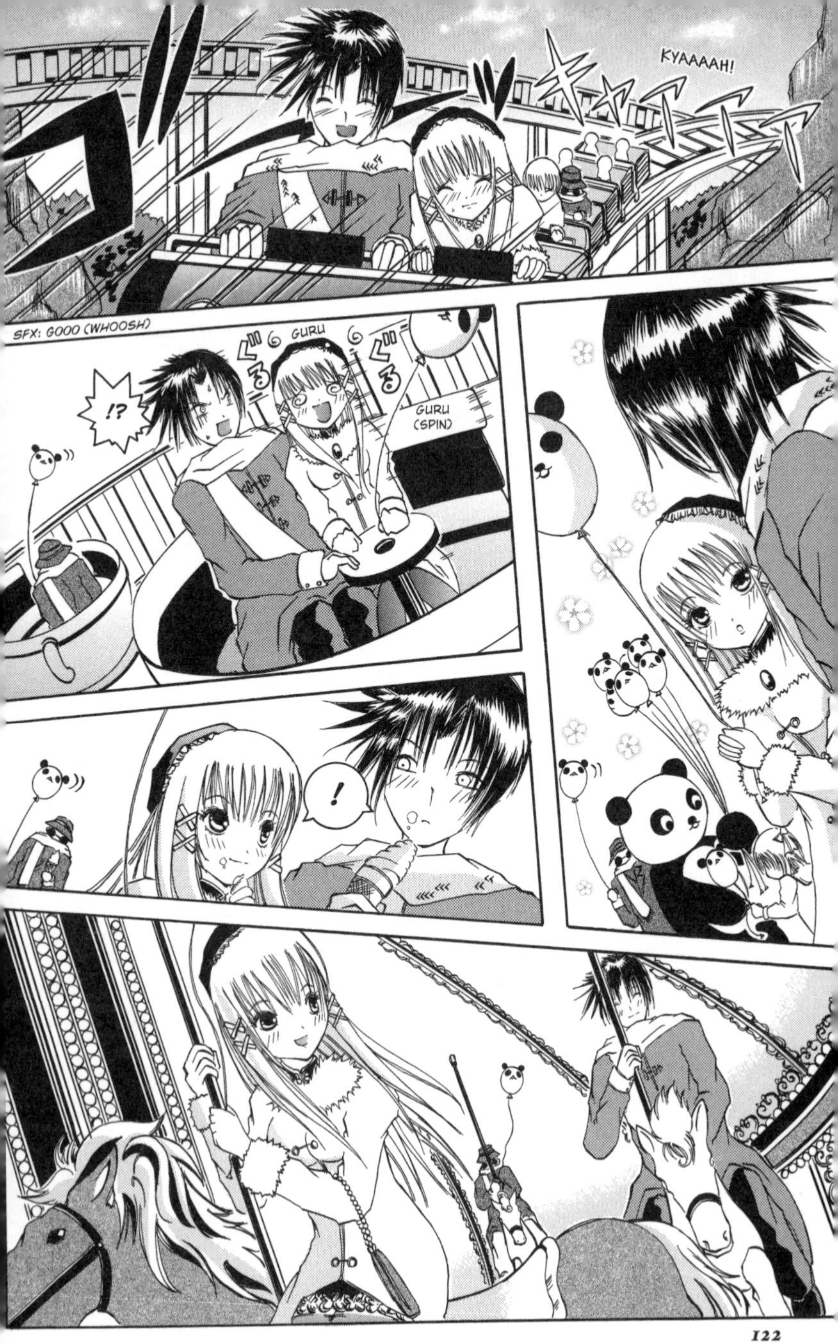
KYAAAAH!
SFX: GOOO (WHOOSH)
GURU
!?
GURU (SPIN)
!

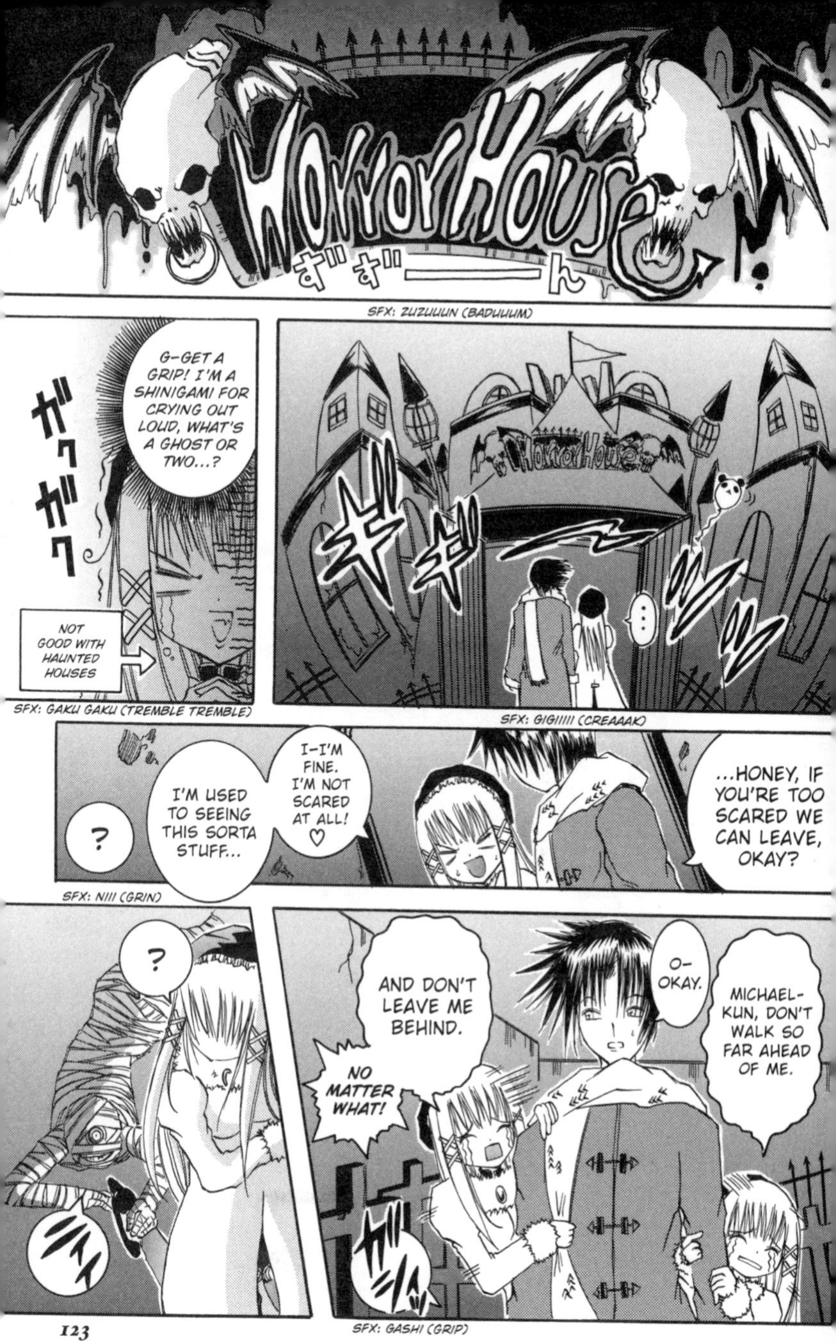
Horror House
SFX: ZUZUUUN (BADUUUM)
...
SFX: GIGIIII (CREAAAK)
G-GET A GRIP! I'M A SHINIGAMI FOR CRYING OUT LOUD, WHAT'S A GHOST OR TWO...?
ガクガク
NOT GOOD WITH HAUNTED HOUSES
SFX: GAKU GAKU (TREMBLE TREMBLE)
...HONEY, IF YOU'RE TOO SCARED WE CAN LEAVE, OKAY?
I-I'M FINE. I'M NOT SCARED AT ALL! ♡
I'M USED TO SEEING THIS SORTA STUFF...
?
SFX: NIII (GRIN)
MICHAEL-KUN, DON'T WALK SO FAR AHEAD OF ME.
O-OKAY.
AND DON'T LEAVE ME BEHIND.
NO MATTER WHAT!
SFX: GASHI (GRIP)
?

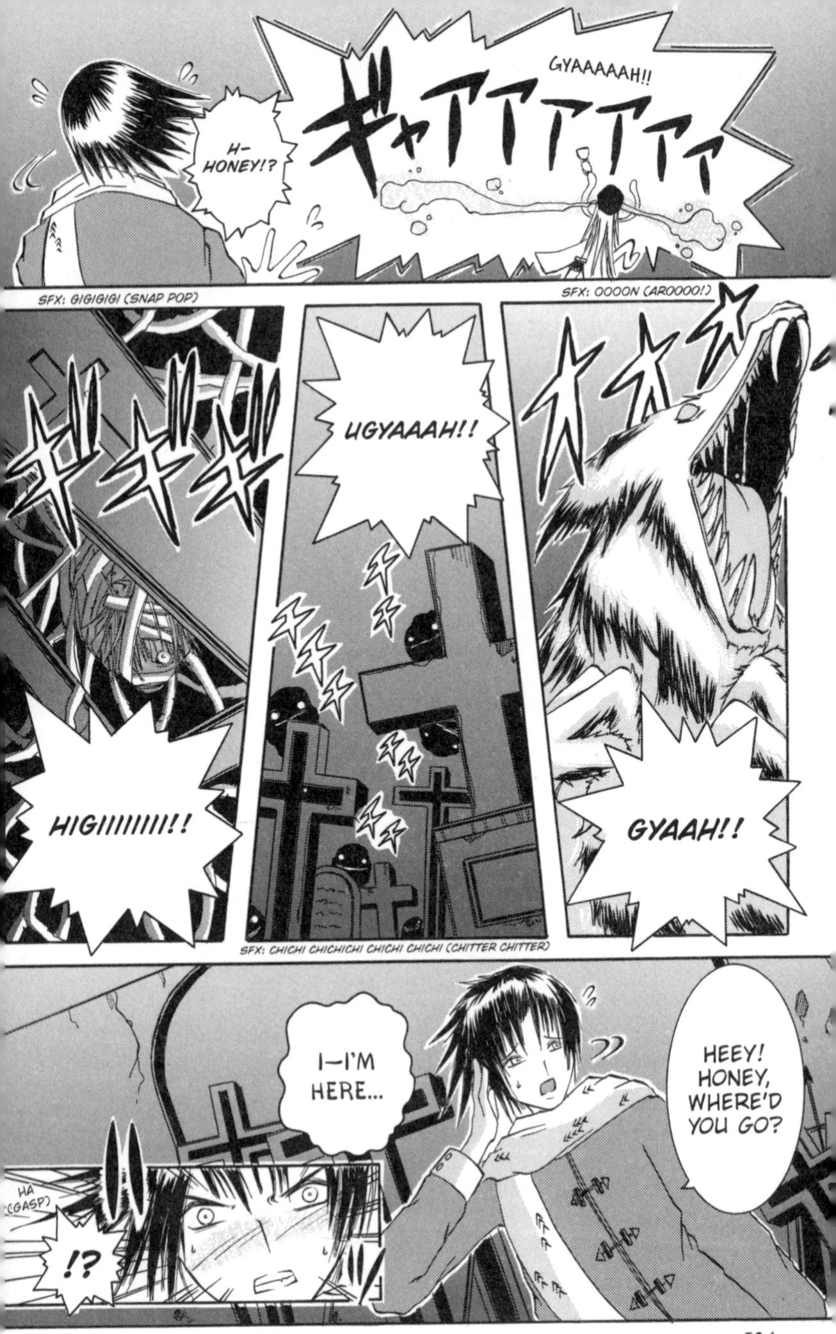
GYAAAAAH!!
ギャアアアアアア
H-HONEY!?
SFX: OOOON (AROOOO!)
GYAAH!!
UGYAAAH!!
SFX: CHICHI CHICHICHI CHICHI CHICHI (CHITTER CHITTER)
SFX: GIGIGIGI (SNAP POP)
HIGIIIIIIII!!
HEEY! HONEY, WHERE'D YOU GO?
I-I'M HERE...
HA (GASP)
!?

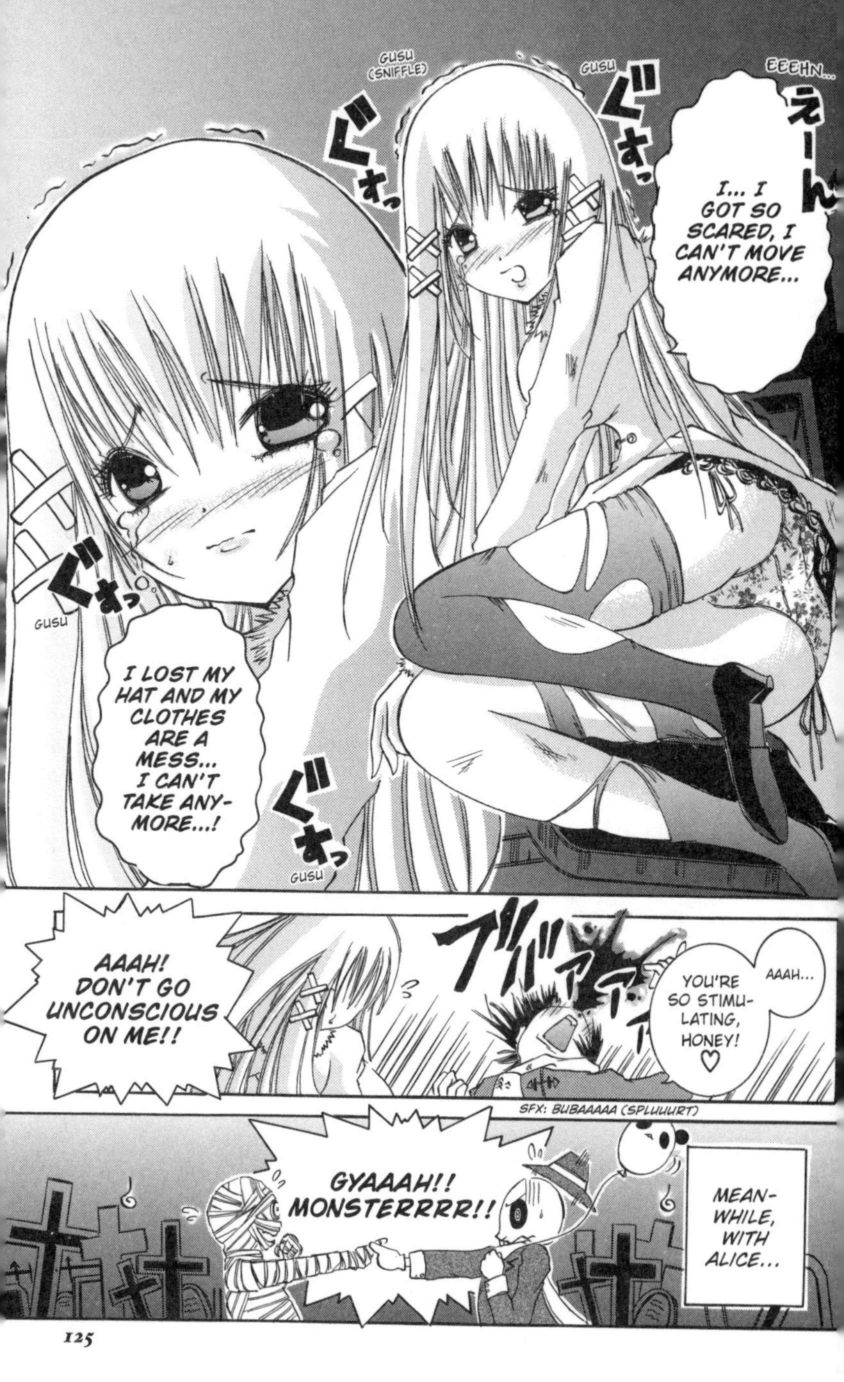

えーん
EEEHN...
I... I GOT SO SCARED, I CAN'T MOVE ANYMORE...
ぐすっ
GUSU
ぐすっ
GUSU (SNIFFLE)
ぐすっ
GUSU
I LOST MY HAT AND MY CLOTHES ARE A MESS... I CAN'T TAKE ANY-MORE...!
ぐすっ
GUSU
AAAH... YOU'RE SO STIMU-LATING, HONEY! ♡
SFX: BUBAAAAA (SPLUUURT)
AAAH! DON'T GO UNCONSCIOUS ON ME!!
MEAN-WHILE, WITH ALICE...
GYAAAH!! MONSTERRRR!!

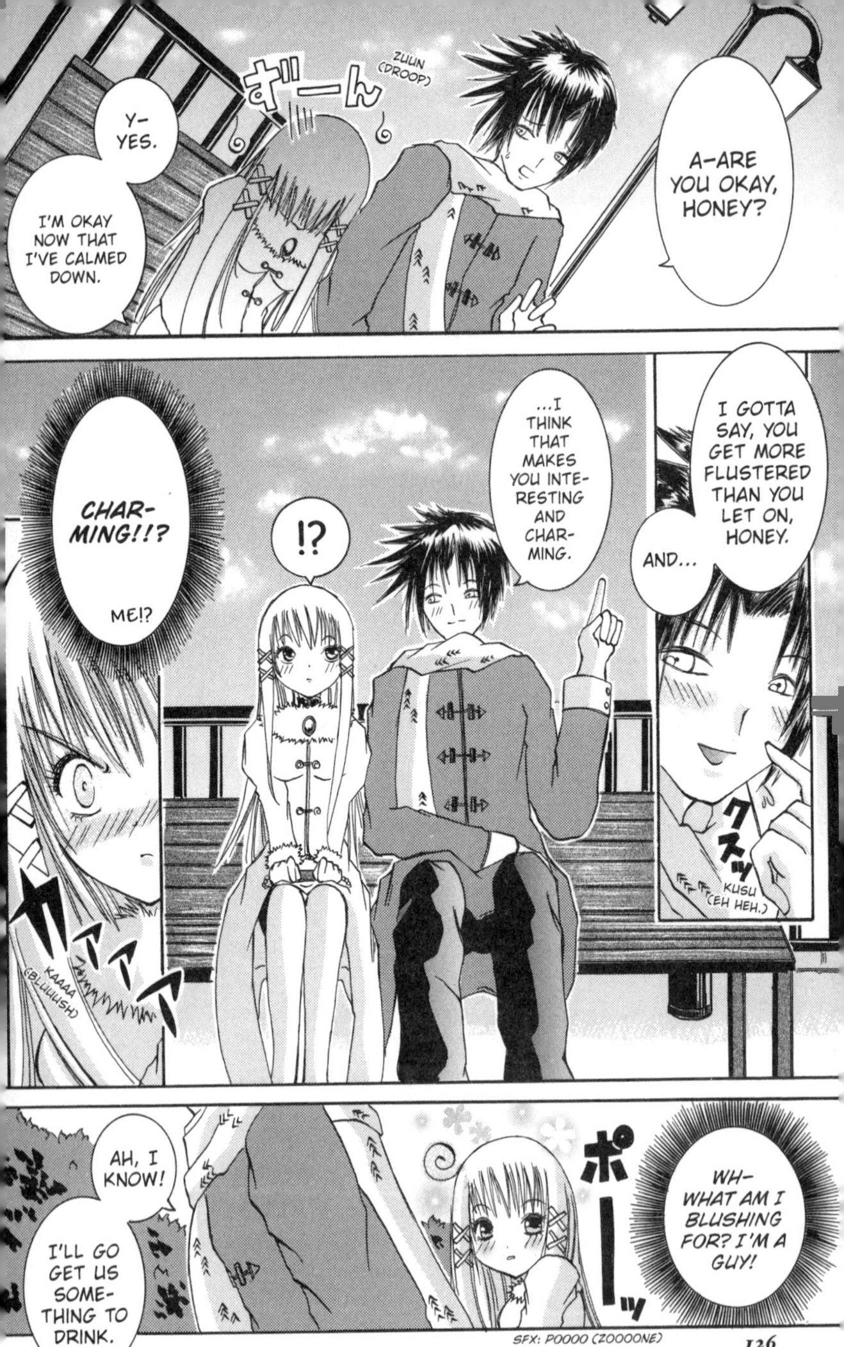
A-ARE YOU OKAY, HONEY?
ZUUN (DROOP)
Y-YES.
I'M OKAY NOW THAT I'VE CALMED DOWN.
I GOTTA SAY, YOU GET MORE FLUSTERED THAN YOU LET ON, HONEY.
AND...
KUSU (EH HEH.)
...I THINK THAT MAKES YOU INTERESTING AND CHARMING.
!?
CHARMING!!?
ME!?
KAAAA (BLUUUSH)
WH-WHAT AM I BLUSHING FOR? I'M A GUY!
AH, I KNOW!
I'LL GO GET US SOMETHING TO DRINK.

SFX: POOOO (ZOOOONE)

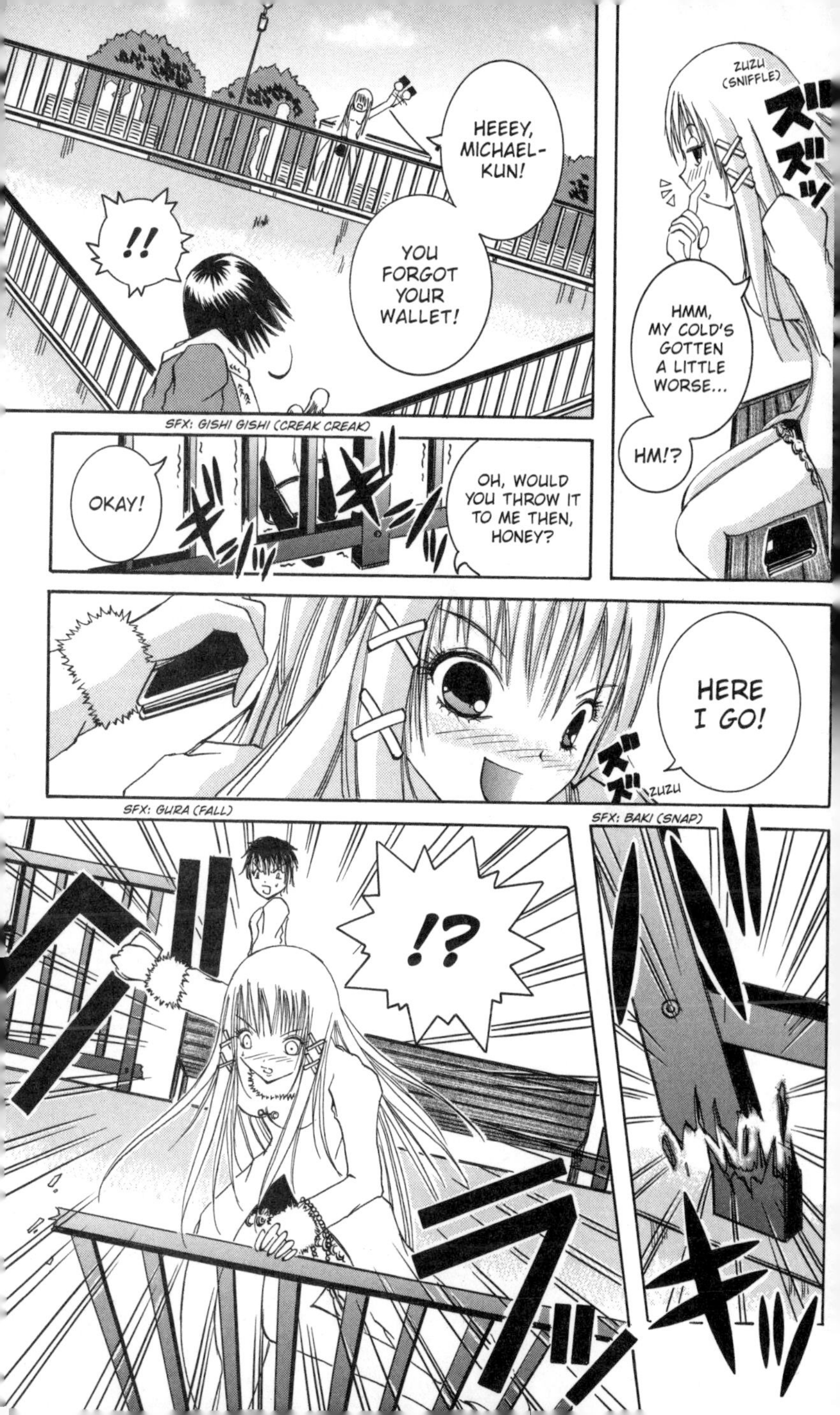
ZUZU (SNIFFLE)
HMM, MY COLD'S GOTTEN A LITTLE WORSE...
HM!?
HEEEY, MICHAEL-KUN!
YOU FORGOT YOUR WALLET!
!!
SFX: GISHI GISHI (CREAK CREAK)
OH, WOULD YOU THROW IT TO ME THEN, HONEY?
OKAY!
HERE I GO!
ZUZU
SFX: BAKI (SNAP)
SFX: GURA (FALL)
!?

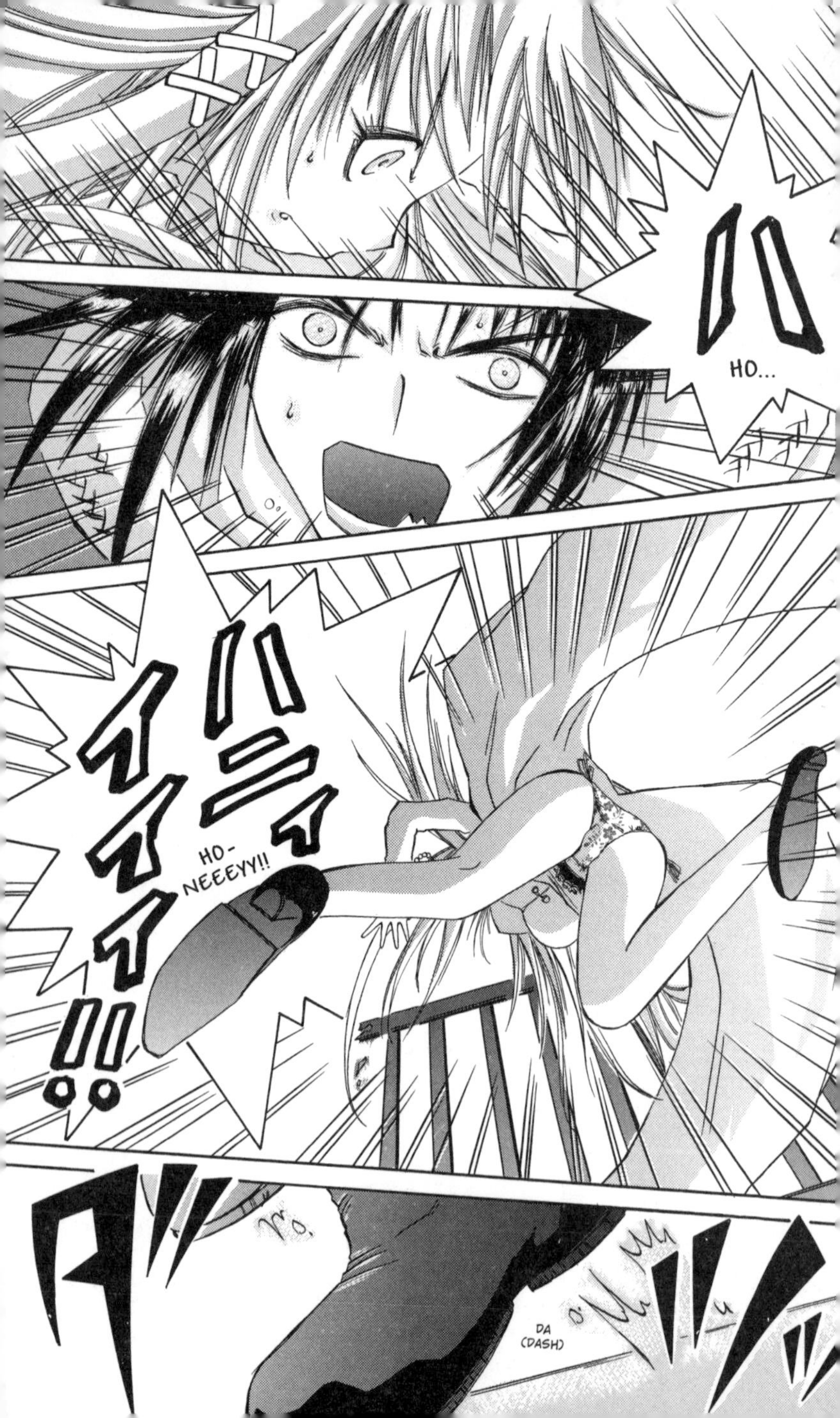
HO...
HO-NEEEYY!!
DA (DASH)

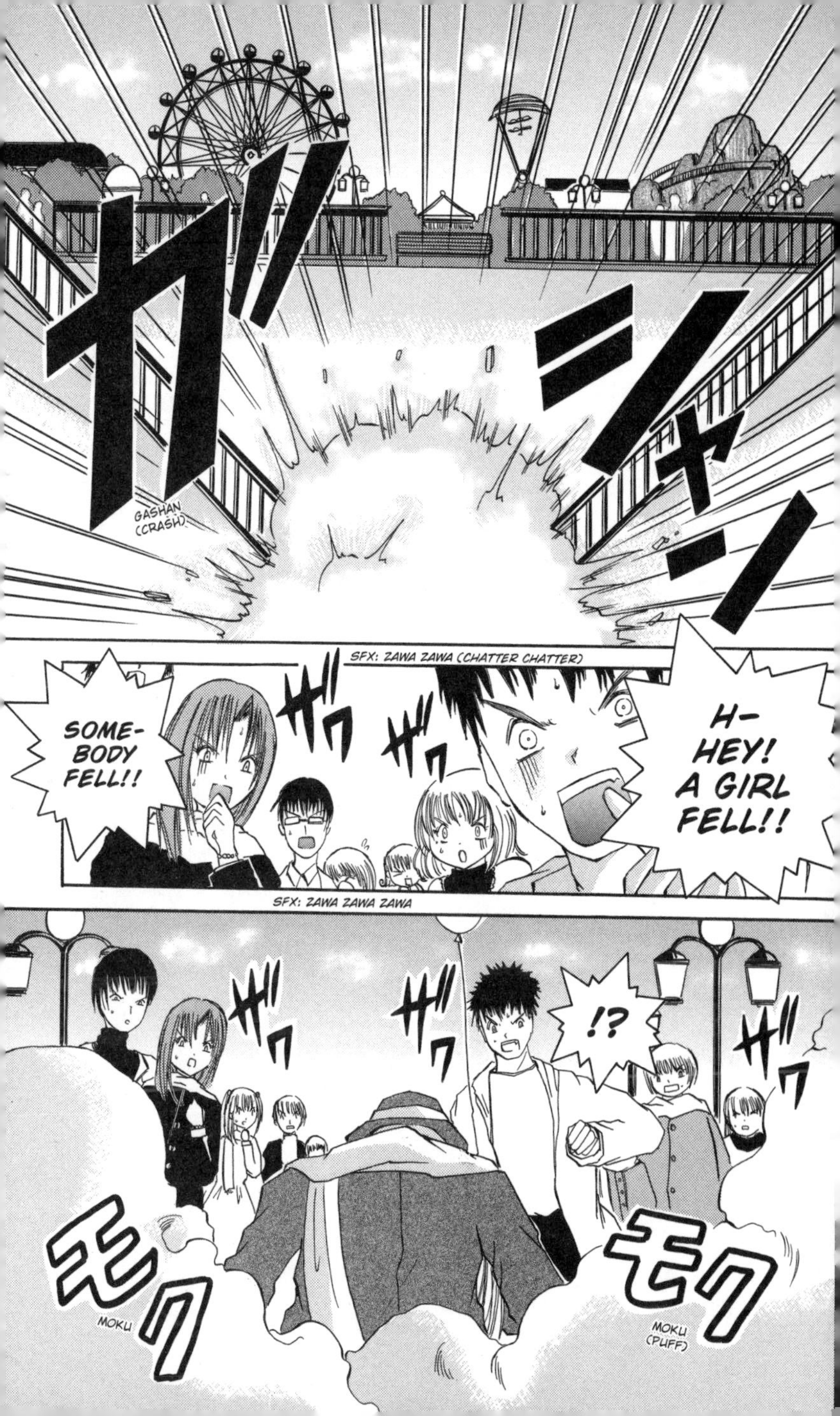
GASHAN (CRASH)
SFX: ZAWA ZAWA (CHATTER CHATTER)
H-HEY! A GIRL FELL!!
SOME-BODY FELL!!
SFX: ZAWA ZAWA ZAWA
!?
MOKU (PUFF)
MOKU

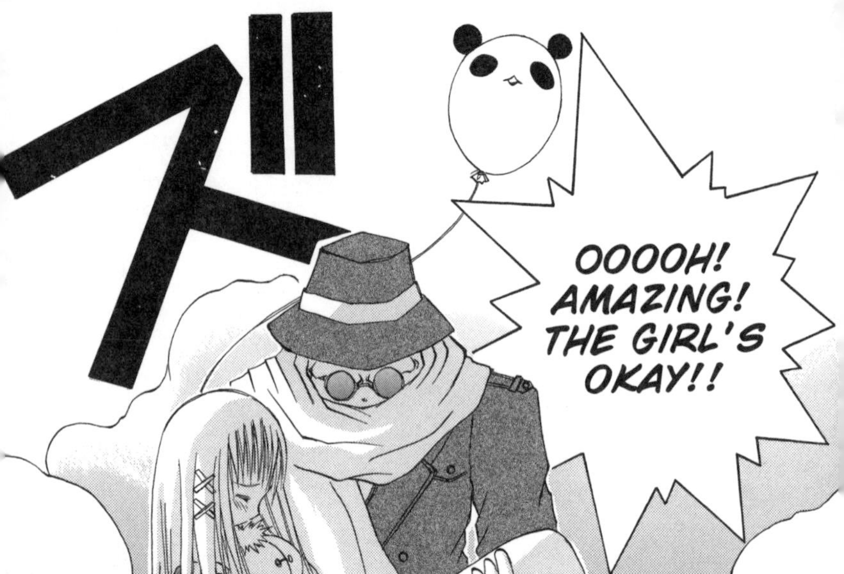
ズン
OOOOH! AMAZING! THE GIRL'S OKAY!!

SFX: ZUN (APPEAR)

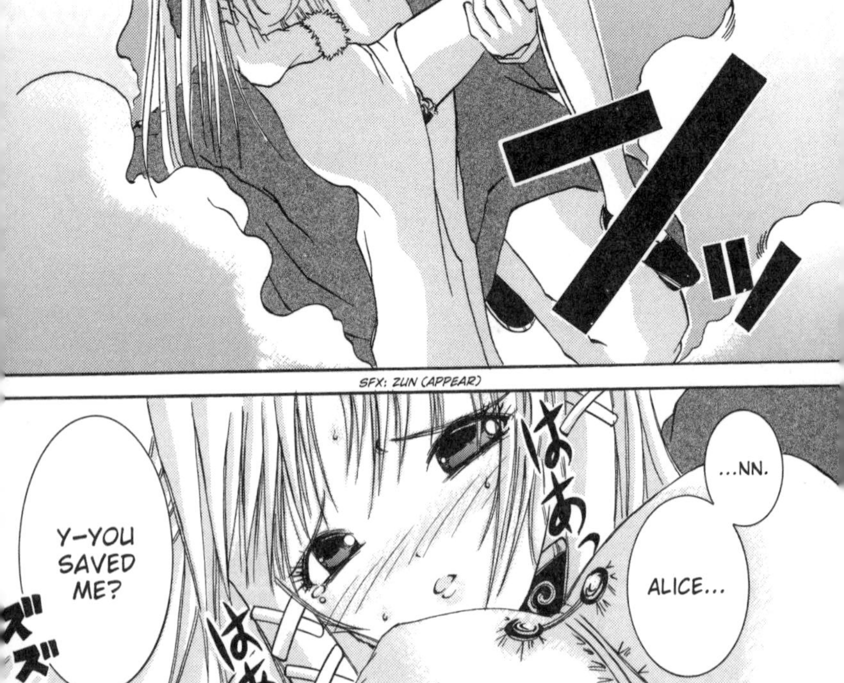
...NN.
ALICE...
Y-YOU SAVED ME?

X: ZUZU... (SNIFFLE...)

SFX: HAA HAA (PANT PANT)

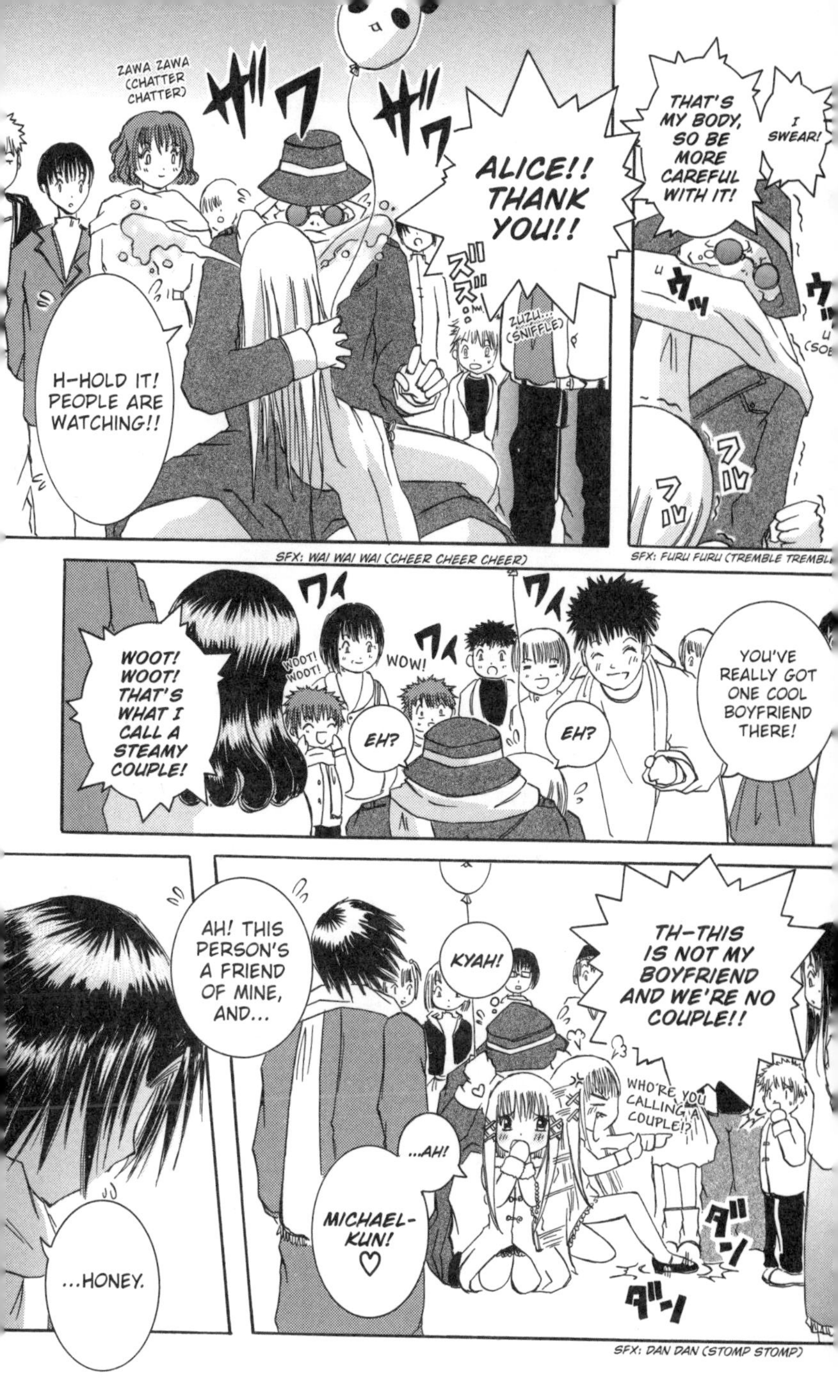
I SWEAR!
THAT'S MY BODY, SO BE MORE CAREFUL WITH IT!
U
U (SOB
SFX: FURU FURU (TREMBLE TREMBL
ALICE!! THANK YOU!!
ZUZU... (SNIFFLE)
ZAWA ZAWA (CHATTER CHATTER)
H-HOLD IT! PEOPLE ARE WATCHING!!
SFX: WAI WAI WAI (CHEER CHEER CHEER)
YOU'VE REALLY GOT ONE COOL BOYFRIEND THERE!
EH?
EH?
WOW!
WOOT! WOOT!
WOOT! WOOT! THAT'S WHAT I CALL A STEAMY COUPLE!
TH-THIS IS NOT MY BOYFRIEND AND WE'RE NO COUPLE!!
WHO'RE YOU CALLING A COUPLE!?
KYAH!
...AH!
MICHAEL-KUN! ♡
AH! THIS PERSON'S A FRIEND OF MINE, AND...
...HONEY.
SFX: DAN DAN (STOMP STOMP)

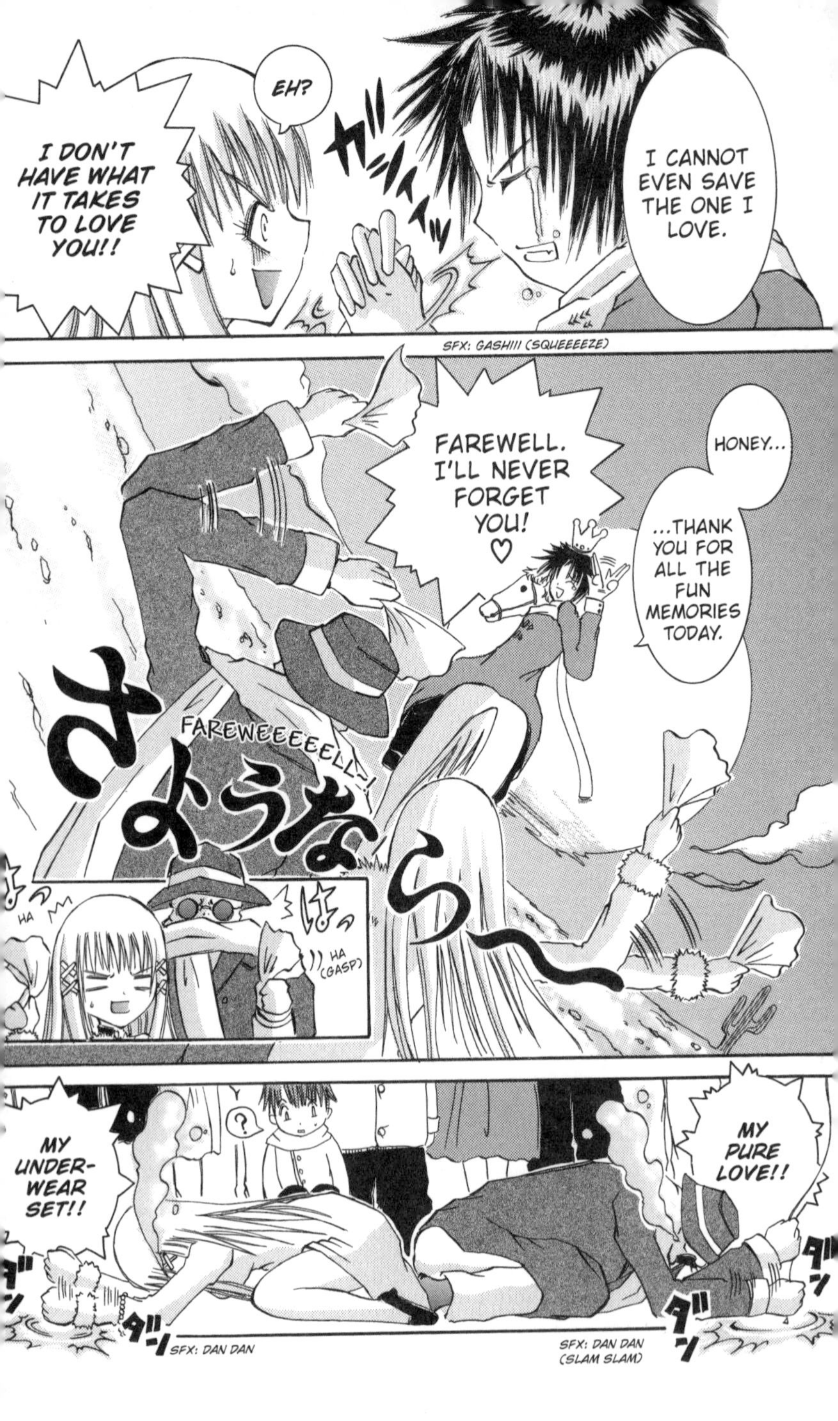
I CANNOT EVEN SAVE THE ONE I LOVE.
EH?
I DON'T HAVE WHAT IT TAKES TO LOVE YOU!!
SFX: GASHIII (SQUEEEEZE)
HONEY...
...THANK YOU FOR ALL THE FUN MEMORIES TODAY.
FAREWELL. I'LL NEVER FORGET YOU! ♡
FAREWEEEEEELL~!
さようなら~
HA (GASP)
HA
MY PURE LOVE!!
SFX: DAN DAN (SLAM SLAM)
MY UNDER-WEAR SET!!
SFX: DAN DAN

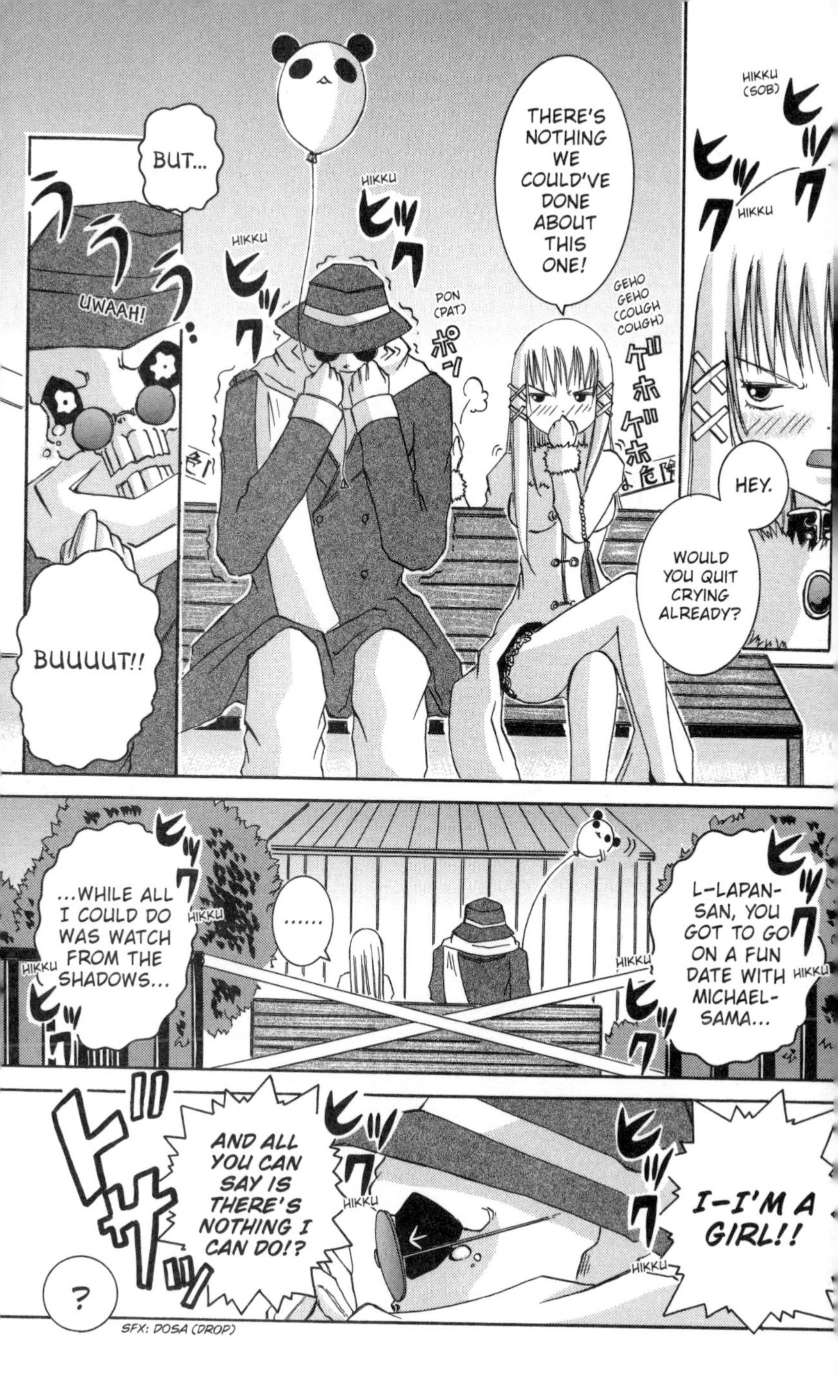
HIKKU (SOB)
HIKKU
HEY.
WOULD YOU QUIT CRYING ALREADY?
THERE'S NOTHING WE COULD'VE DONE ABOUT THIS ONE!
GEHO GEHO (COUGH COUGH)
PON (PAT)
HIKKU
HIKKU
BUT...
UWAAH!
BUUUUT!!
L-LAPAN-SAN, YOU GOT TO GO ON A FUN DATE WITH MICHAEL-SAMA...
HIKKU
HIKKU
......
...WHILE ALL I COULD DO WAS WATCH FROM THE SHADOWS...
HIKKU
HIKKU
I-I'M A GIRL!!
HIKKU
HIKKU
AND ALL YOU CAN SAY IS THERE'S NOTHING I CAN DO!?
?
SFX: DOSA (DROP)

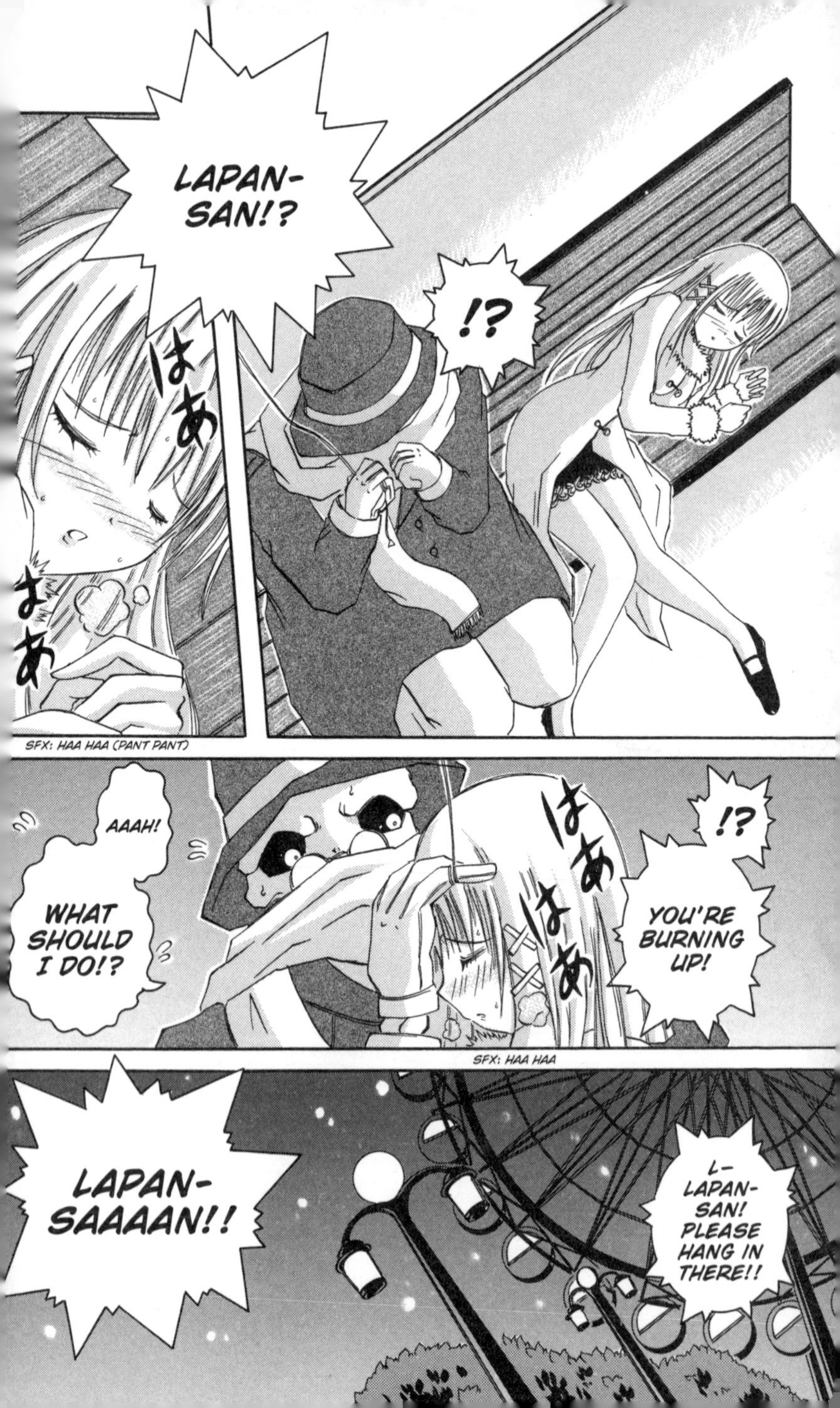
!?
LAPAN-SAN!?
はあ
はあ
SFX: HAA HAA (PANT PANT)
!?
YOU'RE BURNING UP!
はあ はあ
AAAH!
WHAT SHOULD I DO!?
SFX: HAA HAA
L-LAPAN-SAN! PLEASE HANG IN THERE!!
LAPAN-SAAAAN!!

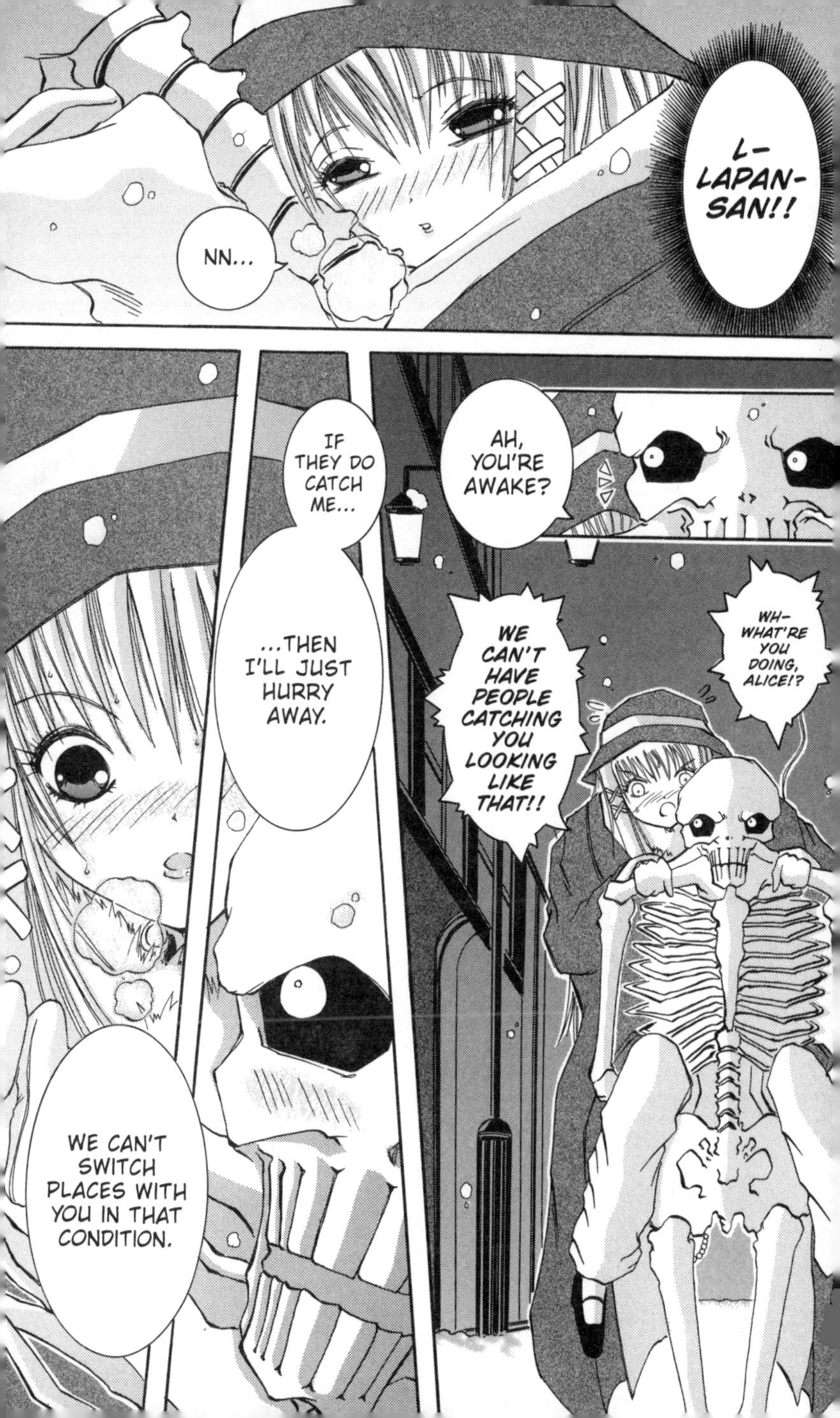
L-LAPAN-SAN!!
NN...
AH, YOU'RE AWAKE?
WH-WHAT'RE YOU DOING, ALICE!?
WE CAN'T HAVE PEOPLE CATCHING YOU LOOKING LIKE THAT!!
IF THEY DO CATCH ME...
...THEN I'LL JUST HURRY AWAY.
WE CAN'T SWITCH PLACES WITH YOU IN THAT CONDITION.

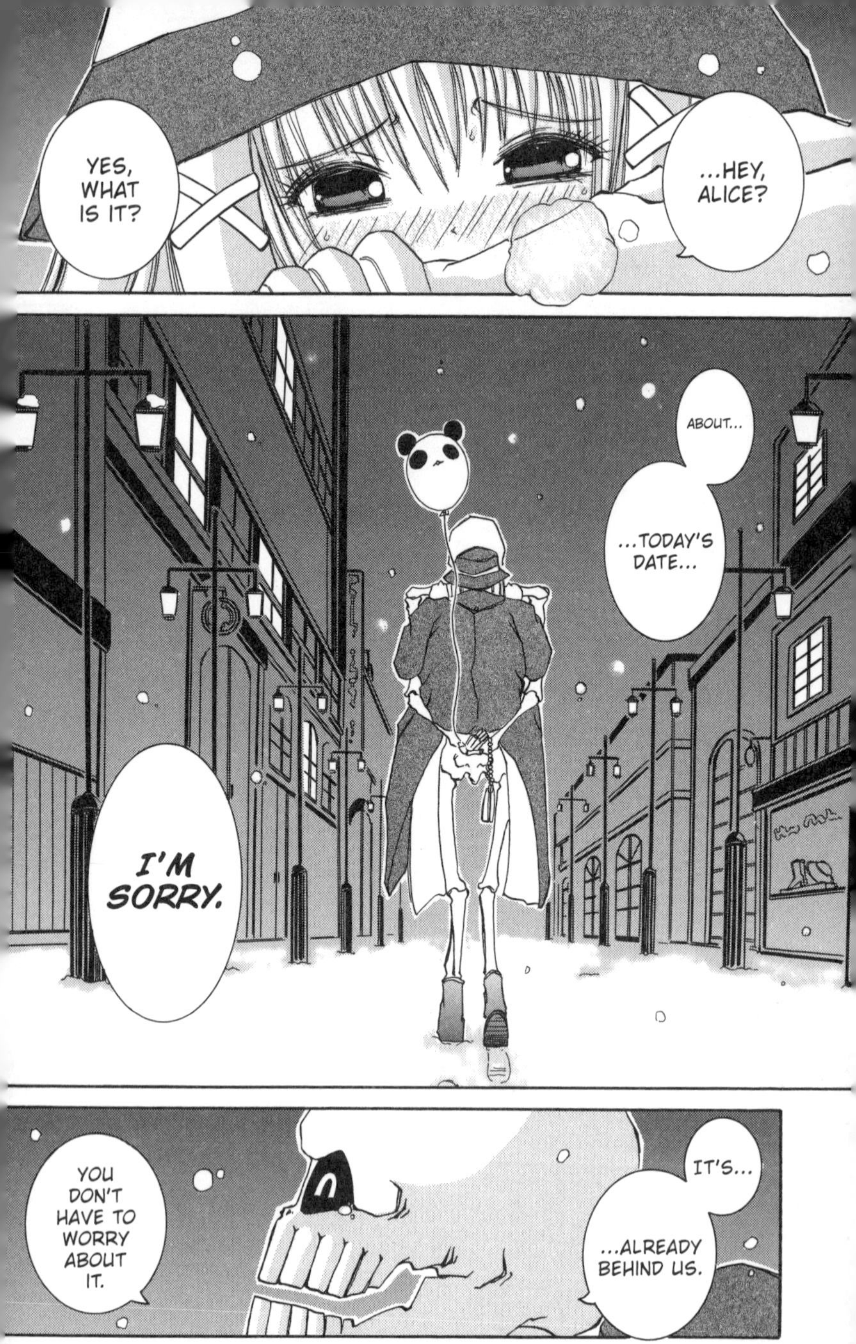
...HEY, ALICE?
YES, WHAT IS IT?
ABOUT...
...TODAY'S DATE...
I'M SORRY.
IT'S...
...ALREADY BEHIND US.
YOU DON'T HAVE TO WORRY ABOUT IT.

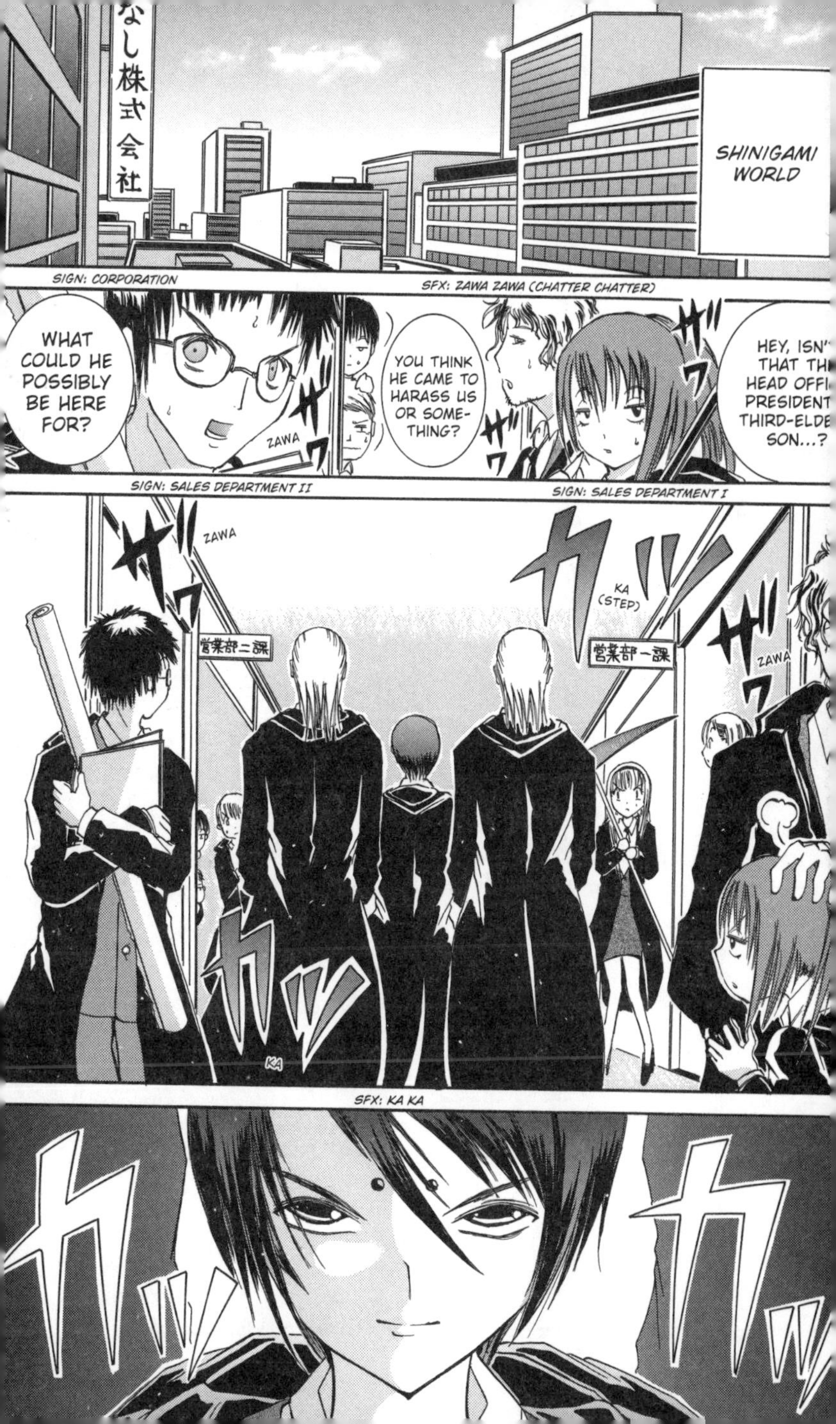

SHINIGAMI WORLD
なし株式会社
SFX: ZAWA ZAWA (CHATTER CHATTER)
SIGN: CORPORATION
HEY, ISN'T THAT TH HEAD OFFI PRESIDENT THIRD-ELDE SON...?
YOU THINK HE CAME TO HARASS US OR SOME-THING?
ZAWA
WHAT COULD HE POSSIBLY BE HERE FOR?
SIGN: SALES DEPARTMENT I
SIGN: SALES DEPARTMENT II
ZAWA
KA (STEP)
営業部一課
ZAWA
営業部二課
KA
SFX: KA KA

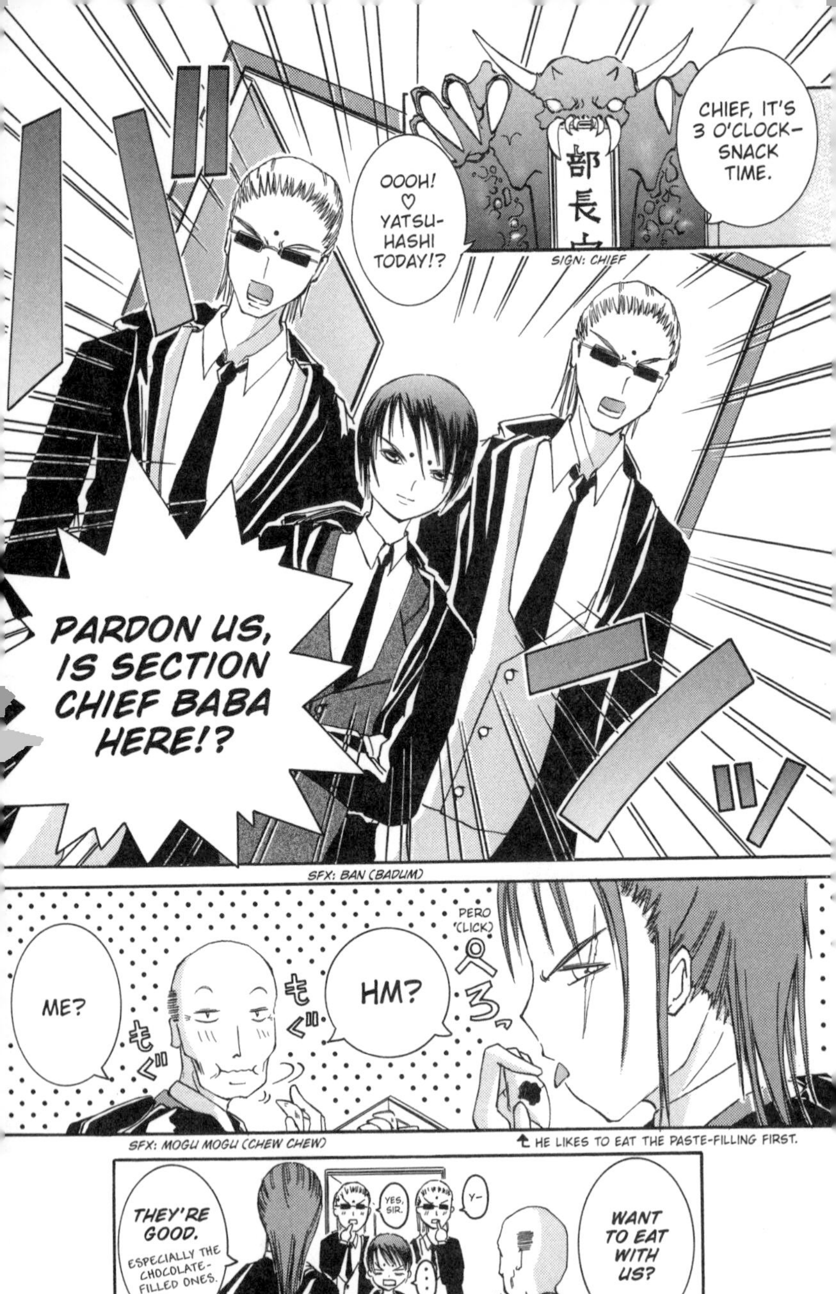
CHIEF, IT'S 3 O'CLOCK—SNACK TIME.
OOOH! ♡ YATSU-HASHI TODAY!?
部長
SIGN: CHIEF
PARDON US, IS SECTION CHIEF BABA HERE!?
SFX: BAN (BADUM)
PERO (CLICK)
HM?
ME?
SFX: MOGU MOGU (CHEW CHEW)
HE LIKES TO EAT THE PASTE-FILLING FIRST.
WANT TO EAT WITH US?
Y—
YES, SIR.
...
THEY'RE GOOD.
ESPECIALLY THE CHOCOLATE-FILLED ONES.

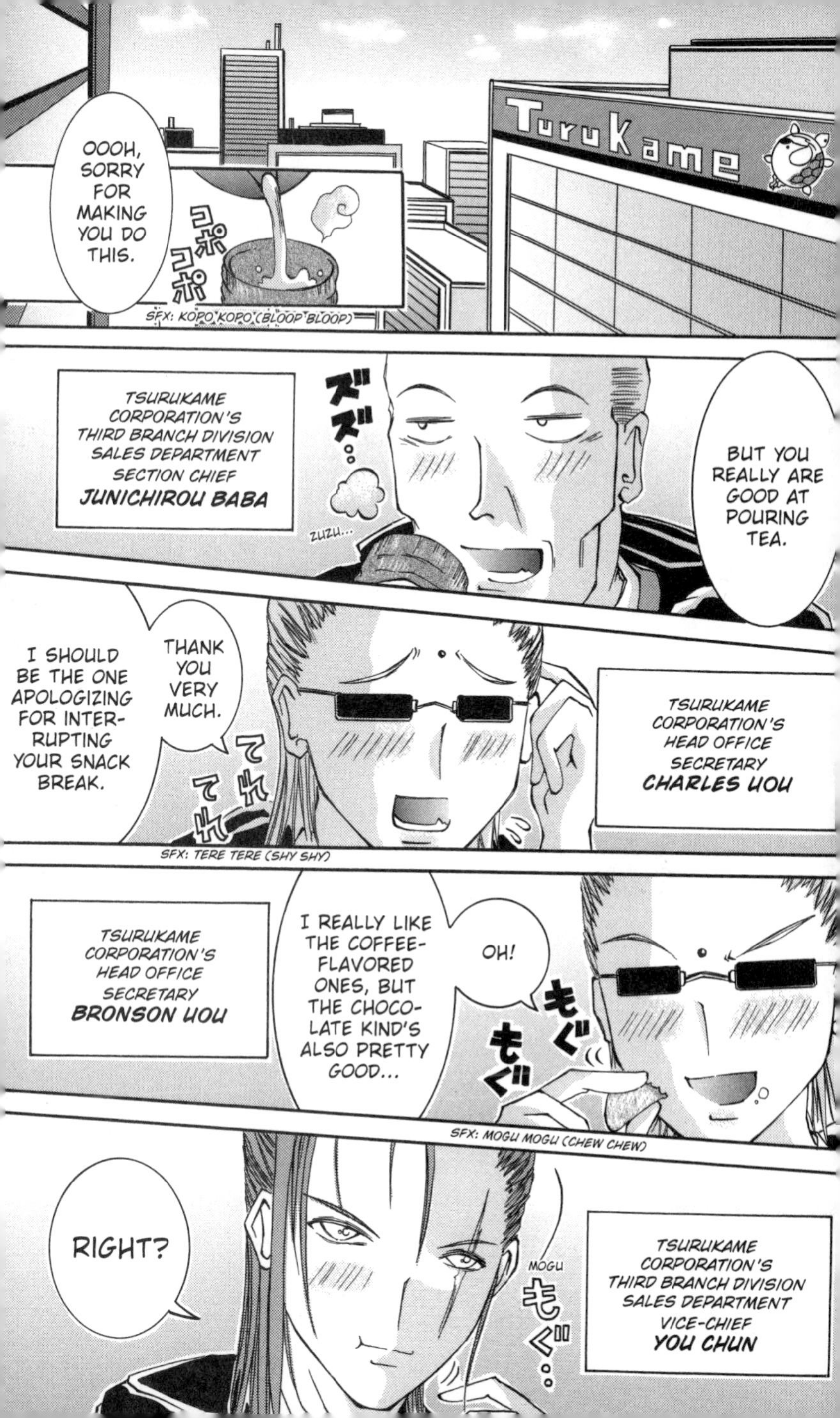
TuruKame
OOOH, SORRY FOR MAKING YOU DO THIS.
コポコポ
SFX: KOPO KOPO (BLOOP BLOOP)
BUT YOU REALLY ARE GOOD AT POURING TEA.
ズズ。。
ZUZU...
TSURUKAME CORPORATION'S THIRD BRANCH DIVISION SALES DEPARTMENT SECTION CHIEF **JUNICHIROU BABA**
TSURUKAME CORPORATION'S HEAD OFFICE SECRETARY **CHARLES UOU**
THANK YOU VERY MUCH.
I SHOULD BE THE ONE APOLOGIZING FOR INTER-RUPTING YOUR SNACK BREAK.
てれてれ
SFX: TERE TERE (SHY SHY)
OH!
I REALLY LIKE THE COFFEE-FLAVORED ONES, BUT THE CHOCO-LATE KIND'S ALSO PRETTY GOOD...
もぐもぐ
TSURUKAME CORPORATION'S HEAD OFFICE SECRETARY **BRONSON UOU**
SFX: MOGU MOGU (CHEW CHEW)
TSURUKAME CORPORATION'S THIRD BRANCH DIVISION SALES DEPARTMENT VICE-CHIEF **YOU CHUN**
MOGU
もぐ。。
RIGHT?

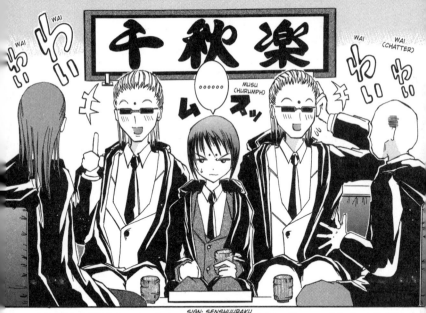

WAI
WAI (CHATTER)
MUSU (HURUMPH)
......
WAI
WAI
SIGN: SENSHUURAKU
TSURUKAME CORPORATION'S HEAD OFFICE SALES DEPARTMENT HEAD CHIEF **UMENOSUKE TSURUKAME**
...HEY!
SFX: BIKU (STARTLE)
HEY, CAN YOU HEAR ANYTHING?
SOMETHING ABOUT CHOCOLATE AND COFFEE...
YOU IDIOTS!! WE DIDN'T COME HERE FOR SNACK TIME!!
!?
SIGN: SECTION CHIEF'S OFFICE

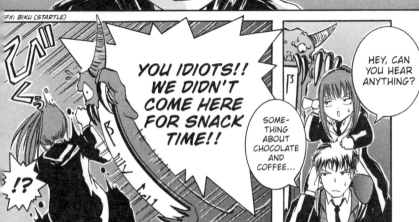

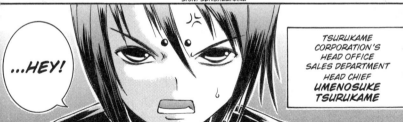

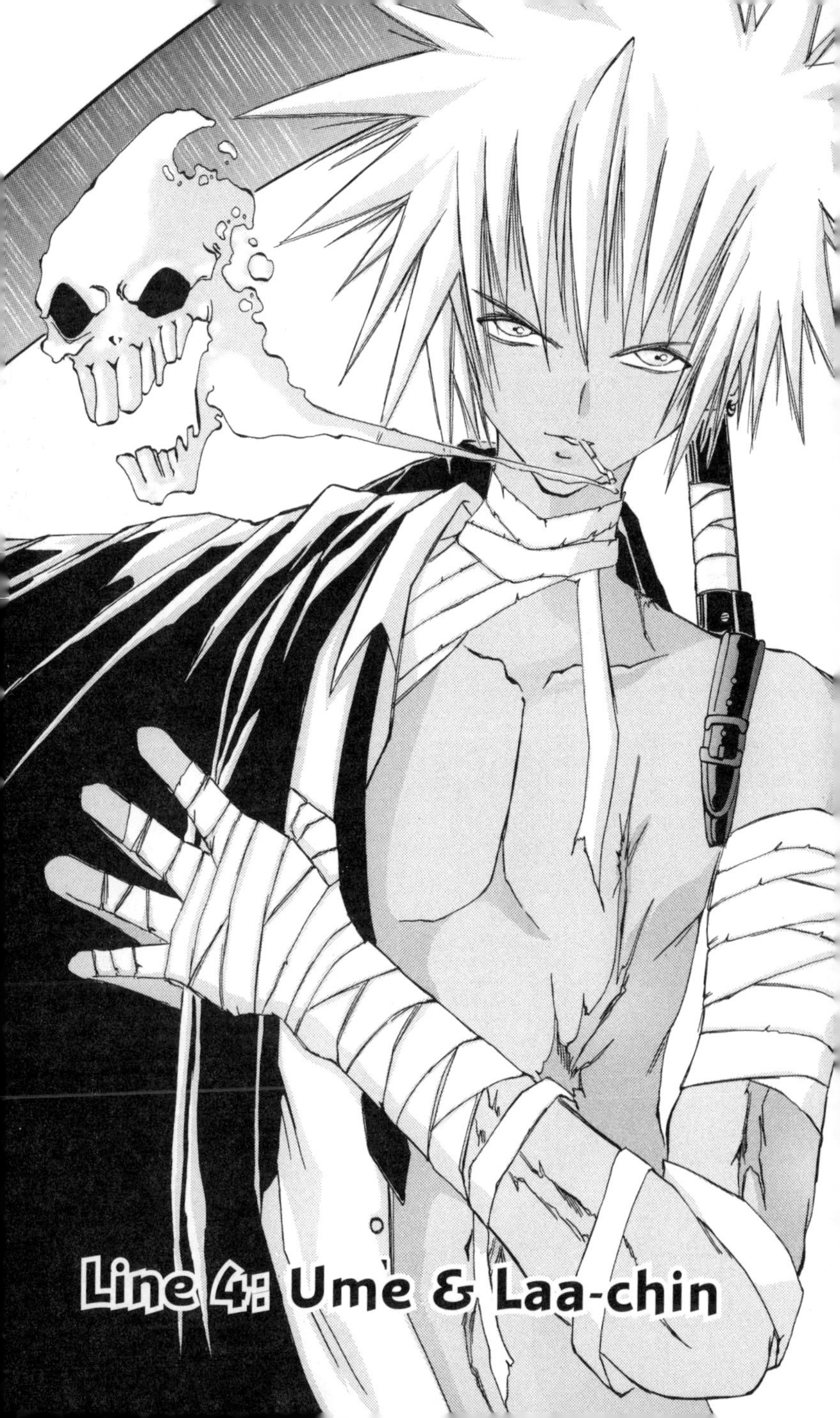
Line 4: Umè & Laa-chin

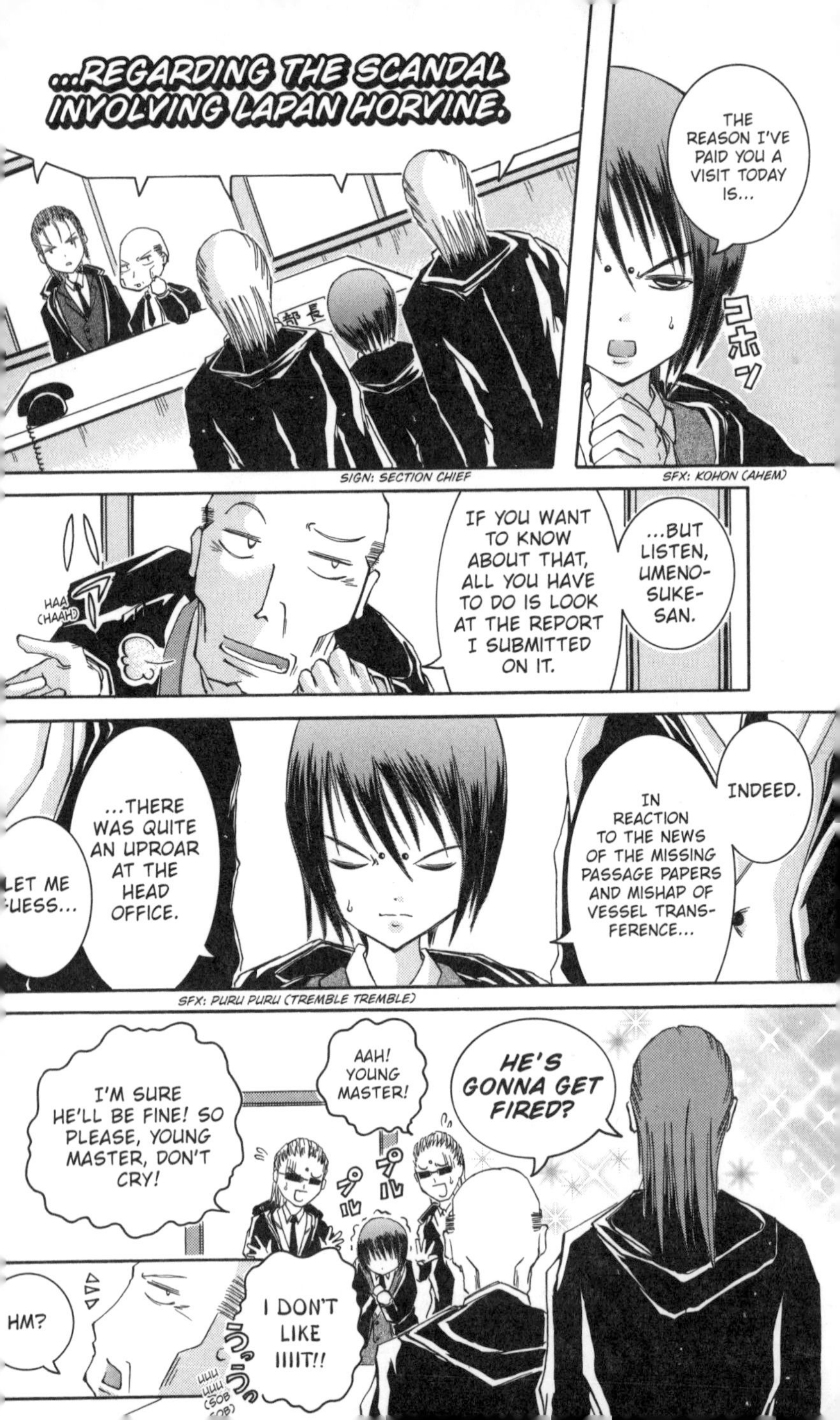
THE REASON I'VE PAID YOU A VISIT TODAY IS...
SFX: KOHON (AHEM)
...REGARDING THE SCANDAL INVOLVING LAPAN HORVINE.
SIGN: SECTION CHIEF
...BUT LISTEN, UMENOSUKE-SAN.
IF YOU WANT TO KNOW ABOUT THAT, ALL YOU HAVE TO DO IS LOOK AT THE REPORT I SUBMITTED ON IT.
HAA (HAAH)
INDEED.
IN REACTION TO THE NEWS OF THE MISSING PASSAGE PAPERS AND MISHAP OF VESSEL TRANSFERENCE...
...THERE WAS QUITE AN UPROAR AT THE HEAD OFFICE.
LET ME GUESS...
SFX: PURU PURU (TREMBLE TREMBLE)
HE'S GONNA GET FIRED?
AAH! YOUNG MASTER!
I'M SURE HE'LL BE FINE! SO PLEASE, YOUNG MASTER, DON'T CRY!
I DON'T LIKE IIIIT!!
UUU UUU (SOB SOB)
HM?

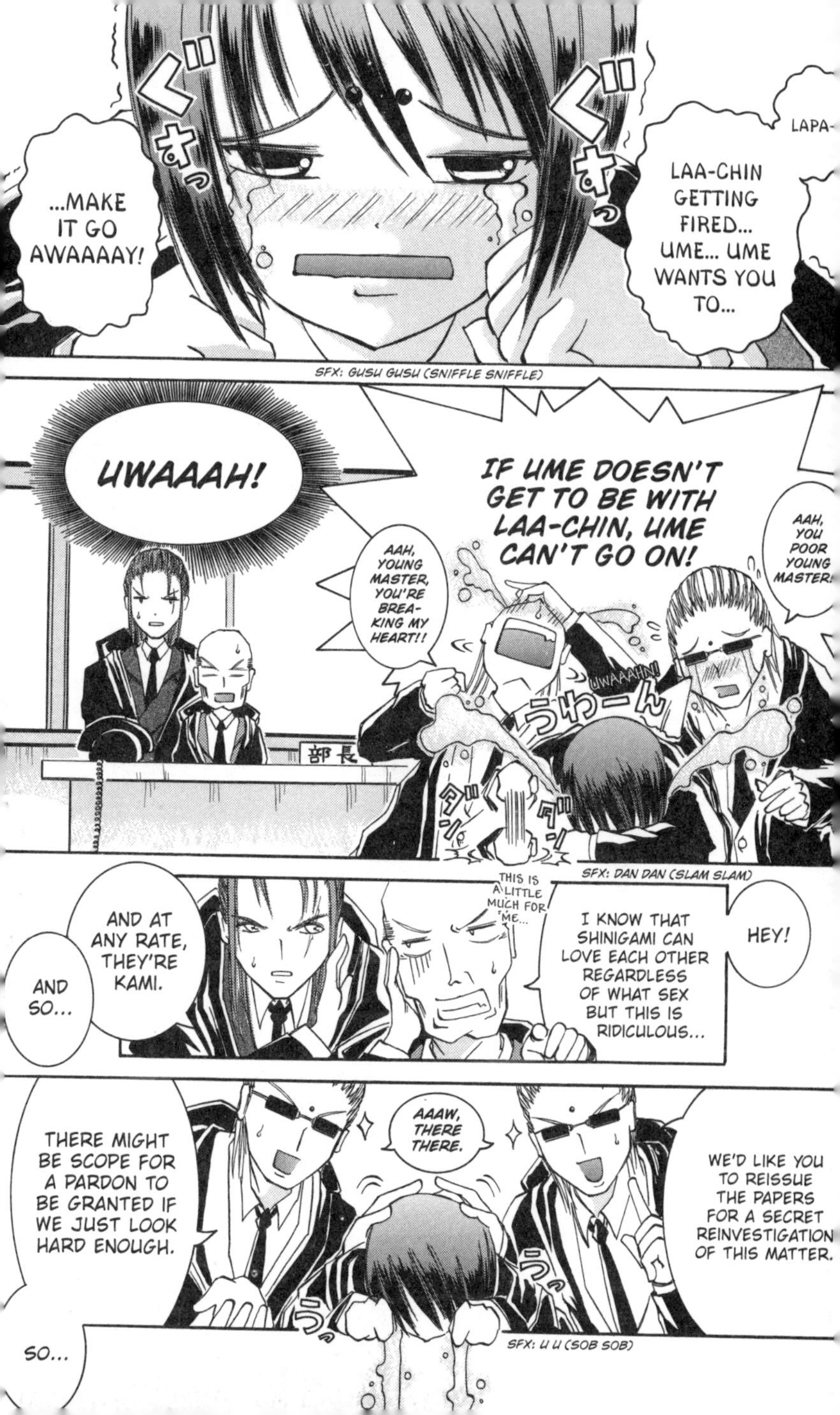
LAPA-
LAA-CHIN GETTING FIRED... UME... UME WANTS YOU TO...
...MAKE IT GO AWAAAAY!
SFX: GUSU GUSU (SNIFFLE SNIFFLE)
AAH, YOU POOR YOUNG MASTER!
IF UME DOESN'T GET TO BE WITH LAA-CHIN, UME CAN'T GO ON!
UWAAAHN!
AAH, YOUNG MASTER, YOU'RE BREA-KING MY HEART!!
UWAAAH!
部長
SFX: DAN DAN (SLAM SLAM)
HEY!
I KNOW THAT SHINIGAMI CAN LOVE EACH OTHER REGARDLESS OF WHAT SEX BUT THIS IS RIDICULOUS...
THIS IS A LITTLE MUCH FOR ME...
AND AT ANY RATE, THEY'RE KAMI.
AND SO...
WE'D LIKE YOU TO REISSUE THE PAPERS FOR A SECRET REINVESTIGATION OF THIS MATTER.
AAAW, THERE THERE.
THERE MIGHT BE SCOPE FOR A PARDON TO BE GRANTED IF WE JUST LOOK HARD ENOUGH.
SO...
SFX: U U (SOB SOB)

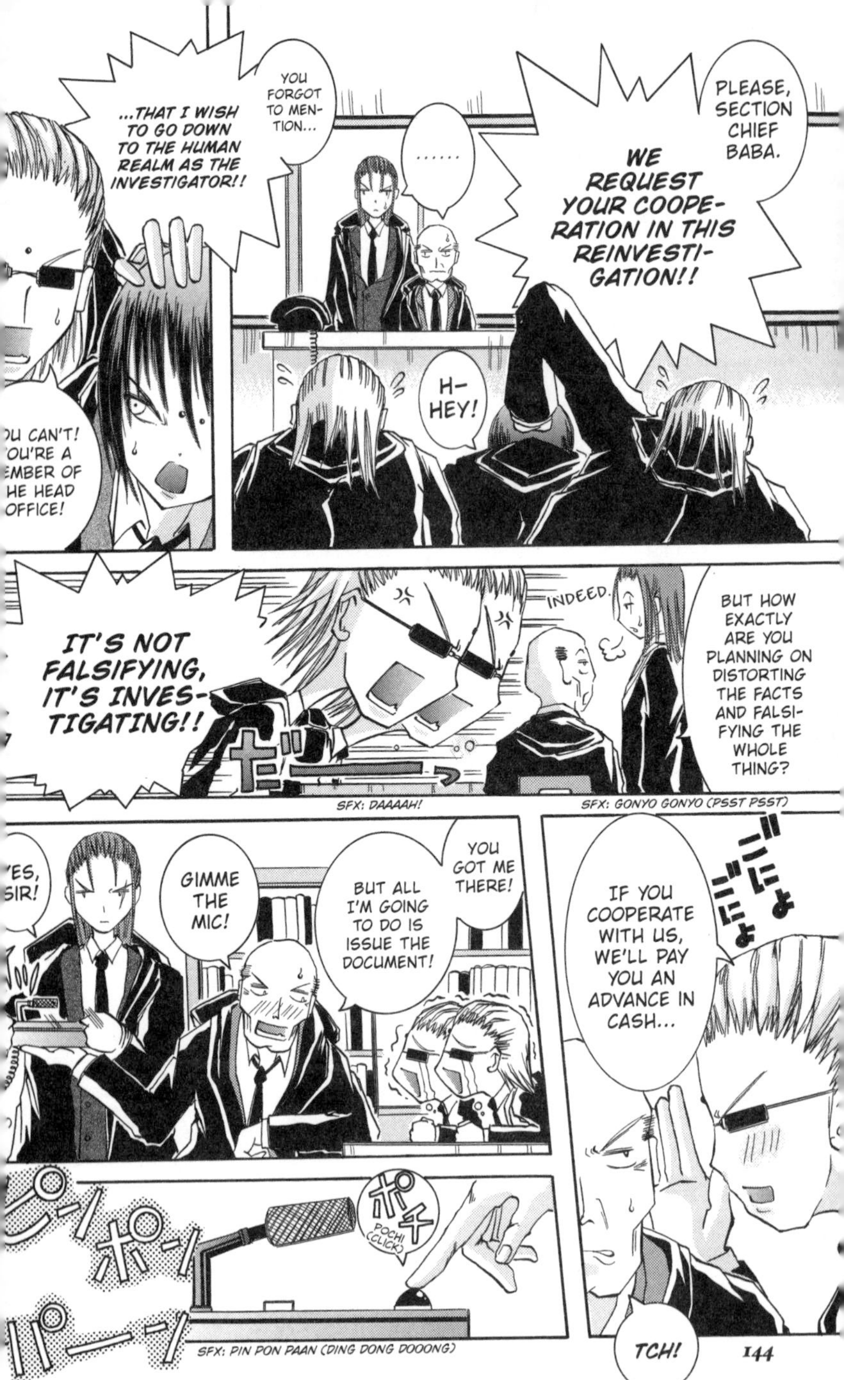
PLEASE, SECTION CHIEF BABA.
WE REQUEST YOUR COOPERATION IN THIS REINVESTIGATION!!
......
YOU FORGOT TO MENTION...
H-HEY!
...THAT I WISH TO GO DOWN TO THE HUMAN REALM AS THE INVESTIGATOR!!
U CAN'T! OU'RE A EMBER OF HE HEAD OFFICE!
BUT HOW EXACTLY ARE YOU PLANNING ON DISTORTING THE FACTS AND FALSIFYING THE WHOLE THING?
INDEED.
SFX: GONYO GONYO (PSST PSST)
IT'S NOT FALSIFYING, IT'S INVESTIGATING!!
SFX: DAAAAH!
ごにょごにょ
IF YOU COOPERATE WITH US, WE'LL PAY YOU AN ADVANCE IN CASH...
TCH!
YOU GOT ME THERE!
BUT ALL I'M GOING TO DO IS ISSUE THE DOCUMENT!
GIMME THE MIC!
ES, SIR!
ポチ
POCHI (CLICK)
ピーンポーンパーン
SFX: PIN PON PAAN (DING DONG DOOONG)

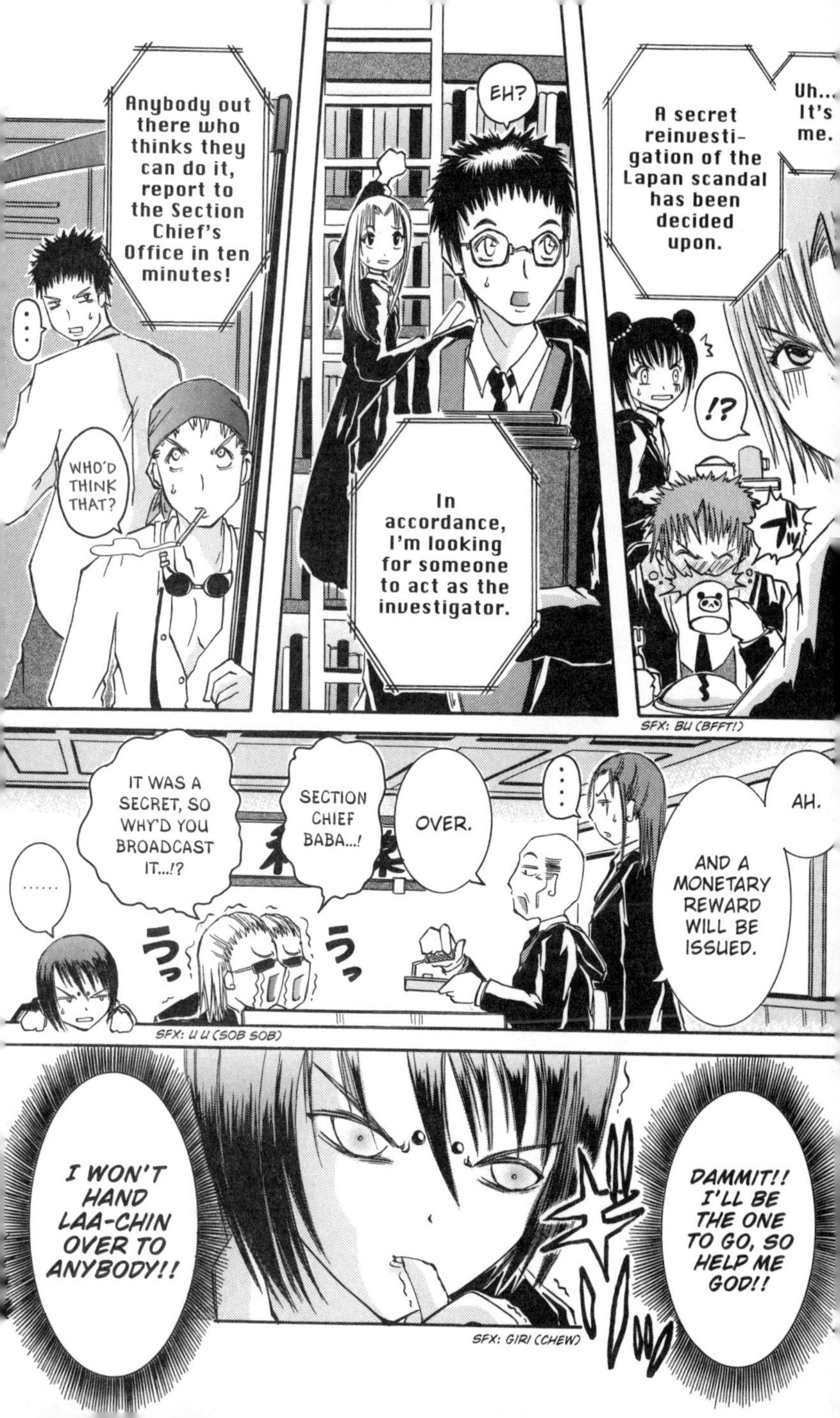
Uh... It's me.
A secret reinvestigation of the Lapan scandal has been decided upon.
!?
SFX: BU (BFFT!)
EH?
In accordance, I'm looking for someone to act as the investigator.
Anybody out there who thinks they can do it, report to the Section Chief's Office in ten minutes!
...
WHO'D THINK THAT?
AH.
AND A MONETARY REWARD WILL BE ISSUED.
....
OVER.
SECTION CHIEF BABA...!
うっ
IT WAS A SECRET, SO WHY'D YOU BROADCAST IT...!?
うっ
......
SFX: U U (SOB SOB)
DAMMIT!! I'LL BE THE ONE TO GO, SO HELP ME GOD!!
I WON'T HAND LAA-CHIN OVER TO ANYBODY!!
SFX: GIRI (CHEW)

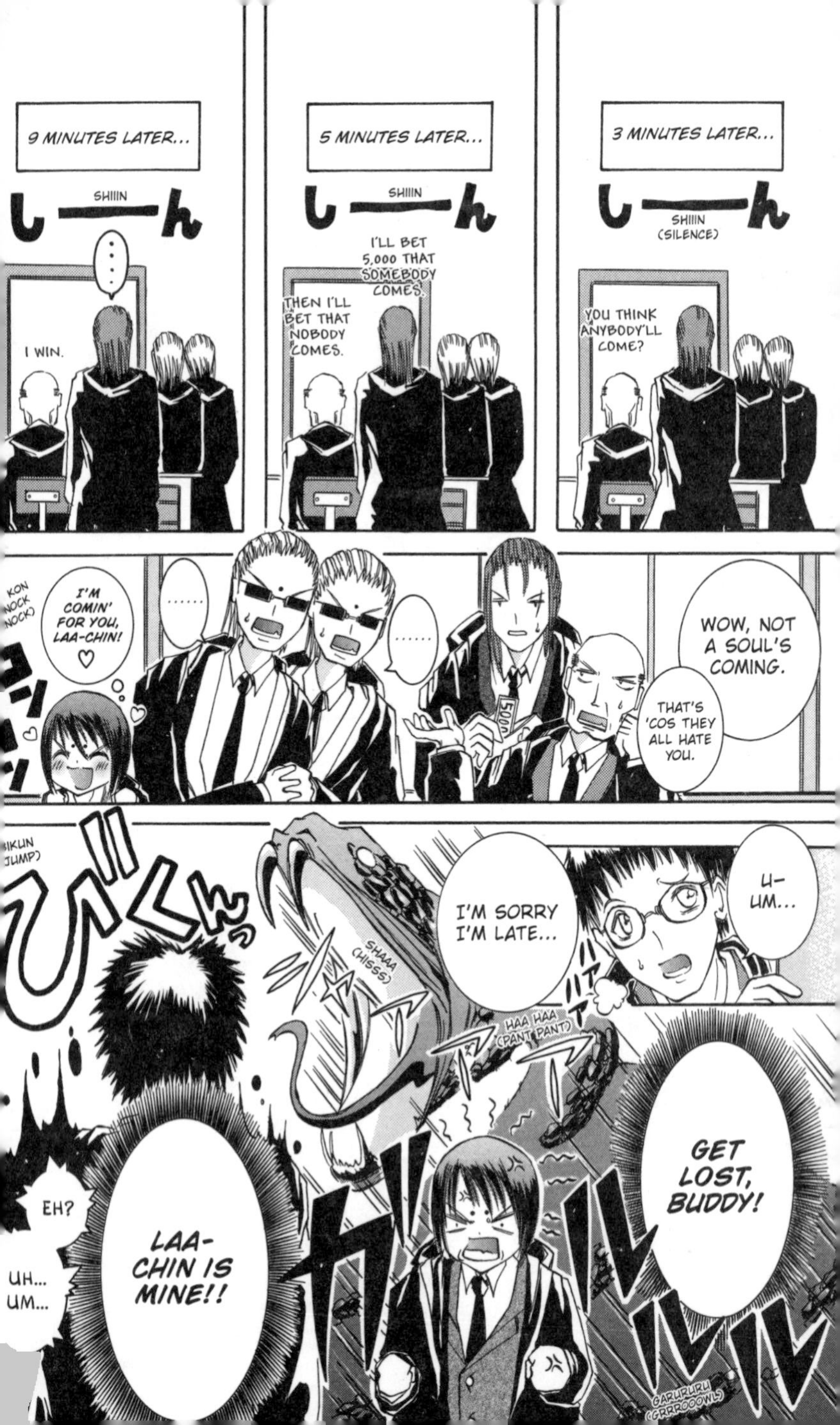
3 MINUTES LATER...
SHIIN (SILENCE)
YOU THINK ANYBODY'LL COME?
5 MINUTES LATER...
SHIIN
I'LL BET 5,000 THAT SOMEBODY COMES.
THEN I'LL BET THAT NOBODY COMES.
9 MINUTES LATER...
SHIIN
...
I WIN.
WOW, NOT A SOUL'S COMING.
THAT'S 'COS THEY ALL HATE YOU.
......
......
I'M COMIN' FOR YOU, LAA-CHIN! ♡
KON NOCK NOCK)
U-UM...
I'M SORRY I'M LATE...
HAA HAA (PANT PANT)
SHAAA (HISSS)
GET LOST, BUDDY!
GARURURU (GRRROOOWL)
LAA-CHIN IS MINE!!
IKUN JUMP)
EH?
UH... UM...

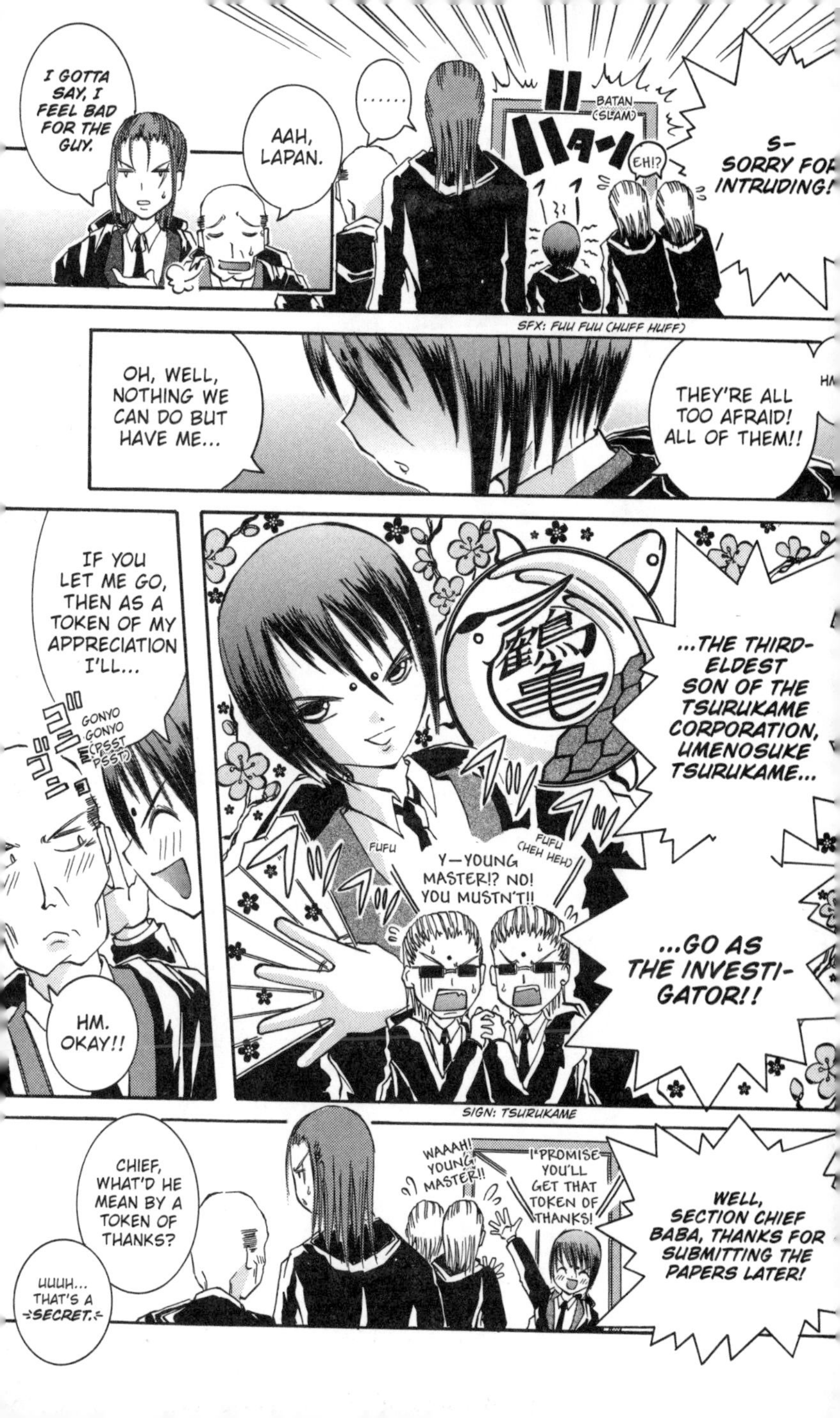
S- SORRY FOR INTRUDING!
EH!?
BATAN (SLAM)
......
AAH, LAPAN.
I GOTTA SAY, I FEEL BAD FOR THE GUY.
SFX: FUU FUU (HUFF HUFF)
THEY'RE ALL TOO AFRAID! ALL OF THEM!!
OH, WELL, NOTHING WE CAN DO BUT HAVE ME...
...THE THIRD-ELDEST SON OF THE TSURUKAME CORPORATION, UMENOSUKE TSURUKAME...
FUFU (HEH HEH)
Y—YOUNG MASTER!? NO! YOU MUSTN'T!!
FUFU
...GO AS THE INVESTIGATOR!!
IF YOU LET ME GO, THEN AS A TOKEN OF MY APPRECIATION I'LL...
GONYO GONYO (PSST PSST)
HM. OKAY!!
SIGN: TSURUKAME
WELL, SECTION CHIEF BABA, THANKS FOR SUBMITTING THE PAPERS LATER!
I PROMISE YOU'LL GET THAT TOKEN OF THANKS!
WAAAH! YOUNG MASTER!!
CHIEF, WHAT'D HE MEAN BY A TOKEN OF THANKS?
UUUH... THAT'S A SECRET.

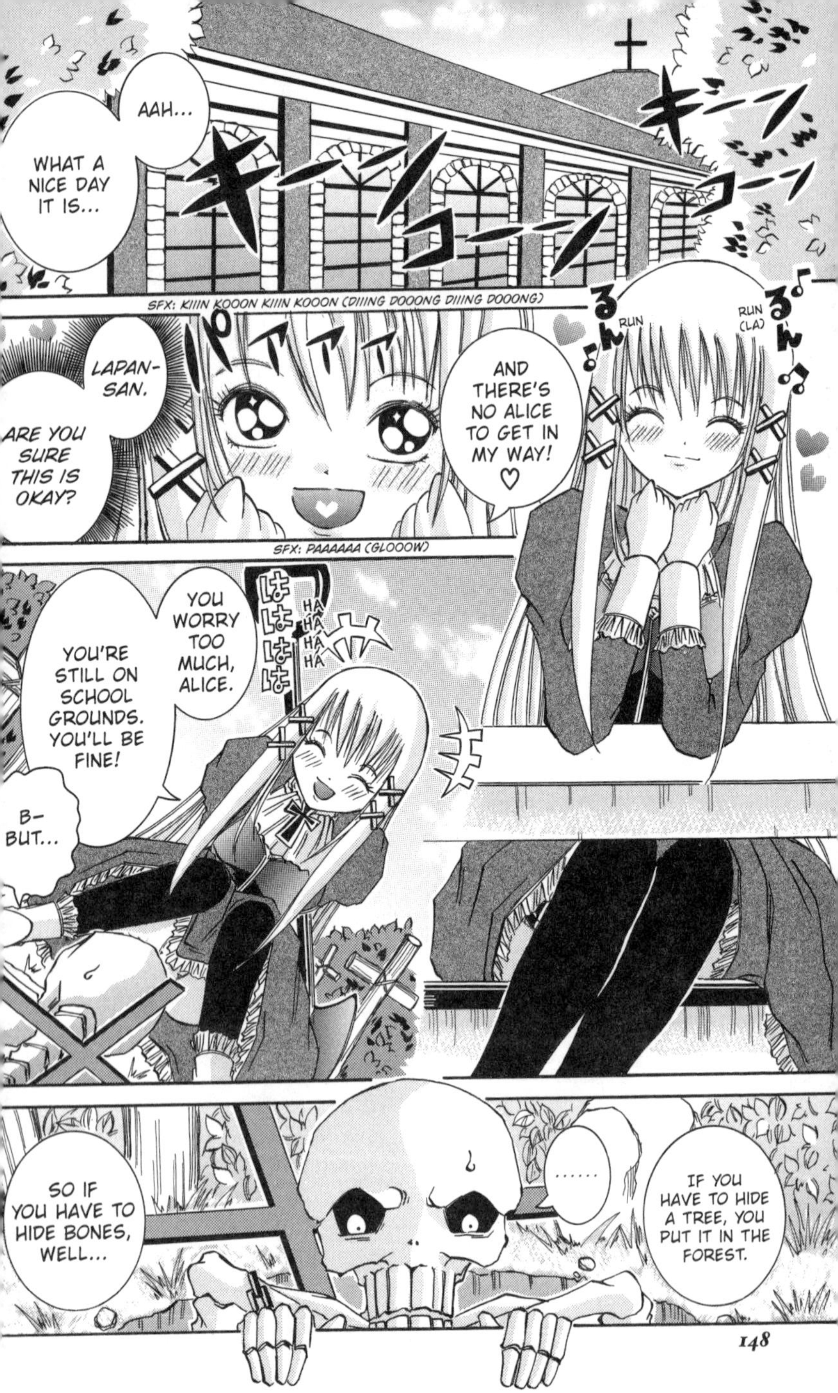
AAH...
WHAT A NICE DAY IT IS...
SFX: KIIIN KOOON KIIIN KOOON (DIIING DOOONG DIIING DOOONG)
RUN (LA)
RUN
AND THERE'S NO ALICE TO GET IN MY WAY! ♡
LAPAN-SAN.
ARE YOU SURE THIS IS OKAY?
SFX: PAAAAAA (GLOOOW)
YOU WORRY TOO MUCH, ALICE.
HA HA HA HA
YOU'RE STILL ON SCHOOL GROUNDS. YOU'LL BE FINE!
B-BUT...
IF YOU HAVE TO HIDE A TREE, YOU PUT IT IN THE FOREST.
......
SO IF YOU HAVE TO HIDE BONES, WELL...

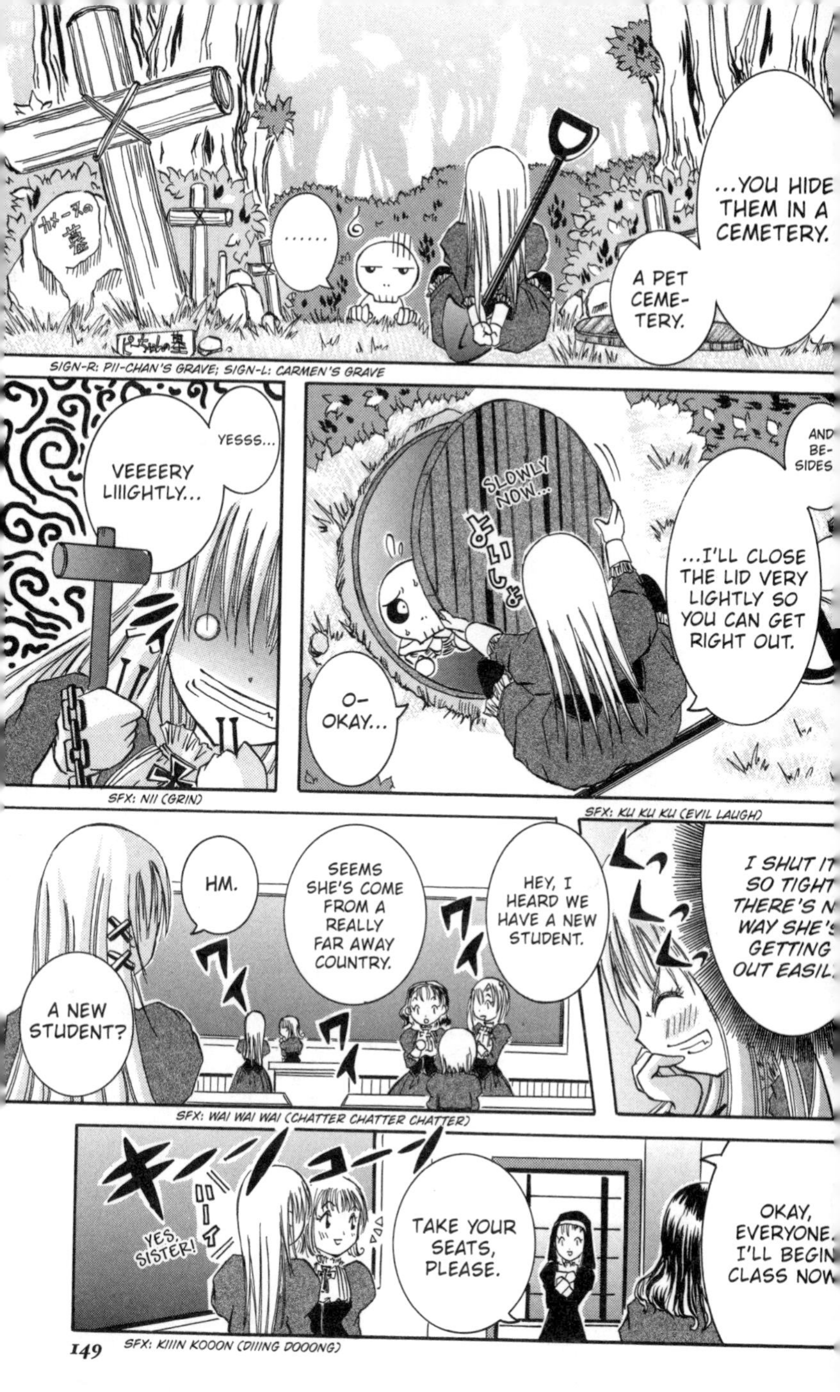
...YOU HIDE THEM IN A CEMETERY.
A PET CEMETERY.
......
SIGN-R: PII-CHAN'S GRAVE; SIGN-L: CARMEN'S GRAVE
AND BESIDES
...I'LL CLOSE THE LID VERY LIGHTLY SO YOU CAN GET RIGHT OUT.
SLOWLY NOW...
よいしょ
O-OKAY...
YESSS...
VEEEERY LIIIGHTLY...
SFX: NII (GRIN)
I SHUT IT SO TIGHT THERE'S N WAY SHE'S GETTING OUT EASIL
SFX: KU KU KU (EVIL LAUGH)
HEY, I HEARD WE HAVE A NEW STUDENT.
SEEMS SHE'S COME FROM A REALLY FAR AWAY COUNTRY.
HM.
A NEW STUDENT?
SFX: WAI WAI WAI (CHATTER CHATTER CHATTER)
OKAY, EVERYONE. I'LL BEGIN CLASS NOW
TAKE YOUR SEATS, PLEASE.
YES, SISTER!
SFX: KIIIN KOOON (DIIING DOOONG)

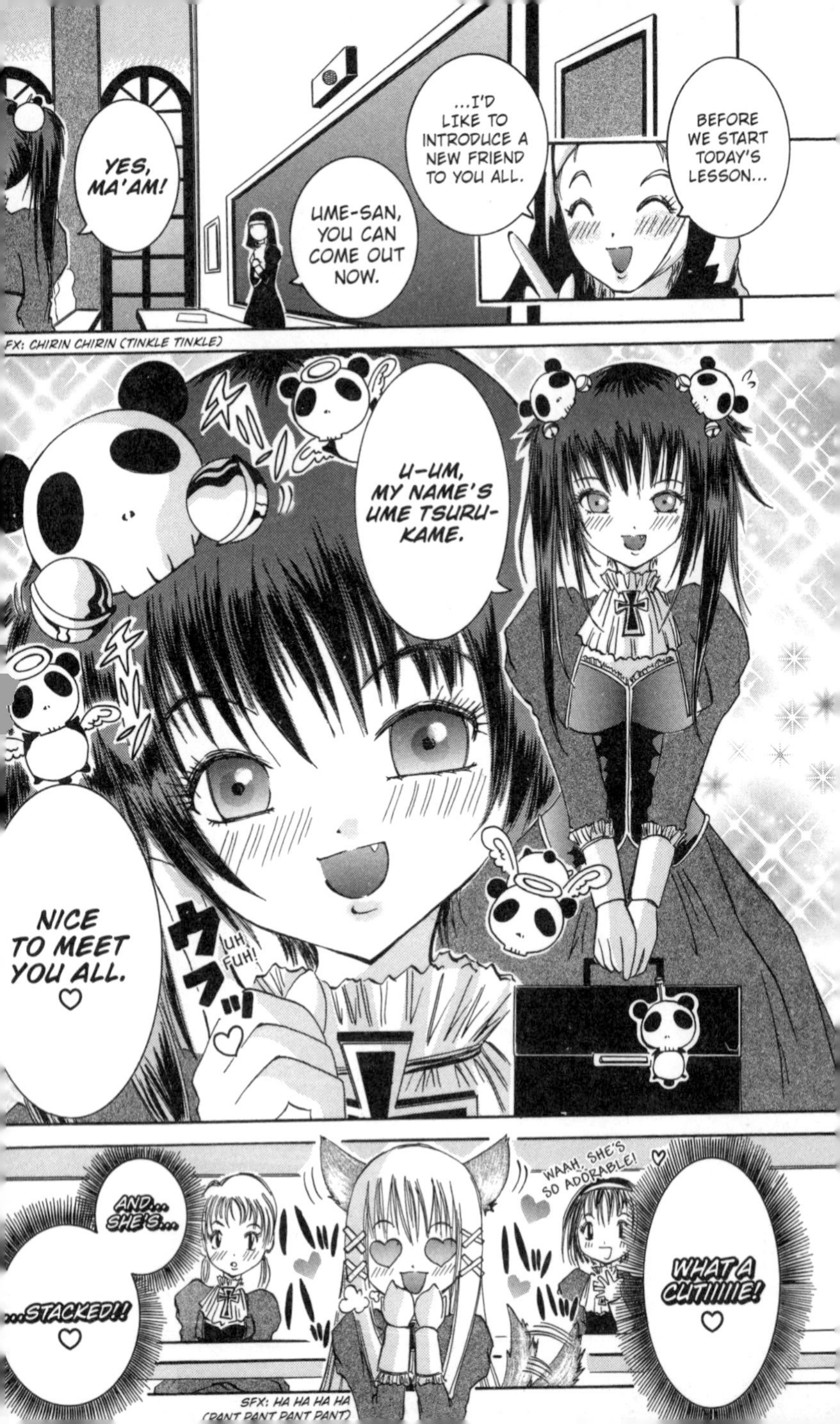

BEFORE WE START TODAY'S LESSON...
...I'D LIKE TO INTRODUCE A NEW FRIEND TO YOU ALL.
UME-SAN, YOU CAN COME OUT NOW.
YES, MA'AM!
FX: CHIRIN CHIRIN (TINKLE TINKLE)
U-UM, MY NAME'S UME TSURU-KAME.
UH FUH!
NICE TO MEET YOU ALL. ♡
WHAT A CUTIIIIIE! ♡
WAAH, SHE'S SO ADORABLE! ♡
AND... SHE'S...
...STACKED!! ♡
SFX: HA HA HA HA (PANT PANT PANT PANT)

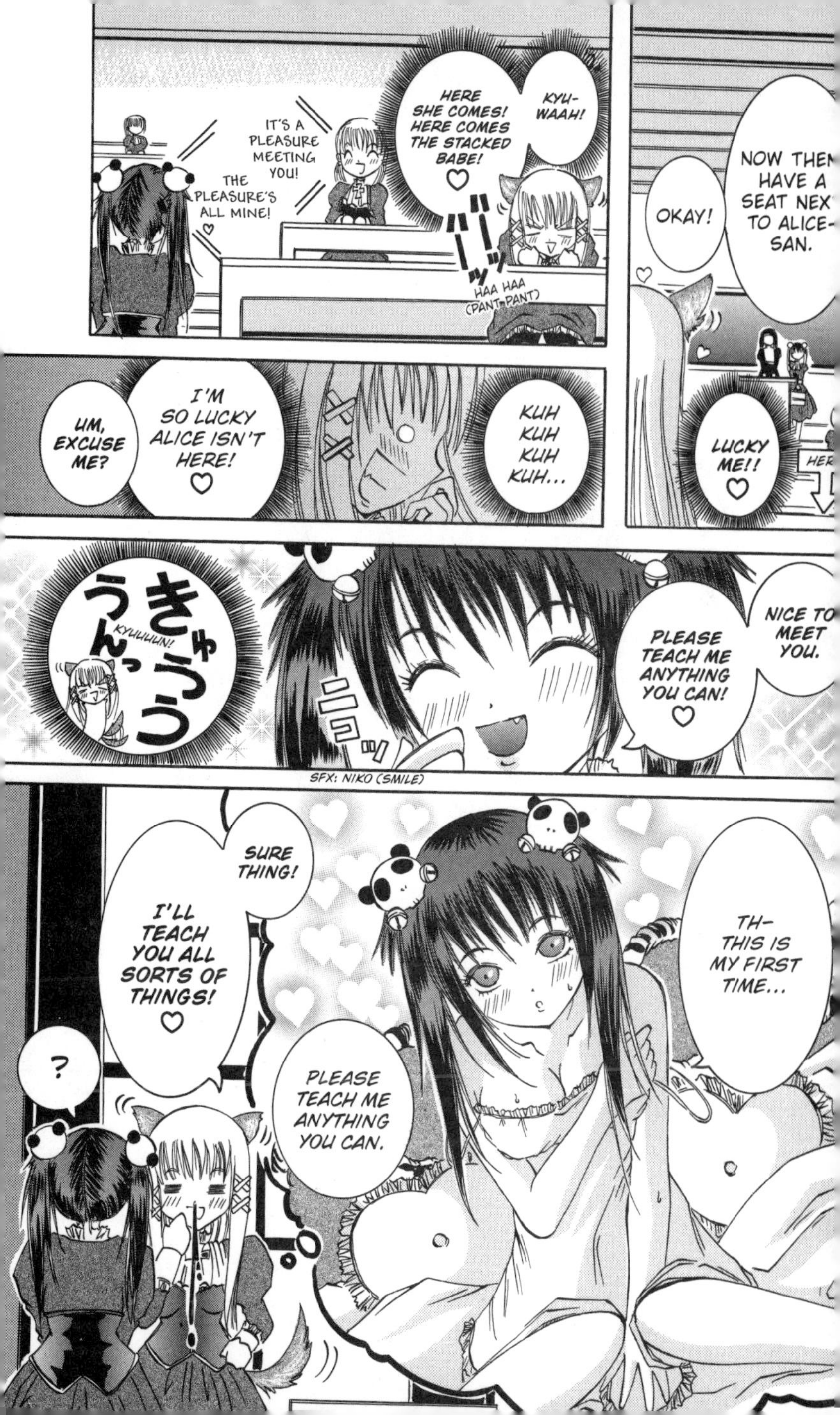
NOW THEN HAVE A SEAT NEX TO ALICE-SAN.
OKAY!
LUCKY ME!! ♡
HER
KYU-WAAH!
HERE SHE COMES! HERE COMES THE STACKED BABE! ♡
IT'S A PLEASURE MEETING YOU!
THE PLEASURE'S ALL MINE! ♡
HAA HAA (PANT PANT)
KUH KUH KUH KUH...
I'M SO LUCKY ALICE ISN'T HERE! ♡
UM, EXCUSE ME?
NICE TO MEET YOU.
PLEASE TEACH ME ANYTHING YOU CAN! ♡
きゅうううんっ
KYUUUUN!
SFX: NIKO (SMILE)
TH- THIS IS MY FIRST TIME...
PLEASE TEACH ME ANYTHING YOU CAN.
SURE THING!
I'LL TEACH YOU ALL SORTS OF THINGS! ♡
?

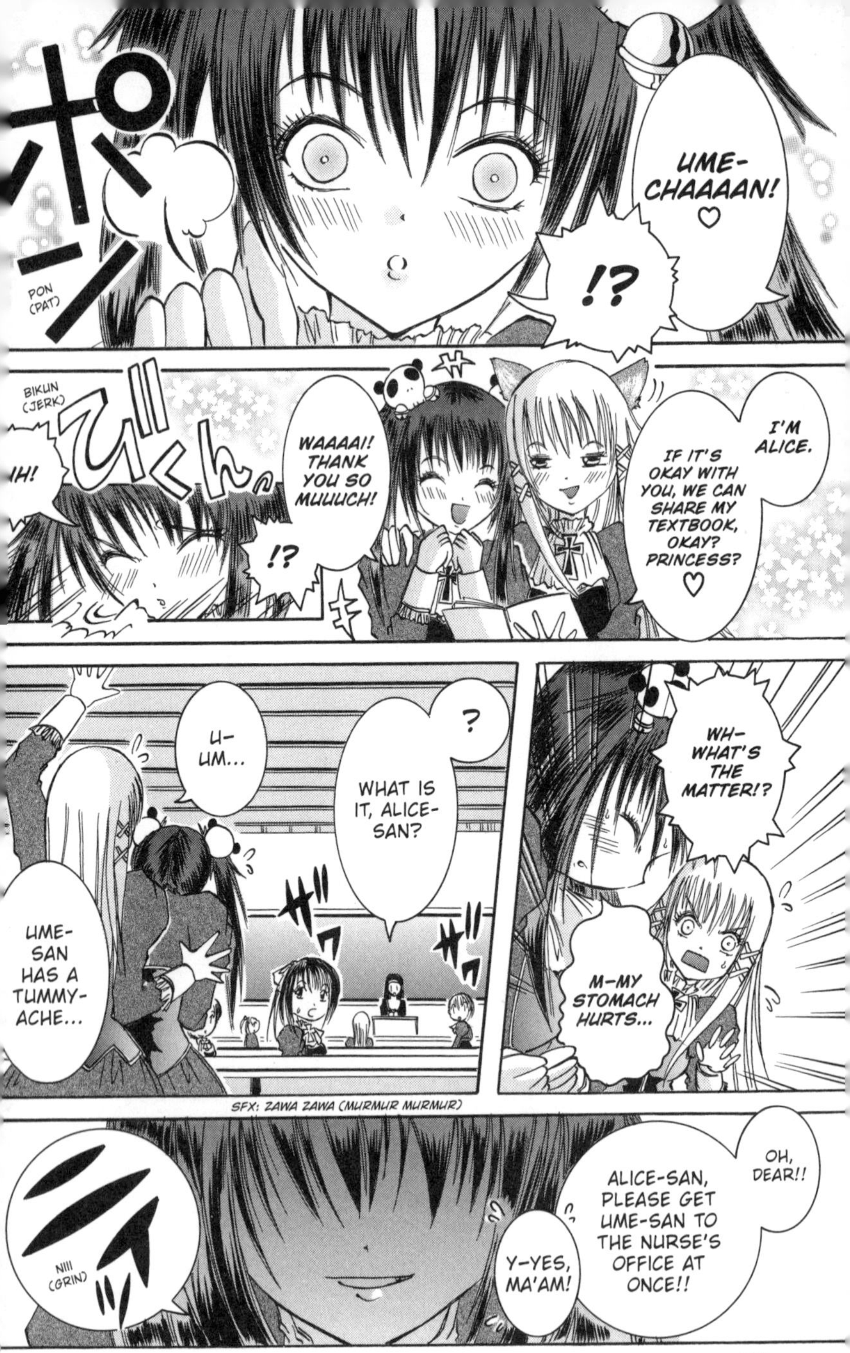

UME-CHAAAAN! ♡
!?
PON (PAT)
I'M ALICE.
IF IT'S OKAY WITH YOU, WE CAN SHARE MY TEXTBOOK, OKAY? PRINCESS? ♡
WAAAAI! THANK YOU SO MUUUCH!
!?
BIKUN (JERK)
WH-WHAT'S THE MATTER!?
M-MY STOMACH HURTS...
?
WHAT IS IT, ALICE-SAN?
U-UM...
UME-SAN HAS A TUMMY-ACHE...
SFX: ZAWA ZAWA (MURMUR MURMUR)
OH, DEAR!!
ALICE-SAN, PLEASE GET UME-SAN TO THE NURSE'S OFFICE AT ONCE!!
Y-YES, MA'AM!
NIII (GRIN)

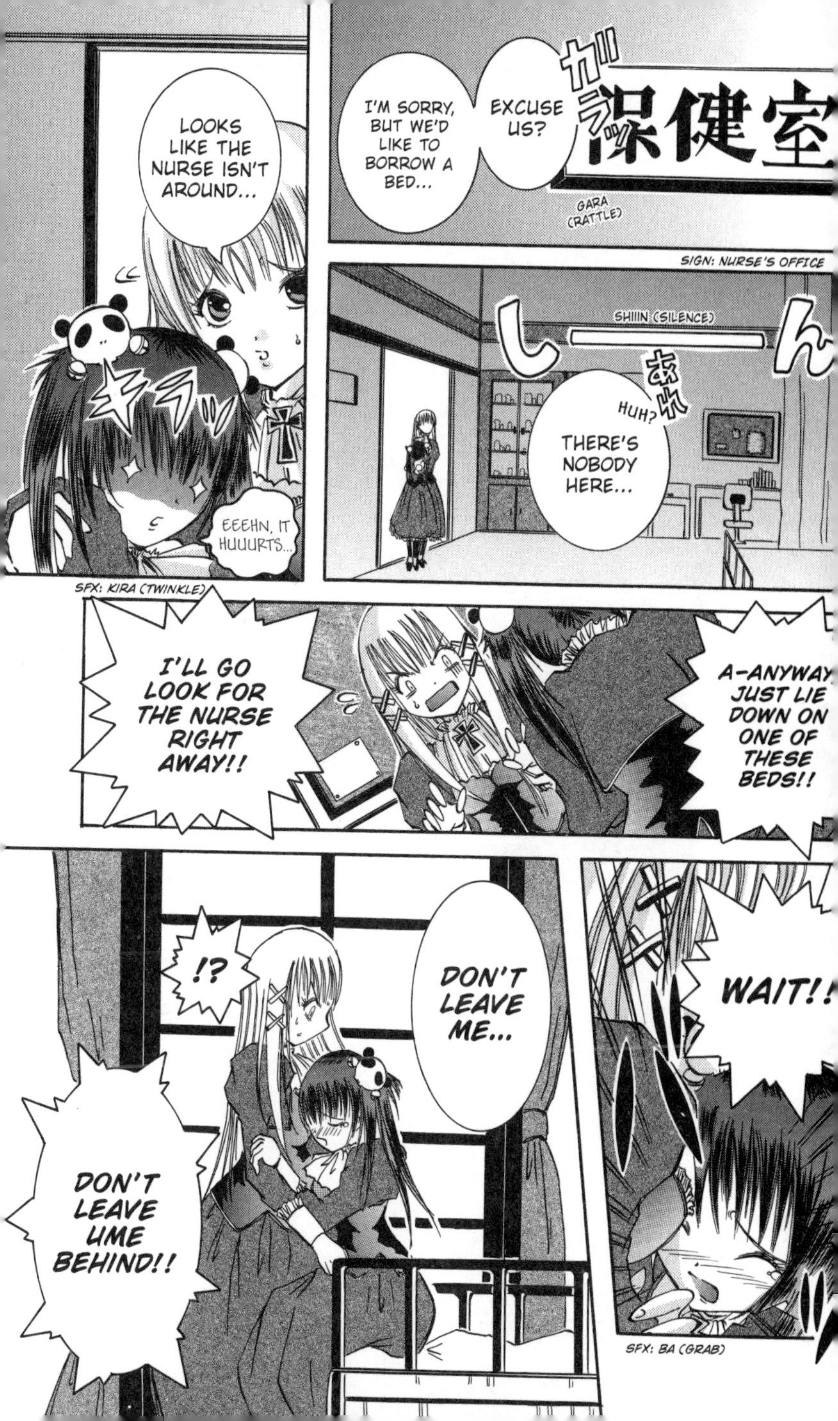

ガラ
保健室
EXCUSE US?
I'M SORRY, BUT WE'D LIKE TO BORROW A BED...
GARA (RATTLE)
SIGN: NURSE'S OFFICE
しーん
SHIIIN (SILENCE)
あれ
HUH?
THERE'S NOBODY HERE...
LOOKS LIKE THE NURSE ISN'T AROUND...
EEEHN, IT HUUURTS...
SFX: KIRA (TWINKLE)
A-ANYWAY JUST LIE DOWN ON ONE OF THESE BEDS!!
I'LL GO LOOK FOR THE NURSE RIGHT AWAY!!
WAIT!!
SFX: BA (GRAB)
!?
DON'T LEAVE ME...
DON'T LEAVE UME BEHIND!!

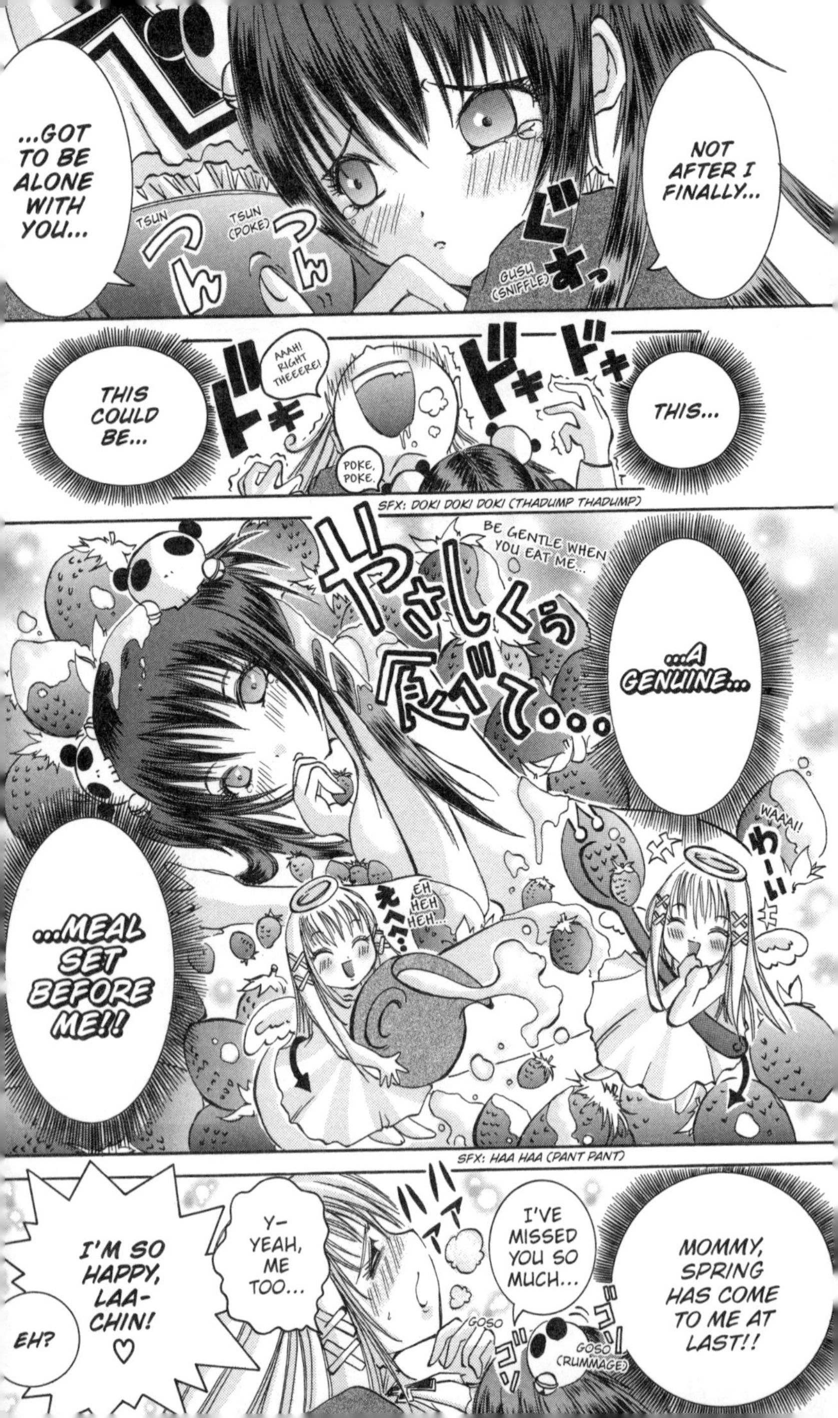
NOT AFTER I FINALLY...
GUSU (SNIFFLE)
TSUN
TSUN (POKE)
...GOT TO BE ALONE WITH YOU...
THIS...
AAAH! RIGHT THEEERE!
POKE, POKE.
THIS COULD BE...
SFX: DOKI DOKI DOKI (THADUMP THADUMP)
...A GENUINE...
BE GENTLE WHEN YOU EAT ME...
WAAAI!
EH HEH HEH...
...MEAL SET BEFORE ME!!
SFX: HAA HAA (PANT PANT)
MOMMY, SPRING HAS COME TO ME AT LAST!!
GOSO
GOSO (RUMMAGE)
I'VE MISSED YOU SO MUCH...
Y-YEAH, ME TOO...
I'M SO HAPPY, LAA-CHIN! ♡
EH?

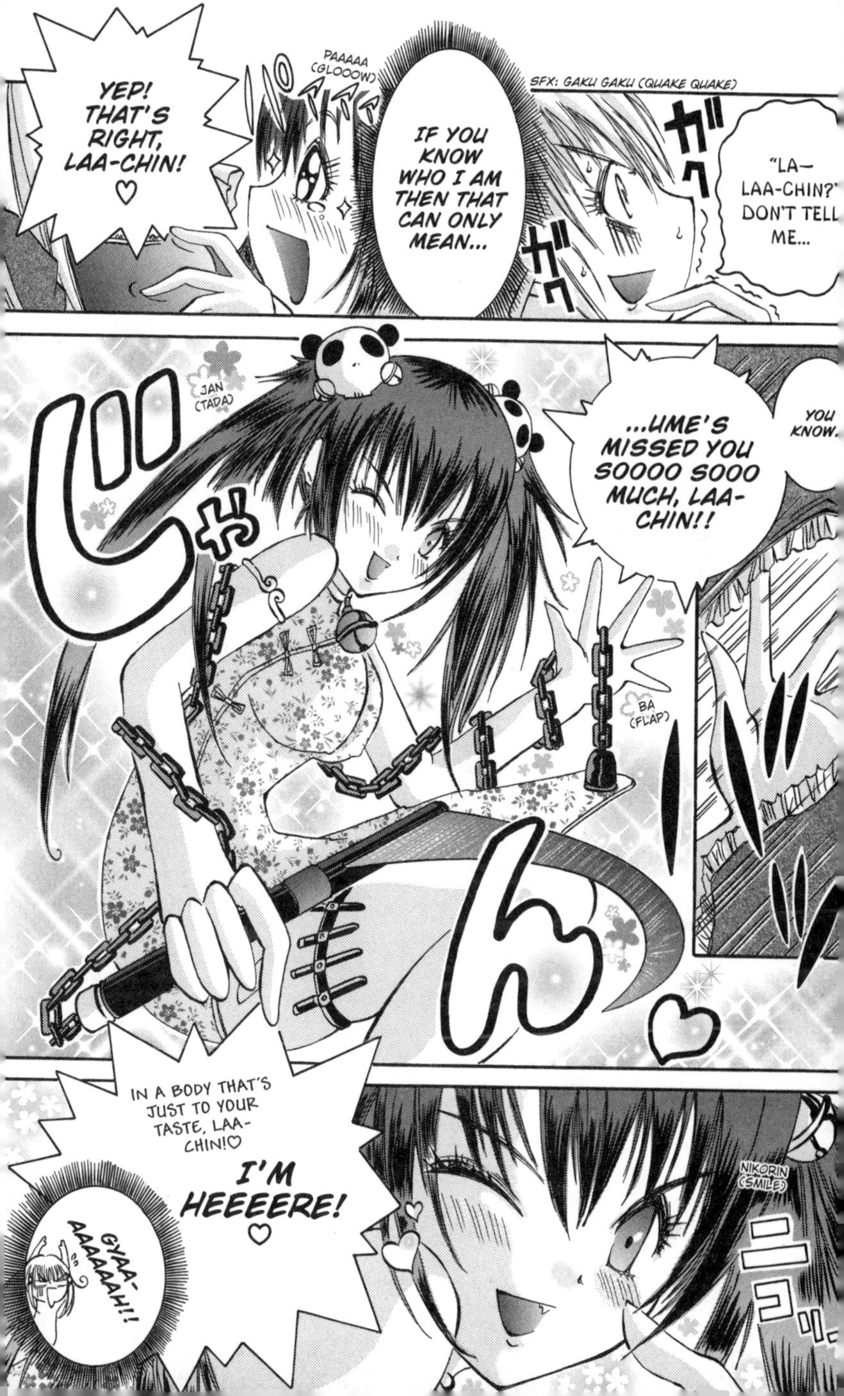
SFX: GAKU GAKU (QUAKE QUAKE)
"LA— LAA-CHIN?" DON'T TELL ME...
IF YOU KNOW WHO I AM THEN THAT CAN ONLY MEAN...
PAAAAA (GLOOOW)
YEP! THAT'S RIGHT, LAA-CHIN! ♡
YOU KNOW.
...UME'S MISSED YOU SOOOO SOOO MUCH, LAA-CHIN!!
BA (FLAP)
JAN (TADA)
NIKORIN (SMILE)
IN A BODY THAT'S JUST TO YOUR TASTE, LAA-CHIN!♡
I'M HEEEERE! ♡
GYAA-AAAAAAH!!

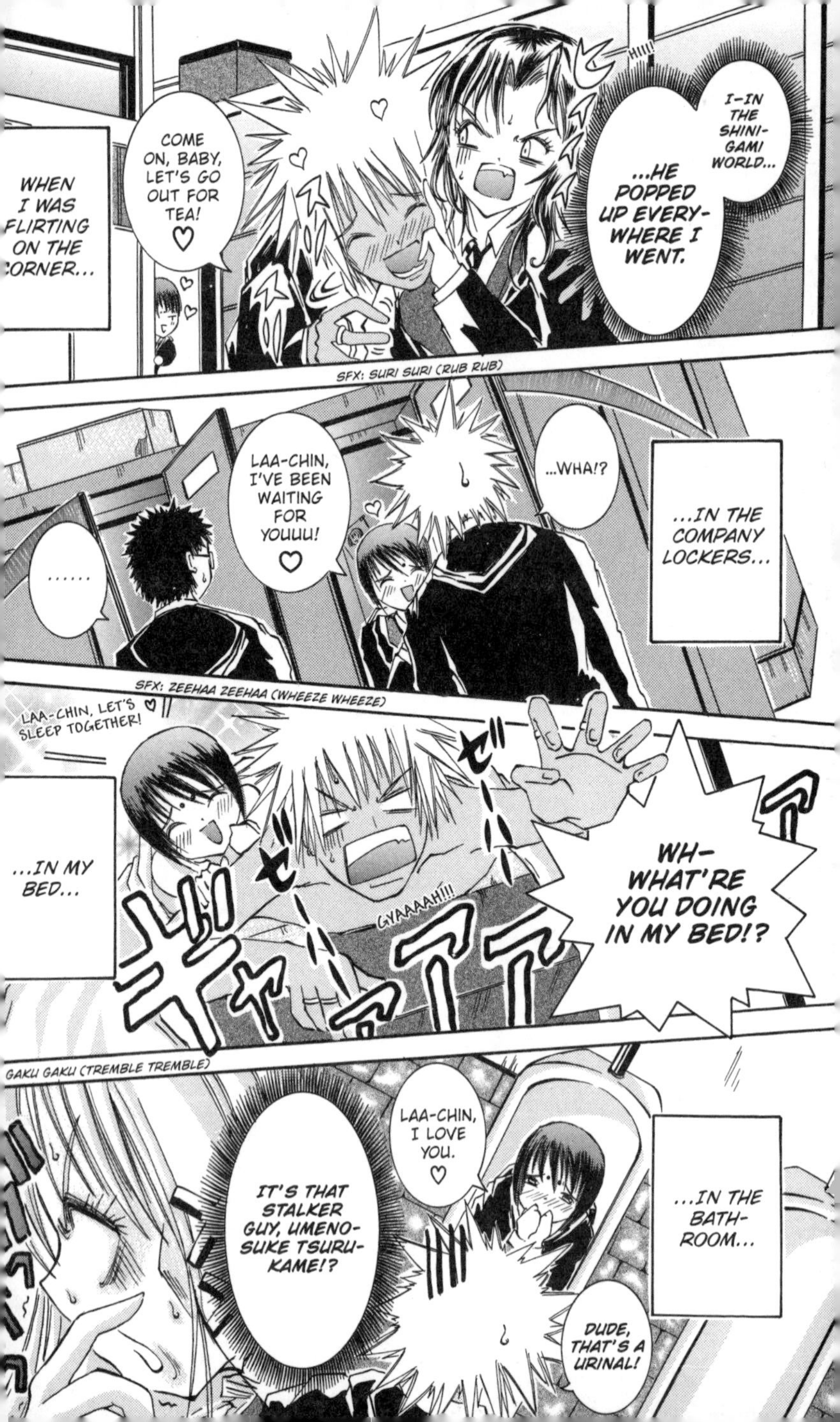
HIII!
I-IN THE SHINIGAMI WORLD...
...HE POPPED UP EVERYWHERE I WENT.
COME ON, BABY, LET'S GO OUT FOR TEA! ♡
WHEN I WAS FLIRTING ON THE CORNER...
SFX: SURI SURI (RUB RUB)
...IN THE COMPANY LOCKERS...
...WHA!?
LAA-CHIN, I'VE BEEN WAITING FOR YOUUU! ♡
......
SFX: ZEEHAA ZEEHAA (WHEEZE WHEEZE)
WH-WHAT'RE YOU DOING IN MY BED!?
GYAAAAH!!!
LAA-CHIN, LET'S SLEEP TOGETHER! ♡
...IN MY BED...
GAKU GAKU (TREMBLE TREMBLE)
...IN THE BATHROOM...
LAA-CHIN, I LOVE YOU. ♡
DUDE, THAT'S A URINAL!
IT'S THAT STALKER GUY, UMENOSUKE TSURUKAME!?

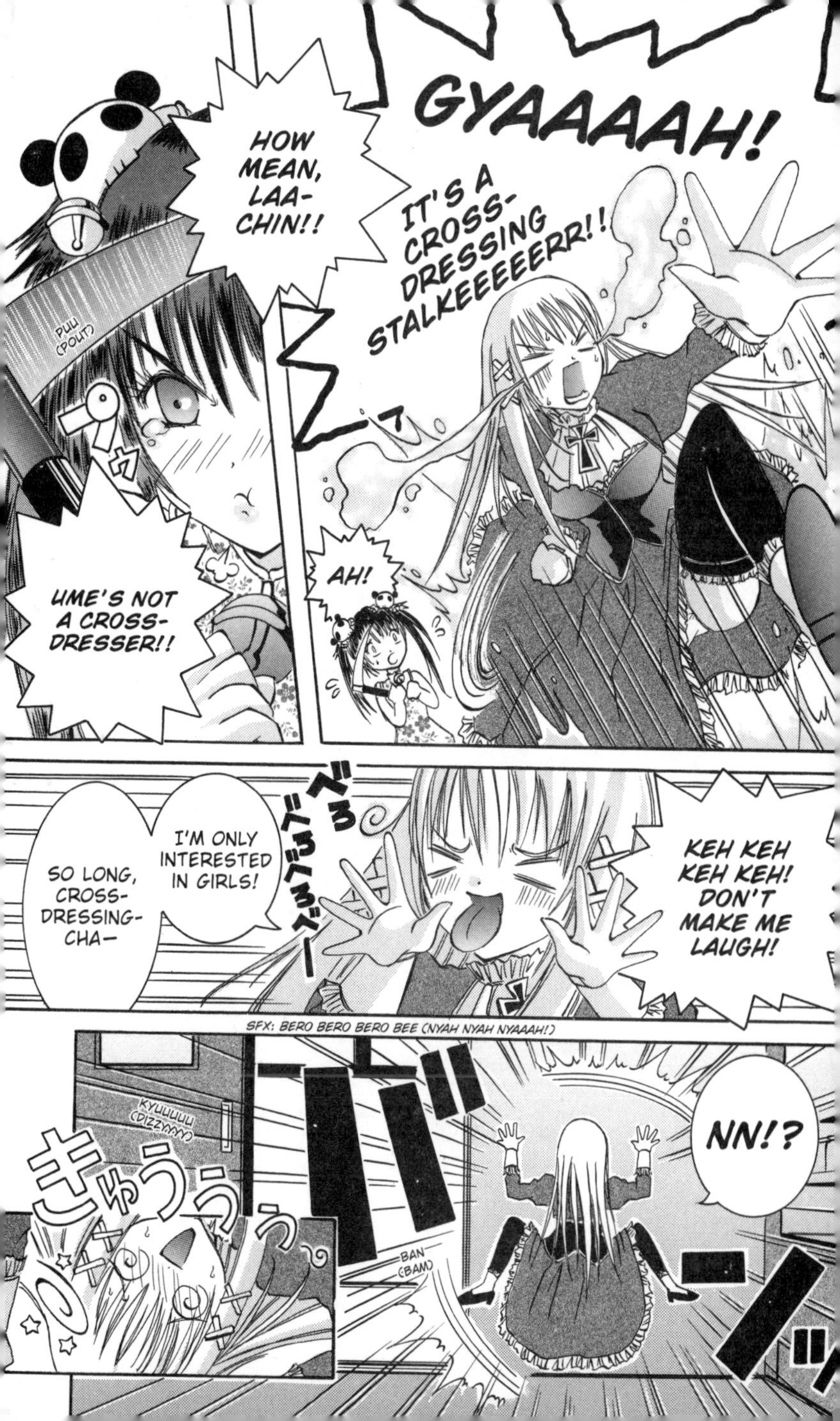
GYAAAAAH!
IT'S A CROSS-DRESSING STALKEEEEEERR!!
AH!
HOW MEAN, LAA-CHIN!!
PUU (POUT)
UME'S NOT A CROSS-DRESSER!!
KEH KEH KEH KEH! DON'T MAKE ME LAUGH!
べろべろべろべー
I'M ONLY INTERESTED IN GIRLS!
SO LONG, CROSS-DRESSING-CHA—
SFX: BERO BERO BERO BEE (NYAH NYAH NYAAAH!)
NN!?
BAN (BAM)
KYUUUUU (DIZZYYYY)
きゅううう

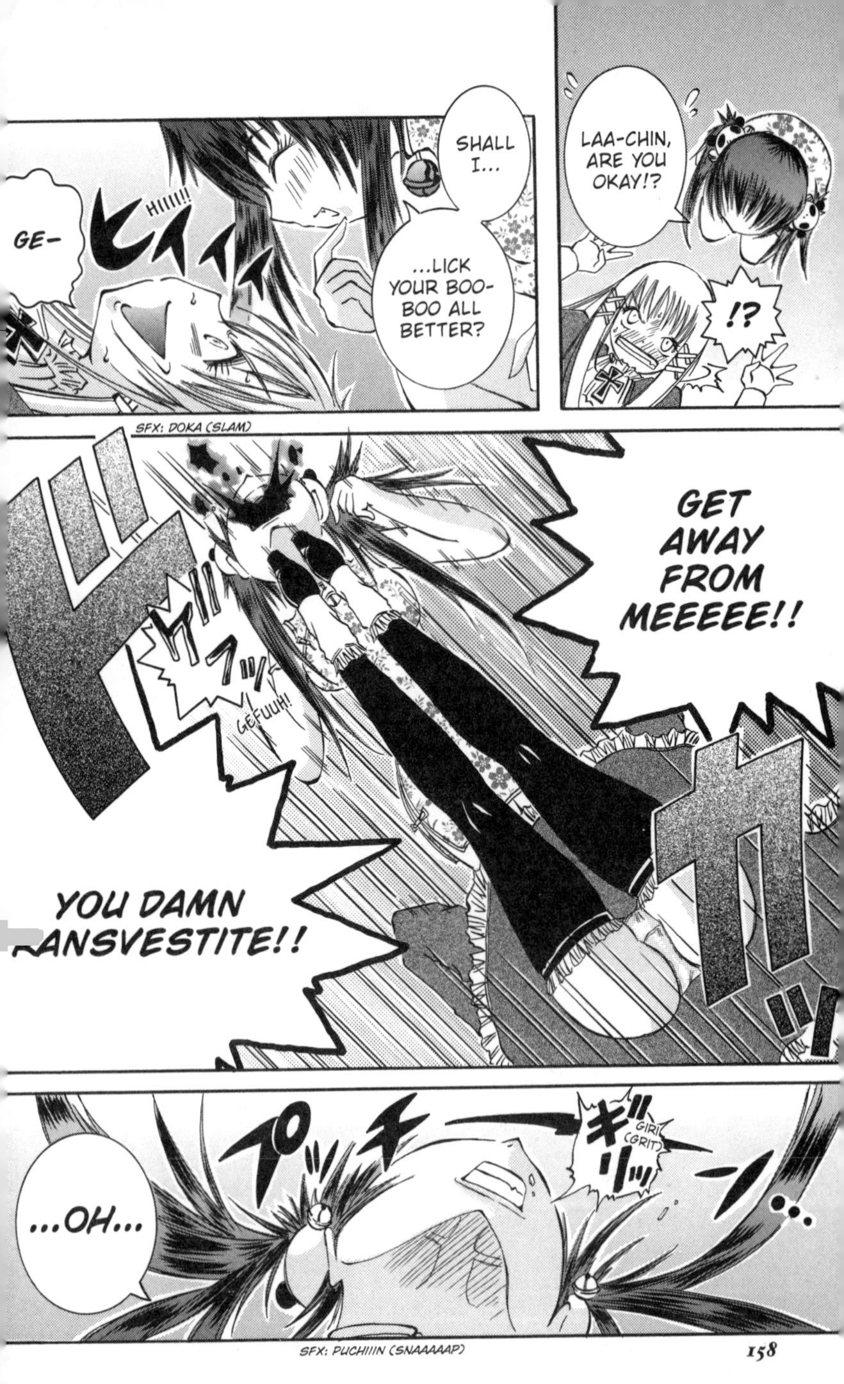

LAA-CHIN, ARE YOU OKAY!?
!?
SHALL I...
...LICK YOUR BOO-BOO ALL BETTER?
HIIIII!!
GE-
SFX: DOKA (SLAM)
GET AWAY FROM MEEEEE!!
GEFUUH!
YOU DAMN ANSVESTITE!!
GIRI (GRIT)
...OH...
SFX: PUCHIIIN (SNAAAAAP)

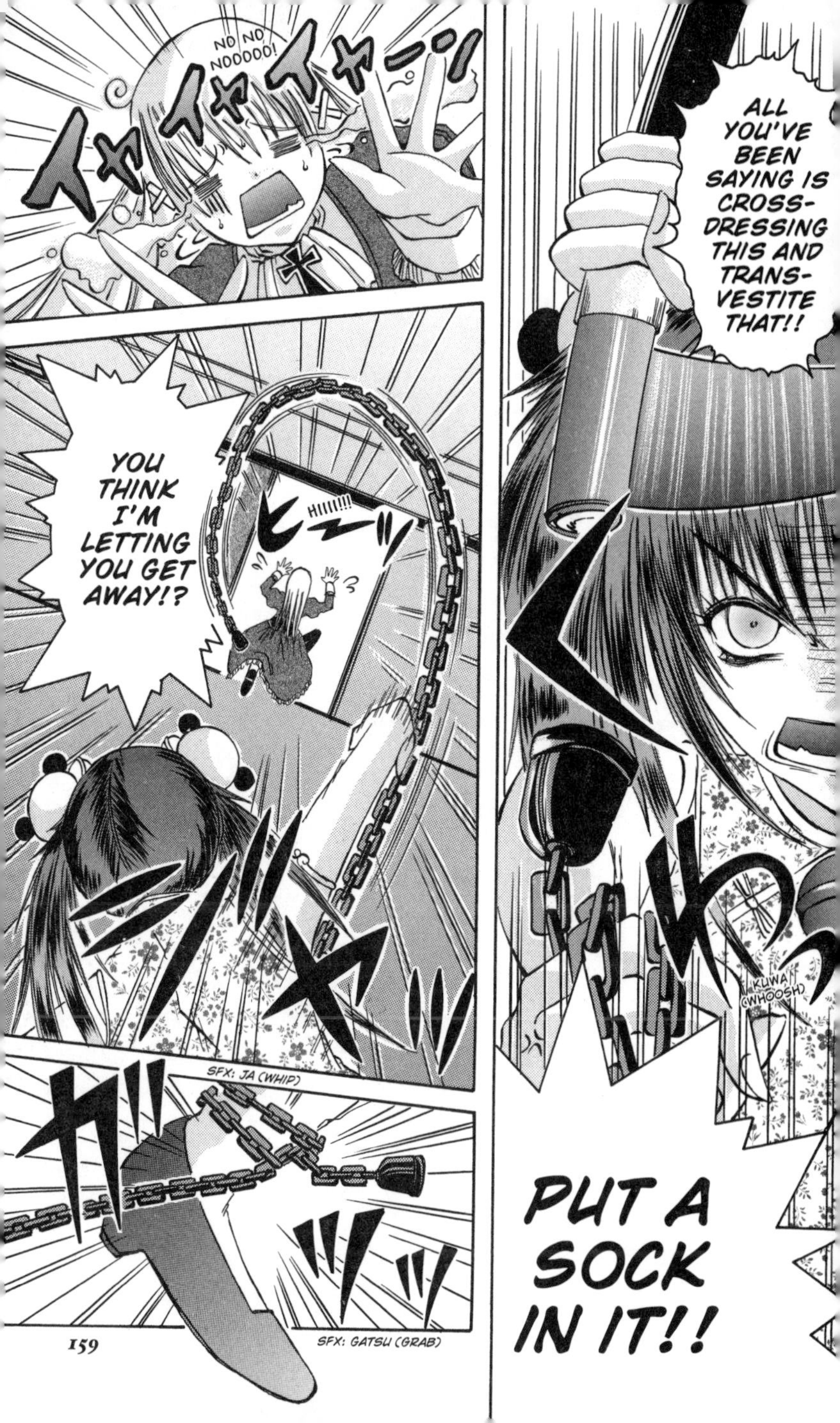
ALL YOU'VE BEEN SAYING IS CROSS-DRESSING THIS AND TRANS-VESTITE THAT!!
KUWA!! (WHOOSH)
PUT A SOCK IN IT!!
NO NO NOOOOO!
YOU THINK I'M LETTING YOU GET AWAY!?
HIIII!!!
SFX: JA (WHIP)
SFX: GATSU (GRAB)

D-DAMMIT! THE DOOR OF LIGHT'S...

ZURI (CRAWL)

ZURI (CRAWL)

...JUST A LITTLE FURTHER...!

BITAN (TRIP)

BU (OOF!)

SFX: GOGOGOGOGOGO (RRRRRUMBLE)

LAAAA-

-CHIN! ♡

A-WA WA

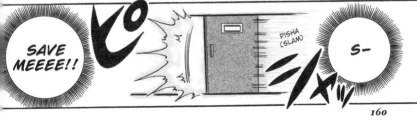

SAVE MEEEE!!

PISHA (SLAM)

S-

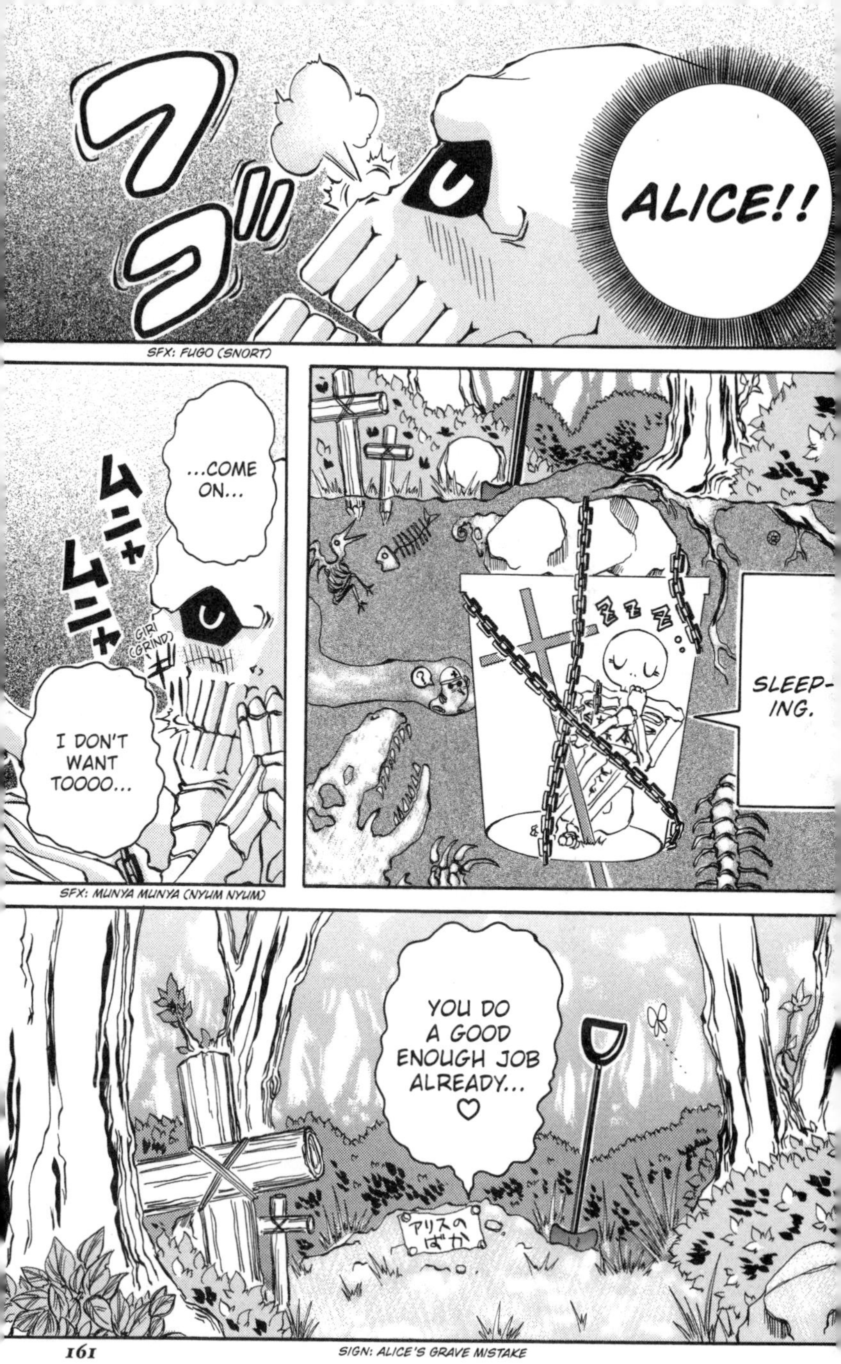
フゴ
ALICE!!
SLEEP-
ING.
ムニャ
ムニャ
...COME
ON...
GIRI
(GRIND)
I DON'T
WANT
TOOOO...
YOU DO
A GOOD
ENOUGH JOB
ALREADY...
♡
アリスの
ばか

SFX: FUGO (SNORT)

SFX: MUNYA MUNYA (NYUM NYUM)

SIGN: ALICE'S GRAVE MISTAKE

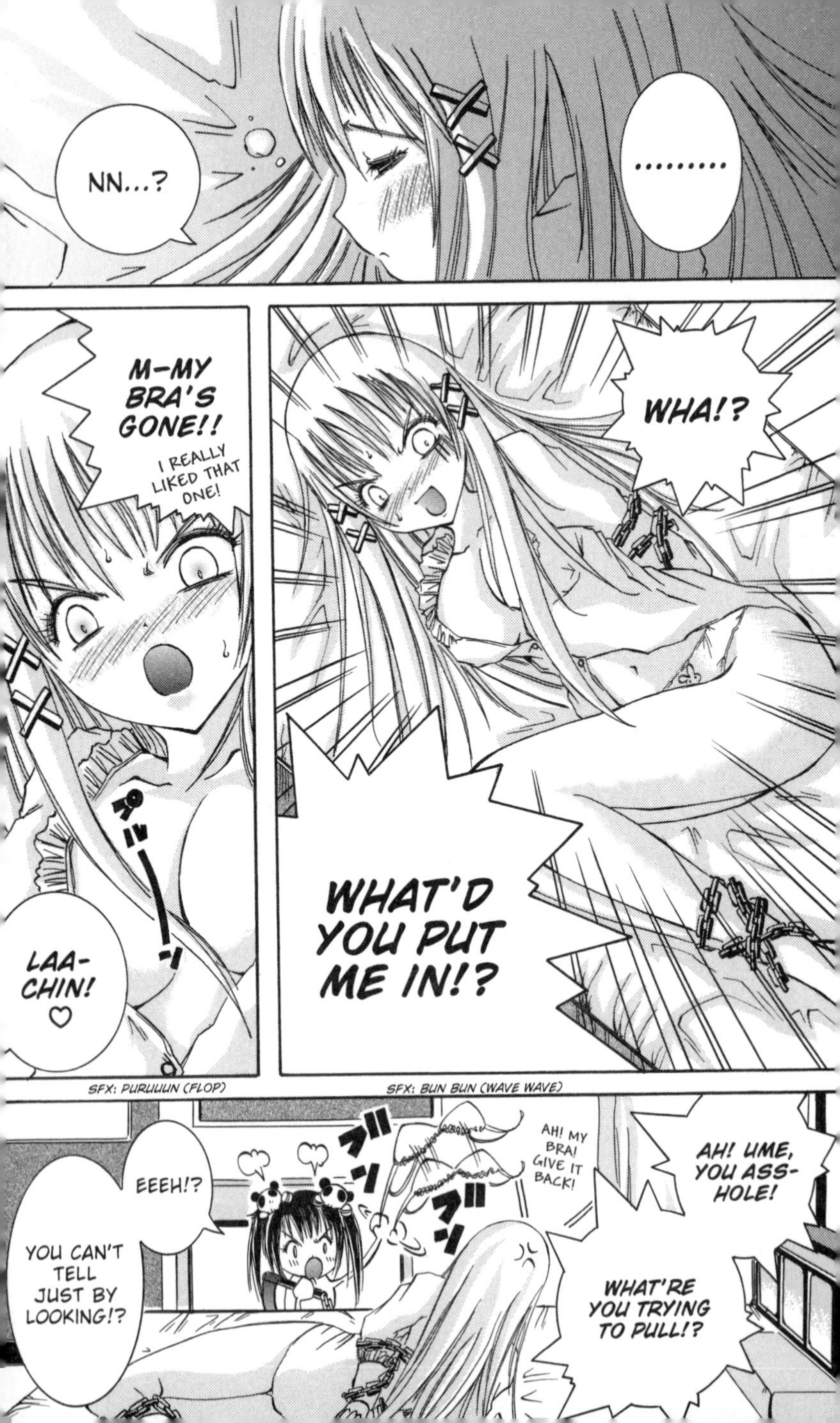
....
NN...?
WHA!?
WHAT'D YOU PUT ME IN!?
SFX: BUN BUN (WAVE WAVE)
M-MY BRA'S GONE!!
I REALLY LIKED THAT ONE!
LAA-CHIN! ♡
SFX: PURUUUN (FLOP)
AH! UME, YOU ASS-HOLE!
AH! MY BRA! GIVE IT BACK!
WHAT'RE YOU TRYING TO PULL!?
EEEH!?
YOU CAN'T TELL JUST BY LOOKING!?

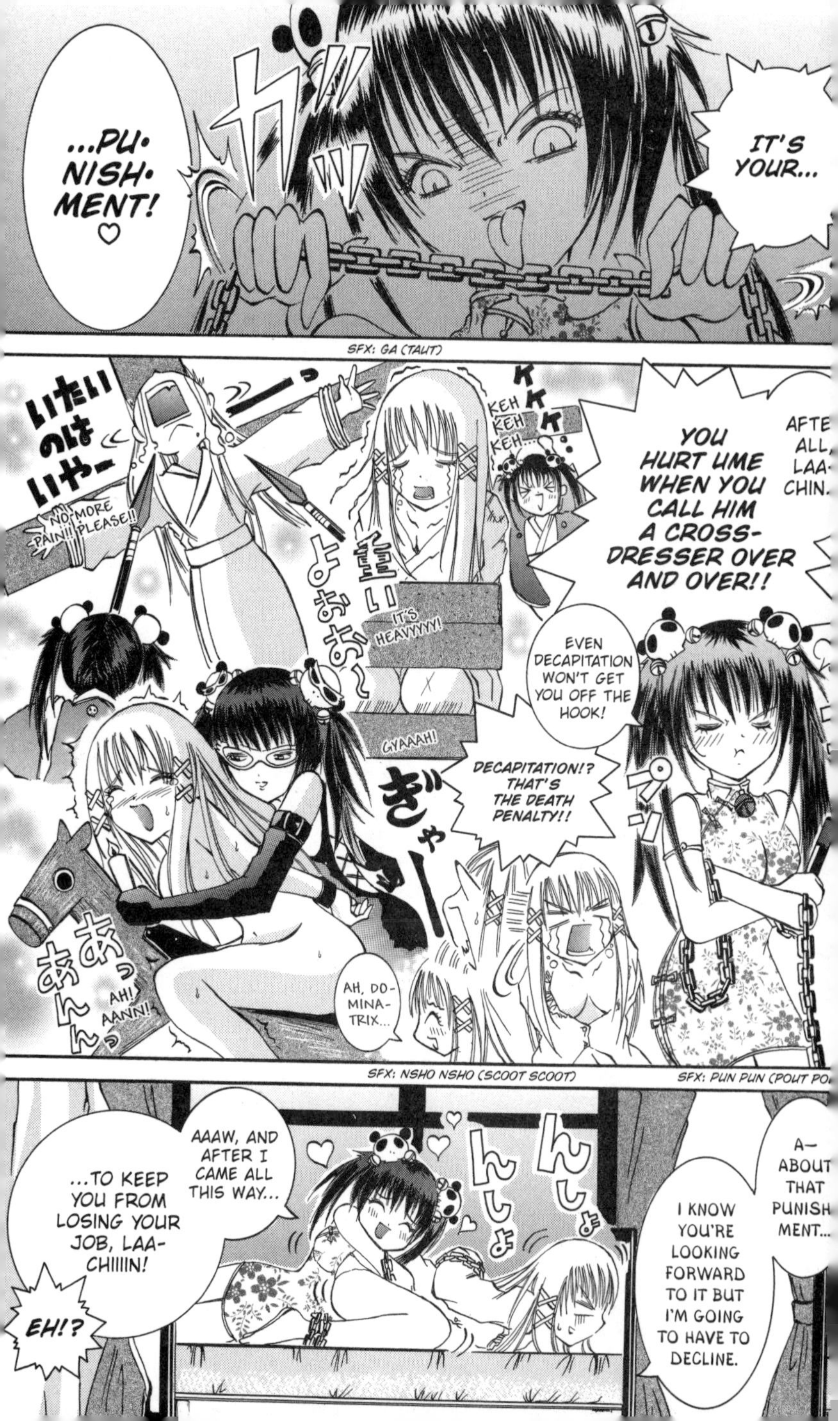
IT'S YOUR...
...PU•NISH•MENT! ♡
SFX: GA (TAUT)
AFTE ALL, LAA-CHIN.
YOU HURT UME WHEN YOU CALL HIM A CROSS-DRESSER OVER AND OVER!!
KEH KEH KEH...
いたいのはいやー
NO MORE PAIN!! PLEASE!!
重いよおお〜
IT'S HEAVYYYY!
EVEN DECAPITATION WON'T GET YOU OFF THE HOOK!
DECAPITATION!? THAT'S THE DEATH PENALTY!!
ぎゃー
GYAAAH!
AH, DO-MINA-TRIX...
あっあんんっ
AH! AANN!
SFX: PUN PUN (POUT PO
SFX: NSHO NSHO (SCOOT SCOOT)
A—ABOUT THAT PUNISH MENT...
I KNOW YOU'RE LOOKING FORWARD TO IT BUT I'M GOING TO HAVE TO DECLINE.
んしょんしょ
AAAW, AND AFTER I CAME ALL THIS WAY...
...TO KEEP YOU FROM LOSING YOUR JOB, LAA-CHIIIIN!
EH!?

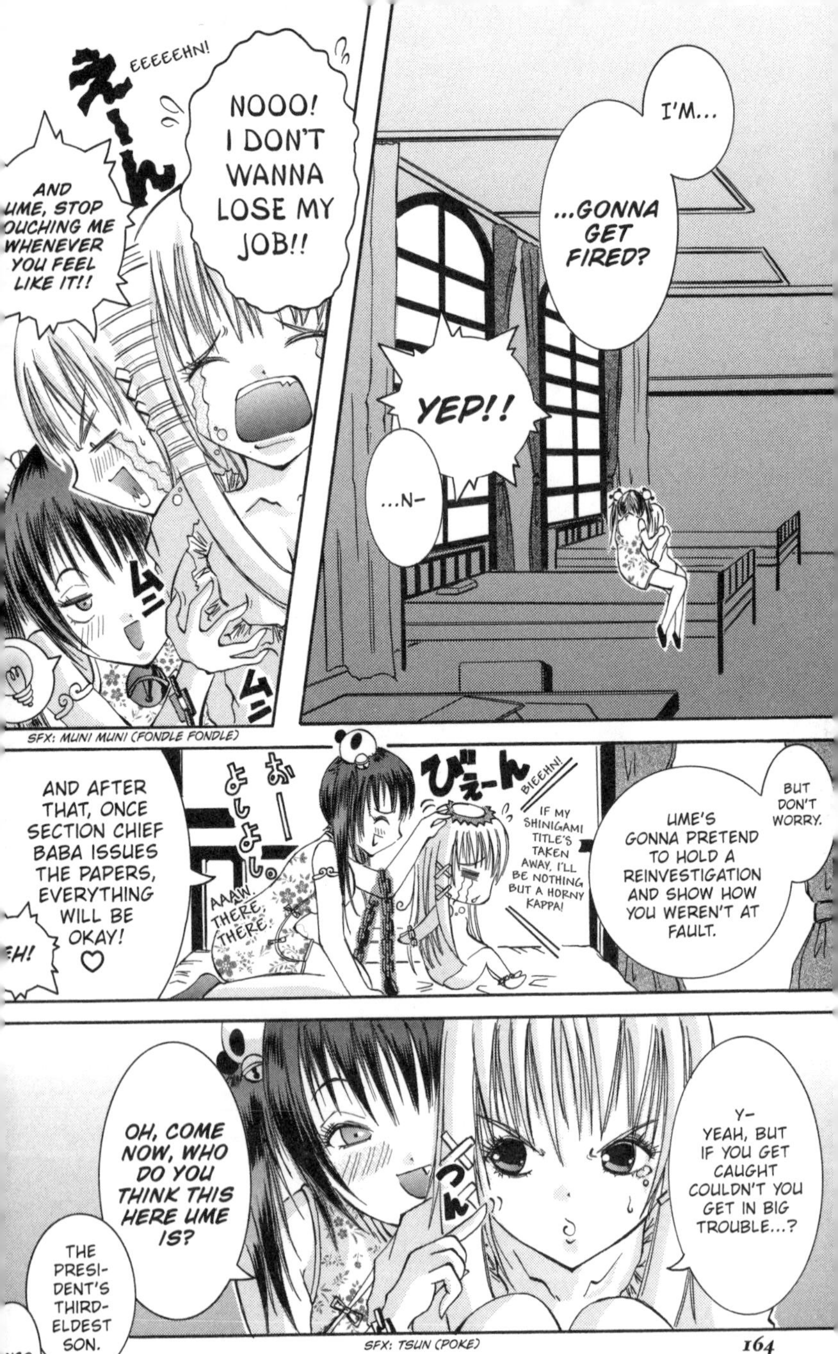
I'M...
...GONNA GET FIRED?
YEP!!
...N-
NOOO! I DON'T WANNA LOSE MY JOB!!
EEEEEHN!
AND UME, STOP TOUCHING ME WHENEVER YOU FEEL LIKE IT!!
SFX: MUNI MUNI (FONDLE FONDLE)
BUT DON'T WORRY.
UME'S GONNA PRETEND TO HOLD A REINVESTIGATION AND SHOW HOW YOU WEREN'T AT FAULT.
BIEEHN!
IF MY SHINIGAMI TITLE'S TAKEN AWAY, I'LL BE NOTHING BUT A HORNY KAPPA!
AAAW. THERE THERE.
AND AFTER THAT, ONCE SECTION CHIEF BABA ISSUES THE PAPERS, EVERYTHING WILL BE OKAY! ♡
Y- YEAH, BUT IF YOU GET CAUGHT COULDN'T YOU GET IN BIG TROUBLE...?
OH, COME NOW, WHO DO YOU THINK THIS HERE UME IS?
THE PRESIDENT'S THIRD-ELDEST SON.
NGO.
SFX: TSUN (POKE)

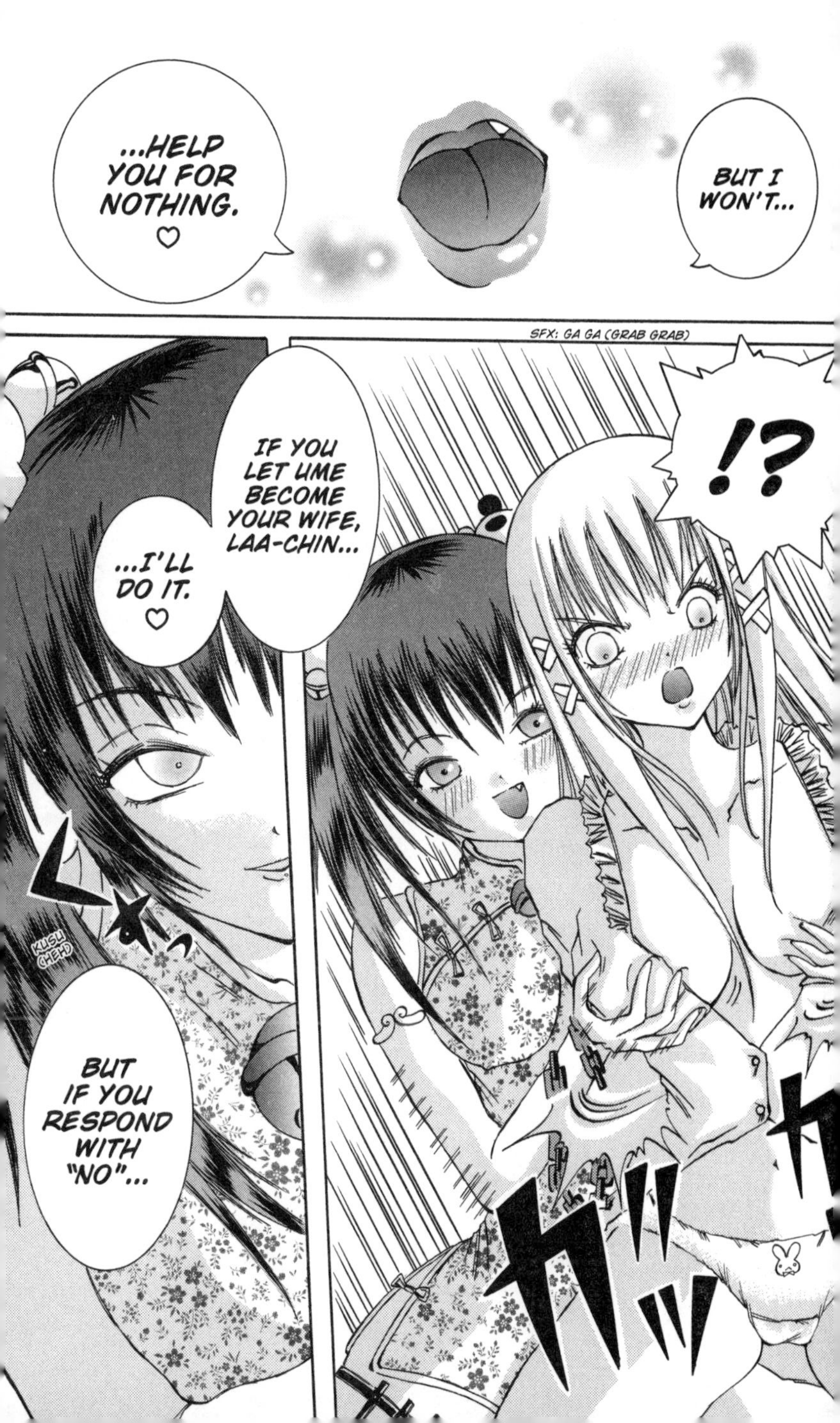
BUT I WON'T...
...HELP YOU FOR NOTHING. ♡
SFX: GA GA (GRAB GRAB)
!?
IF YOU LET UME BECOME YOUR WIFE, LAA-CHIN...
...I'LL DO IT. ♡
KUSU (HEH)
BUT IF YOU RESPOND WITH "NO"...

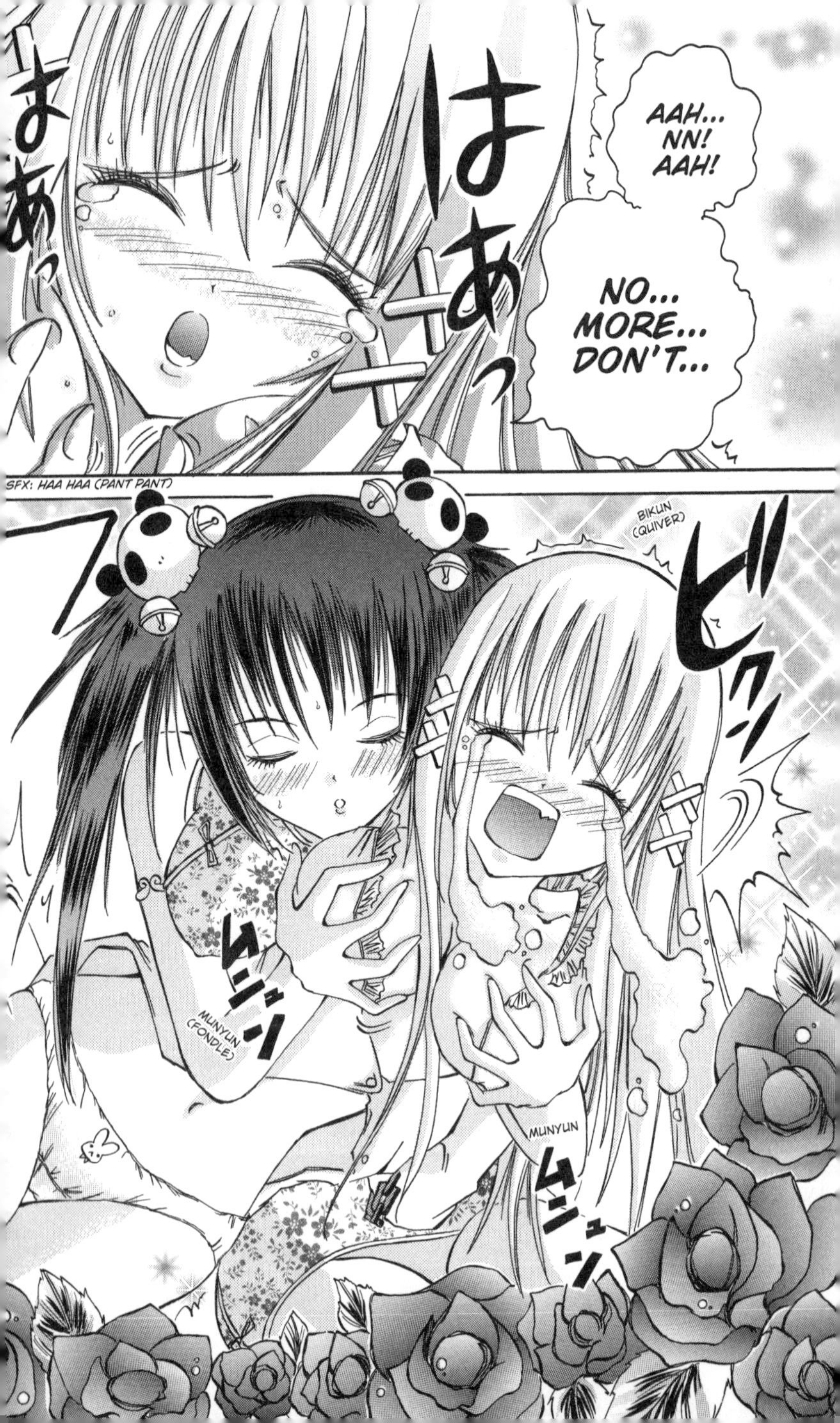
AAH... NN! AAH!
NO... MORE... DON'T...
はあっ
まあっ
SFX: HAA HAA (PANT PANT)
BIKUN (QUIVER)
ビクッ
MUNYUN
ムニュン
MUNYUN (FONDLE)
ムニュン

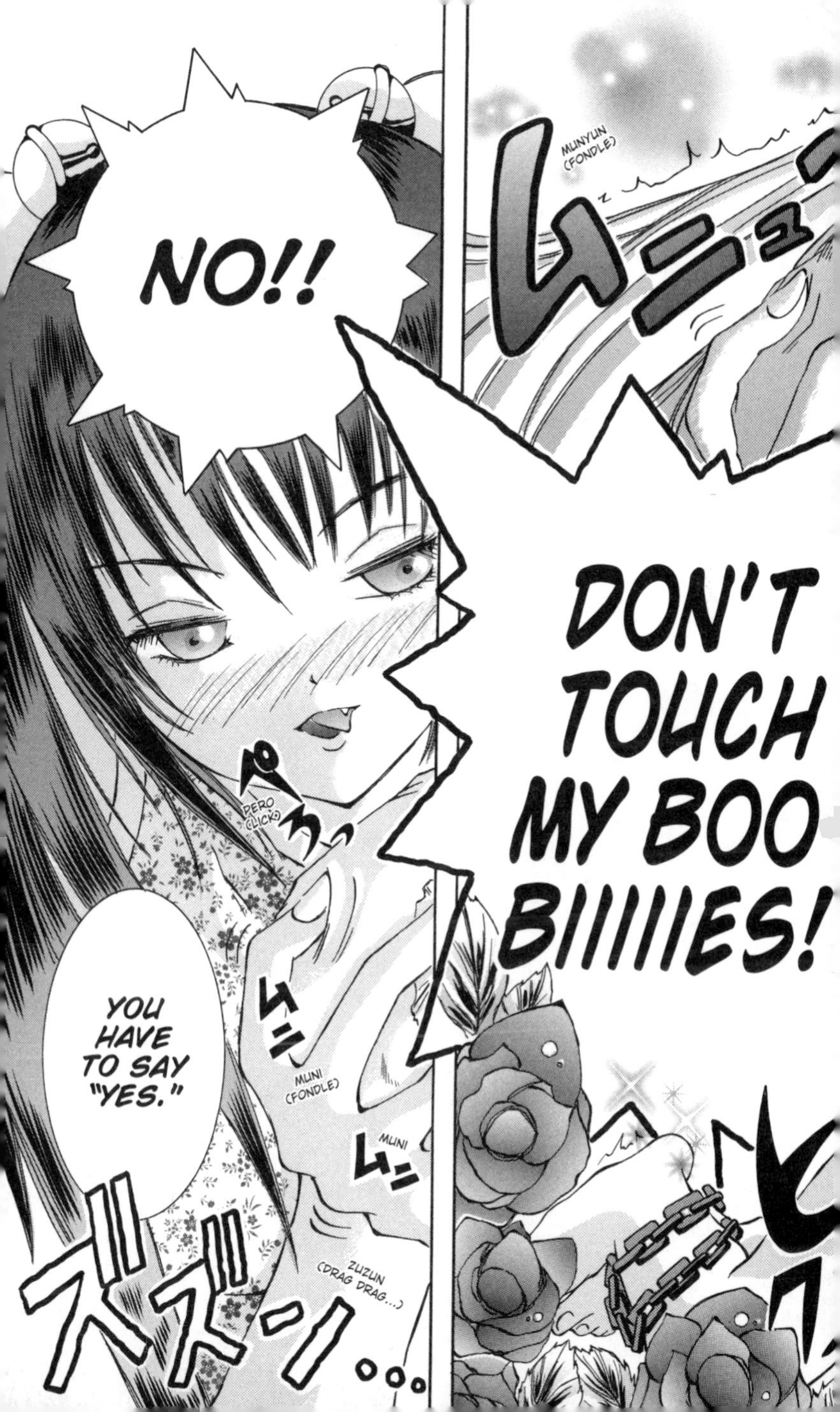
MUNYUN (FONDLE)
DON'T TOUCH MY BOOBIIIIES!
NO!!
PERO (LICK)
YOU HAVE TO SAY "YES."
MUNI (FONDLE)
MUNI
ZUZUN (DRAG DRAG...)

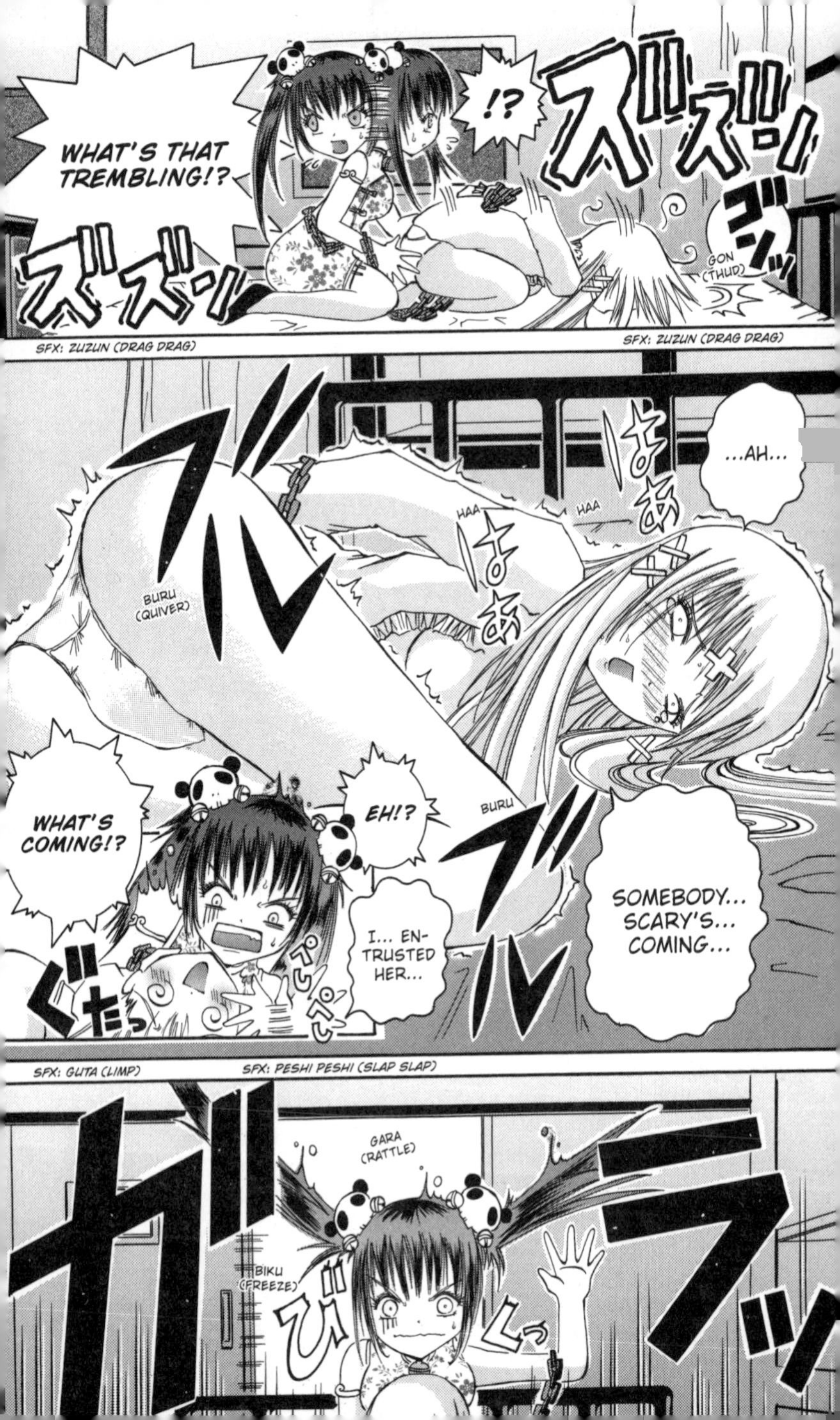
!?
WHAT'S THAT TREMBLING!?
GON (THUD)
SFX: ZUZUN (DRAG DRAG)
SFX: ZUZUN (DRAG DRAG)
...AH...
HAA
HAA
BURU (QUIVER)
SOMEBODY... SCARY'S... COMING...
BURU
EH!?
I... EN-TRUSTED HER...
WHAT'S COMING!?
SFX: GUTA (LIMP)
SFX: PESHI PESHI (SLAP SLAP)
GARA (RATTLE)
BIKU (FREEZE)

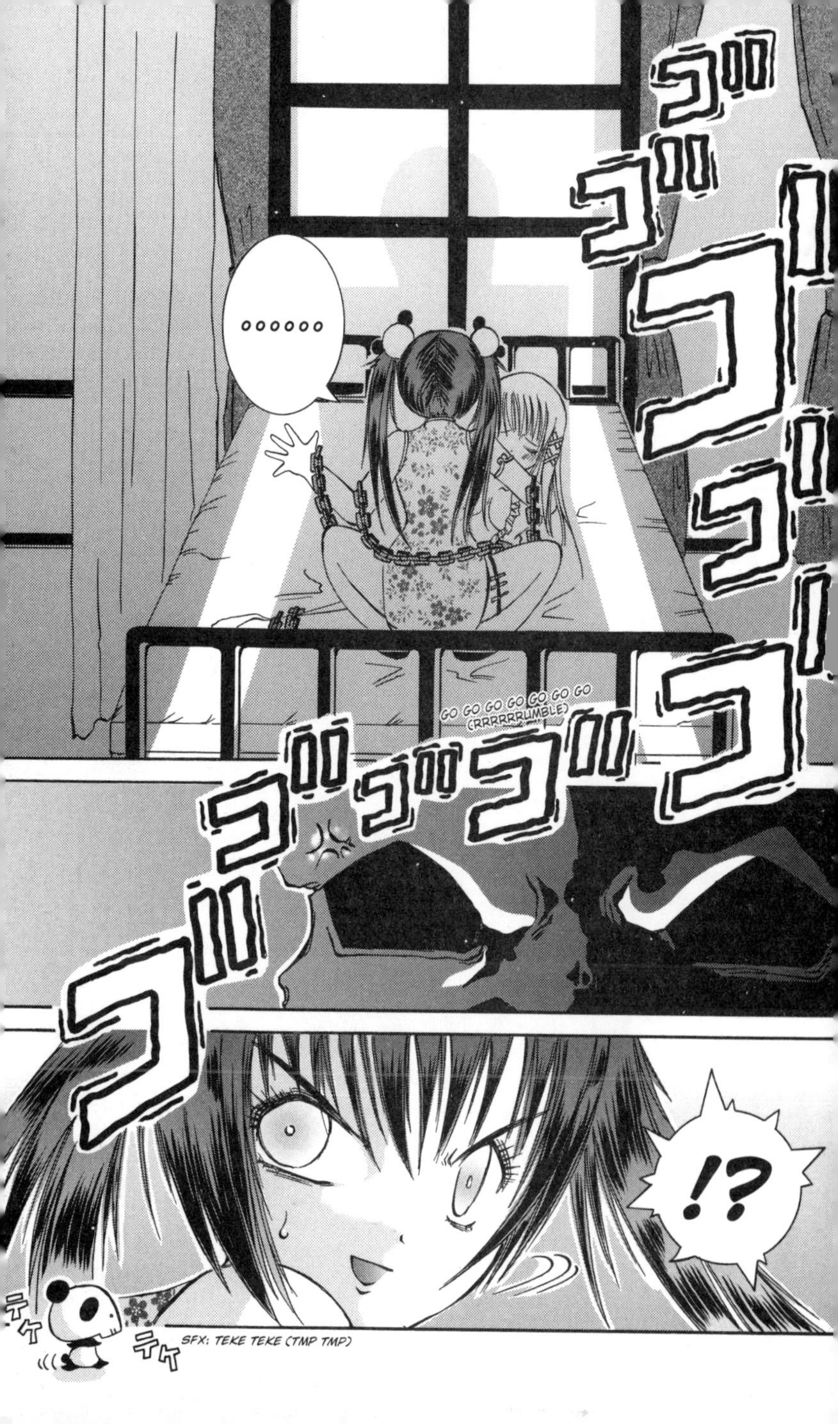
oooooo
GO GO GO GO GO GO GO
(RRRRRRUMBLE)
!?
テケ テケ
SFX: TEKE TEKE (TMP TMP)

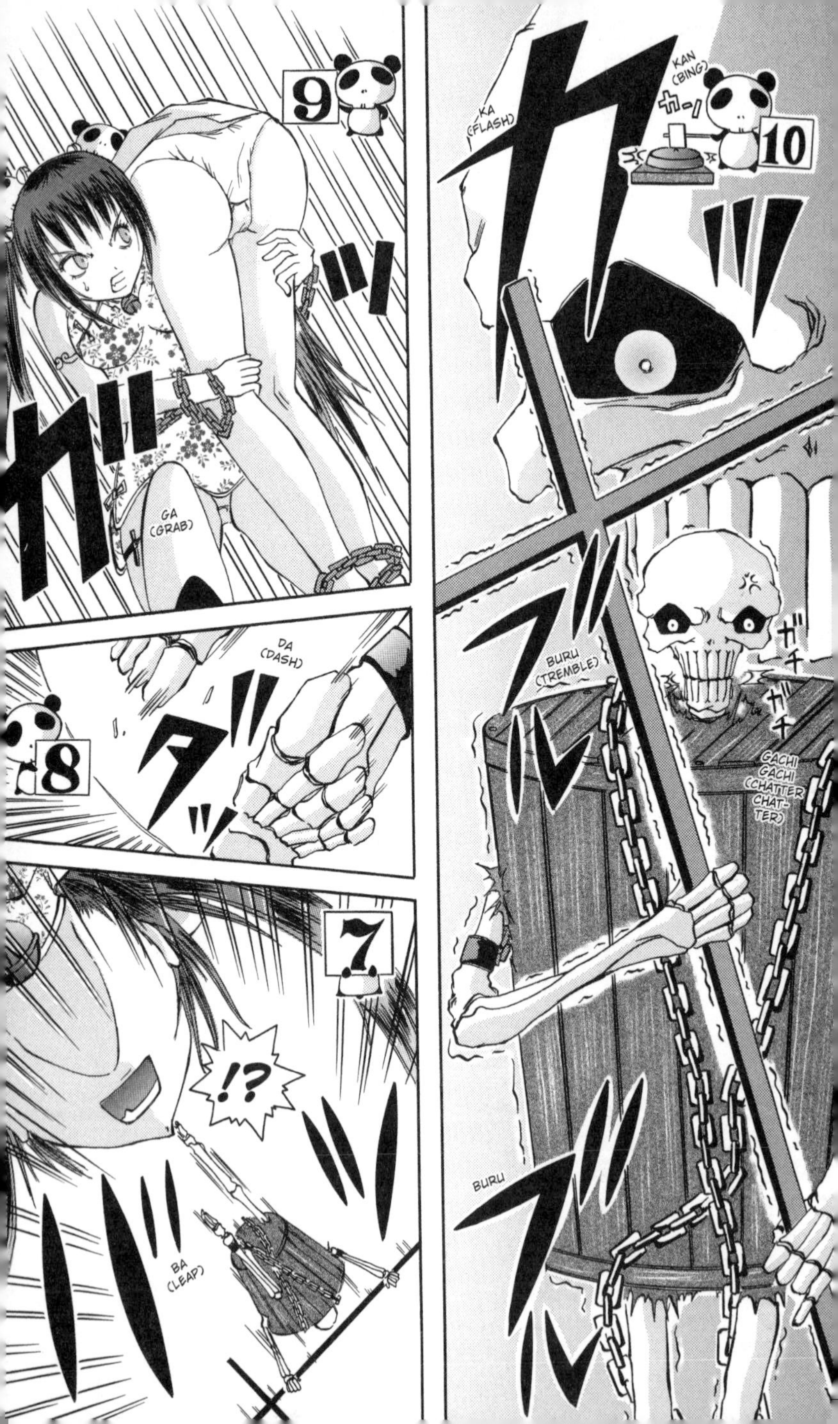

KA (FLASH)
KAN (BING)
10
BURU (TREMBLE)
GACHI GACHI (CHATTER CHAT-TER)
BURU
9
GA (GRAB)
DA (DASH)
8
7
!?
BA (LEAP)

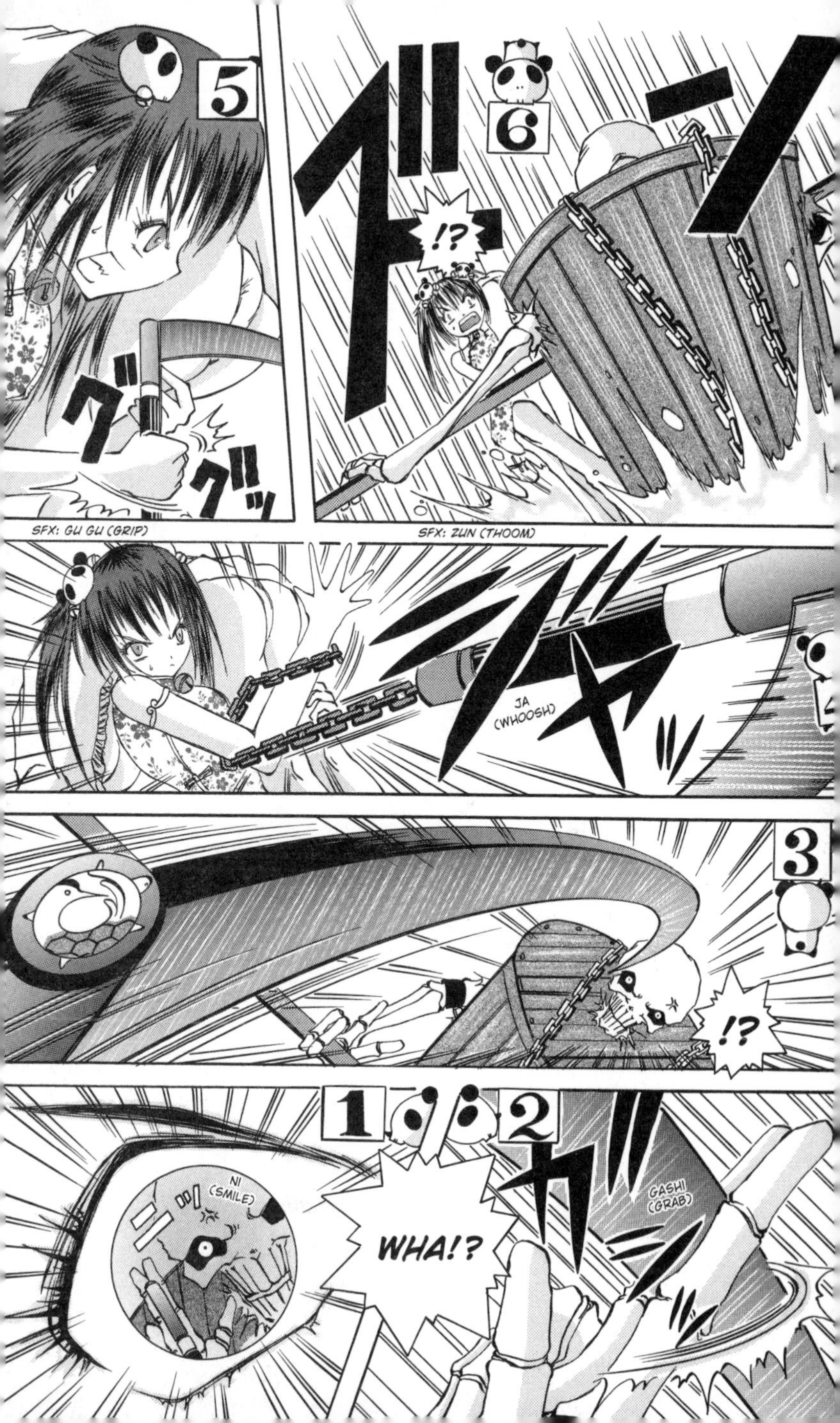
6
!?
SFX: ZUN (THOOM)
5
SFX: GU GU (GRIP)
JA (WHOOSH)
3
!?
1
2
GASHI (GRAB)
NI (SMILE)
WHA!?

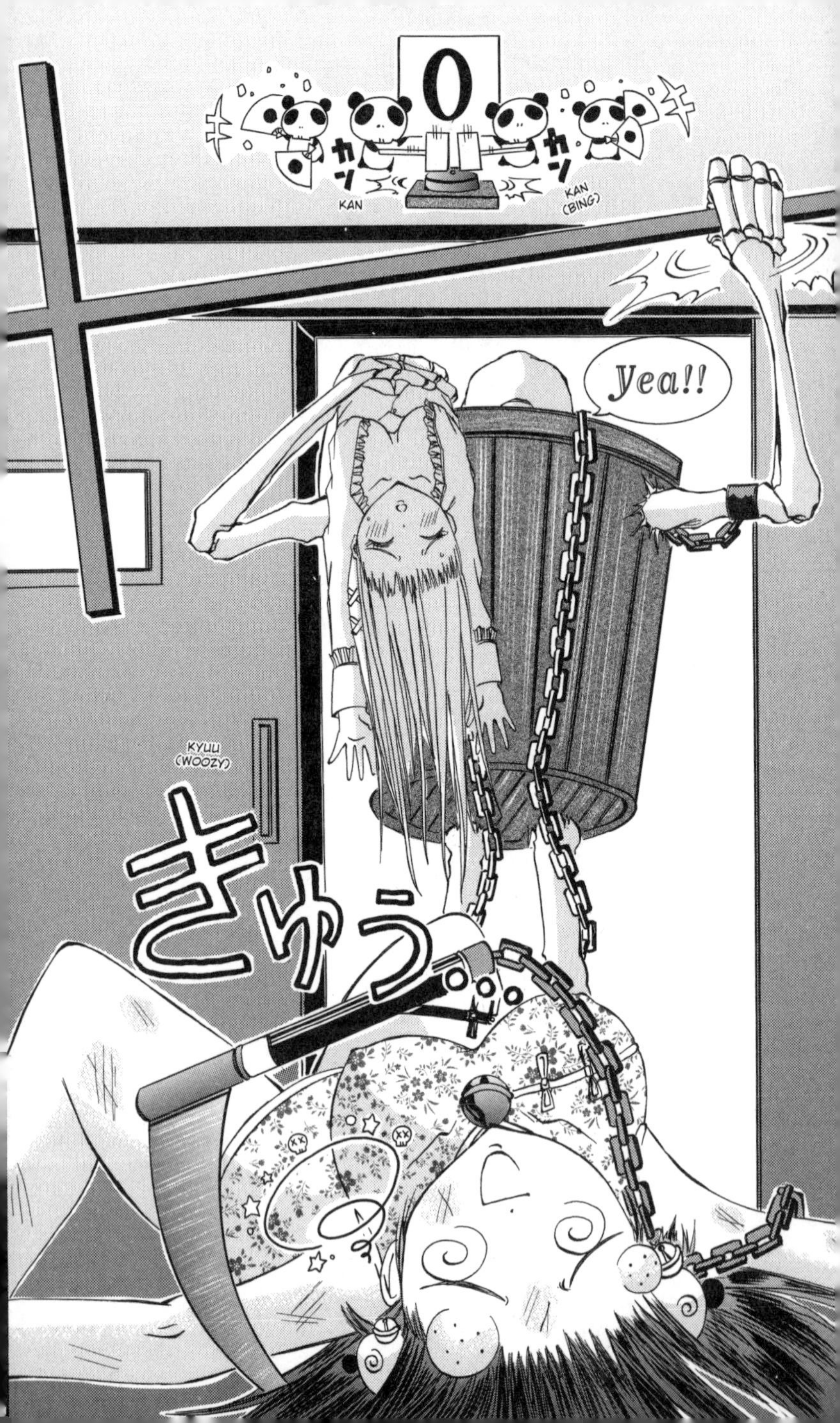
0
キ
カン
KAN
カン
KAN (BING)
キ
Yea!!
KYUU (WOOZY)
きゅう

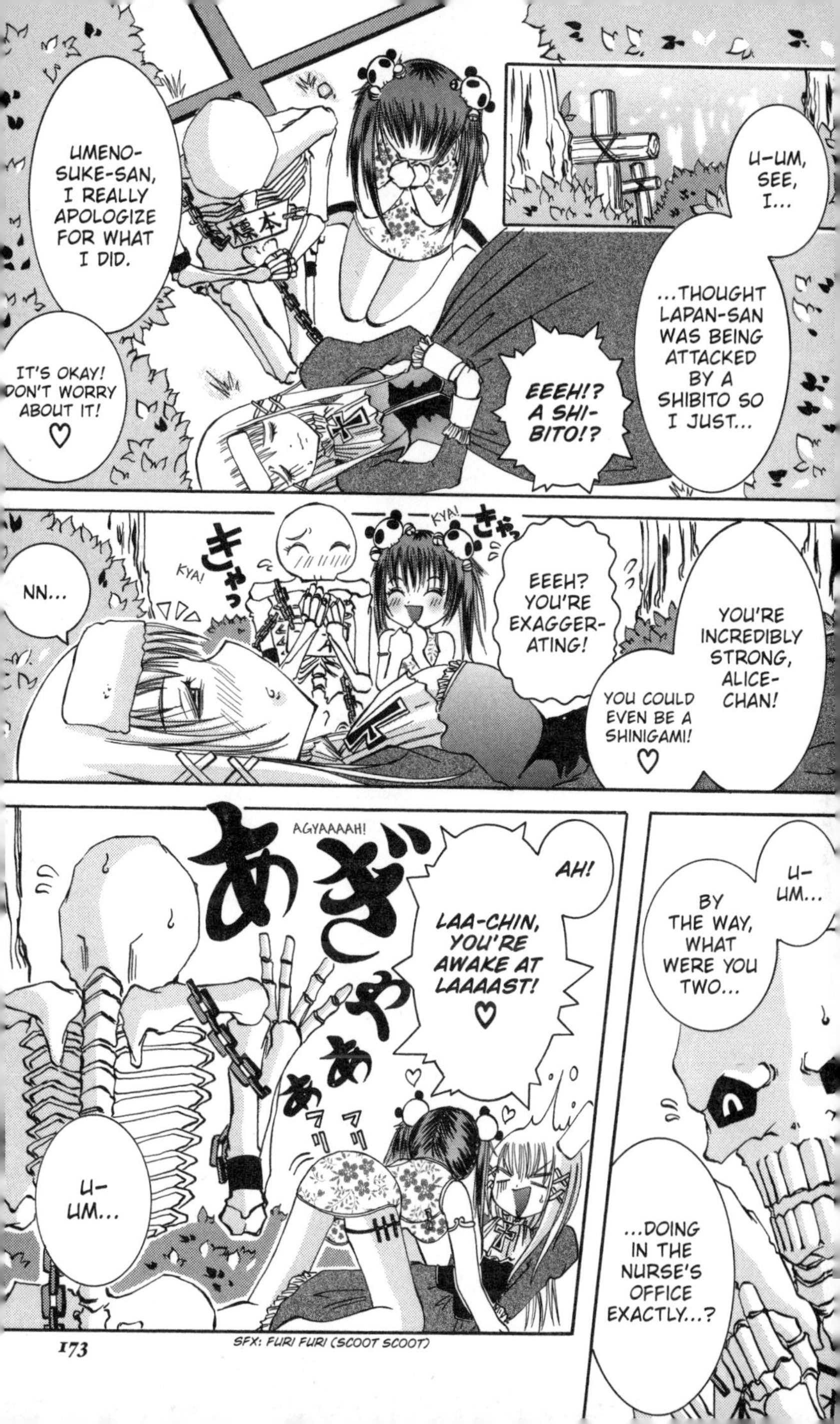
U-UM, SEE, I...
...THOUGHT LAPAN-SAN WAS BEING ATTACKED BY A SHIBITO SO I JUST...
EEEH!? A SHIBITO!?
標本
UMENO-SUKE-SAN, I REALLY APOLOGIZE FOR WHAT I DID.
IT'S OKAY! DON'T WORRY ABOUT IT! ♡
YOU'RE INCREDIBLY STRONG, ALICE-CHAN!
YOU COULD EVEN BE A SHINIGAMI! ♡
EEEH? YOU'RE EXAGGERATING!
きゃっ
KYA!
きゃっ
KYA!
NN...
U-UM...
BY THE WAY, WHAT WERE YOU TWO...
...DOING IN THE NURSE'S OFFICE EXACTLY...?
AH!
LAA-CHIN, YOU'RE AWAKE AT LAAAAST! ♡
あぎゃあああ
AGYAAAAH!
U-UM...
ふりふり

SFX: FURI FURI (SCOOT SCOOT)

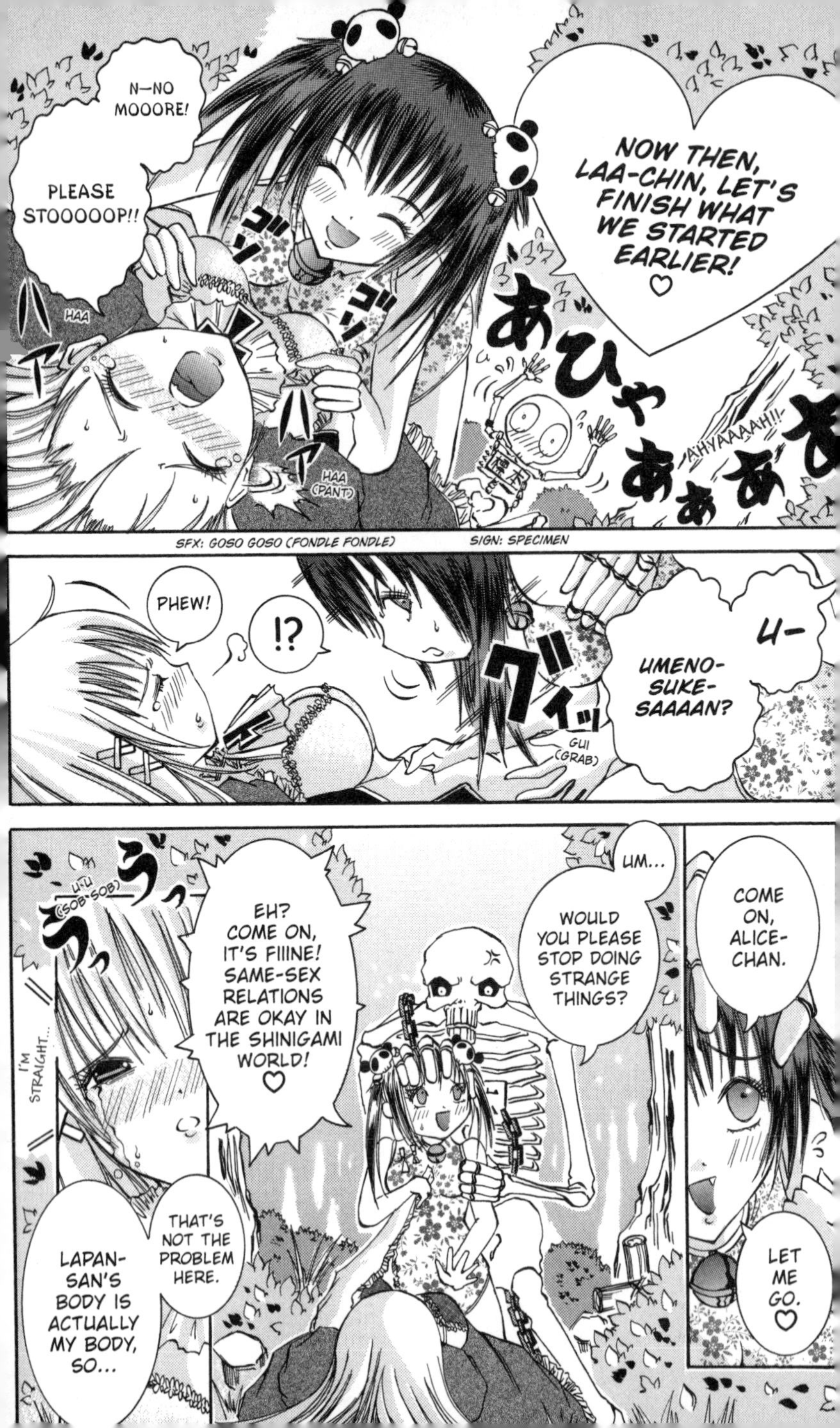
NOW THEN, LAA-CHIN, LET'S FINISH WHAT WE STARTED EARLIER! ♡
AHYAAAAH!!
N—NO MOOORE!
PLEASE STOOOOOP!!
HAA
HAA (PANT)
SFX: GOSO GOSO (FONDLE FONDLE)
SIGN: SPECIMEN
U-
UMENO-SUKE-SAAAAN?
GUI (GRAB)
!?
PHEW!
COME ON, ALICE-CHAN.
LET ME GO. ♡
UM...
WOULD YOU PLEASE STOP DOING STRANGE THINGS?
EH? COME ON, IT'S FIIINE! SAME-SEX RELATIONS ARE OKAY IN THE SHINIGAMI WORLD! ♡
U-U (SOB SOB)
I'M STRAIGHT...
THAT'S NOT THE PROBLEM HERE.
LAPAN-SAN'S BODY IS ACTUALLY MY BODY, SO...

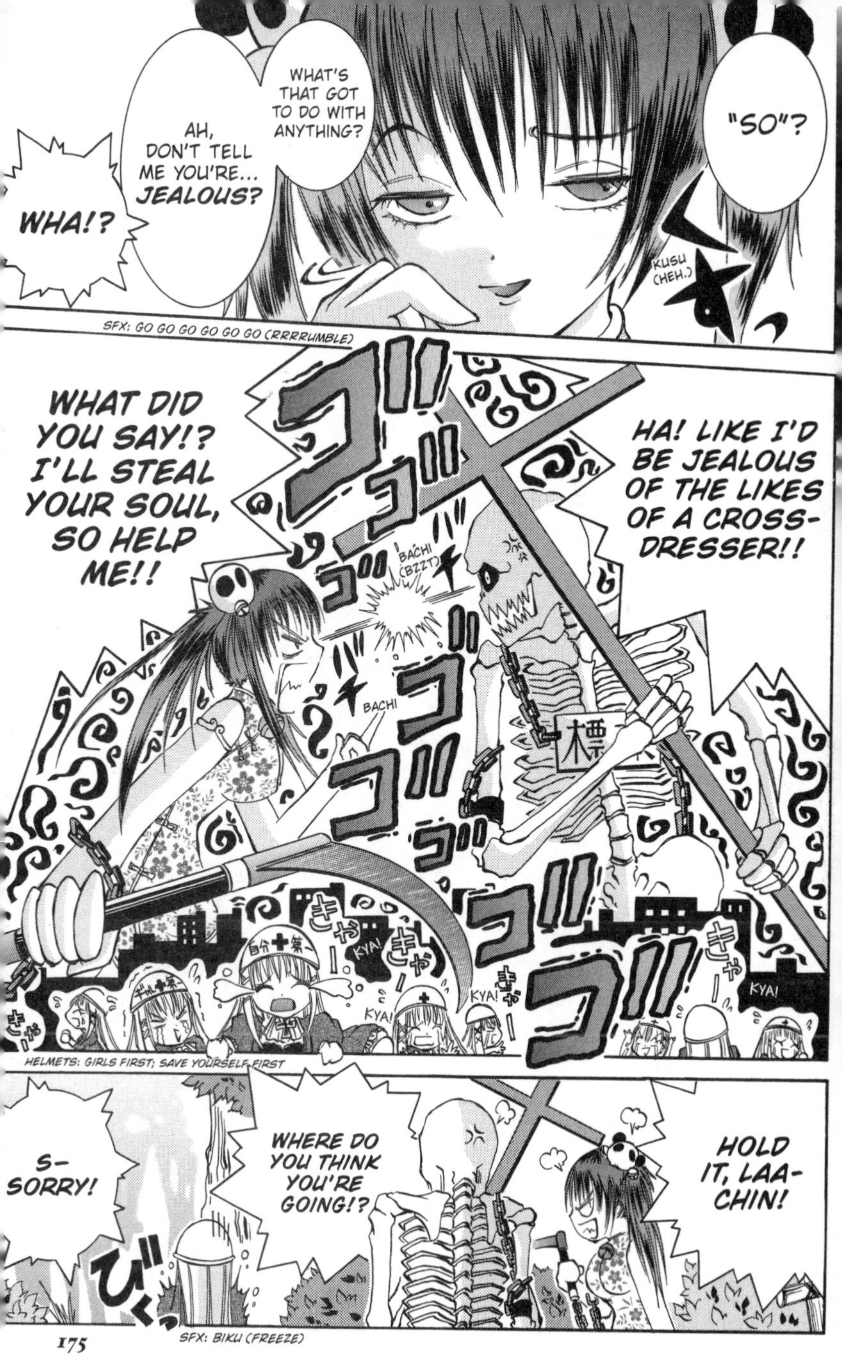
"SO"?
KUSU (HEH.)
WHAT'S THAT GOT TO DO WITH ANYTHING?
AH, DON'T TELL ME YOU'RE... JEALOUS?
WHA!?
SFX: GO GO GO GO GO GO (RRRRUMBLE)
HA! LIKE I'D BE JEALOUS OF THE LIKES OF A CROSS-DRESSER!!
WHAT DID YOU SAY!? I'LL STEAL YOUR SOUL, SO HELP ME!!
BACHI (BZZT)
BACHI
KYA!
KYA!
KYA!
KYA!
HELMETS: GIRLS FIRST; SAVE YOURSELF FIRST
HOLD IT, LAA-CHIN!
WHERE DO YOU THINK YOU'RE GOING!?
S-SORRY!
SFX: BIKU (FREEZE)

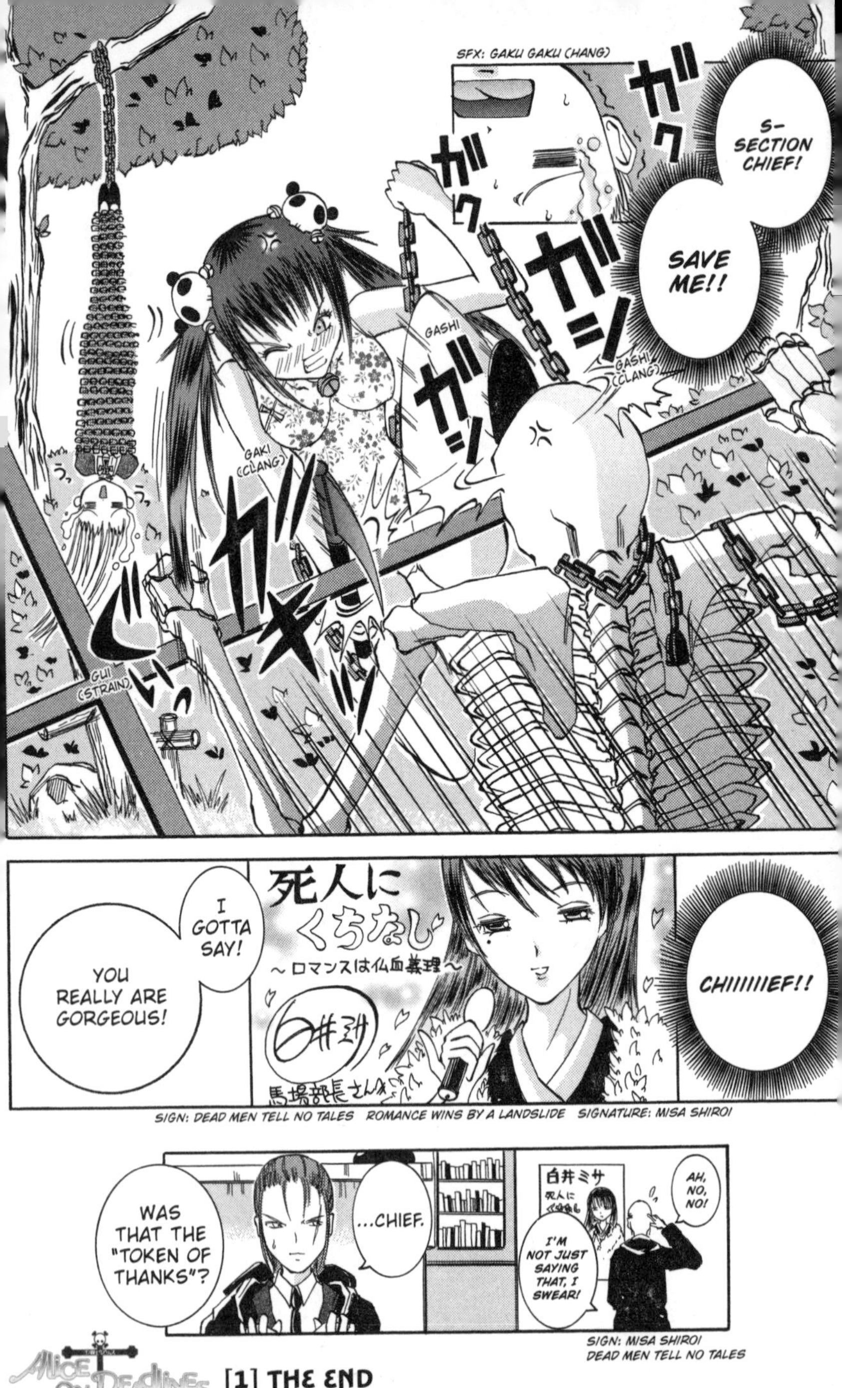

SFX: GAKU GAKU (HANG)
S-SECTION CHIEF!
SAVE ME!!
GASHI (CLANG)
GASHI
GAKI (CLANG)
GUI (STRAIN)
CHIIIIIIEF!!
死人に
くちなし
～ロマンスは仏血義理～
馬場部長さんへ
I GOTTA SAY!
YOU REALLY ARE GORGEOUS!
SIGN: DEAD MEN TELL NO TALES ROMANCE WINS BY A LANDSLIDE SIGNATURE: MISA SHIROI
白井ミサ
AH, NO, NO!
I'M NOT JUST SAYING THAT, I SWEAR!
...CHIEF.
WAS THAT THE "TOKEN OF THANKS"?
SIGN: MISA SHIROI
DEAD MEN TELL NO TALES

ALICE ON DEADLINES [1] THE END

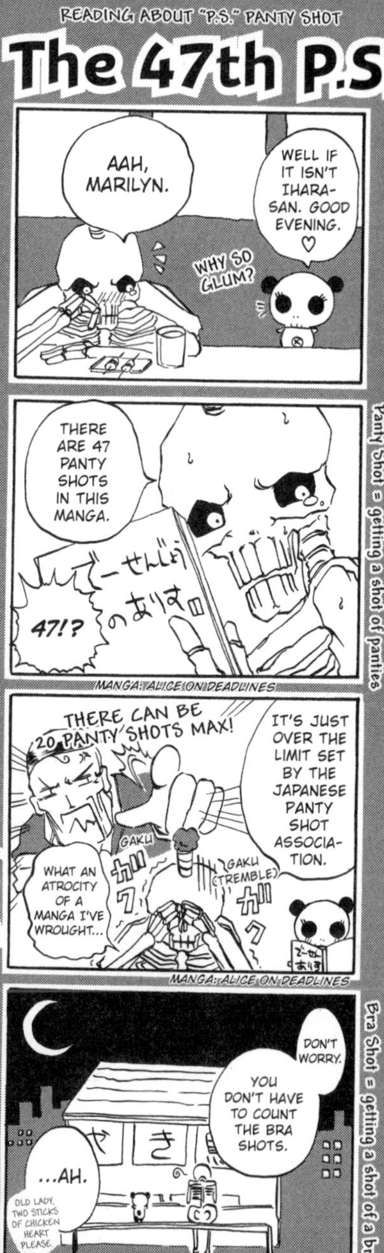
READING ABOUT "P.S." PANTY SHOT
The 47th P.S.
AAH, MARILYN.
WELL IF IT ISN'T IHARA-SAN. GOOD EVENING. ♡
WHY SO GLUM?
THERE ARE 47 PANTY SHOTS IN THIS MANGA.
47!?
MANGA: ALICE ON DEADLINES
Panty Shot = getting a shot of panties
IT'S JUST OVER THE LIMIT SET BY THE JAPANESE PANTY SHOT ASSOCIATION.
THERE CAN BE 20 PANTY SHOTS MAX!
WHAT AN ATROCITY OF A MANGA I'VE WROUGHT...
GAKU
GAKU (TREMBLE)
MANGA: ALICE ON DEADLINES
DON'T WORRY.
YOU DON'T HAVE TO COUNT THE BRA SHOTS.
...AH.
OLD LADY, TWO STICKS OF CHICKEN HEART PLEASE.
SIGN: YAKITORI
Bra Shot = getting a shot of a bra

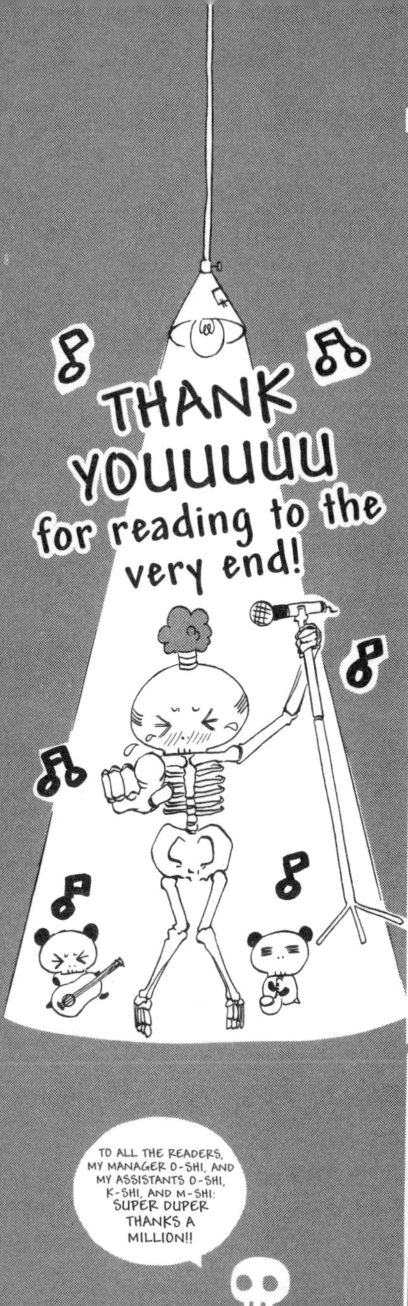
THANK YOUUUUU for reading to the very end!
TO ALL THE READERS, MY MANAGER O-SHI, AND MY ASSISTANTS O-SHI, K-SHI, AND M-SHI: SUPER DUPER THANKS A MILLION!!

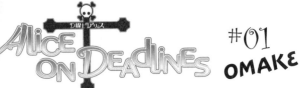

ALICE ON DEADLINES

D線上のアリス

#01 OMAKE

FILMING ALICE

撮影上のアリス。

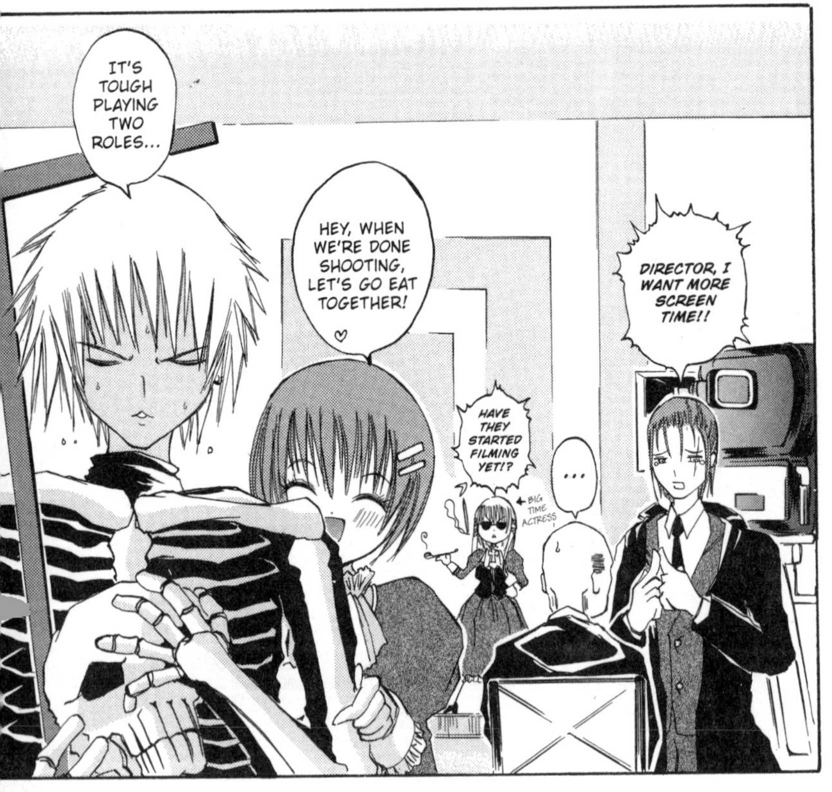

DIRECTOR, I WANT MORE SCREEN TIME!!
...
HAVE THEY STARTED FILMING YET!?
← BIG TIME ACTRESS
HEY, WHEN WE'RE DONE SHOOTING, LET'S GO EAT TOGETHER! ♡
IT'S TOUGH PLAYING TWO ROLES...

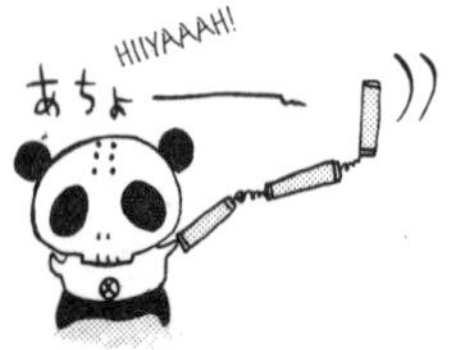

HIIYAAAH!
あちょー

MEATY ALICE

ムキムキアリス

......

UMM...

UH...

GATAN
(SLAM)

ガタン

フン!!
HMPH!

AND NOW FOR A SNEAK PEEK INTO

D線上のアリス

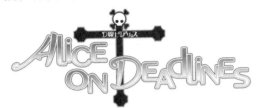

ALICE ON DEADLINES

VOL. 2...

WHERE THE LECHERY GETS TURNED UP TO 11!

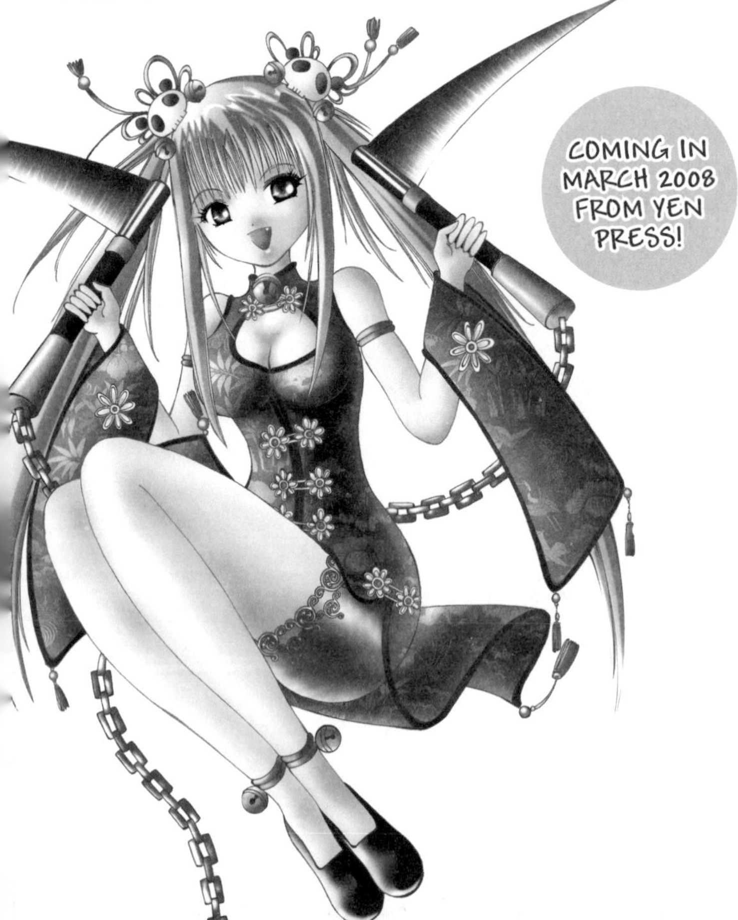
COMING IN MARCH 2008 FROM YEN PRESS!

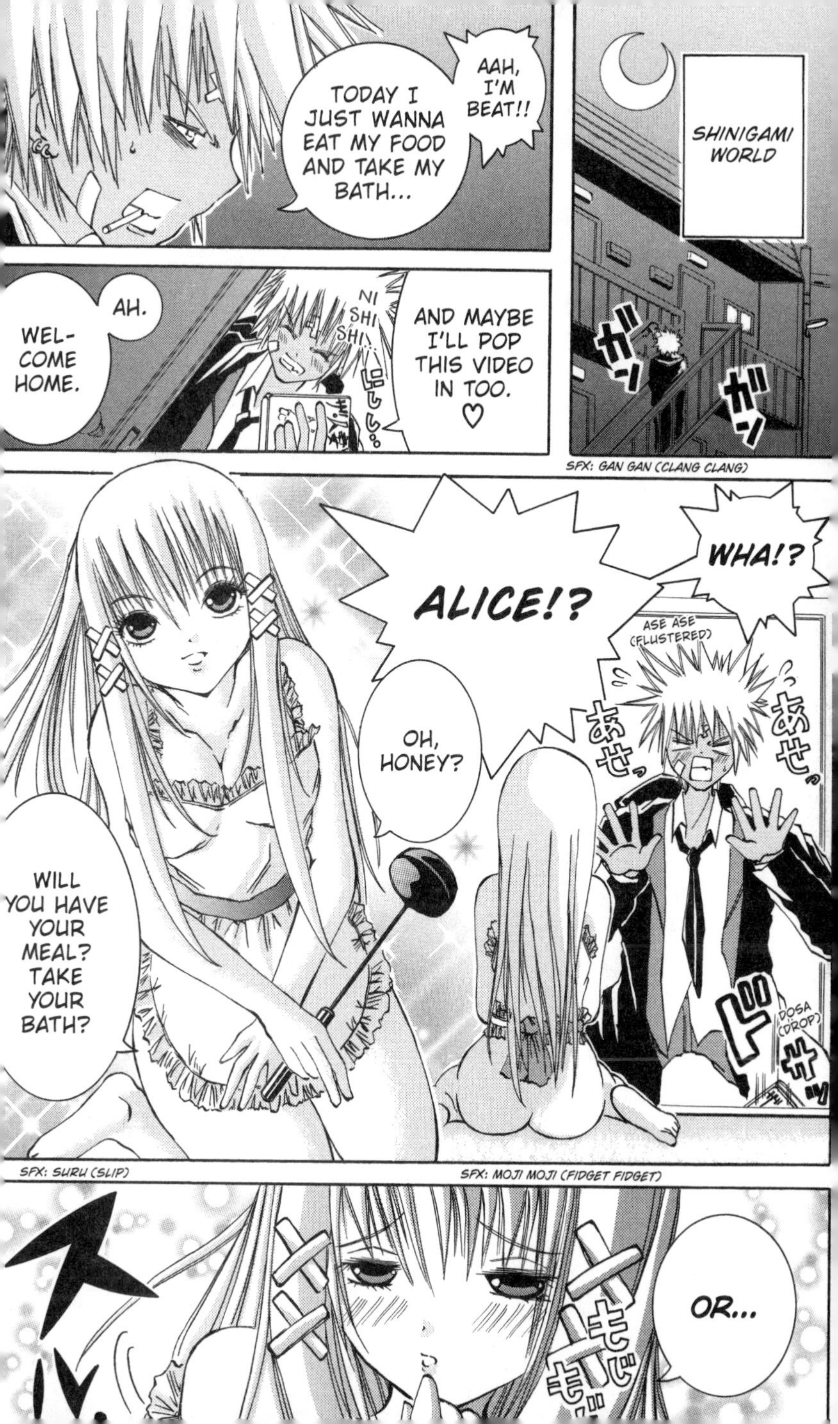
SHINIGAMI WORLD
SFX: GAN GAN (CLANG CLANG)
AAH, I'M BEAT!!
TODAY I JUST WANNA EAT MY FOOD AND TAKE MY BATH...
AND MAYBE I'LL POP THIS VIDEO IN TOO. ♡
NI SHI SHI...
AH.
WEL-COME HOME.
WHA!?
ALICE!?
ASE ASE (FLUSTERED)
OH, HONEY?
WILL YOU HAVE YOUR MEAL? TAKE YOUR BATH?
DOSA (DROP)
SFX: SURU (SLIP)
SFX: MOJI MOJI (FIDGET FIDGET)
OR...

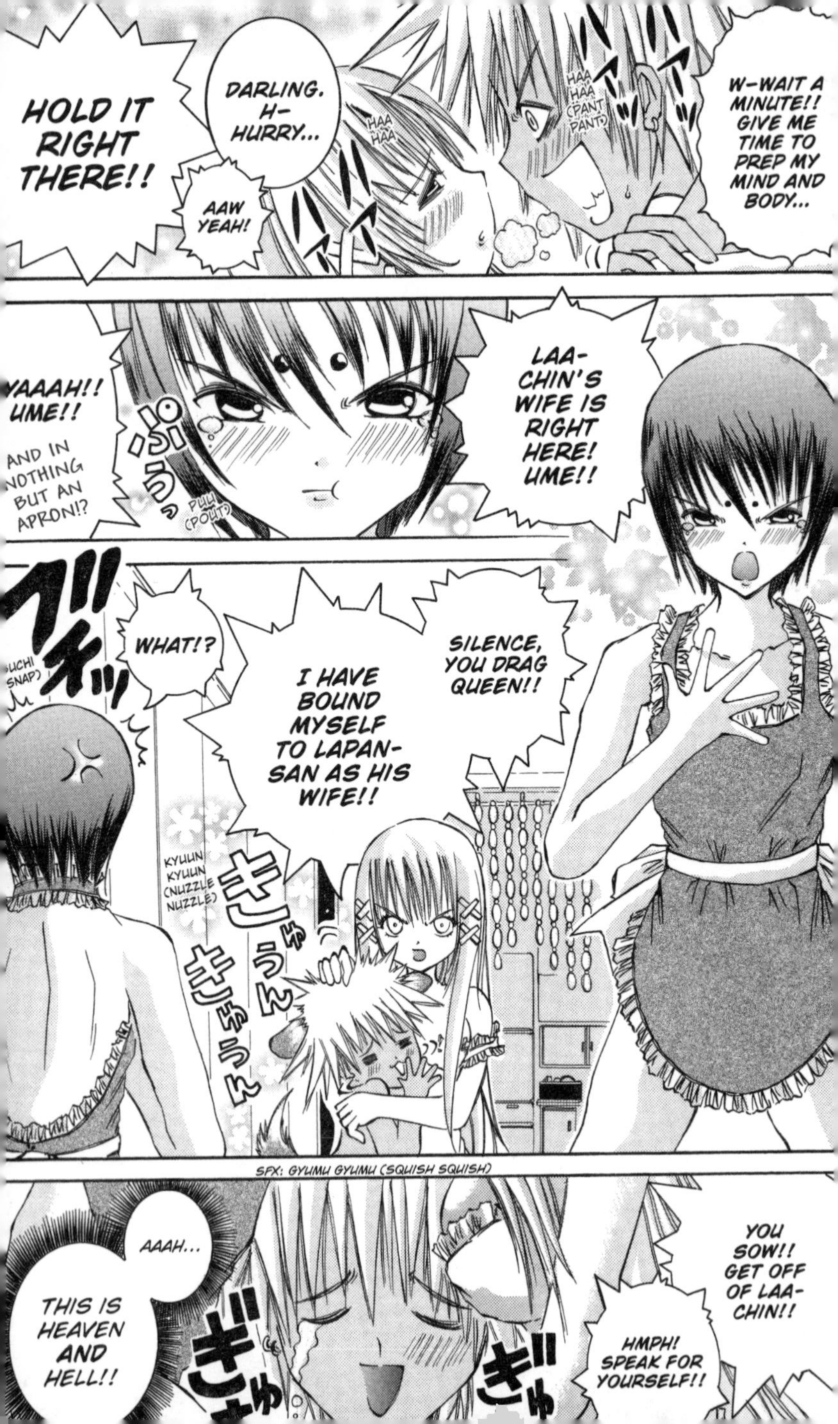

W-WAIT A MINUTE!! GIVE ME TIME TO PREP MY MIND AND BODY...
HAA HAA (PANT PANT)
DARLING. H-HURRY...
HAA HAA
AAW YEAH!
HOLD IT RIGHT THERE!!
LAA-CHIN'S WIFE IS RIGHT HERE! UME!!
ぷぅっ
PULU (POUT)
YAAAH!! UME!!
AND IN NOTHING BUT AN APRON!?
SILENCE, YOU DRAG QUEEN!!
I HAVE BOUND MYSELF TO LAPAN-SAN AS HIS WIFE!!
WHAT!?
ブチッ
SNAP)
きゅうん きゅうん
KYUUN KYUUN (NUZZLE NUZZLE)
SFX: GYUMU GYUMU (SQUISH SQUISH)
YOU SOW!! GET OFF OF LAA-CHIN!!
HMPH! SPEAK FOR YOURSELF!!
ぎゅ ぎゅ
AAAH...
THIS IS HEAVEN AND HELL!!

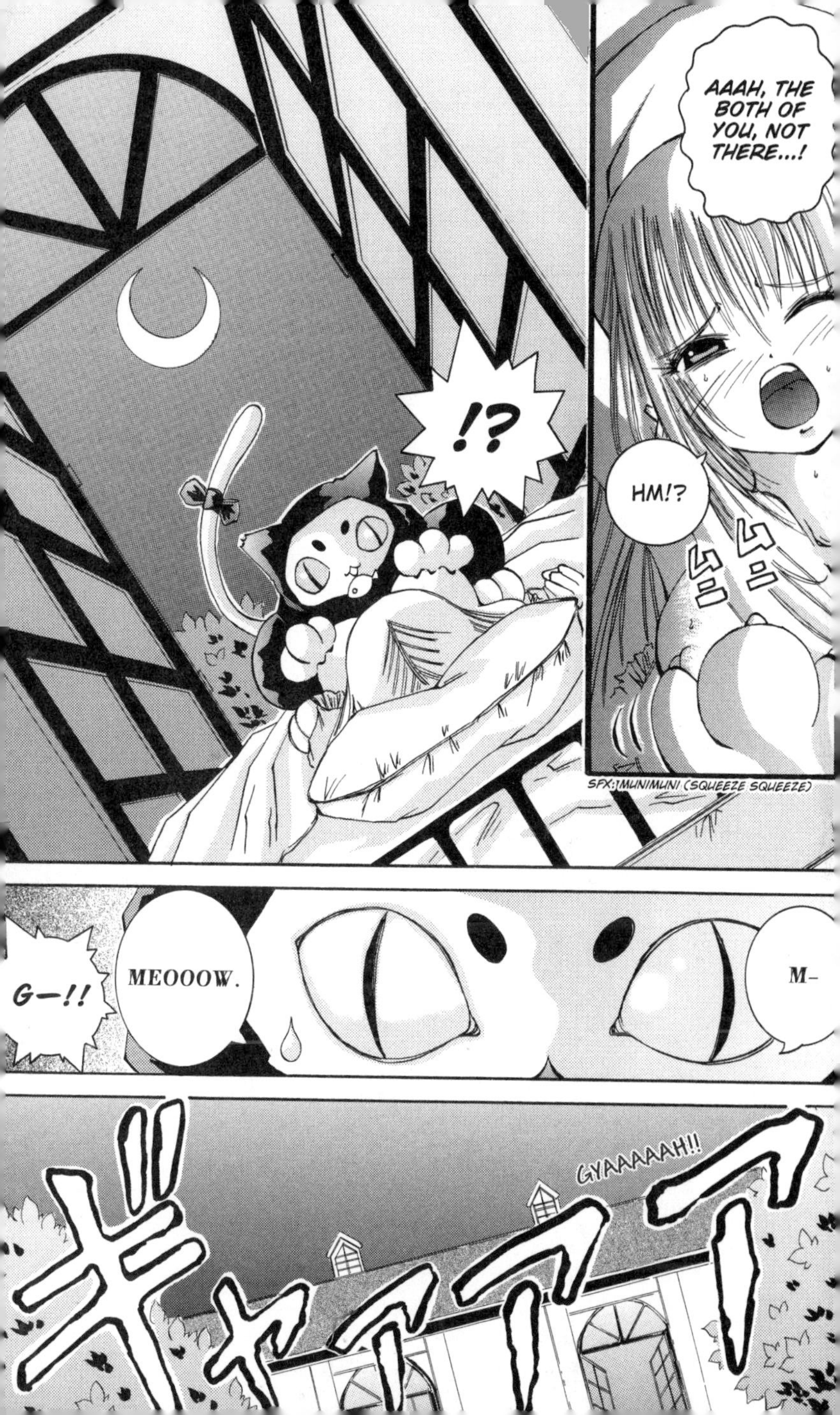
AAAH, THE BOTH OF YOU, NOT THERE...!
HM!?
SFX: MUNIMUNI (SQUEEZE SQUEEZE)
!?
M–
MEOOOW.
G–!!
GYAAAAAH!!

Line 5: The Cat Burglar & the Black Butterfly

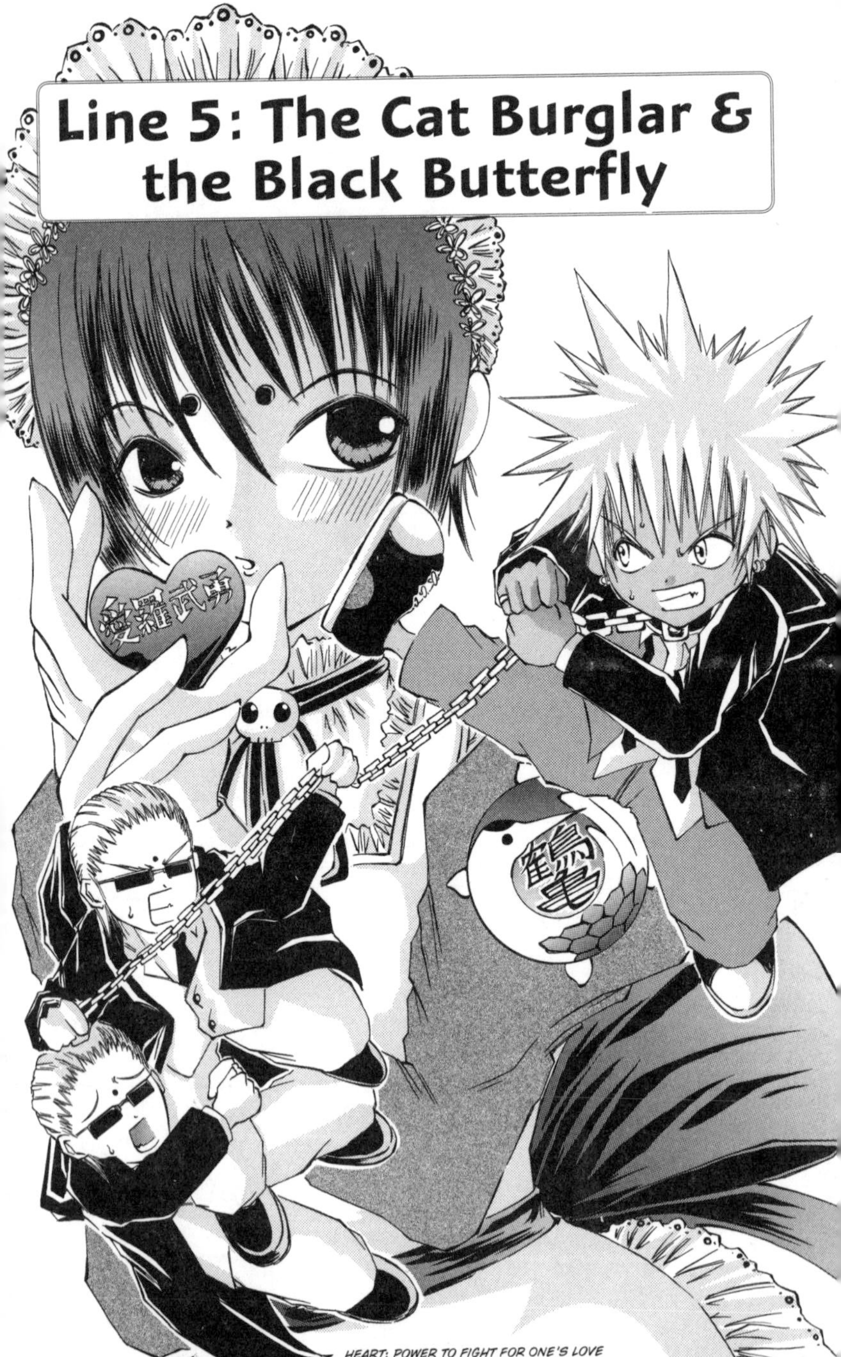
愛羅武勇

HEART: POWER TO FIGHT FOR ONE'S LOVE
SIGN: TSURUKAME

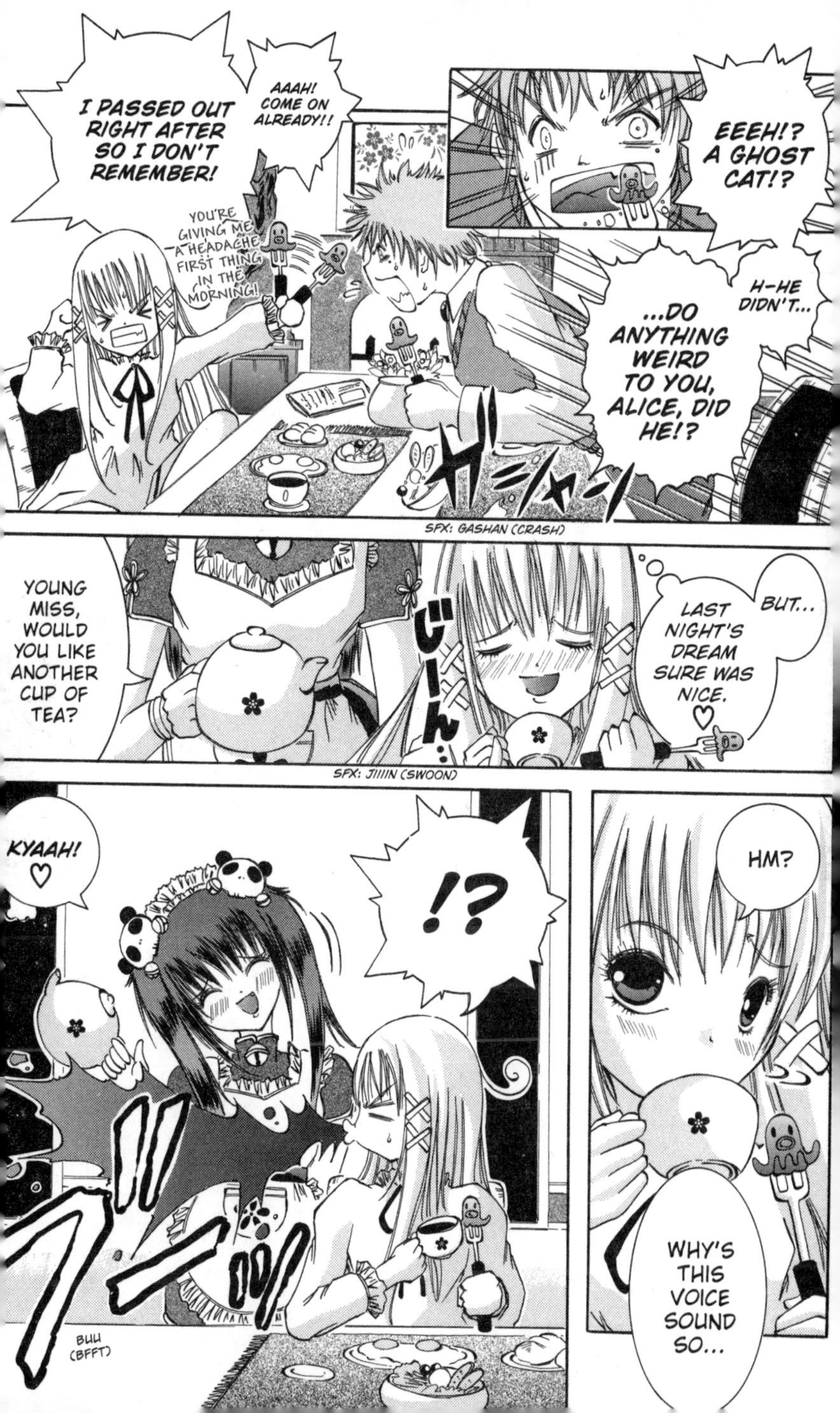
EEEH!? A GHOST CAT!?
H-HE DIDN'T...
...DO ANYTHING WEIRD TO YOU, ALICE, DID HE!?
AAAH! COME ON ALREADY!!
I PASSED OUT RIGHT AFTER SO I DON'T REMEMBER!
YOU'RE GIVING ME A HEADACHE FIRST THING IN THE MORNING!
SFX: GASHAN (CRASH)
BUT...
LAST NIGHT'S DREAM SURE WAS NICE. ♡
YOUNG MISS, WOULD YOU LIKE ANOTHER CUP OF TEA?
SFX: JIIIIN (SWOON)
HM?
WHY'S THIS VOICE SOUND SO...
!?
KYAAH! ♡
BUU (BFFT)

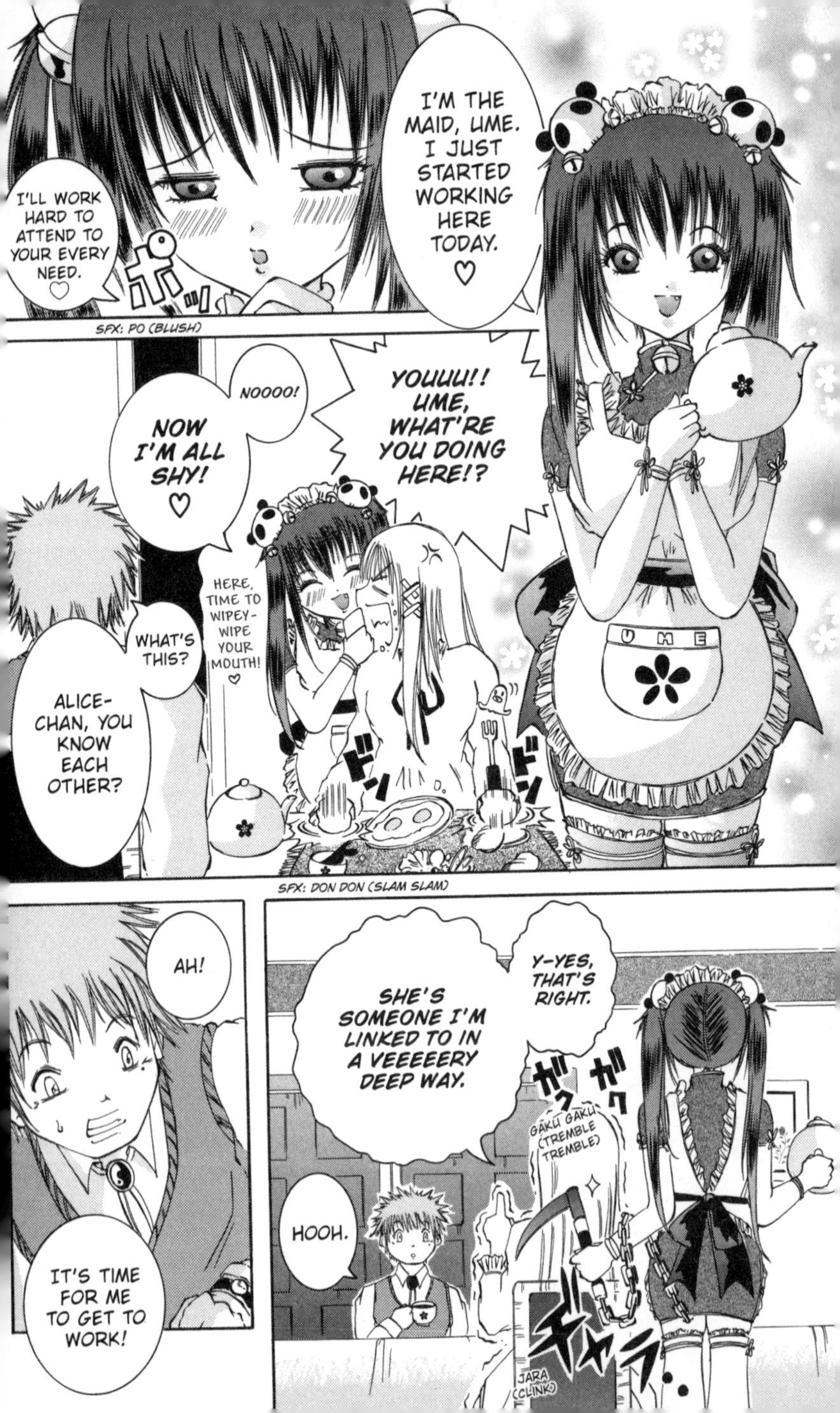
I'M THE MAID, UME. I JUST STARTED WORKING HERE TODAY. ♡
I'LL WORK HARD TO ATTEND TO YOUR EVERY NEED. ♡
SFX: PO (BLUSH)
YOUUU!! UME, WHAT'RE YOU DOING HERE!?
NOOOO!
NOW I'M ALL SHY! ♡
HERE, TIME TO WIPEY-WIPE YOUR MOUTH! ♡
WHAT'S THIS?
ALICE-CHAN, YOU KNOW EACH OTHER?
SFX: DON DON (SLAM SLAM)
SHE'S SOMEONE I'M LINKED TO IN A VEEEEERY DEEP WAY.
Y-YES, THAT'S RIGHT.
GAKU GAKU (TREMBLE TREMBLE)
HOOH.
JARA (CLINK)
AH!
IT'S TIME FOR ME TO GET TO WORK!

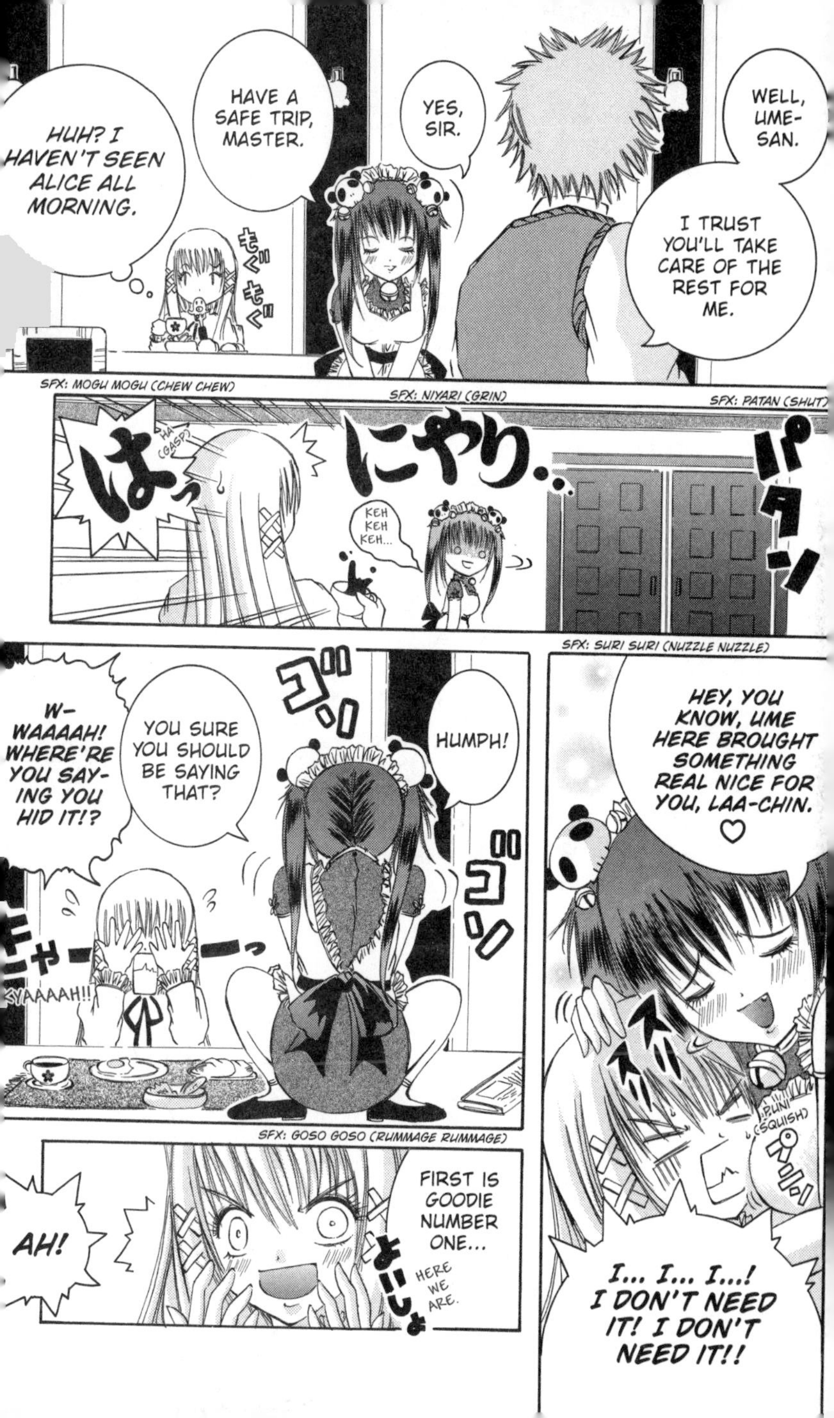
WELL, UME-SAN.
I TRUST YOU'LL TAKE CARE OF THE REST FOR ME.
YES, SIR.
HAVE A SAFE TRIP, MASTER.
HUH? I HAVEN'T SEEN ALICE ALL MORNING.
もぐもぐ
SFX: MOGU MOGU (CHEW CHEW)
パタン
SFX: PATAN (SHUT)
にやり…
SFX: NIYARI (GRIN)
KEH KEH KEH...
はっ
HA (GASP)
HEY, YOU KNOW, UME HERE BROUGHT SOMETHING REAL NICE FOR YOU, LAA-CHIN. ♡
PUNI (SQUISH)
I... I... I...! I DON'T NEED IT! I DON'T NEED IT!!
SFX: SURI SURI (NUZZLE NUZZLE)
ゴソ
HUMPH!
YOU SURE YOU SHOULD BE SAYING THAT?
W-WAAAAH! WHERE'RE YOU SAYING YOU HID IT!?
ゴソ
ニャーーっ
SYAAAAH!!
SFX: GOSO GOSO (RUMMAGE RUMMAGE)
FIRST IS GOODIE NUMBER ONE...
よいしょ
HERE WE ARE.
AH!

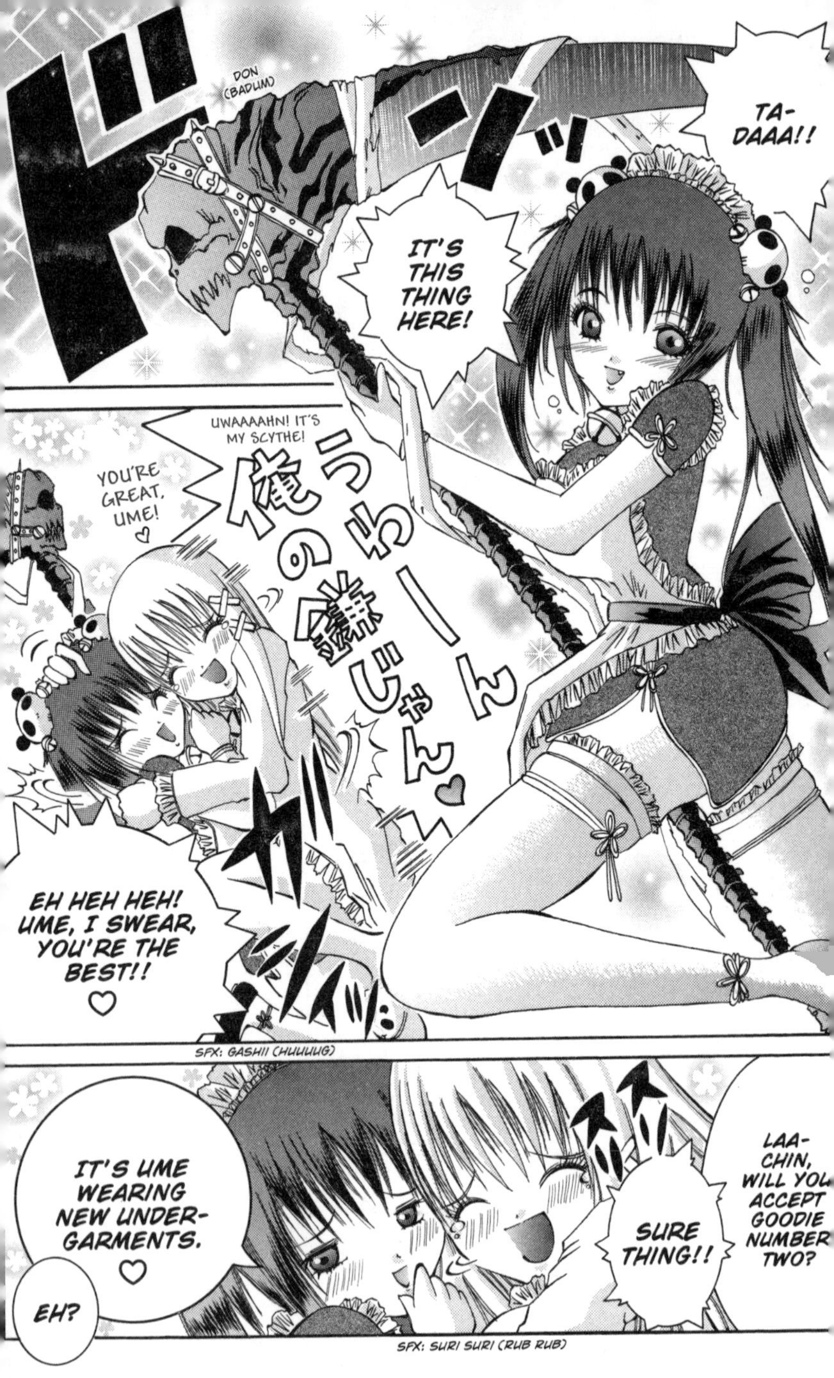
TA-DAAA!!
IT'S THIS THING HERE!
DON (BADUM)
UWAAAAHN! IT'S MY SCYTHE!
うわーん 俺の鎌じゃん♥
YOU'RE GREAT, UME! ♡
EH HEH HEH! UME, I SWEAR, YOU'RE THE BEST!! ♡
SFX: GASHII (HUUUUG)
LAA-CHIN, WILL YOU ACCEPT GOODIE NUMBER TWO?
SURE THING!!
IT'S UME WEARING NEW UNDER-GARMENTS. ♡
EH?
SFX: SURI SURI (RUB RUB)

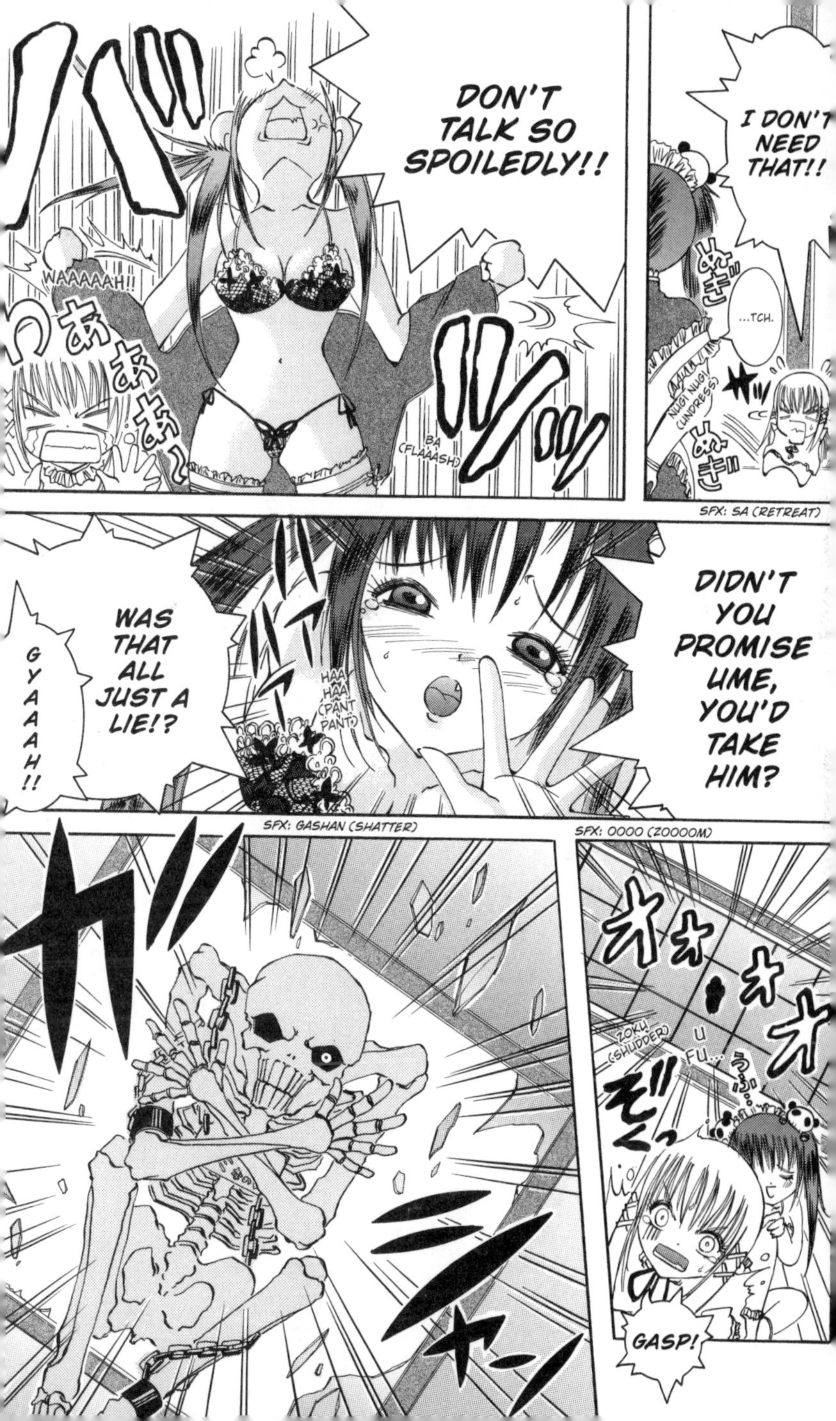
I DON'T NEED THAT!!
NUGI NUGI (UNDRESS)
...TCH.
SFX: SA (RETREAT)
DON'T TALK SO SPOILEDLY!!
WAAAAAH!!
BA (FLAAASH)
DIDN'T YOU PROMISE UME, YOU'D TAKE HIM?
HAA HAA (PANT PANT)
WAS THAT ALL JUST A LIE!?
GYAAAAH!!
SFX: OOOO (ZOOOOM)
U FU...
ZOKU (SHUDDER)
GASP!
SFX: GASHAN (SHATTER)

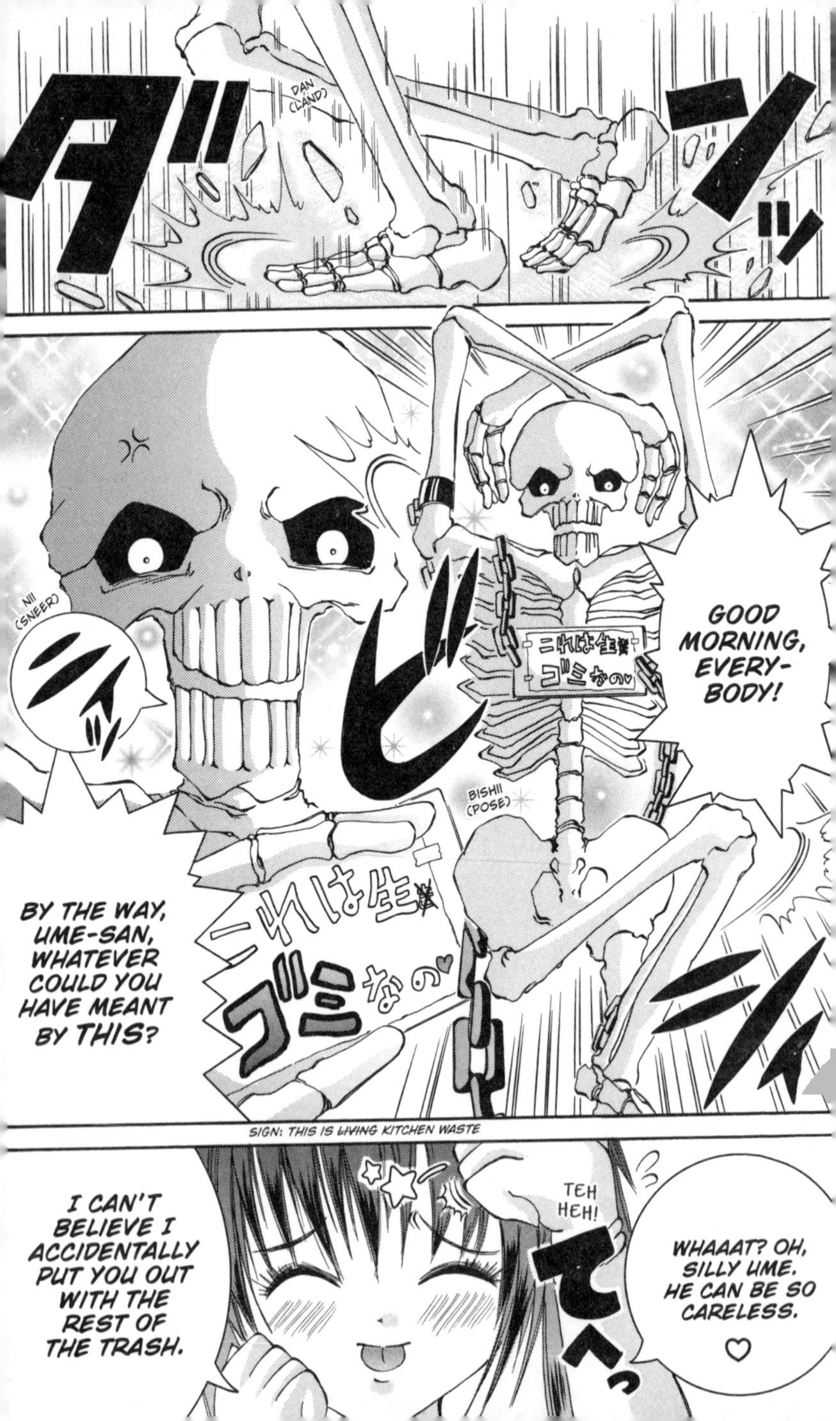
DAN (LAND)
GOOD MORNING, EVERY-BODY!
BISHII (POSE)
これは生ゴミなの♥
NII (SNEER)
BY THE WAY, UME-SAN, WHATEVER COULD YOU HAVE MEANT BY THIS?
SIGN: THIS IS LIVING KITCHEN WASTE
WHAAAT? OH, SILLY UME. HE CAN BE SO CARELESS. ♡
TEH HEH!
I CAN'T BELIEVE I ACCIDENTALLY PUT YOU OUT WITH THE REST OF THE TRASH.

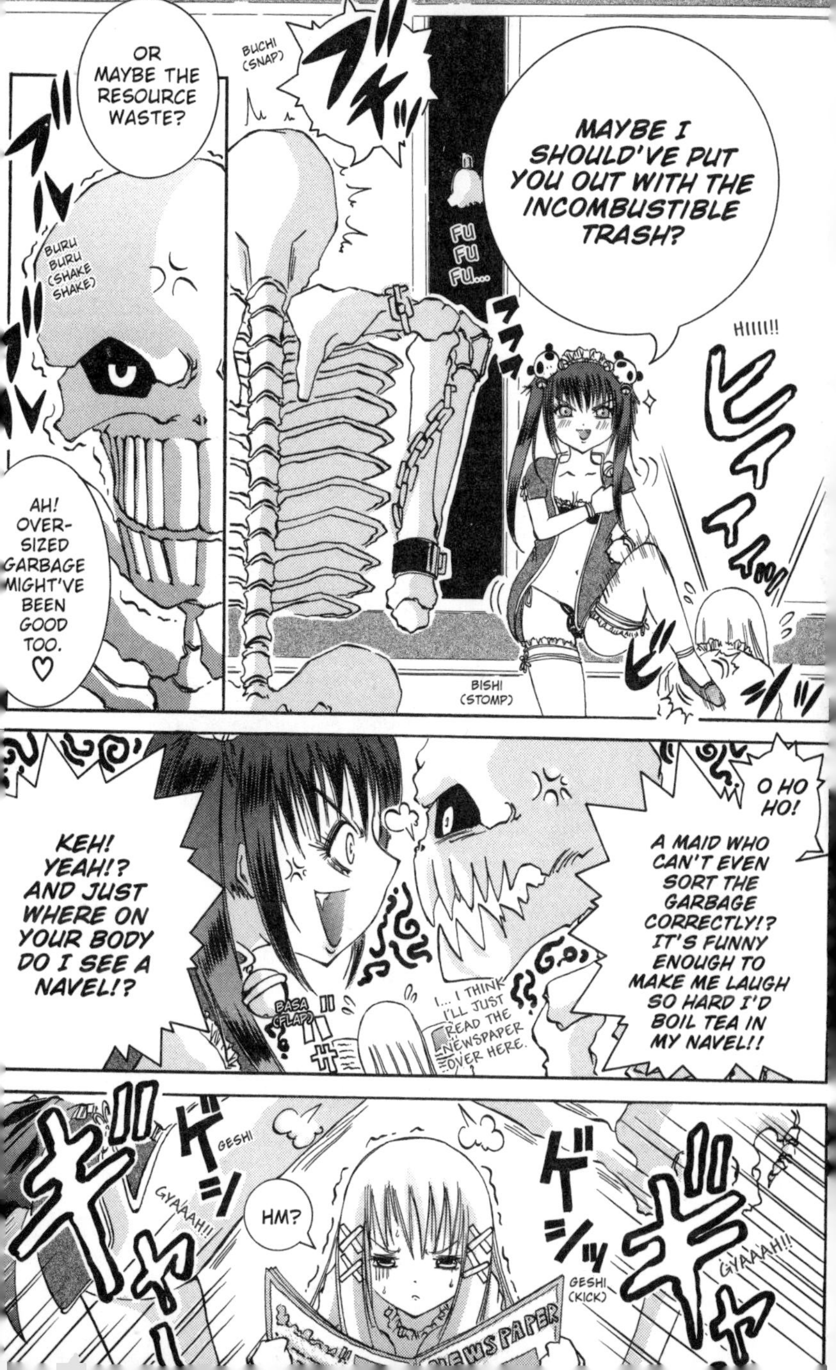
MAYBE I SHOULD'VE PUT YOU OUT WITH THE INCOMBUSTIBLE TRASH?
HIIIII!!
BUCHI (SNAP)
FU FU FU...
BISHI (STOMP)
OR MAYBE THE RESOURCE WASTE?
BURU BURU (SHAKE SHAKE)
AH! OVER-SIZED GARBAGE MIGHT'VE BEEN GOOD TOO. ♡
O HO HO!
A MAID WHO CAN'T EVEN SORT THE GARBAGE CORRECTLY!? IT'S FUNNY ENOUGH TO MAKE ME LAUGH SO HARD I'D BOIL TEA IN MY NAVEL!!
I... I THINK I'LL JUST READ THE NEWSPAPER OVER HERE.
BASA (FLAP)
KEH! YEAH!? AND JUST WHERE ON YOUR BODY DO I SEE A NAVEL!?
GYAAAH!!
GESHI (KICK)
HM?
NEWSPAPER
GESHI
GYAAAH!!

TRANSLATOR NOTES

PAGE 3
SHINIGAMI LITERALLY MEANS "GODS OF DEATH." THEY'RE SIMILAR TO REAPERS IN WESTERN CULTURE.

PAGE 10
SHIBITO IS WRITTEN WITH THE KANJI FOR "CORPSE" AND "PERSON" AND IS THUS AN APT WORD FOR THE ENTITY LAPAN IS SENT TO THE HUMAN REALM TO COLLECT.

PAGE 119
LAPAN (AS ALICE) TENDS TO SPEAK TO THE PRINCE IN THE **THIRD PERSON** TO COME OFF AS EXTRA CUTE.

PAGE 138
YATSUHASHI IS A FAMOUS KYOTO DELICACY. THESE LITTLE PASTRIES HAVE RICE-FLOUR SKINS AND CAN BE FILLED WITH RED BEAN, CINNAMON, AND GREEN TEA PASTE.

PAGE 139
THE SHINIGAMI ORGANIZATION IS KNOWN AS **TSURUKAME**, A SYMBOLIC NAME SINCE THE TWO CHARACTERS MAKING UP THE NAME ARE "CRANE" AND "TURTLE"— TWO ANIMALS THAT SYMBOLIZE LONGEVITY AND GOOD FORTUNE. THIS IS PRETTY IRONIC CONSIDERING THEIR COMPANY DEALS WITH DEATH AND THE AFTERLIFE!

PAGE 140
SENSHUURAKU IS A FORMAL WAY TO DENOTE THE LAST DAY OF A MULTI-DAY PERFORMANCE OR EVENT WITH ALL THE CLOSING FESTIVITIES. FOUND HERE, IT REFERS TO THE END OF ONE'S LIFE WHEN ONE COMES INTO THE SHINIGAMI WORLD.

PAGE 143
KAMI MAKES UP PART OF THE WORD "SHINIGAMI," WHERE IT MEANS "GOD." BUT THIS REFERS NOT TO AN OMNISCIENT GOD AS IN THE CHRISTIAN FAITH, BUT TO THE MANY SPIRITS IN JAPANESE SHINTOISM THAT PLAY VARIOUS ROLES.

PAGE 149
PII-CHAN IS A GENERIC NAME FOR A BIRD, SIMILAR TO HOW "ROVER" IS COMMON FOR DOGS.

PAGE 161
ALICE'S GRAVE MISTAKE IS A PLAY ON WORDS. ORIGINALLY THE PLAQUE READ "ALICE NO BAKA" WHEN IT SHOULD HAVE READ "ALICE NO 'HAKA'" CHANGING "ALICE'S GRAVE" TO "ALICE'S STUPID."

PAGE 164
KAPPA ARE CREATURES FROM JAPANESE MYTHOLOGY THAT RESEMBLE FROG-MONKEYS AND ARE NOTORIOUS PRANKSTERS. THEIR MORE HEAVY PRANKS CAN EVEN INCLUDE RAPE, WHICH IS WHY LAPAN SUGGESTS HE'S ALMOST FALLEN TO THEIR STATUS.

PAGE 177
YAKITORI IS A GRILLED CHICKEN DISH IN JAPAN THAT COMES SKEWERED ON LITTLE STICKS.

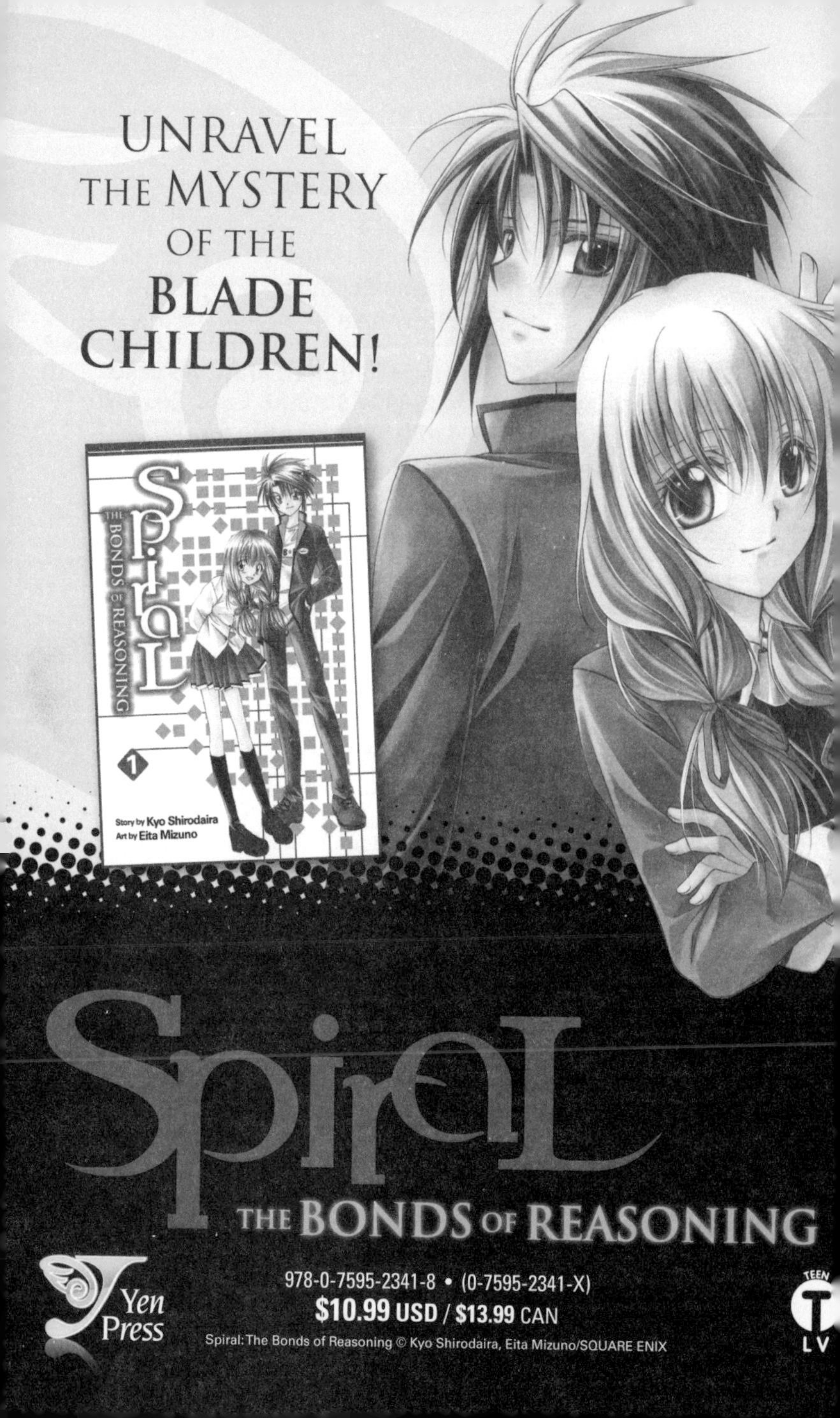
UNRAVEL THE MYSTERY OF THE BLADE CHILDREN!
Spiral
THE BONDS OF REASONING
1
Story by Kyo Shirodaira
Art by Eita Mizuno
Spiral
THE BONDS OF REASONING
Yen Press
978-0-7595-2341-8 • (0-7595-2341-X)
$10.99 USD / $13.99 CAN
Spiral: The Bonds of Reasoning © Kyo Shirodaira, Eita Mizuno/SQUARE ENIX
TEEN
T
LV

ALICE on Deadlines
by Shirō Ihara

Translation: Christine Schilling
Lettering: Fawn Lau

ALICE on Deadlines © 2005 Shirō Ihara / SQUARE ENIX. All rights reserved. First published in Japan in 2005 by SQUARE ENIX, CO., LTD. English translation rights arranged with SQUARE ENIX CO., LTD. and Hachette Book Group USA through Tuttle-Mori Agency, Inc.

Translation © 2007 by SQUARE ENIX CO., LTD.

Yen Press
Hachette Book Group USA
237 Park Avenue, New York, NY 10017

Visit our Web sites at www.HachetteBookGroupUSA.com and www.YenPress.com.

Yen Press is a division of Hachette Book Group USA, Inc. The Yen Press name and logo is a trademark of Hachette Book Group USA, Inc.

First Edition: November 2007

The characters and events in this book are fictitious. Any similarity to real persons, living or dead, is coincidental and not intended by the author.

10 9 8 7 6 5 4 3 2 1

WOR

Printed in the United States of America